# My Life,
# a Roller Coaster
# Ride

First publication by Footprint Press 2025
email: megancarr@hermanus.co.za

Copyright © Megan Carr 2025

Cover design and page layout by Anthony Cuerden
Email: ant@flyingant.co.za

Printed by Print on Demand
Email: tertius@printondemand.co.za

ISBN: 978-0-6398050-7-8

All rights reserved. No part of this publication may be reproduced, stored, manipulated in any retrieval system, or transmitted in any mechanical, electronic form or by any other means, without the prior written authority of the publishers, except for short extracts in media reviews. Any person who engages in any unauthorised activity in relation to this publication shall be liable to criminal prosecution and claims for civil and criminal damages.

# My Life, a Roller Coaster Ride

The life and times of
## Megan Carr

*A ride shared with my family*

Tony, Carole, Peter & Leanne, Andrea

Sean & Nicole, Camilla & Lee, Alexandra & Olli

Matthew, Nicola, Sebastian, Nicholas and Beatrix Kate.

Brothers Milton, John, Christopher and families

Daniel, Crystal and Melanie, my 'adopted' family.

\* \* \*

I Salute Adele Lucas,

my best friend and Business Associate.

A fifty-eight year friendship and

four generations of our families.

\* \* \*

Special thanks to Carole,

Peter and Sebastian for

their editing support.

\* \* \*

My thanks to Anthony Cuerden, talented designer of this book, who went the extra mile with his eye-catching cover, paragraph headings and picture-juggling to produce this reader-friendly memoir.

# Contents

| | |
|---|---|
| Author's Note | 6 |
| Foreword | 8 |
| Prologue | 10 |
| My Family | 11 |
| 30 Pivotal People and Times in my Life | 12 |
|     Part One. Early Days | 17 |
|     Part Two. Courtship and Marriage | 46 |
|     Part Three. Career, Business and Family | 86 |
|     Part Four. Start of Megan Carr Promotions | 126 |
|     Part Five. Move to Cape Town | 280 |
|     Part Six. Retirement Years and Writing | 329 |
| Postscript | 358 |
| Appendix | 362 |
| About the Author | 378 |

My Life, a Roller Coaster Ride

# Author's Note

**Looking back.** Now, at the age of ninety-two, with time to relax and review my life, I am in awe of how much I have packed into those many years.

How blessed I have been with a loving family and lifelong friends.

**This is the extraordinary life of an ordinary woman.** A double life as a mother of four and businessperson, illustrated to bring the stories to life.

Friends have labelled me the ultimate *'Survivor'*. I can never decide if that is a compliment or an insult. It smacks of failing in order to survive. So… I'll give them the benefit of their good intentions as friends, because failure, to me, is not an option.

**Survival.** I have had many near misses. Breach birth feet first. Almost died of pneumonia at six months. Almost bankrupt in 1975. Almost murdered in my bed by a burglar in 1994. Breast cancer and mastectomy in 2002. Cardio Myopathy when Tony, my eldest son died in 2013. Three months after my 90th birthday, I underwent a TAVI (Trans Aortic Valve Implant). The heart valve implant was no less than a miracle, surviving a brief cardiac arrest in the process. They got me back 'with one Zap'. When I opened my eyes after the two hours in la la land, still groggy, I asked Dr. Andre` Phillips, the Anaesthetist, "Are you Saint Peter?" That went viral throughout the Cardiac Unit.

**Survivor.** I could almost include my first view of the top of Table Mountain, upside-down in the pictured 1937 Piper Cub plane during 'The Great American Air Circus' which I was publicising in 1979. I was strapped in the front seat. Lindsay Hess, the American stunt pilot, then flipped to right side up, switched off the engine and, with the propeller stopped, we glided powerless back to the Ysterplaat Military Air Base 8 kms away. In fact, the plane rolled to a stop on exactly the same ground mark it started from. *'A point of pride'*, I was told.

I was always an optimist, always saw the funny side of things and utterly expected that everything would turn out just fine.

In theatrical terms, whatever the obstacles, it would be 'Alright on the Night'.

# Author's Note

**Ideas roulette.** Just as well, because there is something of a gambler in me. Always open to a calculated risk on a good idea. Not the Casino kind. In telling you my story, I will miss out the dreary bits and get on the Rollercoaster, trusting in my luck and synchro destiny, with all its mystery, which has toyed with me, to my delight, over the years.

**Synchro destiny.** When you think of someone and the phone rings and there they are. Or strange coincidences which can't be explained. Almost as if the Universe is playing games with us. I give some examples in the book.

**Magnificent obsession.** I have lived by the principle which I discovered in a novel in my early twenties. It was Lloyd C. Douglas's story *Magnificent Obsession,* published in 1929.

The essence is about anonymous philanthropy. Be kind. Be good to others, privately. Just do it. No bragging. No reward expected. The good and the bad you do, comes back to you tenfold. Some call it 'Paying Forward' or 'Karma'.

**The Five-Seven-Ten Principle.** Musing on a theme for my story, I identified with Dr. Phil's '5-7-10 Principle'. Five Pivotal People. Seven Critical Choices. Ten Defining Moments - those lightbulb flashes. My numbers differ from Doctor Phil's. I've had more of each, but then, I have lived a lot longer than he.

Any regrets? A complete waste of time.

**1937 Piper Cub plane during 'The Great American Air Circus'.**

# My Life, a Roller Coaster Ride

# Foreword

Megan Carr seems to have packed several lifetimes into her 92 years. They are filled with the most extraordinary collection of adventures, most of them but not all related to the world of public relations and promotions. At the height of her career someone referred to her agency as "one of the hottest tickets in town".

From her earliest days she had the ability to win the confidence of South Africa's leading business community, and her friendships with some of its outstanding figures became life-long. Her longest professional and personal association was with the irrepressible Adele Lucas, and together they broke into a male-dominated domain as early as the 1960s. Sol Kerzner invited both to brainstorm a corporate name for his new hotel empire, and then showed them an empty stretch of bushveld in the Pilanesberg which, two years later, he transformed into Sun City and the Lost City. His Maharani Hotel in Durban owes its name to Megan.

After her amicable divorce from Peter Carr in 1972 she set up on her own as Megan Carr Promotions or MCP. It certainly put paid to male chauvinist pigs. Three years later she became involved in a promotion that nearly bankrupted her but ironically also made her name nationally as well as abroad. She accepted an invitation from Los Angeles to stage an annual charity event in Johannesburg termed 'Celebrity Tennis', in aid of the International Actors' Benevolent Fund.

To everyone's astonishment Elizabeth Taylor and Richard Burton agreed to come, as did former Beatles drummer Ringo Starr, never mind that they couldn't play tennis. So did Kennedy-in-law and 'Rat Pack' member Peter Lawford and Dean Martin's son Dino. The event also involved a 'Banquet with the Stars' fund-raising auction in the Carlton Hotel, followed by a safari into the Kruger Park and Chobe Game Park.

At one memorable moment Burton's pants split stepping down from a light aircraft. "Help", he whispered to Carr, covering his backside with a newspaper. She shoved him into a bungalow, gave him a towel to wrap himself in, told him to take off his pants, and sewed them up with the emergency kit she always kept in her handbag. "It remained Richard's and my private joke," she writes. "Until now."

That wasn't the end of her association with 'stars'. When the Fiat motor company unveiled their new Mirafiori in South Africa, Carr organized the launch with the specific assignment of 'managing' Gina Lollobrigida.

# Foreword

Meanwhile, nearer home, Raymond Ackerman entrusted her with the job of promoting his then new Pick 'n Pay hypermarkets – another friendship that continued over many years.

In the 1990s Megan moved to Cape Town (where I first met her) and had the nightmare experience of being attacked in her Muizenberg home one night. Though badly beaten up she talked the intruder out of raping her by reminding him of his mother and grandmother. A resourcefulness and resilience that had served her throughout her professional life, saved her personally when she most needed it.

She went on for years thereafter to organise Alpha Power seminars and even fire-walking, once again inviting volunteers to do nothing that she, her son, daughters, grandson and granddaughter, were not prepared to demonstrate first.

As in everything else in her action-filled life, she led from the front.

**John Scott,**
Former *Cape Times* editor, author, columnist and good friend.

# My Life, a Roller Coaster Ride

# Prologue

**"She'll always land on her feet"**, prophesied her father as she was born feet first late on a Sunday afternoon 30th April 1932.

When the doctor finally arrived after finishing his game of tennis, mother, Mattie, was in labour distress and father, Alf, was frantic and helpless as he awaited the arrival of the tardy doctor.

After a quick examination the doctor shook his head and said it was very serious and that Alf would have to choose between saving the mother or the child. Alf made it quite clear that, having enjoyed his tennis, he would now have to finish the delivery and save both mother and child. Or else!

**"What shall we call her?" They had planned for a 'Clive'.** They had listened to Megan (Margaret) Lloyd George making a speech on the radio. "Let's call her Megan", they both agreed. It was a most unusual name at that time. Family histories had always had traditional English and Scottish names. Nothing Welsh.

**Megan Yuill Steer** had started on her Rollercoaster life.

**Why Roller Coaster?**
After this rocky start, followed by a happy, uneventful childhood, life hotted up from mid-teens onward. Ups and downs, twists and turns, smiles and tears, the title fits the story.

The nature of this book illustrates the story of my life, my family and the many people, events, stray episodes and links which bounced in from the labyrinth of my memory, having affected and enriched my life.

**History, events and life trends.**
I marvel at how times have changed over the years, and how I have managed to stay current in whatever I do.

*Your orderly mind will be tested. As was mine.*
*Enjoy the ride!*

# My Family
## as of January 2025

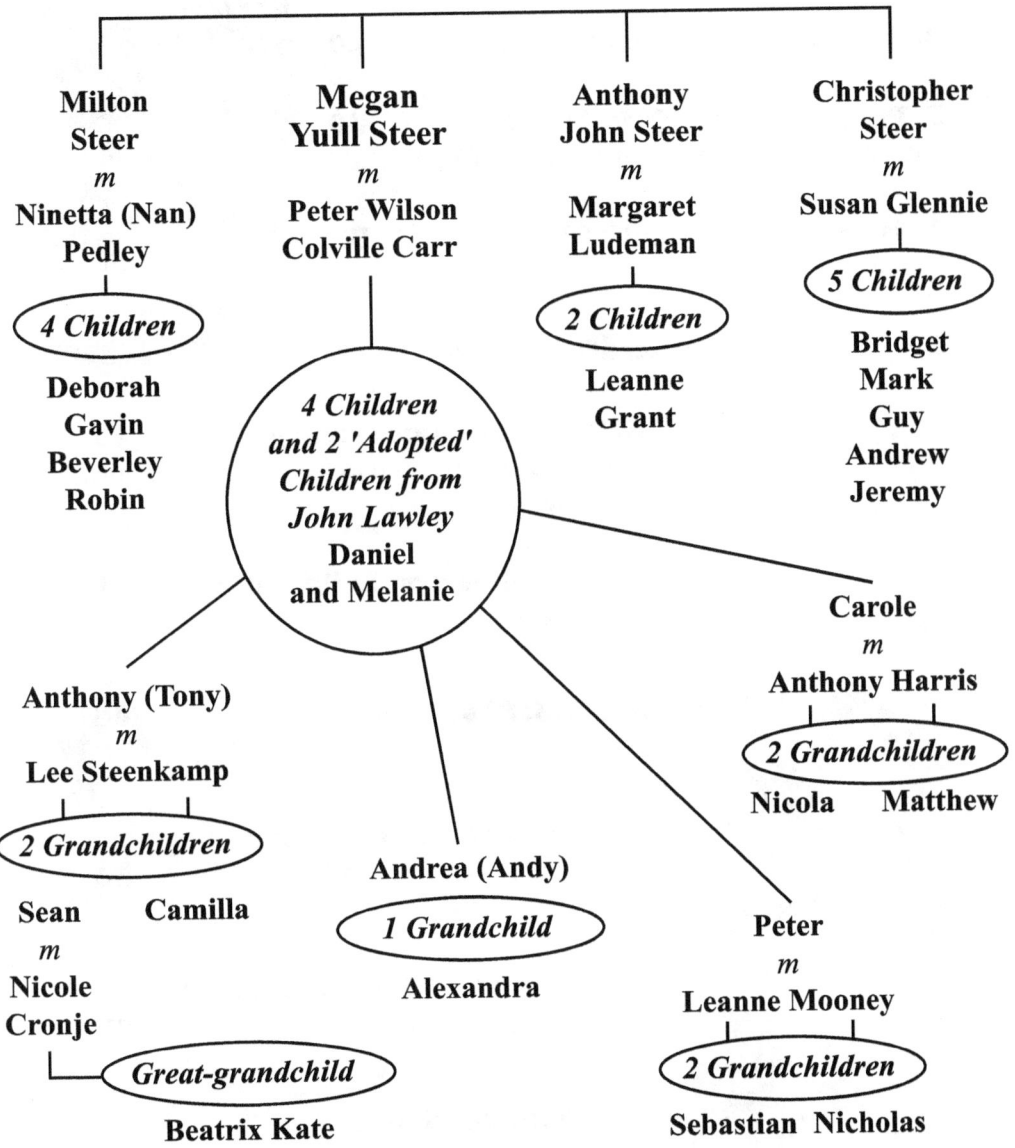

My Life, a Roller Coaster Ride

# 30 Pivotal People and Times in my Life

**1. Father and Mother**     17

**2. Childhood and World War 2**     20

**3. Pivotal person Kitty Dumas**     30
Latin and English teacher at St. Anne's College.

**4. First Critical Health Choice**     33
Not to take up smoking.

**5. 1951. Grande Tour after Matric**     35

**6. Back in Johannesburg**     41
The princess turns into a frogess and becomes a secretary.

**7. Pivotal Person Leila Reitz.**     45
Early mentor.

**8. 1953. 21st Birthday**     46

**9. Courtship and Marriage to Peter Carr in 1954**     50

**10. Birth of Anthony Colville Carr and first home**     57

**11. 1958. Birth of Carole Elizabeth Yuill Carr**     61

## 30 Pivotal People and Times in my Life

**12. 1962. Pivotal Person Angus Collie**    **62**
Chamber of Mines PR, who taught her PR and Event Management.

**13. 1964. Birth of Peter Alfred Colville Carr**    **77**

**14. Second Home**    **79**
115 Katherine Street, Sandown.

**15. 1968. Adele Lucas. Pivotal Person**
Together, they pioneered live promotions in the male dominated business and advertising world of the sixties and seventies. Adele's company, was A&J Promotions with partner, Jenifer Williams, wife of tennis promotor, Owen Williams.    **86**

**16. 1966. Birth of Andrea Colville Carr**    **87**

**17. 1966. Circus Premiere, 1st major event**    **87**
'Stars and Sawdust' was what we named our spectacular Circus, black tie, Premiere with The Monday Club, raising a large sum for Woodside Sanctuary.

**18. 1969. Pivotal person Sol Kerzner**
also starting out with only one hotel, Beverly Hills. Sol worked with Megan and Adele, personally coaching them in running the 'Perfect Seminar'. He also took them to view the property he had purchased, to become Sun City a year later. All three pioneers in their fields.    **107**

**19. 1971. The Wombles**    **123**
Megan is offered the Agency for The Wombles of Wimbledon by their creator Lisa Beresford – wife of the BBC Tennis Commentator Max Robertson.

## My Life, a Roller Coaster Ride

### 20. 1972. Megan divorces Peter and sets up Megan Carr Promotions    126

Suddenly a single mother of four and managing a new business. The first promotion was the launch of Oil of Olay with Orchids, which led to a thriving In-Store Marketing business. Further live promotions followed, with such as Shell, BP. Cabana Beach, Miss Worlds, 320 West Street, Fiat Mirafiori, Chitty Chitty Bang Bang machines and others.

### 21. 1975. Celebrity Tennis    167

Elizabeth Taylor, Richard Burton, Ringo Starr, Peter Lawford, Dino Martin Jr., John Marley, The Three Degrees and The Monkees. It was a make and break event.

### 22. 1976-77. Pivotal person John Lawley    202

the brief love of her life. When he died suddenly, Megan 'adopted' his two children and was introduced to Raymond Ackerman.

### 23. 1977-1988. Pivotal Person Raymond Ackerman    214

Pick 'n Pay became my client 1977 to 1988. In those years I launched several Hypermarkets and taught their promotional staff to run promotions and events. He believed in the power of promotions, they were one of the 'Four legs of his table' The *Financial Mail* quoted Raymond as saying:

> "I regard Carr as an extension of myself in promoting my Hypermarkets."

### 24. Promotions    201

### 25. 1980. Fun and Fundraising for The Wildlife Society    242

## 30 Pivotal People and Times in my Life

**26. Chroma Television          258**
State-of-the-Art TV and Video Post-Production House. Introducing Chroma to the Advertising and Video Production industry.
A Porsche was part of Megan's package.

**27. The Move to Cape Town          280**

**28. 1993-2002.
Alpha Mind Power Seminars          293**
Pivotal Person, Peter Heibloem.
Fire Walking. As a natural option to offer Alpha graduates, we introduced Fire Walking, already used by such companies as Coca Cola as a motivation aid. MCP conducted Fire Walks in Cape Town and Windhoek.

**29. 2002. Brain Gym Seminars
with Carla Hannaford          309**
(US Education Consultant to Bill Clinton)
(2002 Brain Gym). Carla's mission was to discourage the use of Ritalin to control hyperactive children with her alternative left-right brain recognition, cross-movements and exercises. MCP Brain Gym seminars directed at schools and parents.

**30. 2007 – 2019.
Pivotal person
Gerry Leumann          334**
Property manager and Social P.A to Swiss summer visitor to SA, Gerry Leumann. Pivotal person in her retirement years.

# Part 1

## Early Days

# 1. Early Days

## My Father

**Alfred William Steer** was born in Pietermaritzburg, Natal, April 1900, to English immigrant parents Alfred John William and Elizabeth (Price) Steer. Both of high standing in their community.

My father started out as a journalist in Standerton, then a thriving town. He joined Evelyn Haddon & Co in 1931. The Johannesburg branch consisted of three staff with ten in the Cape Town Head office.

His natural business acumen, patent integrity, talent in dealing with people and personal charisma, built up the company to be the largest printing supply house in the Southern Hemisphere. Listed on the JSE in 1968 as he retired as MD to become Executive Chairman.

Alf was a wonderful father and ahead of his time in parenting. He spared the rod but never spoiled the child. He made sure we exploited our talents and abilities.

My Father, Alf To know him is to understand me.

In World War 1: Alf contracted Malaria with complications called 'Black Water Fever' and was honourably discharged at the age of eighteen in 1918.

He remained in frail condition for a few years. This made him health conscious ever after. Ahead of his time, in health matters, he believed in exercise, discipline in diet, 'early to bed and early to rise'. He smoked the occasional social cigarette or cigar.

As a father of four, he listened to our points of view and never put us down for our silly ideas. His favourite quoting sources were strangely eclectic such as American philosophers, Ralph Waldo Emerson and Walt Whitman. He verbalised Shakespeare, Dickens and Wordsworth. And Churchill, of course. He could sing every tricky word of Gilbert and Sullivan's operettas.

With our dad, we always listened to BBC quiz programmes 'My Word', 'My Music' and the South African 'Test the Team'. Unlike me, he didn't enjoy 'The Goons'.

# My Life, a Roller Coaster Ride

## My Mother

**Mattie** (Martha) **Steer** (Born Low) in Kirkcaldy, Scotland. September 1908. Immigrated to South Africa with her parents James and Martha (Armour) Low.

She was governess to a Scottish family living near Standerton. It was there she met Alf Steer. They married in the Johannesburg St. Mary's Cathedral Chapel in 1930.

Mattie was a true Scot. Hard working and practical. Strict with the children, but also a truly amazing wife and selfless mother of four. Megan, Milton, John and Christopher.

Her steady and loving parenting provided a solid foundation for our life development and ultimate success.

**We dared not argue with Mattie.** In many ways I, and later my daughter Carole, were similar. When Mattie set her mind to something, she was immovable.

For example, when Alf encouraged her to go out more, she joined the Old Johannian Women's Bowling Club. Not only did she win championships, she became Bowls Captain. Then the Club, recognising her organising skills, invited her onto the Old Johannian Club Committee with Alfie.

As is the nature of things, Alf started complaining that she was 'never at home'. She gave up bowls and resigned from both committees. By then she was also busy with the grandchildren.

She was a devoted mother and grandmother. After my divorce, she

**My Mother, Mattie** An immovable force.

*The Praying Lady*, Giovanni Fasciotti.

# 1. Early Days

supported me with lifts and child sitting as I, the single mother of four, developed my business. Without the support of Mattie, I doubt that I would have been as successful running my very demanding company.

Mattie insisted that the grandchildren call her 'Mattie' and not 'Grandma'. She started something. My grandchildren call me Meg or Megan, except for Alex, Nicola and Matthew and their significant others. They call me 'Morning' or 'Morns'.

This started in 1995 when Alex was two. Andy, Alex and I lived in the same house on Marina da Gama. Alex would climb the stairs to my bedroom early each morning, knock on the door, and I would call out "Morning". She must have thought that it was my name and has called me 'Morning' ever since. In fact, for the next thirty years. Now Olli, her fiancé calls me 'Morning'.

**Mattie had an eye for beautiful art.** In 1940, when I was eight, there was a knock on the door and there stood Italian artist, Giovanni Fasciotti. He begged my mother to buy his beautiful painting as he needed money to return to Italy as war had started.

She bought it on the spot at his asking price. I have it today and feel it is equal to Da Vinci's Mona Lisa. Or better! I saw the Mona Lisa in the Louvre when I was nineteen, when we could view it up close. After the big build-up, I was slightly disappointed, beautiful as it is.

**Schools and commuting.** Most mothers, in the forties, did not drive. Fathers did the morning school lifts. After school, coming home or going to extra murals on our own was by bus. Double-deckers, red and white with no advertising on the sides.

The bus to Cyrildene was number 23. We always knew someone on the bus, almost social interaction. Bussing involved much walking to and from the bus stops and destinations.

John, my brother, met Margie, his future wife, on that Number 23 Cyrildene Bus.

We had a monthly set of bus tickets and didn't have to carry cash. If, by chance, we forgot or lost our tickets, the conductor always gave us a free pass with a stern warning. We all got to know each other. Regular Drivers, Conductors and fellow passengers. Milton went to Marist Brothers, a mile away, so had to walk a mile home.

Sundays, there were no buses. Dad didn't drive us to the St. Aidan's Church Morning Service. He was in the choir for 'Evensong'.

Church was mandatory. A three mile walk each way. No escape.

He sang in the Church choir at Evensong under the direction of organist Roger O'Hogan. My singing services were not required in the world of boy choristers. Later my younger brothers, John and Christopher, also joined the choir for services, weddings, funerals and some Confirmations. I think they were paid a shilling per social appearance.

Milton's youngest son, Robin, had the voice of an angel. Milton booked his two boys, Gavin and Robin, into the Drakensberg Boys Choir.

Sadly, this never came to be for six year-old Robin. He electrocuted himself in a freak accident. Coming in to wash his hands in the kitchen sink for piano practice, it happened as he touched the metal sink. The careless ironing lady had trailed the iron cord over the live stove plate. touching the metal sink.

Milton sponsored Robin's place at Drakensburg Boys to a talented young Zulu boy as a memorial to Robin.

The family never quite got over it. I know I wept seeing the small white coffin at St. Luke's church.

Nan, his mother, spent the next few years campaigning for electrical safety in the home, although a better circuit breaker would not have saved him.

## 2. Childhood and World War 2

**1939.** I was seven when war was 'Declared'. I remember when Johnny Minnaar was driving June and me to school in his black Jaguar SS Swallow sports car. June asked "Dad, what does 'declared' mean?". His answer didn't mean a thing to us, whatever it was.

**Wartime in South Africa.** The only time the fighting war really touched us was vicariously through family and friends who 'joined up' and went 'Up North' to join the Allied Forces. My uncle, James Low, Mattie's only brother, joined the Medical Corps and was wounded in action carrying a wounded soldier on a stretcher, under enemy fire, to the hospital tent.

**Dunkirk** had us all rivetted to the radio and cinema newsreels, African Mirror and Gaumont British News. But as a child it seemed rather remote, it was just 'news'.

**1942 Alfie bought a citrus farm** near Rustenburg for what he jokingly called a safe escape in case of German invasion! More realistically we enjoyed, lots of chicken, eggs, milk, fruit and meat as well.

We ran wild on the farm. Milton was eight, I was ten. John was only

# 1. Early Days

three, so he didn't join us. We could play anywhere. Swim in the Selons river, climb trees, help with the animals, ride the donkeys, feed the chickens, collect the eggs and work in the dairy.

We were not allowed to milk the cows, but when the milk got to the dairy, the cream was separated and some of it churned into butter. Our job was winding the wooden churning handle, feeling triumphant as we saw the little globs of butter forming.

Once a half pound of butter had formed, we would be allowed to roll and pat it into a brick. If we were expecting guests for dinner, our job was to cut the butter into tiny cubes then roll each one between two grooved paddles into pretty little butter balls for the table.

There was no fridge or electricity at the farm, but we had two very effective cooler cages which we called 'safes'. They stood outside under the cool grape vines. Each Safe was about a meter cubed, like a bird aviary on legs.

The sides were double lined with chicken wire with charcoal and pumice interlined. By pouring water over the coal-packed wire walls, it created evaporation and caused a vacuum cooling effect, keeping everything on the shelves crisp and fresh.

**July school holiday was also harvesting time.** The old Kodak box camera photograph below reveals us seated on the ox wagon.

We helped pick the oranges, lemons and naartjies, then graded them by size, weeding out the less perfect fruit for our own use. Then packed them into net orange bags then labelled each bag with our market code. The Wagon was drawn by four oxen and 'driven' by Abe, Dawid and Johannes, who walked all the way.

Alfie, Megan, John and Milton on their way to Market.

## My Life, a Roller Coaster Ride

**Two little kiddies went to market.** Once loaded we climbed onto the wagon to deliver the hundreds of orange pockets to the market in Koster. It was a very slow journey with lots to see along the way.

With heaps of fresh citrus in all its forms, we spent many happy hours in the kitchen helping our mother make marmalades, fruit preserves and lemonade. Our family's standard, and highly prized, gift to family and friends at food rationing time.

*Did you know that the word Marmalade got its name from Mary Queen of Scots? She had Consumption (TB). The Royal kitchen staff kept preserved citrus to give her when she had bad attacks. They would call out 'Ma'am Malade' (Madam is Sick) and feed her up on the orange Vitamin C preserves.*

Nature is smart, giving us this citrus fruit which ripens in winter when we most need it for colds and flu.

Despite randomly diving stark naked into the river pool to splash around, we were never allowed to go anywhere barefoot because of the scorpions and other denizens of farm life.

**Wartime 1942. "This is the BBC".** At six o'clock each evening on the farm, we would leave the house and all climb into our black slope-backed Ford to listen to the war news on the car radio. Our only radio on the farm. Very scratchy but audible. It helped if one of us stood outside in the cold, holding the aerial.

The broadcast always started with the words "This is the BBC" and continued into the detail of the many planes shot down, London bombing casualties, German casualties. The Nazis in those early days seemed to be winning the fight, bringing doom and gloom. Churchill called Nazis 'Naazies' instead of 'Naatsies'.

Our two main farm staff were Abe and Dawid who always clustered around the car with their families, listening to the news in English, which they hardly understood, about a far-off war which didn't mean a thing to them. They had never ever heard a radio broadcast and always shook their heads and said "Haaw, Baas" to my dad when they heard a man's voice coming out of the car dashboard.

**Religion.** I had my first experience of religious zealots at the farm. We children sometimes bathed in the river without costumes. We just ripped off our clothes and jumped in, sliding down the waterfall and dive-bombing each other. One day we went to swim and found that our river pool had been filled with long spiky prickly pear plants. There was a message in

# 1. Early Days

Afrikaans saying that God would punish us for swimming naked.

Our father was furious. He complained to the neighbour about this unneighbourly act, who replied saying "lightning would strike you down".

My Dad gave up the unequal struggle. He got into his car and laid a charge against him at the Police Station in Koster, for his illegal act of water pollution. He didn't use the party line phone because everyone listened in.

**Prickly pear retribution.** Reluctantly, the cops came to the farm and made our unneighbourly neighbour, fully clothed and wearing shoes, wade waist-deep in the spiky water, personally, dragging every single cactus out and away, safely off our property. Then having to rake the floor of the pool for spikes.

I wondered how he would explain this to St. Peter upon arrival at the pearly gates to make his case to get into heaven.

We did ask ourselves the question. How did he know we were swimming in the nude on our own private tree-lined property? Binoculars? Hot line from God?

However, our other neighbours were very friendly. They even honoured us by inviting us to their Tuesday evening Bible Meetings at their house. Redemption was at hand, even if we struggled with 'Die Bybel' read in Afrikaans.

**Presbyterian Mattie** excused herself and the boys. Alfie and I, out of neighbourliness and interest, went along. About ten of us would sit around their long kitchen table with Bibles at the ready. The hour-long meeting would proceed with many references to Corinthians 2 or Matthew 5 verse 3 followed by praising of the Lord. After some time, we all held hands in the circle, a final prayer and the long awaited 'Amen'. *( so be it)*.

After this, the women would rush around providing strong coffee and biskuit (rusks) on perfectly set trays. This, as the men talked about farming and local affairs. No one ever mentioned the thorny subject of the other neighbour and the prickly pears, who never attended if they knew we would be there. Praise the Lord!

**Afrikaans.** The local *lingua franca* was Afrikaans, and we soon became proficient. This was a big plus when it came to schoolwork, as Afrikaans was one of the two set languages for Matric. Later in life, it came in handy when I was taking VIP visits to the mostly Afrikaans-speaking, gold mines. Equally useful when I was working with the Defence Force in Pretoria.

Alfie was raised in Natal (now Kwa-Zulu Natal) where Afrikaans was hardly used. He found that Afrikaans language proficiency was very useful

# My Life, a Roller Coaster Ride

in business. At the end of the war, Alfie decided that farming was not for him, and sold the farm.

**My days at Observatory Girls Primary, were happy and uneventful.**
The Head Mistress was Miss Cheshire. She always seemed to lean forward. I wondered if her large bosom and small bottom could have something to do with her posture. Or maybe it was just because she was always in a hurry.

**Music.** My school education was supplemented by music-loving parents wanting the very best for us. Classical piano lessons once a week with Miss Fleischer, down the road from home. Lots of scales, chords, practicing but little in the way of happy tunes. At eleven, I was sent to the glamorous Gertrude Walsh who had a slot on morning radio. That was much more to my taste, and I learnt to play 'syncopation' in recognisable tunes.

**Great expectations.** At this stage my father bought us a baby grand piano. A beautiful Rosewood instrument. It took pride of place in our lounge, and always looked inviting. The piano stool could fit two small ones, and we made a lot of noise. Milton was much more musically talented than me. Between us many hours were spent playing *chopsticks* duets and the latest tunes.

**Dancing.** For at least four years. Mattie and I bussed to town weekly for dancing lessons with Ivy Conmee. Ballet, Tap and Folk dancing. I loved dancing and in later years took up Ballroom.

**Deportment classes** for 'Young Ladies' took up another afternoon of the week. The exotic René Lacey was the only one to go to. Book balancing on head and footsteps in a very straight line. "If you walk on a beach", she said, "Your footprints should always be in a straight line". I still check on this every time.

> *I divert in context but out of chronological order for a 'Defining Moment'.*

**In the '70s** I met René Lacey's handsome son Richard. He was Adele's husband, Bob Lucas's good friend. Bob told me that Richard needed help getting his book ready for publication. Bob asked me if I could help him? I had just bought a sexy little Olivetti portable typewriter and dying to use it on a real project.

**The Beautiful Street.** Richard was battling to get his book done. He had written it in longhand on a lined pad and needed it typed, double spacing,

# 1. Early Days

in duplicate with a blue carbon sheet between two Bond pages. The top page to go to his publisher and a carbon copy to file. The title of the book 'Mooi Street, The Beautiful Street' A little bit of Johannesburg history. Sitting at his dining table, he dictated it from his rough manuscript. We edited and corrected the grammar and punctuation as we went along. Then each proofed it without benefit of a trained editor.

**Defining moment.** From that day onwards, I knew that I would one day be a writer. Seeing the slim published book, the fine print and glossy cover became a seminal moment in my life. I met up with Richard thirty years later, in the 90's, when we visited as pals. He was an actor and had a house in Loader Street. As a favour to Adele, I acted as her letting agent for her two Loader Street houses. Richard and I were part time neighbours in that magical Street in central Cape Town.

**Craft beer.** Richard's hobby was making his own 'craft' beer. He kept dubious buckets of smelly bubbly stuff in his bathroom. He insisted, after sieving it through a pillowcase, that we pour ourselves a glass to taste. It was cloudy and greyish. Quite revolting. I teased him that it tasted like he's sieved it through old socks. He always laughed at my jokes.

**1945.** End of Prep school, end of the war. Towards the end of those gentle and orderly Prep School years my parents decided that I should proceed to Boarding School. They selected St. Anne's Diocesan College, Hilton, Natal. The College could only accept me in standard seven, so I spent 'Standard Six', the first year of high school, at Highlands North High. This worked out very well for me. I found that I could hold my own in a Co-Ed class. I also started doing well in the gymnasium, competing in inter school vaulting and bars. I never could climb up a rope or do triple running somersaults or cartwheels along the floor.

**Dad loved swimming.** He taught me to swim when I was four when we went camping at Maloney's Eye. At twelve, he sent me for coaching to a trainer who was famous for doing the Cape Town to Robben Island nine-mile solo swim. I spent a good deal of after-school hours at the Olympic-size Patterson Park Swimming Pool where I was also taught to dive.

**Meg the diver.** Soon I was competing not only in crawl 100-yard races, but also high diving competitions. The diving moves were Pike, Tuck, Somersault, Swallow and Twist. I never had the courage to try the Reverse Somersault. For the first time in my life, I was suddenly aware of being somewhat competitive.

# My Life, a Roller Coaster Ride

My first heartthrob - Denis Compton.

**Denis Compton.** Out of the blue, that year, I discovered cricket. Dad and Milton also loved cricket, so we went to all the big local and international matches. I fell in love with the English Captain Denis Compton. I had his picture on my wall and in my private journal. I found myself somehow getting to the old Wanderers Ground near Ellis Park, for all the games, catching a lift back home with dad on his way back from work.

**1951. Our Grande Tour in UK.** As a special treat we went to a cricket match at Lords, the Marylebone Cricket Club (MCC) grounds with its club house walls festooned with boards and the familiar names of cricket captains and test players.

I thought the silk Club ties were what you might call 'garish' with broad red and yellow diagonal stripes. I looked it up. Only members are allowed to wear the tie and they currently pay sixty pounds to buy one. Available from the MCC Club or from 10 Savile Row.

My PR friend Dick Foxton proudly wears his MCC tie. In 2018, he courted and became engaged to our beloved South African Public Protector, Thuli Madonsela.

Other cricketer friends in my life were Basil Crews, Arthur and Cyril Tayfield and Dick Westcott. Barrie Richards rode a bike in our VIP relay race at Kyalami 1979.

**July school holidays.** The July holidays were big. Our chance to get out of very cold, dry, brown Johannesburg and off to green, warm Scottburgh, Natal.

Dad bought us a luxury Eccles caravan and we always went South to the Scottburgh Caravan Park almost on the beach. He would pick me up

# 1. Early Days

from St. Anne's and Milton from St. Charles in Maritzburg and in a few hours we were there. The boys camped out in a tent.

In Scottburgh we would sit on the lawns sloping down to the beach with a protected rock pool in the sea. Two Johannesburg boy schools, Jeppe High and King Edward High schools set up holiday camps, so there were always more boys than girls.

Supervised dance evenings were the weekly highlight. Boys came into my consciousness. That was when I learned ballroom dancing. Something I loved then and now. I also got to jive and boogey with the best of uninhibited teenage energy.

**Beauty pageant.** Another highlight beach event was a beauty pageant. The recreation master would persuade about twenty girls, sunbathing on the grassy slopes, to line up and march up and down for inspection. We had numbers pinned on our tops and voting papers were handed out to everyone else. We were wearing our one-piece costumes. No Bikinis in those days. The local news rag snapped off photos and became part of the selection panel for finals.

It was a two-weekend event. The first ten were selected. Then five semi-finalists were weeded out and paraded. I made top five of a motley lot. Being young and tanned helped! The finals would be at a dance the following weekend. Unfortunately, or fortunately, we trailed back to Johannesburg the following Saturday, so I never got to know my beauty queen fate.

**John, Meg, Chris, Milton.** (photo taken with our basic Brownie camera)

# My Life, a Roller Coaster Ride

A pity as I rather fancied the winning prizes – a fat shopping voucher at the local beachwear shop, a voucher for the local hairdresser and dinner for two at the best restaurant. At the age of seventeen this was heady stuff. Apart from the publicity and fame. I never found out who won.

**A Scottburgh diversion. Perla Siedle Gibson.** The Lady in White. My 'aunt' by marriage was Perla Siedle Gibson She was famous throughout the war years by going down to the Durban Docks, dressed in a flowing white gown, and big floppy hat.

As the Troop Ships, loaded with soldiers, sailed off to war, Perla with her magnificent contralto voice and only a megaphone to help, sang the well-known song "We'll Meet Again – don't know where, don't know when, but I know we'll meet again some sunny day " tra la la and other famous war songs. They called her South Africa's Vera Lynn.

(She didn't sing the funnier war song "Kiss me goodnight, Sergeant Major, Sergeant Major be a mother to me", sung by George Formby, which I am pleased to say I remember very clearly, because it made us laugh.).

There was never a dry eye amongst the thousands of anxious families on the dock, waving 'good-bye' to the soldiers and sailors aboard. Some never to return. Perla never missed a troop departure throughout the five years of the war. The whole world knew and loved her.

Her life-size statue can be seen at the Durban Museum.

**Perla Siedle Gibson** as related to our family was Perla's husband's brother, Guy Gibson, was married to Alf's feisty younger sister Eva. (He was not the famous Guy Gibson, Wing Commander of 'Dam Busters' fame).

Our family Guy Gibson was taken prisoner of war at Tobruk. I remember

Lady in White Statue, outside Durban Museum.

The real Lady in White along Durban Docks, singing to the troops.

# 1. Early Days

that we always sent him comfort food parcels together with letters and drawings about life back home. Letters in and out were always censored for national security. We'd find whole paragraphs, lines or names blacked out. However hard we tried we never could read even one deleted word.

When Guy returned home after the war, rather shaky and thin as a stick, he refused to talk about the prison camp, but always told us how much our parcels and letters had meant to him and kept up his spirits.

He was not one who tried to escape. Far too gentle for that.

**1947. Boarding school.** Before Milton and I started Boarding School, we had this family photo taken. I went off to St. Anne's and Milton to St. Charles. The younger boys, John and Christopher, went to St. John's College.

**Legendary school train.** St. Anne's was the start of my social life, a Tsunami hit me.

Each term started and ended on the school train. Electric trains from Park Station to Howick. At Howick it switched to a steam engine. I just knew that after Howick, we had to keep the windows firmly closed to avoid soot coming in.

The train was for St. Anne's girls and one or two Epworth College girls, then Hilton and Michaelhouse boys. Who knows what the train did after it dropped us off at Balgowan station for Michaelhouse then Hilton Road Station for Hilton College and St. Anne's College.

The train always departed Park Station at 8pm sharp. Parents would dutifully hang around the train for half an hour before, as we stowed our luggage in the girls' first class four berth compartments. Then back out

Back: Megan, Alfie, Milton. Front: John, Christopher, Mattie.

onto the platform for last minute parental instructions, "don't forget to write, don't forget to brush your teeth". Then there was the five-minute whistle, and we would all pile into the train and hang out of the windows for last hugs and kisses, as if we were going away for life.

**Sabotage.** I remember once, when the five-minute whistle blew, we waited and waited. The train didn't move. Parents looking at their watches because of their dinner bookings. After an eternal twenty minutes, another five-minute whistle blew, and the train finally pulled off. A few days later we heard that my friends, Johnny and Dave (Michaelhouse) had disconnected the engine from the carriages for a rich dare. Somehow, they didn't get expelled. We all loved them for it.

The girls' carriage was nearest the front of the train, then the dining carriage followed by the boys' carriages. Boys and Girls were not allowed across the dining car barrier.

Not a chance. Every time the train slowed through stations, the boys would climb out of their windows, run along the train roof and slide into the windows of the girls' carriages, and the party was on. There was no privacy for romantic trysts. The train was too crowded. So, no 'Funny Business'. We didn't even think about that.

**Music man.** Pat Crozier was crazy about music – and about me. His sister, Marion, came aboard the train with his wind-up record player and records ready for our side of the train party. Pat and his pals would blow in through the windows, wind up the music and we would all dance in the corrridors.to Fats Domino, Little Richard and the Boogie-woogie hits of the time.

The Dining Car was mixed boys and girls, always packed to the gills chatting and dancing into the wee small hours till we were kicked out by the weary Train Inspector. At the Howick twenty-minute stop, changing engines, being the last Station before school, we all went back to our own compartments to freshen up and look angelic for the bus ride to school.

I counted twenty-one such epic train journeys over the years.

# 3. Pivotal Person  Mrs. Kitty Dumas
Middle aged with a small round face and beaky nose. French born, she was small with dark brown eyes, olive skin and short black-grey hair. Through her, I discovered my own potential. "You are no better or worse than others. So don't get any fancy ideas of superiority. Don't cave to snobs and bullies".

# 1. Early Days

Later, in business, I would use her technique of thinking out-of-the-box and using think-tanks. Her way of opening and exercising our developing minds. It also helped me become a more open-minded mother, allowing more physical and intellectual freedom.

**Matric.** I coasted through college. Never top or bottom of the class, except in English, Latin and Afrikaans which kept my averages up. History, Science, Geography and Maths were always average.

**The St. Anne's 40th Reunion.** The last time I saw St. Anne's was in 1990 when I attended a 40th Reunion. Amazingly almost all our class of 1950 were still alive, well and very glamorous.

We were told to meet outside the chapel at ten o'clock. Having travelled from Johannesburg, I strolled to the chapel, just in time.

My first thought was 'who are all these old women?'

Then I heard Wendy Wickee's naughty laugh and knew I was in the right place. What a joyful two days we had.

The Class of 1950 had arrived from all over the world, Canada, Australia, England, Mauritius and all corners of SA and Zimbabwe. There had only been twenty-three girls in our class.

**My good friends and future links** Carole Ann Brink, who married Gogh Charlewood, a fashionable Johannesburg Gynae.

Molly Bristow. She became the mother of Anthony Harris who married my daughter, Carole. Molly died when Anthony was in his teens, and so

St Anne's 40th Reunion, class of 1950 were still alive and well and very glamorous.

# My Life, a Roller Coaster Ride

never knew that we were co-grandmothers to Carole's two children Nicola and Matthew Harris.

**Boyfriends and letters.** Everyone wrote letters. Sadly, now, a lost art. After lunch we would assemble in the school hall where the letters would be distributed. No privacy respected. My mother's letters would arrive like clockwork every Friday. I would write a letter home every weekend. But the real excitement was the love letters from boyfriends.

The prefect in charge of the post would make a meal of it. "Megan Steer, Michaelhouse" "Megan Steer – Hilton", with a few from Johannesburg. And each one would mean writing a reply. Never a letter from my brothers.

**Letters.** In those days, can be compared to Cell phones and social media today. Everyone wrote and received letters. It was our social medium as we weren't allowed to make phone calls. Sharp prefect eyes would not give us a chance to write letters in evening Prep hours, so precious afternoon and weekend free time would have to be devoted to correspondence.

**Matric dances.** The end of the Matric year meant several Matric dances. Each school had theirs carefully spaced so as not to clash or overlap. When the school dance was at one of the boys' schools, the girls were always chaperoned by a teacher.

Our dress code was specific and inspected before take-off. No off-the-shoulder dresses and bra straps always had to be securely safety-pinned so as not to reveal themselves. The dress would always be floor length with no ankles peeping out. No high heels.

Worst of all, no make-up. We would do each other's hair with many pin curls. To redden our lips, we would rub them with Dettol for days till they were red and sore.

Then Vaseline them to make them shine – tasting awful.

For the Michaelhouse Dance, Pat and I had different partners. It was bad manners to swap partners – unless they both agreed. His and mine didn't, so we two had to be satisfied with only two dances all evening whilst gazing soulfully at each other across the ballroom.

**Holiday parties.** In the holidays we could always rely on parties, tennis afternoons, swimming at the Country Club, and going to the movies. Almost always in groups as the boys didn't yet have their licences to drive. So, it was up to the mothers and fathers to do lifts.

## 1. Early Days

**1951 Debutante Spring Ball.** Megan Steer and Marion Crozier curtseying to Governor General, His Excellency Ernest Jansen and Mrs. Jansen.

It was customary for 'school leaver' girls to be 'presented' to the Governor General at the Spring Ball. He represented King George VI as South Africa was still in the British Commonwealth.

**1975. Carole Carr.** When it came time for Carole to become a debutante, she had just turned seventeen.

South Africa was out of the Commonwealth. So, The Debs were presented to Sir Harry and Lady Bridget Oppenheimer – at that time being a kind of South African 'royalty'.

Since then, such British custom has been lost to South African society.
In Andy's time – no Debs Spring Balls.

## 4. First Health Critical Choice

Not to take up smoking, having watched my mother smoke fifty a day all my life, I decided never to smoke. All my friends were rushing off to buy ciggies. They teased and cajoled, but it was not for me.

It may be one of the reasons that, here I am at ninety-two, with lungs and arteries in reasonably good shape. Only an Aortic heart valve scare, now fixed and in good working order.

**Megan Steer and Marion Crozier curtseying to the Governor General.
His Excellency Ernest Jansen and Mrs. Jansen.**

# My Life, a Roller Coaster Ride

However, my little four-year-old, Carole had other ideas. You must admit she looks cute and very pleased with herself. Note the 'diamond' ring and attitude in the picture below.

What was I thinking? Buying children sweets which looked like cigarettes? Or any sweets at all. I made her dress.

My liberal mother was a dedicated smoker and was happy to share cigarettes with our teenage children.

In those days, everybody smoked. Every film had the stars smoking. Movie houses were filled with smoke. The projector beam tunnelled through clouds of it, swirling above our heads. So perhaps I did smoke at the movies, other people's smoke.

At the half time intervals, an usherette would come down the aisle with a tray hanging from a strap around her neck, selling cigarettes and sweets. I never saw her selling matches or lighters. That was standard equipment in every pocket and handbag.

The Smoking 1960's. Long cigarette holders came into fashion after Audrey Hepburn elegantly used one in 'Breakfast at Tiffany's'. By now

1951. My debutante picture in *The Star*.

My four year-old daughter Carole, smoking a sugar ciggie.

# 1. Early Days

they were really in Vogue. Filtered cigarettes had come in. No-one thought of the health aspect.

My Last Cigarette was my first cigarette. When Milton and I were ten and twelve, we stole two ciggies from Mattie's pack, plus some watermelon to disguise the tell-tale breath. We hid behind the chicken run at the bottom of the garden, puffing away at our first illicit cigarettes. Milton loved it, I did not. We swallowed some watermelon before returning to the house. I was very sick and never smoked or enjoyed watermelon again. Milton smoked till the day he died, very young at 47. Not directly from smoking. A heart attack from teenage Rheumatic Fever. In retrospect, the watermelon was unnecessary. Mattie, always with a ciggie at the ready, could never have noticed the smoky breath on her two children. But I'm surprised she didn't notice the guilty faces or the missing two cigarettes.

This non-smoking mother and father produced four children, all of whom smoked. A lot.

## 5. 1951 The Grande Tour after Matric

Imagine the excitement when Alfie announced that he, Mattie and I would be taking a three-month long trip abroad. I was almost nineteen years old.

We boarded the 24 000-ton Italian cruise ship named the *Gerusalemme* at Durban Harbour. Destination Brindisi, Italy. It was a fourteen-day excursion up the East Coast of Africa stopping at Beira, Zanzibar, Mombasa, Kenya, Aden in Yemen, then finally Port Suez at the start of the Suez Canal. At this point we had three days in Cairo, joining the ship at Port Said, the other end of the canal. We disembarked at Brindisi at the heel of Italy.

**Defining moment.** It was then that I fell in love with Egypt. We had two nights at the magnificent Shepherds Hotel (which later sadly burnt down) and made the most of our short stay exploring the Pyramids, Luxor, it's markets and museums. I vowed that I would return some day. This I did forty-seven years later, in 1998 with my daughter, Carole.

MD of Haddon's, Alf was on holiday on this starting voyage. His business meetings would only take place weeks later. He was a magical fellow traveller. He knew everything about everywhere. He did his homework on the history and culture of wherever we went ashore. My school Latin was of some help on board the ship, more in recognising and understanding rather than communicating.

The Italians were not interested in speaking English. Thought it a very difficult language. I didn't mention the problems with Latin with its declensions *Amo amas amat amamis amatis amant*, all about love. Nothing understood if not the correct pronunciation. I say 'Bus' but should say 'Booss' for them to understand.

**Defining moment.** The next love affair was with Italy. Naples, the Isle of Capri, Pompei. I was not allowed into one of the Pompei ruin chambers as they told my dad that the wall paintings were not suitable for young ladies. Yes, I did get to see them many years later and, correct, they were not suitable for an innocent young woman in the year 1951.

Our private special guide in Rome was a small gem of a man. Professor Leonardo. He got us into some forbidden places and because he was a University Professor, his English was quaint, and good. Every English word he said ended in an 'uh'. We sat in the seats of the Colosseum and studied the underground exposed passages as he described how it worked behind the scenes of a working arena. We could almost hear the cries of the crowds, the rumbling chariots and the galloping horses.

**A random memory on a return to Rome in 1970.** I was involved in business with Alitalia Airlines and Alfa Romeo, bringing them into our travel and motoring promotions, I enjoyed many trips to Italy (Business Class) for meetings at their head offices. Mario Giorgi was the head of Alitalia, South Africa.

**Emergency.** In June 1970 my father, Alf, was on the *SS Canberra*, a holiday cruise ship, with Mattie. Upon disembarking for a day trip in Lisbon, he had a massive heart attack. He was rushed to the British Hospital. Mattie then stayed at The British Club.

Our family decided that I should immediately go to support Mattie and be there for him. It was July high season in Europe. It was also the World Cup Football time so I couldn't get on any flights. In desperation, I phoned Alitalia's MD, Mario Giorgi and begged for help. I said we would pay whatever it cost. Mario called me back within the hour and said I was booked on an Alitalia flight the next morning. They called it the 'Africa Shrinker', one of the few daytime flights in those days.

Not only did he book me a return ticket, Business Class, from Johannesburg to Rome, but set up an overnight stop at The Inghilterra 5 Star hotel in Rome, near the Spanish Steps. He also booked me on to Lisbon with Air Portugal the next morning and even booked a taxi to get me to the airport.

## 1. Early Days

**Mario Giorgi was a class act.** When I returned home from Italy, two weeks later, I called to thank him and asked to settle the account, he laughed and said – 'no charge it is our pleasure. Somehow, he even knew that my dad had pulled through and claimed some credit for this, saying that seeing me must have helped his recovery.

Amusing memory. I must report an incident on this trip. On the flight to Rome, I sat next to a very attractive businessman. We got talking and talking – as one does on a long day trip, with no night-time to nod off. We both discovered that we would only catch our connections the next day. So, he invited me to dinner. He picked me up at the hotel, and we found ourselves at a restaurant called Romulo e Remo.

Romulo e Remo was to be found in an underground cave down many narrow winding dimly lit steps. I wondered briefly what was going on. Inside, it sounded like mostly Italian diners.

Pain in the neck? Our table for two was next to a small dance floor and a four-piece band was playing something very Italian. We ordered and chatted. I noticed that the four band musicians all had crooked necks. They were lively enough so we assumed that it was simply chronic disability. A charity gig.

When dessert was served, I pointed to the band and asked the waiter what was wrong with the band, and miming that they couldn't keep their heads up. He laughed and said, "No worry, *Signora*, they are listening to the World Cup football semifinals on their earphones".

**Lisbon.** When I arrived in Lisbon, I took a taxi to The British Club where Mattie was staying, round the block from the British Hospital. The doors were massive. Three meters high and solid. It was the weekend. I rang the bell, I hammered with my fists, still no reply. So, I crossed the road where I saw a sentry on duty outside the Presidential Palace. He didn't understand English. I managed to convey the word 'Hospital' and he pointed up the road. Now here was a problem! Luggage and no Taxi. I simply couldn't lug two suitcases up the road. So, I just parked them next to the Sentry, rifle at his shoulder, assuming they would be safe for a while. He looked straight ahead making me invisible.

Up the road I went. The blocks are long in Lisbon. As I reached the corner, Lo and behold, Mattie almost bumped into me. Mattie apologised politely and walked on. She did not know I was coming. When I called out "Mom", she stopped in her tracks not believing her eyes. Then the crying and hugging started. We turned back to the hospital and saw a very frail

## My Life, a Roller Coaster Ride

looking Alfie all plugged into the ICU machines. The amazing Cardiologist said, my arriving was the turning point in his recovery.

I spent a week in Lisbon. Very beautiful and quite grand. It reminded me a little of Paris. After visits to Dad, Mattie and I did a few day trips and enjoyed the annual flower parade, where all the districts of the country join the miles of street pageantry, each region featuring its unique magnificent flora.

Then Rome for two nights. After a token business meeting with Alitalia Head Office, to justify my trip. I was back at the Inghletere Hotel. I was awoken in the middle of the night with what sounded like riots outside. I opened the shutters and window. The noise was deafening. People running around. Cars blaring their horns. Kids in their pyjamas winding their noisy hand ratchets. I phoned Reception to ask what was going on? "We won the World Cup semifinal. Italy will now play the finals with Brazil". I felt we were all winners that night. Listening on the radio back home, the following week, Italy sadly lost the final with Brazil 1 - 4. The Italian euphoria must have switched to mourning.

Sad to report that our dear Mario Giorgi was killed in an aircraft hijacking at an airport a few years later.

**Another cameo.** At that time, we had been staying at the Vaal River house for the July school holidays when news of Alfie's heart attack came. Tony was 14 then Carole 12, Pete 6 and Andy 4.

Our fabulous nanny was Julia, who stayed at the Vaal house with the family as Pete and I commuted daily to our Johannesburg offices. Every time we drove away, this chubby, cheerful lady would run after the car waving goodbye. And when she heard us arriving, would stand at the driveway, running alongside, welcoming us back home.

**Synchro destiny?** I had been anxious to get home, so asked Alitalia Airlines if I could take the Thursday midnight flight instead of the booked Friday evening flight. I was not able to contact Pete to tell him of the change of plan.

On Friday morning, as Peter was leaving for Johannesburg, Julia rushed in saying "You must pick up the madam, TODAY". He patiently explained that I was only leaving Italy today, arriving Saturday morning. In tears she insisted "I saw her arriving". Out of character, Peter decided to placate her and made a call to the airport and was informed that there was an Alitalia flight from Rome due that morning. No passenger information. All credit to Peter, he decided to pass by Jan Smuts airport on his way to work. And

# 1. Early Days

there he found me waiting for a taxi to town. He was very pleased with himself. I was very pleased with him. And impressed with Julia believing in her vision.

**Back to 1951. University of life.** My grande tour at nineteen was a fast-forward education into the wider world. Hobnobbing with high powered businesspeople, whilst acknowledging the role of people who serve behind the scenes. I acquired a taste for luxury and fun. I learned to claim it and fulfil my dad's goal for the very best life had to offer.

He emphasised the value of patience, diplomacy, modesty and generosity. Incidentally, I also experienced the value of a smile and a sense of humour. Both my parents demonstrated and practiced the value of hard work and 'No free Lunches' in life.

After journeying through Italy, Switzerland and France, we hopped over to England and almost immediately sailed across to Scandinavia where my dad's real business started.

We landed in Gothenburg where Alf had his first business meetings. Haddon's imported printing machines and paper from Scandinavia. His supplier, Jan Liebig, and his gorgeous wife, Annie, invited us to dinner at a restaurant called 'The Henriksberg'. I had my first experience of Schnapps thrown back and the eye-engaging *"Skal"* toasts with fine Smorgasbord cuisine.

Now, this fine restaurant had a party trick. You can imagine an innocent non-drinker tasting her first Schnapps, and a dessert wine. Suddenly the framed pictures on the walls showing majestic schooners in full sail started splashing over high seas in and over the waves. The boats in the pictures were moving. I thought I would be seasick.

All eyes at the table were on me trying not to laugh. Very funny ha-ha. Fun at my expense and, much later, I had to have a laugh at myself.

After dinner we were invited to a downstairs lounge for liqueurs and coffee. It was also an open platform for anyone wishing to perform on the small stage.

Stand-up comedy, singers, piano, tango dancers. This night they happened to have a pianist who kept sending the waiter across to ask me for a request to play. I sent a few across and I felt he was hitting on me. All innocent fun and very flattering.

**Midnight caller.** We all walked across the park to our hotel and off to bed. In the middle of the night my room phone rang. It was the pianist. He had followed us to the hotel, somehow got my name and room number and introduced himself as James Rawlings. We chatted for two hours and agreed to meet the next day for coffee.

Of course, Mattie stuck to me like glue. So, it was coffee for three twice that day and the day after. He was a young English businessman spending two years in Scandinavia developing his own Import Export company. On the third day he invited Mattie and me on a day trip to Tivoli Gardens amusement park. After coffee, he asked Mattie and me to ride on the Ferris Wheel. Mattie declined.

**First marriage proposal.** Jamie and I rolled up into the sky. On the way up he told me that he was twenty-nine, had a very successful business and that he had fallen in love with me. At the very top, he went on his knees and proposed.

He had a temporary ring. Shock and confusion from me. I was very tempted as he was very attractive, and I was a romantic. What to say? Obviously, I got through it and asked for time. "It's too soon, I'll have to think about it". I was due to leave the next day for Stockholm. He said he would follow me till I agreed.

I didn't dare tell the parents but did give him our next stop details. So, it became a telephone romance for another week. When we eventually got to the Stockholm railway station leaving for Oslo, Jamie arrived from Gothenburg with flowers, a book to read (I remember it was called *The Cardinal* by Henry Morton Robinson), and a letter promising his undying love. My first serious romance, only one kiss at the station, my first marriage proposal and then farewell forever. But not for him. He sent flowers to our London Hotel and phoned every day. I realised I would have to get real and accept the futility of a long-distance romance. Very long distance as we were about to sail for home. Heady stuff. It was over.

**Stockholm.** My dad's biggest supplier of printing machinery also owned the Volvo factory. So, we had a beautiful black Volvo for our stay in that magnificent city. I loved the pale wooden clean designs of the furniture. I loved the free and easy temperament of the people I met. It seemed to be a perfect society. The Corporation owner, whom his staff called 'President Alm' had a daughter, Birgitta, my age. We got along so well that they invited me to stay with them for a year. However, my parents thought the 'free and easy' aspect of the people would be a risk for their young daughter. So, politely declined.

# 1. Early Days

**Frogner Park Sculpture.**

**Frogner Park, Oslo.** How different was Oslo and the Norwegians. Serious and a little conservative. Rather like the Scots. At least that is what I thought until we visited the Frogner Park. We walked up a long avenue of fifteen magnificent massive standing sculptures depicting naked people entangled in all sorts of sexual poses, men juggling babies and columns of every entanglement you can imagine.

**First duvet.** It was my first experience of the Midnight Sun and down duvets. We had only known cotton quilts and counterpanes and blankets as bedclothes. I asked if I could take one home with me. But with much travelling still on the cards, they thought it impractical. It would be another forty years before I got my first duvet.

The rest of the trip was two weeks in England, mostly London. Then back home via the west coast of Africa on the SS *Carnarvon Castle*. I had sailed around the African continent Durban to Durban.

## 6. Back in Johannesburg
**Reality. The princess turned into a frogess.**
It was July 1951. I attended a Secretarial College. A modest career plan, far removed from my old dream of becoming a doctor. Women were not encouraged to be doctors in those days. And to be honest, my academic track record was underwhelming.

After graduating as a secretary at the end of November, I decided I needed pocket money. So, I got a job in the Toy Department at John Orr's in the centre of Johannesburg. I was paid ten pounds a week (add about two 00s in 2024 values). I had to pay for my bus tickets and was required to give 10% to my parents for board and lodging. Now, having a job, my monthly pocket money stopped but I still had enough to meet friends for milkshakes and movies and modest little luxuries like make-up, hairdresser and buying fabric to make myself new evening dresses. I had become a good seamstress like my mother.

It was considered good parenting and lessons in life to make the children realise the value of money and to take nothing for granted. This was very hard for me after the supreme luxury of the overseas trip. My parents requested the same from Milton. However, they became soft on the next two laat-lammetjies, John and Chris who never had their salaries docked for their board and lodging.

**1952. Anglovaal.** My first real job. I was placed in the Anglo Alpha Cement and Union Lime Division. The Swiss M.D. was Mr. Hans Byland and his perfect secretary was Mrs. Parker who was the 'office mother'. Very reassuring to have that person around in your first real job.

Formal wear to work. Suits, skirts, blouses. Matching shoes, belts, sometimes gloves – and always a hat. I had at least ten hats in my cupboard. We always wore stockings held up by a suspender belt. Stockings were called 'Nylons'.

Nylons were quite expensive, so we were always careful not to get 'ladders'. If a ladder started, we would stop the run in its tracks with a little nail varnish base coat. If that damage control was done whilst on the leg, it stuck the stocking to the leg skin and had to be unstuck when undressing. Or, if colour varnish was all we could find at the moment, it could only be used on ladders or nicks under the shoe or under the skirt, out of sight. We always bought two matching pairs of nylons at a time so that if one stocking laddered, we could match it up as a spare.

Nylon was so strong that it was almost indestructible. Bad for business. So, the industry produced a flimsier thread to ensure a bigger profit through bigger turnover. Which brings to mind the Arwa Parys Airfield, which I launched in 1971. (See Arwa story later)

1960. Vance Packard wrote a book, *The Waste Makers*, about disposable goods, consumerism and planned obsolescence, which applies in this case.

I worked at Anglovaal for four years till I was expecting Tony. My leaving present was a case of a dozen Stuart Crystal goblets. I still have five of them sixty-nine years later. Never tossed in the sink. Used daily, I wash them myself.

# 1. Early Days

**1952. Alf and Mattie decided we should move to a new house.**
I remember our excitement when we moved about one mile away to the north. It was top of the mountain with a long view almost to Pretoria and to the East, on an acre of land extending downwards both sides of the mountain. On the north down-slope, we blasted a place in which to build the swimming pool with an infinite view North.

The house had four bedrooms and a conservatory. The kitchen had a massive Aga stove. There were double staff quarters at the side and a Billiard Room over the double garage. We all lived there till we married. Mattie and Alfie lived there till 1970.

'Shaftholme' 19 Grace Road, Mountain View.

**Michael Claude Reitz.** In 1952, my second year at Anglovaal, I met the most magical man. He was a partner in his late father's law firm Deneys Reitz, Hersov and Menell on the ground floor of the building. Not far from the elevators. He was 29-year-old Mike Reitz. Tall, blond, blue eyed with a big mischievous smile. Not shy.

He would contrive to be near the elevators when I arrived and left and soon plucked up the courage, as he confessed, to invite me to lunch.

Soon we were dating seriously. He had graduated from Cambridge with a law degree. My mother loved him as he impressed her with his easy grace and manners.

Every week we would go to the Country Club for the Saturday evening dances. Mostly with newly married mutual friends Henry and Isobel Hunt. (Of the Williams Hunt and Herbert Evans families). Or meet at the Club on weekend afternoons to swim and lie in the sun. And, of course, we saw

# My Life, a Roller Coaster Ride

General Wavell, Field Marshall Jan Smuts, High Commissioner Deneys Reitz and Leila Reitz.

Headstone Deneys and Michael Reitz in Pilgrims Rest.

Twenty-two years later, 1975, Peter Murrough, Sales Director for Leyland, talking to Rowland Emett at my Chitty Chitty Bang Bang Exhibition.

# 1. Early Days

each other almost every day, being in the same office building.

Soon we realised that we were getting very serious, to the extent that he introduced me to his mother, Leila, widow of the famous South African soldier, lawyer, author, historian and politician Deneys Reitz.

In those days young men would have to do part time military service in the Citizen Force. He was a pilot and would be called up for flyovers or air exercises, which he loved.

Michael was called up for a fly past at a Nationalist Party Convention. He was a conscientious objector to this but had to go. Whilst fooling around in the air, he and a fellow pilot clipped wings and fatally crashed to the ground.

My mother woke me on Sunday morning to tell me that Mike had crashed and died. I was in shock and zombied around for months. I couldn't even bring myself to attend his funeral at their family plot near Barberton.

However, after a month or so, Leila and I met regularly at her home, till she moved away from Johannesburg.

## 7. Pivotal Person Leila Reitz

Leila Reitz became a pivotal influence in my life. In consoling each other, she took me under her wing and taught me some valuable life lessons.

Leila Reitz's own life legacy is impressive. First female member of the S.A. Parliament representing Parktown 1933 to 1943. She fought for Women's Rights.

But, to me, she was simply Mike's mother. She urged me always to fight for my position in life.

Leila said, "you don't have to be like a man to do it. Be yourself. Always stand your ground, in the nicest possible way, of course".

Leila was also the dutiful wife of her famous husband. He became the S.A. High Commissioner to London. She accompanied him as the lady Ambassadress. He died in 1944. Leila died in 1959.

# Part 2
# Courtship, Marriage and Family

## 8. 1953. My 21st Birthday

The photograph below shows me cutting the Lucky Horseshoe cake. Famous organist and family friend, Roger O'Hogan, the party toastmaster, and my parents' friend, all having a good laugh.

As a special optional extra, the photographer borrowed the stole, matching my dress, and hand-coloured the photo exactly to match.

The only colour photo in the white, leatherbound album of the birthday evening.

My gift from my parents was a bundle of Haddon's shares, which came in handy buying the Athol and Sandown houses.

**My Dress.** My fabulous soft gold organza off the shoulder dress was 'The New Look', three quarter length and, of course, an orchid pinned at the shoulder. A gift from my parents. In those days orchids were special, highly prized and a token of love.

I had never made a speech before, but I was told that my birthday

Mattie, Roger O'Hogan, Megan, Alfie.

## 2. Courtship, Marriage and Family

speech in reply to the main toast was amusing. They likened me to my dad for being able to address a room full of people.

Peter was a good dancer but always with a soppy look on his face. Looks like we are dancing standing still. Never let a dance stand in the way of conversation. See pic on page 49.

You can see he got his money's worth at the barber! Strange because he had really nice slightly curly hair which he kindly passed on to our children.

**Speeches.** I have never sought to make speeches of any kind. My Birthday speech was my first but by no means my last. When, years later, addressing busloads of international visitors en route to mines, it didn't bother me and I could do it in both languages with some ease. I always made sure that I had a handful of 'funnies' as the best way to get people's attention and to keep them awake.

**Rosebank Secretarial College.** For many years, I was the annual guest speaker at the Graduation Ceremony of the College.

It happened after I had made my mark in business. The Head of the College felt I could motivate the students to use their new skills as a 'foot in the door' to anywhere they wanted to go.

I was always introduced as "Megan Carr who started out her career as a secretary – and look where she is now".

**Engagement.** Peter and I were engaged, July of 1953. I chose a 1.5 carat solitaire diamond, set in gold. Long engagements in those days.

**1954. The Marriage.** 10th February 1954. We married and were together for exactly eighteen-years. We had four children. Anthony, Carole, Peter and Andrea. Thereafter seven grandchildren and one great granddaughter. We divorced almost amicably in 1972.

I was happily divorced. He was later happily married to Vanda Henderson. Mother of three. Our two families lived amicably apart.

1983, Vanda and I even travelled by car to Grahamstown to visit Andy at DSG (Diocesan School for Girls) for the Founders' Day weekend. Andy with her mother and stepmother visiting together, caused some amusement.

My wedding dress was designed by the currently fashionable Ivor Kirsten, who also did Mattie's soft grey floor-length gown.

Betty Carr looked elegant in a floor-length burgundy gown and matching hat. I had two bridesmaids, Yvonne Jowett and Jane Lennox, dressed in soft watermelon pink. Also produced by Ivor Kirsten.

# My Life, a Roller Coaster Ride

## 2. Courtship, Marriage and Family

**No Colour Film.** The professional party photographs are all in black and white.

Opposite: My family, school friends, Anglovaal friends, boyfriend, Peter, and many old boyfriends with their partners. Our social set.

Left: Mattie, Alfie and Me.

Bottom Left: Peter was a good dancer but always with a soppy look on his face. Dancing behind us, Carole Ann Brink (later Charlewood) with her boyfriend at the time, Graham Greathead. Carole Ann was tall and handsome.

Bottom Right: My fabulous soft gold organza off the shoulder dress.

**Wedding at St. Aidan's Church 1954.** Despite pouring rain, It was a most beautiful wedding, dancing into the wee small hours at the Old Johannian Club.

Strangely, it was fashionable in those days, to get married midweek. It was 5pm on a Thursday. The service was at St. Aidan's Church and the reception for 120 friends and family.

Peter's Best Men were Peter Packer and Peter Hartford (three Peters from Cape Town). Sadly, for Peter the Groom, Peter Packer, his childhood best friend, couldn't make it as his wife, Glenda, was ill with measles. Peter, an E.N.T. Specialist, felt he might also be infectious.

Peter Packer was the son of author Joy Packer and Admiral Sir Herbert Packer, Commander in Chief of the British Navy, South Atlantic, stationed at Simonstown. Joy's book 'Pack and Follow' told of her nomadic life as his navy wife. Peter was raised by 'Granny Petersen', Joy's mother.

I cut the wedding cake, then climbed onto a bench and threw the bouquet. It was caught by Jane Lennox who soon married. I threw the rose-embroidered garter, which was caught by Geoff Robin, who also soon married Joan Polson. All had attended my 21st birthday party. We left the wedding in Johnny Minnaar's Fishtail Cadillac, shamelessly plastered with shaving cream 'Just Married' messages, dragging tin cans. Confetti everywhere. Confetti is no longer allowed at churches, for obvious reasons.

## 9. Courtship and Marriage

**Early 1953. Synchro destiny.** my office friend June Leslie was dating a handsome Canadian Peter Murrough. They decided that it was time for Peter's flat mate, Peter Carr, to meet me, June's office friend.

# 2. Courtship, Marriage and Family

1953, June and Peter set up blind date lunch for Peter Carr and me at His Majesty's Cellar restaurant, central Johannesburg. Table for four. When I arrived, there were the three of them waiting for me. Peter and June introduced me to Peter Carr. He was twenty-eight, I was twenty years old.

My first impression of Peter Carr was handsome, good smile, somewhat arrogant. I didn't immediately take to him but kept an open mind. After the starter, Peter and June abandoned us to get on with lunch.

I learnt that Peter had been a Spitfire Pilot at the end of the war followed by three years at the University of Cape Town. Medicine and Dentistry, but never graduated.

Our date went reasonably well but I was not 'bowled over'. Not only had the lunch date been set up, but they had also invited Peter and me to join them at a Sunday picnic at Retief's Kloof Resort. It was a most beautiful day and the company, relaxed and welcoming.

We all left as evening was setting in. Peter drove me home, to be met by an angry Mattie at the front door. She said that my evening date had been sitting around for half an hour, waiting for me.

I'd quite forgotten. Peter scurried off fast. I quickly showered, changed and, out I went with Ian to our weekly ballroom dancing classes. The last thing I felt like doing!

**Motorbike courting.** Peter started inviting me out and I included him in my dating diary.

On our dates, he would pick me up in his car at the Grace Roadhouse, then off to his place where we would switch to his BSA Bantam 127 motorbike which he called *Fidget'* Sometimes we would go off to open fields, Pete teaching me to ride. Then I graduated to jumping ditches and doing slaloms set up with stones.

We'd go for picnics with a thermos of coffee and chocolate shortbread biscuits.

Evening dates, we went by car. That Christmas, he bought himself a bigger bike, a blue Tiger 500 and taught me to ride it. It was quite scary after little Fidget. One day, I was driving, he sat pillion. I took off so fast that he fell off the back and I went on wildly, round and round, too scared to do anything but hold on till I remembered to close the throttle.

**Brother fury and embarrassment.** My brother, Milton, was disgusted at my motor bike antics. Mattie had always said "Ladies don't ride motorcycles". He didn't tell her about the illicit rides as yet unbeknown to our parents. He warned me never, ever, to let any of his friends see me

# My Life, a Roller Coaster Ride

behaving so badly. Not a smart thing to say which amounted to a dare.

One Saturday, Milton went to play tennis at his girlfriend Maureen Baker's house across Linksfield Ridge. Peter and I decided to pay them a visit on the *Tiger*. Me on pillion.

Then disaster happened. As we biked noisily up the Bakers' driveway, their Doberman dog chased after us and nipped me on my bum. Mrs. Baker came out and, in a moment, had me bending over a basin as she bathed and treated the small wound. It attracted a crowd of white-clothed tennis players all giggling to the mortification of poor Milton. Never to be forgiven by him.

**Going nowhere.** Peter became a regular around the house with or without an invitation. He once quoted to a friend "If the daughter you would win, on the mother first begin". So, he would visit Mattie even if I wasn't there. I was going everywhere. Often, I would return from an evening date, and he would rush out, hug me and ask if we had had a good evening. Not good for the dates. Soon they dropped off one by one and Peter became part of the furniture.

**About doctors and engineers.** Peter followed his War service as a spitfire pilot with three years at the University of Cape Town doing two years of Medicine, then switched to Dentistry. Peter hated them both. (Silly Billy Carr, his son was a born engineer.) Peter dropped out of university.

He became a Buyer in a small Mining House in Johannesburg, far from

Peter's Spitfire. He'd managed to wangle a Spitfire with CA _R.

Cecil Colville (Billy) Carr, Peter's father.

## 2. Courtship, Marriage and Family

his folks in Cape Town. It so happened that his best friend Peter Packer had married a wonderful girl, Glenda Orr, heir to her father's small Mining House. She managed to secure the job for Peter.

He was very articulate and smart and seemed to be doing quite well. Then suddenly he announced that he had switched jobs and became a car salesman at the big Chev and Opel franchise, Williams Hunt. He had a love affair with cars and bikes and suddenly seemed more fulfilled with his work.

**Easter 1953. Meet the folks.** He drove me to Cape Town in his Vauxhall Velox to meet his parents. Daunting. I heard them whisper to him "Please, don't get serious with a Johannesburg girl". But we had drifted into a serious relationship. No intimacy; Separate bedrooms, in those days, intimacy waited for marriage.

**Peter's family background.** Joseph Wilson ('JW') Carr was Peter's grandfather, Born in 1865, north of Durham in Chester. His father, George Carr, died early and his mother married Joseph Graham, who managed the nearby Penshaw Railway Station.

In his early twenties, Joseph (JW) emigrated to the Cape Colony to start a new life in South Africa. His life is a success story.

His first job was lighting the evening lamps on the platforms at the Cape Town railway station, soon being promoted to 'Traffic Manager'.

He married Sarah Jane Colville Scott in 1893. JW was transferred to the small Karoo town of Steytlerville. Here Sarah Jane gave birth to Cecil Colville Carr. Cecil was nicknamed 'Billy'.

1899 the second Anglo Boer had begun. When it became dangerous for

**Look-alikes Spitfire Pilot Peter Carr and grandson, Chef, Matthew Harris.**

## My Life, a Roller Coaster Ride

women and children to remain in such a remote region, JW sent Sarah Jane and young Billy to live in the newly built Mount Nelson Hotel in Cape Town in1900, where they lived until the war ended in 1902.

JW joined the British Forces and went on to hold the rank of Major in the Colonial Imperial Railways Regiment. He was awarded several medals including clasps for his service in the Cape Colony, the Orange Free State and the Transvaal.

JW, Sarah Jane and Billy moved to Johannesburg after the Boer War ended. This transfer was a Railways promotion.

**The Tin Temple.** Billy attended the St. John's Preparatory School, which was nicknamed, 'The Tin Temple' since it was an Anglican school built from tin sheeting.

St. John's later moving from Joubert Park in Johannesburg to the suburb of Houghton in 1905. Billy went right through to matriculate there in 1912. He sailed by ship to England in 1913, to study Medicine at Durham University.

In 1914, when World War 1 started, Billy had to pause his studies midway, to join the Durham Light Infantry. He was offered two choices. To go to France, where the life expectancy of a soldier was 19 days, or go to North Africa where he stood a better chance of survival. Wisely, Billy

The Tin Temple. St. John's Preparatory School, nicknamed,
'The Tin Temple' since it was an Anglican school built from tin sheeting.

## 2. Courtship, Marriage and Family

chose the Africa option and was assigned to the Warwickshire Yeomanry Regiment with the rank of Second Lieutenant, Signaller. In this unit he trained in Cavalry as he was a good horseman.

He was sent, first to Egypt and then to Palestine, to fight against the Germans and their Kurdish allies.

Billy participated in one of the most famous and successful battles of WW1 in Huj near Be'er Sheba, close to Jerusalem, under the command of General Allenby.

In WW1, 'JW' Carr served in the 2nd Brigade of the South African Railroads and Harbours Division. He was promoted to Major and earned the DSO (Distinguished Service Order).

After the war, he was mentioned in Dispatches by General Louis Botha to Winston Churchill. He earned many more medals in the course of his military career, holding the rank of Lieutenant Colonel before retiring from the SAR&H in 1925.

At that time, he was Assistant General Manager of the SAR&H, second in charge to Sir William Hoy.

**Heirloom.** On his retirement from SAR&H, he was presented with an engraved Ceremonial Sword, which Peter inherited, and which always proudly hung on our dining room wall. Peter treasured JW's DSO medal, which we kept in the safe.

He also inherited a mahogany travelling writing chest with a brass disc engraved 'Sir John Colville', which must have belonged to Sarah Jane's father. Sadly, this was stolen in a burglary at our Sandown house in 1972.

**1918. After the war** Billy returned to Durham University to complete his medical studies, including his internship at the St Andrews Hospital in Newcastle, where he qualified as a doctor in 1919.

Betty Blackwell was a nurse in the war between 1915 and 1918. She was stationed at Salonika in Greece where she became seriously ill and discharged from army service. Both Betty and Billy received many war medals for their service. She continued her nursing in Newcastle which is where she met Billy.

Billy bought a motorbike with a sidecar for them to travel around the countryside and go on picnics together in their hospital off-duty hours.

Billy returned to South African to take up residence in 'Iowa' his house in Grove Avenue Claremont.

Betty travelled in the Edinburgh Castle to join him in Cape Town where they were married in St. Georges Cathedral a week later.

# My Life, a Roller Coaster Ride

Billy became a highly respected General Practitioner in the Southern Suburbs of Cape Town and became Secretary of the Cape Medical Society.

The practice was run from his home surgery and Betty was his Nurse-Receptionist. She gave birth to their only child, Peter in 1924.

**Billy loved fishing.** His annual break was fishing with a group of friends, some of them Doctors, at a remote coastal retreat called 'Blombos'. So remote, that the final stretch to reach the cottage was by ox wagon. Young Peter would join him there when school permitted.

Billy said that when on holiday, if people knew that you were a doctor, they'd always talk about their health problems, so no holiday at all. So, a complete getaway was necessary.

Peter and I visited them at Blombos, on our honeymoon and were proudly presented with an orange bag full of fresh oysters off the rocks, for lunch.

Peter Carr was a weekly boarder at Diocesan College (Bishops) from the age of eleven. He signed up for UCT Medical School in 1943. but put medical studies on hold and attended flight school at Youngsfield, Cape.

WW2 was already in its fifth year, and he wanted to be part of it. He received his 'Wings' and qualified as a Fighter Pilot. He joined the Allied Forces in Italy, North Africa and Palestine in late 1944 with the rank of 1st Lieutenant.

**Billy on the rocks.**

## 2. Courtship, Marriage and Family

Peter flew Spitfires and Mustangs – but preferred the Spitfires. He managed to get a plane with the insignia 'CAR R'. He was disappointed not to see much war action as the war was almost over in Europe. His function was to fly reconnaissance missions and to shoot up enemy supply chains.

### 10. 1956. Birth of Anthony and our first home

It was a long labour. I was RH Negative and Peter RH positive. We were warned that this could produce a 'blue baby'.

He didn't turn blue as expected. He didn't look like us, as expected, looking rather puffy and stretched from the pressure, our cheery Doctor Roley, assured us it was the right baby and that the long labour had caused the features to puff and stretch. And he did bear the plastic bracelet with our name on it.

Proud father strutted around saying, "I ordered a Boy", as if it mattered. The Rh-negative factor didn't kick in for any of the four children.

It was a very good time for us.

I left the Marymount early after eight days and then the reality set in. Fortunately, we had sold our Bellevue flat and moved in with my parents at Grace Road.

Help was at hand in the form of my mother, Mattie.

Carole (3) Tony (5).

# My Life, a Roller Coaster Ride

**Athol House being built (Baby Tony asleep in the 1952 Packard).**

**Neighbours and friends, Charles, Italia and David Greig.**

**Our first house.** I was pregnant with Tony, my friend, Italia Greig was also expecting their first child, Charles. They had bought the stables of a subdivided farm in Athol and transformed it into a quaint thatched house on an acre of land.

Italia persuaded me to come over to look at the adjoining plot which had a substantial outbuilding on it. I loved the position and spoke to their architect, Eddie Bock, about the possibility of using the solidly built, concrete flat roofed farm staff outbuilding, as the base for a house. After testing the foundations and walls, he came up with house drawings showing a high-pitched roof with dormer windows and a double volume lounge. We were delighted with the design.

When I took my parents to see the property. They were aghast at how

## 2. Courtship, Marriage and Family

far away 'in the country' it was. They, living in Mountain View and me and their grandchild moving about eight miles away to the north.

I sold some of my 21st birthday shares and bought the property. With the land and building paid for, I was therefore easily able to arrange a bank loan, and the building improvements began.

Owning the house in my name (which needed my husband's signed permission) paid dividends later on.

**1956 – 1964. Athol house.** (Left) Note the newly ploughed upper side garden awaiting lawn. I was expecting Tony when, with a rotavator, I ploughed up the acre of wild veld ready for clearing and levelling by our gardener, Newstone (seen walking at the back of the house).

**5 Owen Road, Athol.** Our next-door neighbours were the Greigs. Up the road were other best friends, Adele and Bob Lucas, who had recently returned from Cape Town with their one-year old daughter, Carolyn, who was born six months before Carole. The start of a lifelong sixty-four year friendship. Longer than their mothers' fifty-eight year friendship.

The builder was a Mr. Heathcote. He was sweet but slack and inefficient. And misnamed. Heath Robinson would have been more appropriate. He went bust after 6 months. Instead of the trauma of re-costing with a new builder, I decided to project manage the building myself. I signed up the, now redundant, Heathcliff artisans and used outside contractors, I got on with it. I was pregnant and happy to have a project to work on.

Our dream home was becoming a reality. An acre of bare garden. 'Lots of potential', as they say in the property adverts. It took almost a year to complete. Tony was born during the time of the building process.

**Back to work.** Tony was three months old, and money was short, so I decided to find a job. I found employment as a temp secretary in a mining house. By foregoing lunch break, I could get away early and be home by five to feed the little one. He had had to be fed my expressed milk by the nanny, four-hourly.

By the time Tony was a year-old we had moved into our fabulous new Athol home with our old friends as neighbours and a garden gate between the two houses. The bond between the two boys was lifelong.

When Carole was born eighteen months later Italia's Christopher soon followed.

The two little boys took no notice of these events.

It is interesting to note that the difference in upbringing for children in the fifties and sixties is that we were comfortable having two live-in servants around as part of the average family dynamic. Our household budget always included wages and upkeep for two servants, broke as we often were. It was simply 'normal'.

All homes, in our area, had a staff house, separate from the main dwelling. Two rooms with a shared bathroom and cooking facility. A female domestic worker/nanny and a house help/gardener. This meant that I could go off to work and the children were cared for. The nannies were a blessing to us all. They were natural and practical mother figures. Not keen on child discipline or any kind of regimentation.

Ours showed a kindness and indulgence which gave the children much more freedom than the old strict Victorian-type parenting.

Currently, those staff quarters have mostly become 'granny cottages.'

**Anthony Colville Carr** was born in 1956. Born weeks late and eventually trained himself to bepunctual. He always asked questions and spent hours in the garden studying ants and beetles.

**Below.** Carole's 6th birthday party. Diana Lucas, Carole, Megan, Tony, Chris Greig. Not in the picture, Carolyn Lucas and Charles Greig.

Shown at the Athol house with Mothers Adele and Italia having tea

Carole's 6th birthday party on the lawn at Athol house.
The table was a door on bricks with a pretty cloth and the little guests all sat on cushions.
Birthday cakes with candles, and we always had a theme. It was all about party food.
As they grew older, there would be dress-up themes like wigs, earrings and hats.

## 2. Courtship, Marriage and Family

inside looking on through the window. Note the two bottles of CocaCola on the table.

Birthday cakes would always have a theme. The drinks were 'Suncrush', a case of mixed soft drinks in small bottles and straws. There would always be ice-cream, ice-suckers and cupcakes. The table was a door on bricks with scatter cushions on the lawn. Everyone dressed up for parties. Dress-up themes for girls like earrings, wigs and fancy hats. In the spirit of the theme, one baby-sister, attending in her carrycot, came dressed as a carrot, wrapped in an orange blanket and a wide green bow tied round her little head.

### 11. Carole Elizabeth Yuill Carr

In 1958, Carole arrived exactly on time and has been on time ever since. Pretty, happy, and smart from day one.

**1962.** I was becoming a little bored, unchallenged and restless. Our funds were limited, and we watched every penny. Yes, pennies, before decimalisation in 1971.

I was driving a green 'Baby Renault' which I loved. Engine at the back and a roof rack. Adele had a green, clapped-out mini minor with doors difficult to open and close. She sometimes had to use the front passenger door as the driver's door was clamped shut. The Greig's were one-up with a black Citroen. Peter, at that time with Williams Hunt Chev and Opal agency, got himself the perk of test-driving new cars before they were delivered. He lorded it over everyone, arriving home in brand new cars. He seldom had to use his own Vauxhall Velox.

Charles Greig (left), Tony (right). Playing with the garden hose around the blow-up pool in the Athol Garden. The two were like twins. Both happy, wilful, bright, mischievous and inseparable.

I was somewhat disenchanted with my marriage. We were simply incompatible, in interests and in parenting. In those days, divorce was frowned upon. Whenever I broached the 'D' word with my mother she went apoplectic and trotted out the usual tut-tuts, "What about the children?". "Don't be silly, it will pass". "Give it your serious attention" or just "Don't be ridiculous". My father was more into clichés "You made your bed, now lie in it". Easily said.

So, I hung in there for another ten years of marriage, putting my own spin on it to make it workable, although not particularly fulfilling. We never quarrelled.

## 12. Pivotal person Angus Collie

I decided to keep my eyes peeled for an interesting part time job. Also to supplement our income, which was simply not enough.

I answered an advertisement for a position at the Chamber of Mines Public Relations division. I had no PR qualification or experience. However, I had been a good secretary before having children and spent time doing voluntary work for charity events. My secretarial experience of four years with Anglovaal was useful, even essential for the advertised job. I also was well recommended by my various employers as a temp secretary.

I was most fortunate to be interviewed and accepted by the Chamber of Mines Public Relations Director, Angus Collie. He was typical of PRs in those days. He didn't care what people thought of him, his ideas or his methods. He was autocratic, brilliant, and effective. His mind was laser sharp. His command of English, supreme. His sense of humour, subtle and interesting. Never unkind. He satisfied the powers, that be, within the Chamber.

It was my pure luck that he equipped me to, later, take on a PR career in my own business. I owe much to him for my future direction and business success. A pivotal person in my business life.

Angus had his moods depending on how much his leg hurt. The more he limped, the more we tip-toed around him. He had been in a car accident some years before, which had left him partly lame. He often walked with a stick, which was the 'tip-toe-signal'. He sometimes used this same handy walking stick to impatiently cut off a phone call in mid conversation. He said, "It's OK, they will just think you were cut-off". He'd then say his piece and limp off.

Angus Collie introduced me to Felicity Fenwick, who managed the VIP and Public Mine Visits. Felicity was regarded as formidable. She was a

## 2. Courtship, Marriage and Family

very capable, but 'difficult' person. A real snob in the office. She was 'one of the boys' in the mines.

Luckily, I was blissfully unaware of her reputation so, as 'fools rush in'. I simply settled in and chose to take no notice of office moods. I have always assumed that people are nice and that I was no threat. So, I breezed in ready to learn the job whatever it took. I ignored the cutting remarks which could have been seen as bullying to a new young apprentice. But I was confident and happy that I could handle anything she threw at me. She did, and I didn't blink an eye, as I got on with it.

In a very short time, we were getting along just fine, almost friends. The job was one of the most interesting I'd ever had in those early days. It involved a certain amount of office preparation and winding up in between visits to mines.

The main job was hosting people from South Africa and all over the world. General public and specialised groups. Taking visitors to the mines was a PR exercise for the mining industry, also for the country, badly in need of good publicity at the time of heightening Apartheid pressures on South Africa.

Every minute that the mines are not at full production can be measured at the financial bottom line. Some of the working mines around Johannesburg were past their prime production, so these were mostly on the list selected for public visits. The mines we visited were usually within a one-hour bus ride from the Rotunda at the Johannesburg Station.

They were mines such as Durban Roodepoort Deep, Luipaardsvlei, Randfontein Estates (which also produced Uranium), Vogelstruisbult (which had a little zoo in the hospital compound). Grootvlei, Nigel, ERPM, East Daggafontein, all on the East Rand.

We, as specials, visited some of the newer mines in the Carletonville area like Blyvooruitzicht and some, which we flew to, such as President Brand in the Free State. Because of high production, mines such as Blyvooruitzicht were reserved for specialised mining industry visits.

In the first month I had to learn the history of the gold mining industry, the mining and refining processes, the various mining groups, personnel, production details and financial history and industry status.

I also learned about the migrant labour, training, leadership programs, aptitude testing, nutritional policy, work safety procedures, the medical facilities and the tribal diversity and influences of the migrant labour force.

The office work involved ordering the luxury forty-seater buses from

# My Life, a Roller Coaster Ride

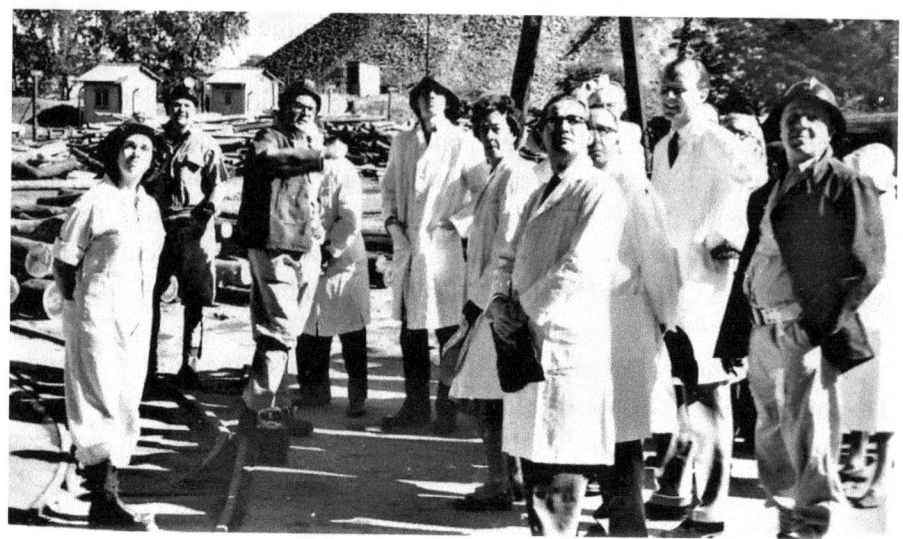

**Mine visit group, Megan front left.**

SA Railways Transport department, liaising with the mines on times and visitor numbers, taking the bookings in the Hollard Street office, doing confirmations, accounts, preparing brochures and information relevant to each mine. Filing reports after each visit. My work week consisted of two underground day visits and a day in the office, Tuesday, Wednesday and Thursday. Perfect to fit in with my home and family life.

Felicity always took the best mines to start with. Later we each had our favourites and fell into a comfortable rotation.

The mine visits were in great public demand with long waiting lists. Imagine at least an eight to twelve-hour day trip, free of charge, including transport, lunch, teas and talks by experts in each of the specialist fields. The mine manager would invariably host a full sit-down lunch.

At lunch, I would select the most appropriate of the visitors to stand up and thank the mine for its hospitality. There always seemed to be an extrovert or two in the mix to choose from. They often asked me for help checking their speeches to get the names and details right.

The PR part of every mine excursion, for me, involved trying to memorise the names and countries of each visitor and jot down notes about them to make their visits more personally enjoyable and relaxed.

If they were defined groups, I would research their specialities, whether they were mining engineers from Texas, teachers from the UK or Brain Surgeons visiting SA on an International Congress. I would adapt the tour accordingly.

## 2. Courtship, Marriage and Family

Doctors, for example, at the mine hospital, the talk would cover specialised medicine for the job. Mine health hazards, cultural requirements and beliefs. On occasion, I would bring in a Sangoma for his or her herbal input and treatments. Angus Collie would allow me this personal interest in remedial medicine. Sometimes, the office booked in famous entertainment people and their entourages. I almost always got the university engineering students and other student groups. Loved them! I rarely got celebrities to begin with. I can't think of any group which was not vitally interesting and interested.

**Crack of dawn.** At 07h00 I would count the booked guests on to the bus. 07h30, sharp, we would drive off. I usually had the same roster of drivers who got to know the mine routines. Once on the open road, I would stand up and give the guests a 10 to 15 minute talk on the mining industry and what to expect of their day.

**Tweetaalig.** Sometimes I would have to do my presentation in Afrikaans. My Afrikaans driver remarked "Jou Afrikaans is goott, maar jou eksent iss terrible". I am fully bilingual and had swotted up on the relevant terminology of my subject.

**The people.** What I loved most about the mine visits was the people. Both visitors and the mining personnel. The miners were generally the 'salt of the earth', so to speak! They lived with danger. They were loyal to each other. A close-knit brotherhood.

Their work friendships were often lifelong. They risked their lives rescuing each other in mine accidents. They were very down to earth and often even a little crude. Even though they expected me to arrive with at least two new jokes per visit – and I hate telling jokes – it became part of my homework to build up a store of them. Luckily my brother Milton was in the print and packaging industry, and I could rely on him for a rich supply of jokes, risqué enough to satisfy my mining friends, but not really 'feelthy' jokes, just not in me. I left those to Felicity which sounded really weird in her frightfully upper-class English accent.

Picture top of page 64 is a small group of visitors at an East Rand mine. Me front left in mining gear.

**Visit programme.** On arrival at the mine, we enjoyed tea and a welcome by the Underground Manager or one of the senior people. Then we would change into boots, yellow waterproof jackets and hard hats. No old Davey carbide lamps on the hats because the mines were reasonably well lit.

## My Life, a Roller Coaster Ride

We'd get into the cages and were 'dropped' down the shaft in a couple of stages at high speed.

**Jokers.** If the visitors happened to be guest miners or engineers, the winch driver would play the fool and drop us like a stone. It was not reassuring to know that the two-inch steel cables could stretch a couple of feet. The 20 people in the cage would bounce up and down a few times before it settled to a stop. Even some hardened men would look ready to throw up.

Some mines, such as ERPM (East Rand Proprietary Mine), the deepest at that time, 3585 meters, had 'incline shafts' between levels. Imagine, dropping down, by cage, vertically for about 200 meters. Then getting into cabled, gravity controlled linked carts on rails at a forty-five-degree incline for another 100 meters down to the next level. The incline shaft was claustrophobic as the sloping tunnel was usually only high enough for a sitting position, much like a roller coaster ride but dimly lit, with acid smelling drips of water spitting down. I always feared that one tiny little outcrop stalactite would take my head off at that speed. The whole procedure would be repeated until we reached the bottom level.

I still have a tiny little raw nugget of gold, embedded in a small pebble of rock, found by one of the miners down there and given to me as a memento. Not enough gold in it to be valuable or illegal, but enough to hold a special memory.

**More jokers.** Some of the miners stand out in my memory. Grootvlei, near Springs, in the East Rand, had an underground manager introduced to me as Aga Nelson. Aga, because he resembled the Arab millionaire playboy The Aga Khan (then married to the actress Rita Hayworth). Aga Nelson was very proud of this resemblance and even exaggerated the look.

**Boo!** The miners always tried to play jokes on Felicity and me. Never played on the visitors. On one visit, Aga Nelson and his cronies lured me away from my visitors in the depths of the mine. They had 'something to show me'… We walked quite a while. They then switched off all their headlight's and ran off leaving me on a pitch-dark stope hundreds of meters underground.

No one can possibly know the darkness of a mine with the lights out. I was determined not to show my terror. I just sat quietly on my haunches, listening to the 'tommy knockers', the crunching of the rock under pressure all around me. The sound was like crackling paper with sometimes a deeper crackle. I didn't like it but decided to make some noise of my own to block it out. So, I started humming a song. That's how

## 2. Courtship, Marriage and Family

my disappointed captors found me when they crept quietly back five long minutes later. They popped a paper bag, to test my heart condition. They triumphantly switched on their headlights to lead this, now blind, singer back to the group.

**Dark places.** I laughed at this enormous 'joke', but to this very day I do not enjoy dark places during daytime, I need, always, to be surrounded by lots of light. I forgave them in my heart. Just pranksters. They didn't forgive me easily for singing and laughing at their joke.

Most of the miners assigned to visitor hosting were the extraverts and characters of the mine. It was important as a PR exercise to keep the guests entertained, relaxed and informed.

**Alfie Skews.** At the gold mine, Luipaardsvlei, the Underground Manager assigned to us was exactly the opposite of an extrovert. A small wiry little fellow, rather shy with a soft voice. Well informed and a very sweet person. I asked the Mine Manager why Alfie Skews was allocated this job as he didn't always seem comfortable in the role of 'front man'. He said to me "I have a story to tell you about Alfie.

Alfie Skews was a Spitfire Pilot during the Battle of Britain. They had been escorting bombers over Occupied France. On the return flight, they were suddenly attacked by German Messerschmitt's. Alfie shot one down. He was recording his hit when he noticed that the German plane had managed to land in a field and was on fire. The pilot was trapped, unable to escape.

No trouble to Alfie, he managed to land near the downed plane, jumped out and struggled, finally, to get the wounded pilot free and drag him away before his plane blew up. Being a small man – and fortunately, so was the fallen German, Alfie squeezed the two of them into the Spitfire cockpit and flew back to base.

He handed over his captive as a prisoner of war and forgot about it. The following week (or two), a 'Peaceful Mission' was declared by the Germans (with pilots it was a gentleman's war). An Iron Cross medal (German Bravery Medal equal to the Victoria Cross) was dropped into England with Alfie Skews name engraved on it, "with their tribute and gratitude". What a story! At my request, he brought it to the mine next visit to show me.

Chivalry still existed especially in the Air Forces of these two warring countries. And on the mines. Indeed, there was more than one type of Gold down that mine.

# My Life, a Roller Coaster Ride

General Adolph Galland.

**Messerschmitts.** Later in the year I had a mine visitor called Adolf Galland. He was a General in the Luftwaffe and highly decorated Ace Messerschmitt pilot. An exceptional man now travelling on business. I told him the Alfie Skews story. He wasn't surprised. He said that there was a very high code of honour amongst the fighter pilots of both sides. They loved flying, not war.

I was so entranced with this intriguing man, that I invited him to have drinks with my husband, Peter, and some pilot friends at our home in Athol that evening. Adolf was delighted to accept.

Peter was a Spitfire pilot towards the end of the war. When I phoned him from the mine, I told him to round up some of his Air Force pals to meet Adolf. Great excitement!

They all knew of him and his 104 victories in the air. That evening about eight men, some with their wives, arrived at our house. The women didn't get a show in. The men spent hours in déjà vu describing their dog fights with their arms flying and getting along like best friends.

A very deep experience for the men.

Each time Adolf Galand visited South Africa, he took me to lunch. On one visit, he presented me with a signed copy of his autobiography titled 'The First and the Last'. It described the daring exploits of the German Fighter squadrons. Needless to say; someone borrowed the book and didn't return it. Available on Amazon and Kindle.

**Messerschmitt.** While I was with the Chamber of Mines and also while on the subject of Messerschmitt's, Peter and I bought a three-wheeler Messerschmitt car just for fun. It was known as a 'Kabinenroller' or

motorcycle with enclosed canvas cabin. It had two wheels in front and one at the back. One front and one back seat. It was convertible by removing the entire top.

It had a motorbike two stroke engine. Four forward and four reverse gears.

## 2. Courtship, Marriage and Family

I was the only non-executive staff member at the Chamber to get a permanent parking bay in the Chamber directors' garage. I could take the lift to my parking place. People more senior than me, had to walk blocks away to their cars. How did I fix this? There was a parking area for motorcycles in the garage. After doing a hard sell, my 'car' qualified with the cycles, and I got the space. Probably also because they liked me, and I didn't mind working odd hours if there was a panic going on.

**Little Red** as she became known, cheerfully parked noisily and neatly in the basement corner, in the company of Rolls Royce's, Mercedes and other luxury cars. I arrived about the same time as the senior management, so I was very visible and regarded with considerable amusement. Maybe even as something of a crank driving this decidedly peculiar and rare vehicle.

I didn't really care what anyone thought. I simply loved not having to walk blocks away to the parking lot. I had ruined every pair of shoes I had, walking, walking.

Of course, there were also drawbacks with the little bubble car. The closed canvas roof lifted over and up, or off altogether. It had a few small holes in the canvas top, so it leaked in the rain. I always carried an umbrella in the car and put it up inside on rainy days.

It was very low-slung, so rather scary in the traffic, drawing up alongside big trucks where the wheels towered over me with hub caps at eye level. I always worried that they wouldn't see me below line of sight in the rear view and side mirrors. When they did see me, they always had something to say. Mostly compliments or smart remarks.

Little Red made me lots of friends. Everyone waved, chatted and talked to me. It was more social than walking the dog.

Felicity did not drive. Sometimes, if our working schedules coincided, I would give her a lift home. In those days, going to work we always wore slim skirts, hats and gloves and looked very smart. It was something of a curiosity to see the two smartly dressed businesswomen hoisting finely stockinged legs over the low door to squeeze into the little torpedo of a car. The tight skirts were a challenge, and we needed good timing to avoid us being seen in this inelegant manoeuvre.

**Elegant cop.** There was, in Johannesburg at that time, a millionaire traffic cop who did point duty, probably as a kind of fetish or a childhood ambition. A *Sunday Times* story about the rich suave Dickie Hoyle showed his dressing room in his Bryanston Mansion (near Sol and Shirley Kerzner), with a whole closet devoted to his six perfectly tailored traffic officer uniforms, complete with highly polished, imported black leather knee high boots. All the trappings of an eccentric, part-time, cop. Eat your hearts out Hitler's SS Gestapo. I never got to meet him personally, but I knew his wife as we both attended Pre Natal classes together. She had been a British ice-skating champion.

**Pssst!** Dickie's regular point duty was at the end of Empire Road as it formed a T-Junction with Oxford Road in Parktown. Although Dickie and I had never actually met, we got to know each other in another way. He seemed to look out for me after five each evening in my Little Red Devil and when he caught sight of me, he would slow the traffic both ways, crouch down on his haunches and wiggle his upturned index finger, beckoning me to carry on driving, turning right into Oxford Road and down to Rosebank. We'd each wave madly to each other. I went up hugely in Felicity's estimation.

**School lifts.** When using *Little Red* for the school lifts, it was something of a challenge. I sat in the single front seat, leaving the backseat at home so that four children could stand up like sardines in the back.

I shudder to think about it nowadays in this era of seat belts. I would be arrested in a flash. But it was only two kms from Sandown Primary to Athol where we lived. At first, my own children were embarrassed by our car, but soon got over it because the other kids loved every minute. Disneyland rides every second week.

**Make-up.** Once I dressed it up for fun. I put long liquorice eyelashes on the front headlights and painted on eyes. Stuck on a pert little nose and luscious lips and had a big bow at the neck. *Little Red* looked really pretty. A bit like an old-fashioned Cupie Doll.

I eventually sold Little Red to a New Yorker who pestered me for it, offering a tempting price. He packed it into a crate and flew it away to make some Americans very happy in its afterlife. They are now valuable collectors' items, some worth millions.

**Back to the mines.** The start of my Eventing career. Being part of the Chamber PR Department meant that we also had to organise industry sporting events and official functions.

Three-day and four-day bowls and golf matches involving all the mines which sent teams and individual representatives. Highly complicated because of the hundreds of competitors involved. Venues, briefings, personality clashes, egos, punctuality, catering, prizes and prizegiving.

## 2. Courtship, Marriage and Family

**Eventing internship.** This was where I had the most useful training in event management. After those numbers, any future event seemed small by comparison.

**Protocol.** The official function was a real eye opener. Everything had to be impeccably set up. Almost like the royals in perfection. Angus Collie became my mentor and friend. He took me under his wing and schooled me in top level corporate etiquette. When it came to table seating our powers of public relations, and patience, were stretched to the limit.

**Egos.** As soon as the invitations went out the phone calls started. Often from the wives reminding us of how important their husbands were and jockeying for the most advantageous places at the tables. We found it best, in the long run, just to agree with everyone and then did exactly what we adjudged correct. It was too late once they were all gathered, to make any changes. Although some of them did try by strolling through the hall and switching the name cards around. We kept a beady eye on this and switched them right back.

**Lesson in diplomacy.** At one of the first banquets I managed, there was a diplomat of the United Nations who was Guest of Honor. The problem was, he enjoyed the banquet more in spirit than he should have and had to be assisted out before the evening was quite over. When we spotted the problem, and the evening was at an end, we sent two top managers to go up and shake hands with him as if congratulating him, then stiff-armed him out without anyone realizing his feet hardly touched the floor. He didn't last very long in that job, and I feel I know why.

For these events, I was able to work with Angus Collie on the press releases and publicity. The best teacher I could have had, which served me well for the rest of my career.

I never had any other formal training in PR and was accepted as an honorary member of PRISA, the Public Relations Institute of South Africa. And the IMM Institute of Marketing Management by virtue of my track record, experience and Collie endorsement.

**Flying visits.** When we started going more regularly into the bigger and busier mines, we chartered Dakota DC 10s, 21 seaters. The smaller mine visit groups were even nicer because we really got to know the visitors who, without fail, loved the experience. We exchanged names and addresses and pledged eternal friendship.

**Bar service.** They were relaxed when the time came for the return flight. The minute we lifted off the ground, 20 fingers would push the service buttons for drinks and a party would start. As there was no stewardess on our chartered Dakotas, I would open the bar and let them D.I.Y. for the next hour.

**Boeing test flight.** The crew of a Boeing 707, in S.A. to demonstrate to SAA for its passenger fleet, were guests on one of my mine visits. I remember one of the names, the Captain, Don Bugsy. Could I forget a name like that?

**First SA Boeing passenger?** When we arrived back from the mine visit, at the Rand Airport, they persuaded me not to go home immediately, but to go for a test joyride with them in the new demo plane. Could I really refuse? We drove across to Jan Smuts. The crew of seven, and I, climbed into the huge plane, belted up, and took off. We decided to *buzz* the Durban beaches. I think it took us about an hour to get there, *buzz* the string of beaches and head back home. We were back in about two hours. I still have the memory of the beaches with hundreds of upturned faces and flying umbrellas. We must have been rather low.

I congratulate myself that I was one of the very first South Africans to fly in a Boeing. It would appear the sales pitch was successful.

**Learning Bridge with Crème de Menthe.** Another interesting guest was Ken Gibson, the red-headed British Trade Commissioner. He had just arrived in Johannesburg for a one-year stint. No friends outside the Embassy. He invited me to a few functions. Amazing how embassy functions all seem to be the same. Then he decided to teach me to play Bridge. Peter refused to play, so he would lie on the floor of Ken's study reading his book while we played. Ken's idea of a good game of Bridge was to open a bottle of Crème de Menthe and drink it out of wine glasses as we played. Not to be recommended as a teaching aid. Horrible sugar hangovers for my early rising job.

Ken had a crazy sense of pure British humour. I adored this physically unattractive but beautiful man. We corresponded regularly after his year was up and he returned to the UK. I was devastated to hear, about two years later, that he had died of Pancreatic cancer. I never did carry on with Bridge and decided to leave it until I had more time on my hands.

**Complimentary voyage.** A very attractive Italian couple who visited a mine with me were Signor and Signora Nachtegal. He was the CEO of the

## 2. Courtship, Marriage and Family

Italian Lloyd Triestino Shipping Line. They were delighted by the whole day's outing at the mine. Signor Nachtegal gave an impassioned speech of thanks at lunch and complimented the mine management on its gracious hospitality.

On the bus ride back, I sat with them, and they asked many questions about South Africa and about me and my family. Very Italian. They said they would visit this country often.

Next morning on my desk, hand delivered, was a huge bouquet of roses and an envelope. In it was a handwritten letter of thanks and two open first class tickets to be their guest, for a week, on any of their ships, which plied the South African coast.

I showed the invitation to Angus Collie and asked what he thought? I knew about the policy of not accepting payment or gifts for the mine visits. After some thought, Angus told me to accept their gift as it would be impolite not to.

**Novel experience for the children.** Of course, I accepted the cruise gift, from Durban to Cape Town returning to Durban. I took four-year old Carole on the first hop and brought Tony back with me from Cape Town. He had been fishing with his father and grandfather at Blombos.

The Italian ship the *Europa*, 28 000 ton cruising ship, reminded me of earlier years, when I was eighteen, and travelled in its sister ship, the *Gerusalemme*, from Durban to Brindisi, Italy.

Carole still remembers the trip. There is something magic about a sea voyage. The captain invited us up to the bridge. Being spoilt rotten comes naturally to we women. I suspect that Signor Nachtegal had something to do with the singular attention.

**The return.** In Cape Town, after a brief visit with my in-laws Billy and Betty Carr, I swopped children with Peter. Six-year old Tony and I sailed back to Durban. Tony thought the ship was the best adventure ever. He had just been fishing with his dad and grandpa and was fishing mad. The Italian crew had no English. Tony had no Italian but, somehow, they never stopped talking and understood each other perfectly.

**Italians adore children.** Starved of them months away from home. Whenever I checked to find out where Tony was, I would find him either helping mix Martinis at the Deck Bar, or fishing with one of the crew out of the lower deck portholes. He didn't want to get off the ship after the three short days.

# My Life, a Roller Coaster Ride

**Family, fun and finance.** My Chamber of Mines job was only three days a week Tuesday to Thursday, and no office homework was required. The exception to this was supervising the rare special events mostly at weekends. So, it was easy to juggle family commitments and chores to fit them in. The excellent salary gave me the opportunity to provide little luxuries for the home and the family.

**The Stauffer Couch.** Adele and I decided it was time to make some extra money. The children were still very young, so we worked from home.

We bought a slimming machine. A Stauffer Couch passive exerciser. A long stretcher-like bed in three sections, with a central rocking pad.

After measuring the client in eight places, she would put on a loose white towelling tunic (made by me) and lie on the bed, bottom on the middle moving pad. We would put a sausage-like sandbag weight over the torso and legs, and then switch on. Wobble-wobble, lying first on her back then on each side. A half hour of this passive exercise would produce very good results, firming up over six or eight sessions. We would triumphantly subtract the 'after' measurements from the 'before' figures and tell them the total centimetres lost. Sometimes between 10cm and 20cm.

For more impressive 'proof', we would also ask them to bring something tight as a starting garment and see how it fitted more loosely after the course. More convincing than mere numbers.

Adele and I took turns week-about at each house. This brought in very

Marlbank parents: (L to R) Mattie, Ron and Betty Hubbard, Johnny and Ruby Minnaar, Alf, looking pensive.

## 2. Courtship, Marriage and Family

nice pocket money for a couple of years. It was when the clients' husbands also asked if they could come and firm-up, that the thought of all that intimate measuring made us sell the machine to friend, Dierdre Sims.

It was Adele's and my first venture into a joint enterprise. By then we had joined The Monday Club, running events to raise money for charity. This led to our private Catering business for private and business functions.

I had taken private Cordon Bleu cookery lessons with teacher Maudie Wooll. We swapped services. I made her a Jersey cloth suit in exchange.

Adele was a natural cook with many cookbooks. Although this made us excellent money, the family sometimes suffered, having to be satisfied with leftovers and takeaways on a busy catering weekend.

**Alfie buys the Vaal River property.** Alfie and Mattie bought 14 Marlbank, the 16 acre, 125 meter river frontage property in July 1964. It was a 120km drive, South of Johannesburg.

It instantly changed our lives for the following 28 years. I was pregnant

**John trying to hit a golf ball across the river. Nobody ever did.**

**Middle House and Boathouse. German Shepherds playing at riverside.**

with Peter when it was bought. He was 28 when I sold my share at the end of 1992.

The actual purchase of 14 Marlbank had a two-family history going back 32 years. At the end of the Marlbank road, known as 'Millionaires Bend', was the Minnaars' beautiful thatched house 'Shangri La', The two families had been friends all my life.

The name 'Shangri La' derives from James Hilton's novel *Lost Horizon*. A story about a place in the mountains, where nobody grows old as long as they don't leave.

Johnny and Ruby owned a popular night club in Johannesburg, 'The 400 Club'. The Minnaar's and Steers went night clubbing almost weekly for years. The two families grew together. Johnny and Ruby with June (only child born in June 1932), Alf and Mattie with Megan (born April 1932).

In those early days, Johnny, a keen boat racer, was always pestering Alf to buy a property near them on the Vaal River. When Johnny let Alfie know that a 16 acre property, at 14 Marlbank, was up for sale, Alfie bought it.

**Three Generations.** The two-family connection continued through three generations from 1930

**Forest Drive.** Turning right off the road to No.14, first impression. Driving through the forest of blue gum and pine trees which cover probably 20% of the property.

**History.** The property had previously been a small dairy farm and consisted of four buildings and a boathouse.

**Middle house.** Mattie and Alfie chose the middle house a two-bedroomed cottage, one bathroom, dining room and lounge with a sunny North facing kitchen. It was situated in the best position with a view of the river.

**The barn.** Megan, Peter, John and Margie, shared the thatched barn on the East side. It had been used for housing, feeding and milking cows, 10 x 8 Meters with only a small separate kitchen. West Cottage Went to Milton. It was a two-bedroom cottage which also had a caravan under a roof.

**Staff quarters and double garage.** In the middle of the property, between, and separate from, the houses. It was a four-room compound, housing the staff, with a double garage workshop, tacked on to the end.

**Renovating the barn.** The floor was concrete, sloping slightly to a 20cm wide runnel canal down the length door to door for the spilled milk and the sluicing water to run outside.

## 2. Courtship, Marriage and Family

**Women in action.** Preggie Meggie and mother, Mattie, returned to the farm two weeks after the purchase with a DIY plan to level the Barn floor. We had ordered cement, stones and river sand, a meter-long spirit level, and a long garden hose to be delivered and many extra buckets and spades. The 80 square meter sloping barn floor was raised up by 2-4 centimetres and levelled smoothly.

**Dairy.** The only side room, at ground level, was the Dairy room for separating the milk and then churning the cream into butter for house use. This left buttermilk which, in turn, was also enjoyed by Alfie and the staff The farm had two sheep, which doubled as lawn mowers.

**Troughs to beds.** John brought our trusty old family retainer/cook/handyman of 30 years, Elias, to work on the dual family Barn house. There were five two-meter feeding troughs. So, they hinged doors onto the wall side of each of the five feeding troughs and turned them into long seats waiting for Dunlop foam mattresses and bolsters. These seats by day, were then transformed into beds at night. By lifting the horizontal door-seats we could use the trough space underneath as bedding storage. We had open plan living, day and night.

John and Peter then, with all family lending a hand, erected a dividing wall.

**The Thunderbox.** There was no inside toilet. The loo was a long drop in a shed outside to the left of the front door under a tree.

We called it 'The Thunderbox'. The seat was an edge-to-edge wooden square with a suitably sized hole in the centre. I don't recall suffering splinters or missing children. Why 'Thunderbox? Because it produced tell-tale echoes depending on the current function of use.

## 13. Birth of Baby Peter

At about this time, on due date. Peter arrived 'into the world' 13th October 1964. He was welcomed by Tony 8 and Carole 6, became the family doll. Spoilt rotten from day one. Until he was 28 years old, he didn't know a world without 'The Vaal'.

**Re purposing the barn.** Suffice it to say, we divided the house in two with a wall. Re-thatched the roof to include dormer windows and put in a kitchen and bathroom with wooden flooring upstairs to house three bedrooms. We plumbed and electrified the house with professionals and suddenly it was a handsome, functional double residence.

**Whitewash.** My special recipe: 50lbs of unslaked lime, 5lbs of suet and 5lbs salt in 20 gallons of water. It boiled up and took a day to cool, ready for use.

Peter Carr Snr, the family handyman's next job was to build the wooden stairs and upstairs balcony. For the stairs, he bought four long Meranti side pieces measured floor to ceiling/floor upstairs. and 14 sturdy Meranti steps all cut to size measure and set to work slotting them in perfectly together.

Baby Peter was two months old when the stairs were finally completed at ground floor level and then hoisted and fixed into place, just in time for Christmas holidays.

The staircase was perfect and lasted for about 30 years till the Barn was demolished by the next owner, Ray Montenegro.

**Orange and more orange.** Decorating the Barn, I felt we could go wild with colour. I found some orange and white cotton curtaining and matching plain orange Swedish cotton fabric for cushions at the fashionable Helen de Leeuw Interiors in Hyde Park Centre. Orange was 'in'. The bold floral design lent itself to the white walls. It lifted the mood instantly. It sang out 'Holiday' not 'Relax'.

Finding the long-stored curtains in an old trunk recently, fifty years later, I thought it would take courage to use them today. I went orange crazy. Table and benches and both barn doors – Orange. When we eventually left, Andy took over the table and benches and the first thing she did was to sand away the orange paint down to the well preserved Oregan wood.

**Sunflower wall print.** Years later, Carole arrived with a gift of a huge metre square blocked print of a single yellow sunflower on a blue background.

**Wood for the stairs on the roof rack of my blue Opel Car-a-Van.**

## 2. Courtship, Marriage and Family

It seemed to smile at you. Perfect and much loved. Placed on the rear wall facing the door. This picture, with the bright curtains, dominated the otherwise all white living room.

## 14. Finding 115 Katherine Street, Sandown House

Whilst enjoying our lovely Athol House, when out and about I couldn't help noticing an unoccupied, rundown property in Katherine Street, Sandown. I was drawn to it and drove in regularly to peek through the dusty windows. It became an obsession. I simply had to have it. No good reason for it.

I managed to track down the owner's home address and insisted Peter drive me there one early evening. The surprised man greeted us at the door and invited us in. I told him I wanted to buy the Sandown house. Shaking his head, he said that he had just accepted a telephone offer that very day.

**On a mission.** To cut the story short, I whipped out an envelope with a Bank Guaranteed cheque in it and told him it was a token of our intent to secure the house. As he hadn't yet met the phone caller or shaken hands on the deal, nothing signed yet, I asked if he would please reconsider and accept us as the new owners. Somewhat bewildered, and even intrigued, he surprised himself by accepting the offer. And the cheque. It was the strangest deal he had ever done and expressed delight that we would be living in the old house because we loved it 'Warts and all'.

We sold the Athol house to Dr. Dennis Kemp, the Johannesburg Coroner. Ten years later, he sold it on to my good friends, Adele's sister,

Sandown House.

Diane, and her husband Simon Valentine and their three children Mark, Grant and Nicola. A very loved house by all who lived in it.

**Sandown House.** Sometimes I set a children's picnic in the garden often with friends.

In summer the apricots were plump and juicy. I made quince jelly and preserve which were delicious. We *scored* grenadillas from the tennis court fence. The rambling garden was the perfect safe playground for the four children for over eleven years.

Over the wall was the untarred Linden Road and Kijlstra Stables which had horses and milking cows. Idyllic and rural. Further down was the Anderson chicken farm.

Note the avocado tree at the corner of the house, the apricot tree and a quince hedge further back, provided fruit but no avocados, till Tony asked around about this problem. He gave the trunk a beating with a chain. Feeling endangered, big fat avocados appeared within months.

The suburb was safe for the children who were free to cycle to their friends' houses – but too far and too dangerous to cycle to school at peak hour. Freedoms fondly remembered in today's crime-ridden society and racing traffic.

**Water tank tower at the gate.** Silver Oak trees and circular gravel driveway, the rambling 1.5 Acre garden. The house name was 'Silver Oaks' for obvious reasons.

**Silver Oaks.**

## 2. Courtship, Marriage and Family

Although, at first, the house and garden were run down, they had a special rural charm. A three bedroomed double story house, with a double staff cottage and a ramshackle garden shed.

In the sprawling overgrown garden was a tennis court with weeds and a massive heavy roller. The blue swimming pool had a flat floor and no filter. It had an inscription 'built in 1919'. The raised, disused water tank at the gate became a watch tower for the children and a place in which to store coal, wood and wheelbarrow.

Soon, the house was cleaned up, painted and redecorated, It was a charming, friendly, home. It had dormer windows in the thatched roof and interesting nooks and crannies and secret hiding places in the roof. Tony made his photographic dark room in one of them. It was child's heaven.

We added a double garage with workshop. The garage became Peter's *Man Cave* with his magnificent workshop filled with every possible state-of-the-art gadget and tool. I have a theory that no family should be without one as a marriage preserver.

Tony and Charles started at different schools but still visited each other regularly entailing many lifts. Life for me was a whirl of work, school, extra murals, home management and a social life for young and old. Our pets were Cleo the elegant Siamese cat, and our beautiful black cat, Victoire (named after a Dior model).

Jane, our lively Boxer, had been shot at the Athol house, by the Anderson's chicken farmer down the road. She had been on a hunting rampage one night and the evidence was out on the lawn strewn with chicken feathers.

**Turning property into cash.** After five years, I sub-divided and sold a half-acre to Peter and Ann Wrighton, which helped pay for private schooling and two brand new cars. A dark green Kombi and a matching green VW Beetle. Life was good.

Peter Wrighton was the M.D. of Premier Milling. We had worked together on a few promotions and, together, we were co-opted by a Sandown Municipal committee to a brainstorming session in the proposed amalgamation of the larger suburbs into a single body. Ultimately, without too much input from us, the Peri Urban Municipality became known as Sandton, devised from 'Sandown' and 'Bryanston'.

**1972.** We moved out of the Sandown house. After the divorce, we'd had a burglary, and I didn't feel safe. Pete had long since moved out with his three guns and ceremonial sword.

# My Life, a Roller Coaster Ride

We moved to the Kambula apartment near Sandton City and rented out the house to Jimmy Thomas, ex Group Editors friend. Kambula was our home for seven years.

**1979.** We moved back to Sandown house for a year before selling it and then buying a townhouse, Kent Downs, near Benmore Gardens.

**The end.** The Katherine Street house was further sold first to Holiday Inns and later to Southern Sun. The old house was demolished. Peter was born in this house in October 1964 and Andrea in October 1966.

When we moved to Sandown house, Tony was eight and Carole was six.

## Kent Downs, Benmore Gardens.

This home has family history. We moved there at the end of 1979. A delightful, new townhouse overlooking an open park with a double garage. Gracie had her own private adjoining room, bathroom and kitchen.

When she retired, Peter took over the room as his private space. Only Pete and Andy in the house with me. Carole and Tony were long since independent. It was at this time that I met John Harvey, who moved in. We were partners for eight years.

Kent Downs, Benmore Gardens.

The complex also had a squash court. I bought two squash racquets for the family. Only Peter and I used the court. Adele gave it a try, but it didn't work for her knees.

**Ackerman.** It was here that I had many a meeting with Raymond Ackerman when we had to have confidential meetings away from business ears. Gracie would make us lunch out on the patio. She would also provide sandwiches and a coke for his chauffeur, waiting out by the car.

Gracie was a proud woman. Raymond would ask for a peanut butter sandwich and a coke. She was in awe of him and would rustle up something good on plates at a set table. And a coke!

## 2. Courtship, Marriage and Family

**Info scandal time.** It was an awkward political time. Remember Eschel Roodie and the Info Scandal? The Government Department of Information, under Dr Connie Mulder, was making overtures to Raymond among many local and international opinion leaders, to change world opinion of the Apartheid regime. This bothered him, putting him on the spot. He just needed someone independent, with nothing to gain, to bounce ideas off, as his own solutions crystalised.

The 'Info Scandal' was also known as 'Muldergate'. It failed and cost Mulder, Eschel Roodie and Hendrik van der Berg (BOSS, Bureau for State Security) their political careers. Eschel Roodie moved to America.

It was at Kent Downs that Tony and Lee had their wedding reception. Andy was happy when her best friend Dusty Bristol and her father, Tony, bought a townhouse in our complex, just a few houses down our road. Andy and Dusty had been best friends since they were seven and are still friends, now in their late fifties. I regard Dusty and her son, Zinzan (named after Zinzan Brookes, the New Zealand rugby player), as part of the family.

We were her soft cushion to fall on when she had trouble with her unkind stepmother. Dusty is now a highly successful businesswoman.

**Pioneers.** The sixties and seventies were not an easy time for women in business management. Male chauvinism was alive and well. Women were a necessity in the typing pool. Thereafter, 'The little woman' belonged at home with the children, ready with slippers and newspaper when the man of the house returned from a hard day's work.

Running the home was not considered a hard day's work. I must admit we had servants to help care for the children and manage the home during the day.

When I dared to enter the man's business world, I followed Leila Reitz's advice: "Do not try to be a man. Your femininity is your best asset. Use it. Work hard, play hard".

# Part 3
## Career, Business and Family

Adele Lucas and Megan at Blues in Camps Bay (circa 2000) enjoying 'Whate Whane' or 'White Wine' to everyone else. Photo by Andy Carr.

## 15. Adele Lucas, a Pivotal Person in my Life

Best friend for 58 years; we were the same age. We had similar ideas on almost everything. Business, Health, Family. However, we were also different in personality, which made it work.

Adele was 'Front of House' enjoyed the limelight. I preferred to organise, in my own way, behind the scenes. She was a marketing genius. I had marketing talent.

We both had original ideas for getting people's attention, especially with the press. In our separate businesses, we often joined forces and complemented each other's skills Adele had the wonderful Bob at her back. Her family of three - Carolyn, same age as Carole, Garth, same age as Peter and Diana somewhere in between.

**Exercise:** I couldn't count the more than thirty-five years of early morning hours that Adele and I jogged together round the block, did our 5BX Canadian Air Force exercises, swam twenty lengths in the Lucas long pool, chatted over a cup of tea and back home by seven a.m. Or beach exercises for many years, at Adele's Uncle Ernest's 'Surf Edge' holiday flats in Ramsgate, where Adele and I would take the young children, once or twice a year, leaving husbands behind.

Adele's parties were legend. Saturday lunches were open

house, home from home. She was an amazing host, a tolerant person, rarely judgmental. Never a swear word.

Born 10th December 1932, Adele's star sign is Sagittarius. When I looked it up in Linda Goodman's Star Sign book, it told me that Adele would absent-mindedly stub her cigarette out in the office paper cups. At a party I saw her absent-mindedly stub her cigarette out in the bowl of peanuts.

**The Monday Club** was a group of thirty invited women 'Socialites'. The Club's charity mission in the sixties, was to adopt the cause of The Woodside Sanctuary's proposed new wing, urgently needed for the home in Cottesloe, Auckland Park. The Sanctuary cares for young people living with mental disorders.

## 16. 1966 Birth of Andrea Colville Carr

**Andrea was born October 1966.** The baby of the family, this pretty, petite apricot blonde arrived at a good time in our lives, living in our Sandown house with its rambling garden.

She attended Sandown Primary School and then on to DSG in Grahamstown. After matriculating, with both Carole and Peter in the film industry, she trained to be a film Make-up Artist and instantly spent almost two years in that capacity, on the set of the Jamie Uys film, *The Gods Must Be Crazy*. Highly efficient, she moved across to become film coordinator in the film *The Adventures of Sinbad* and others.

In the 90s Andy joined MCP as a full partner running the Alpha Mind Power Seminars. She later joined Cell C as a P.A. to top management.

Andy is talented ceramic artist specialising in Raku firing. She kept three beehives, producing honey to share around. She has a daughter, Alexandra Colville Carr, born in 1993.

## 17. Circus Premier - First major event

**Adele Lucas** was voted in as Monday Club Chair. I was nominated Vice Chair. Obviously, we would meet on Mondays. Whilst enjoying a monthly social afternoon meeting over tea (never coffee in those days) at the Inanda Club. We organised regular fundraisers, like Bridge Drives and expensive plate banquets.

Woodside Sanctuary needed a new wing. Adele and I had a brainstorming session and came up with an outrageous idea. We knew it would be a hard sell to the club members. I had always loved Circus since childhood, enhanced since reading Paul Gallico's new novel *Love Let me not Hunger*, so the idea of this project got the juices running.

# My Life, a Roller Coaster Ride

**Circus.** We decided to ask Boswell Wilke Circus if we could stage a Black-Tie Charity Premiere for the start of their season. We had to think big as the amount needed was huge for the club to raise. Bear in mind that, although all the members were financially comfortably well-off, we were never asked to contribute money. Our personal value to the Monday Club was our top-notch business connections who could be approached for support in cash and kind, and our own personal time and skills.

**Stars and Sawdust.** This is where it all started. The Grand Circus Premiere, which we named *Stars and Sawdust*. It was the introduction to Adele's and my promotional careers as a team.

**It was 1966** and we were complete amateurs at organising public events. Adele and I dreamt up something outrageous. Adele presented our Circus Premiere idea to the Monday Club members and made it sound exciting and perfectly manageable. Several members thought the idea 'ridiculous. 'Could never work for our sophisticated society audience' and 'Far too ambitious'. It seemed like it for our relatively small group. In theory, they were right.

I strongly backed our idea which got some traction with the doubters. We got a nervous vote of approval.

We were therefore delegated to manage it. The members were good sports, and we divided up the different aspects of the mammoth undertaking to our bunch of amateurs. We delegated tasks according to wishes and talent. Fortunately for us, in those days, there was no stigma attached to the Circus and performing animals.

Since working with the Circus on this premiere and spending much time with the amazing circus community and their beloved animals, I had my eyes opened to how much love, dedication, hard work and utter devotion I was privileged to witness. They treated their animals like their own children. Good parents with love and kind discipline. I also observed that the animals got excited just before their performances. They are enthusiastic actors and enjoy being on stage.

But we won't go into the tree-hugging and blanket condemnations. I know what I saw and acknowledged my prior ignorance of life in the circus as I saw it. Generalisations are odious and often misguided, even if well intentioned.

I made an appointment for us to see the Boswell Wilke Circus Business Manager, who was also the Circus Ringmaster, Maurice Carré. We had no idea what an amazing two-month adventure we were embarking upon.

## 3. Career, Business and Family

**Maurice Carré** must have been about 35 years old. Tall, slim, handsome and a cheerful personality, larger than life. We also detected an underlying steely core. A 'not to be messed with' personality. Of course, he had to be all those things to enable him to have complete control of a daily audience of 3 000, seated around a challenging circular stage with no backdrop.

He also was the man in charge of the staff comprising only about 50 artists which also included the circus owners, the Wilke's.

The impressive thing about a travelling circus is its quick-change ability and expertise in moving from place to place every few days. It erects an entire entertainment centre in days and hours rather than months as in the real world. It is an exercise in efficiency and excellence.

**How it works.** Everyone in the circus has two or three jobs to do. The Ringmaster is also the business manager, advertising manger, human resources officer and chief accountant.

The Lion and big cat trainer is also the presenter of his acts, looking fierce in his cowboy hat, cracking a whip, disguising his tender heart and burden of his duties. He cannot show fear or weakness but is also loved and respected by his animals and human co-performers. His other important job is to drive the truck and trailer cages with his animals. His duties include the cleaning, fuelling and maintenance of the transport and the trailer cages. He is also in charge of ordering their food and managing their health, accommodation, exercise, safety and general welfare. Each show day he rehearses the act.

Civic Centre grounds, Braamfontein.

# My Life, a Roller Coaster Ride

The Pony act usually has six trained ponies, dressed up in their shiny equipment, feathers and sparkles. They love dressing up. This act has its own ringmaster, and each pony has its own dedicated, skilled trick rider. This team is responsible for its costumes, makeup, pony regalia, equipment, feeding, practicing, transport, accommodation, safety and general wellbeing. Girl riders double at the box office. They assist with ticket sales at the entrance and serve as usherettes and selling programmes. After the show. They tidy up ready for next day's show or start packing up ready for moving to the next stop.

Trapeze artists team up with other circus people and are responsible for the transport and erection of their large and precise high-flying equipment including the safety nets and the maintenance of their trucks.

They are also often called upon for advertising and personal appearances ahead of the circus arrival in a town.

Madame Wilke and her birds. More high flying. She and her husband owned the circus. She has the most amazing act with birds interacting on command with the audience and enchanting everyone. A traditional circus trooper with her faintly foreign accent.

Clowns are almost the stars of the show. Of course, they are smarter than they act. You must be smart to make people laugh. Darlings of the show. Interacting as fillers during stage changes and popping into most of the acts. But never during the animal acts because these must stay focused with no distractions.

Clowns are the main marketing tools used to go ahead of the show appearing at schools and Shopping Centre's to secure advance bookings.

One clown is usually the traditional white-faced clown with a red wig. The other one acts as foil, a bumbling tumbling fool, tripping up and bumping into everything and everyone. In our circus premiere, there was a third clown who walked on very high stilts providing *oohs* and *aahs* high above the audience in the ring. He is also useful when advertising visits on village streets and at schools.

**The Stars and Sawdust Premiere.** To our target Opening Night audience in pre-TV days, radio was the popular form of home entertainment and communication.

We, in our wisdom, asked Maurice Carré if we could introduce famous radio and stage stars into the show to ensure a broader audience. Maurice reluctantly agreed to it as an interesting exercise, and an opportunity to test the flexibility of their normal rigid routine.

## 3. Career, Business and Family

Adele and I approached the prolific radio show producer, Mike Silver. He produced *Squad Cars, Inspector Carr, No Place to Hide, The Creaking Door* and many others. He was a real character. We asked Mike to ride an elephant in the show. He laughed and said, 'I'm a nice sensible Jewish boy. Certainly not. I will never ride an elephant, or any four-legged beast.'

Fair enough. Luckily, we were overheard by the tall mischievous Radio Presenter, Hugh Rouse as he entered one of the SABC sound studios. We heard him shout, "I'll ride the elephant". We accepted instantly. A good start. He wasn't allowed to change his mind. He later had cause to regret this rash decision.

We then approached news reader Mike Todd who agreed to put on a singing 'Barbershop Quartet' involving himself, radio mates, Hugh Rouse (again), Dougie Laws and Paddy O'Byrne. Four well-known voices offering good Music Hall songs.

At that time there was a comedy actor Gabriel Bayman who specialised in jokes speaking and sounding like a Cape Malay Minstrel with all its rhyming language so beloved by his multi-ethnic radio audiences. He agreed to put on an act. We had slight reservations because he was also a well-known drinker. We knew that his drunken acts were not entirely acting.

We decided to get some of the Monday Clubbers to hold the hoops for the ponies to jump through. Diane Valentine and I were two of them. That was all the variety we needed to add to the circus programme. It also brought a lot of free advertising banter over the radio ahead of the show.

Boswell Wilke Circus entered the spirit of the event with their usual gusto. Maurice Carré ordered new satin and sparkling costumes throughout. We borrowed some empty trailers from them and made facades to look like cages to be the food counters for take-away snacks and bar counters for the interval which was part of the profit plan.

**Black Tie.** It was a unanimous club decision to turn the Circus Opening Night into a Black-Tie affair, charge premium prices for the seats and then to sell the tickets. If the tickets were cheap, we would have sold fewer.

The excitement of the show took hold of the club members and families. It went viral.

Because the circus has a sawdust floor and a circular stage with no backdrop, rather than a normal square stage, it obviously has a predominantly forward-facing routine looking onto the expensive seats. We decided to sell only two thousand paid tickets and leave the one third

## My Life, a Roller Coaster Ride

of the seats each side, free of charge for charities, helpers and Monday Club families. Expensive seats in a circus were still a huge challenge. The event itself was a gamble as an unknown entity. Sceptics said that the well-heeled target audience would never allow themselves to be seen at a circus.

Originally, circus was created especially for kids. But we felt that we all had good childhood memories and could take the audience down memory lane. We had to change adult attitudes by making it a social event not to be missed.

After our good start with the radio personalities, we planned to take to the streets and get the show awareness going on the road, at events and public places.

Diane Valentine, (Adele's sister). Megan Carr and Joscelyn Fox (concert pianist).

# 3. Career, Business and Family

Excitement in the club continued building. One Monday Clubber persuaded a friend to make us three larger-than humans, stuffed animals. A lion, a giraffe, and a chimpanzee. We would use these huge mascots to advertise the show on display at shopping Centre's and public events together with Stars and Sawdust banners.

**Blue Angel outfits.** It was my job to design and produce thirty costumes, tailored in sizes to fit the members. Earlier, Marlene Dietrich had starred in the film *Blue Angel*. So, I copied what she wore. A black leotard with white cravat and bow tie, black tailcoat, fishnet stockings, black patent high heeled shoes and black top hat. We expected the Clubbers to supply their own comfortable black shoes.

This picture appeared in *The Star* newspaper, calling us Mrs, Simon Valentine, Mrs. Peter Carr, and Mrs Martin Fox. Then the nitty-gritties to be considered. Seating comfort on the hard circus benches, Food, drinks and programmes with lots of advertising. Hopefully a sponsor or two.

Fortunately, the circus would attend to such things as public address system for our entertainers, and door and stage management.

As always, the long-suffering Monday Club husbands were drawn into the fold. They did what they were very good at. Running the bars and the parking. A novelty as they were Managing Directors, Doctors, Accountants, Lawyers and celebrities in their fields.

The Monday Club divided itself into various sub committees to take charge of the various aspects of the circus project. We had two months to get it together.

Two long cage-fronted counters were decorated, labelled and set up at the entrance. One for the bar. One for takeaway counters. What to serve? Of course, what else but Champagne, Hot Dogs and Hamburgers. Best quality of each.

**Hard seats.** We had a committee to find coloured foam sporting cushions to place on the seats. They also had the job of putting them in place the afternoon of the event all 2 000 of them. Thank heavens for child labour. What fun for our kids to do.

**Bubbly.** Adele and I decided that the audience needed a party starter to get them in the mood. 'Champagne'. We were then still allowed to call it that. We approached Stellenbosch Farmers Winery (SFW). Grand Mousseux was very acceptable and popular. Nice fat bottles. As good, in those days, as any of those locals we buy today. In the sixties, they included a dry sparkling in their range. We offered a part sponsorship advert in the programme and tent banners in return for 1500 bottles of Brut bubbly. They were very happy to use the prestige occasion as a marketing exercise.

Adele and I later mused that this event was a precursor to our eventual business in Promotions and Event Management. We haggled to get 2 000 plastic champagne flutes at cost price and persuaded SFW to set up a table suitably bannered inside the tent entrance. SFW paid for the flutes as part of their promotion.

Each couple arriving would be handed an opened bottle and two flutes to take up to their seats.

With all the basics in place, only two weeks to go and many tickets still to sell, more promotion was needed. Bold and cheeky was the order of the day!

**Rush hour traffic exposure.** We borrowed a Silver Cloud open Rolls Royce from one of the members. Three of us got dressed in our revealing Blue Angel outfits, fastened the three stuffed animals on to the open backrests, placed huge cushions to elevate the three Monday Club Blue Angels into plain view, hoisted a banner advertising the event and booking details and got a student driver in a bowler hat, to take us to town.

Where else but the centre of Johannesburg at traffic peak hour. The three of us were, Adele Lucas, June Bullen and me. We wove in and out of the dense traffic, held up the gawping lines of cars and generally made a nuisance of ourselves whilst waving merrily and answering shouted out questions to all those bored peak victims. We cheered up their lives. We got ourselves photographed and in the newspapers.

I must tell a special story of an incident which happened. Adele was an enthusiastic smoker. But she had to have a little white Royal Mint to suck while she smoked. Horror of horror, during our peak traffic epic, Adele found that she had forgotten to bring her mints – and she needed a cigarette. We spotted a tiny convenience tobacco and sweet shop in Jeppe Street and begged our rather timid chauffeur to stop at the shop in the 'no stopping' zone reserved only for bus traffic.

You might remember that there were 'no stopping at peak times' everywhere in town. 7 – 9 am and 4 – 6 pm. Also in those days, traffic cops on their motor bikes were everywhere. We decided to risk it and asked our driver to go into the shop to buy the mints. (None of us could get out of the car because of our revealing outfits.)

It was then we heard the dreaded 'Brmm Brmm' of a cop on his bike. He parked in front of us and strolled over, warning, "You can't stop here".

# 3. Career, Business and Family

Then he caught sight of three pairs of fishnets and his eyes popped.

Adele snapped into dumb blonde mode, "Oh Officer, I simply must get to the shop to buy some mints, but can't really because I'm wearing these very high heels and this costume...We are trying to raise money for our charity".

June and I pointed to our banner and waved the paw of the stuffed Lion, as Adele fished in her handbag and handed him some money saying, "Please will you just get me a packet of Royal Mints?". He looked amused and shook his head and marched into the shop, and emerging waving the mints and some change.

"I can't believe I'm doing this". He laughed saying, "Follow me", with a roar of his bike and the purring of the Rolls, we followed him, past the heavy traffic, in the bus lanes to cheers from the onlookers. He cheerfully escorted us via many Johannesburg streets for half an hour till it was six o'clock and time to go home.

He was our hero that day.

That escorted ride through town became a talking point and spread the circus premiere news. *The Star* newspaper picture and story caught the imagination. Radio interviews followed, and the tickets started to sell like hotcakes. Within a week we had reached our target.

Our circus friends were also captivated. We were welcomed into the community of the Big Top family, telling us about their amazing lives and adventures. We went into many caravans for a cup of tea and chat. Never for long because they work so hard and love what they do.

**Show time.** At last, the big night in the Big Top arrived. Everything in place. The only unknown quantities were the Stars part of the Stars and Sawdust. Never worked in a circus before but nevertheless, were absolute pros at their game. We had a private front seat box set aside for them and their families, with easy access to the ring for their acts.

The stage nets were up for the Big Cats first act. The sawdust in the entrance foyer, passages and in the ring was carefully raked with tidy rake stripes. The animal smell was faint considering how many there were quietly munching outside the tent.

The circus band was tuning up. A nostalgic, familiar sound. Maurice Carré, the Ringmaster, striding around checking on absolutely everything. Pony trick riders in their strapless sparkly outfits looking spunky and glamorous with lots of stage makeup, ready to usher, sell programmes and working at the box office.

Monday Club members as Blue Angels, all at their stations. What professionalism they exhibited, doing their unfamiliar tasks.

The location of the Big Top was in Braamfontein, where the Civic Centre is today. Lots of space and parking. A team of Monday Club husband volunteers to direct the parking for 600 cars.

With half an hour to showtime, the guests started trickling in looking grand in their black-tie suits and tuxedos, elegant gowns and glittering jewellery. It looked like a vintage Opera audience arriving. No Jeans in sight. No jeans were in fashion yet.

They produced their tickets, and the couples were handed their bottle of bubbly and flutes before being ushered up wooden steps to their reserved numbered seats.

It was a warm dry Highveld June evening. And something strange happened. As more and more people arrived, men wearing their black suits, the static in the dry air made the sawdust cling to their lower dark trouser legs. The illusion of what we saw made us laugh as it appeared that all the men were walking on very short legs. Like walking on their knees. Luckily, they were blissfully unaware of this spectacle. Most of the sawdust fell off once they were seated. A moment in time.

Our Monday Club usherettes put on brave happy faces as they showed the guests up to their seats, negotiating the wooden steps in their stilettos. The band was playing the familiar Souza circus marching music. The atmosphere was electric.

Everyone expressed their emotions at the childhood memories which came rushing back. The music, the sawdust, the circus smell, the sight of the trapeze awaiting the high-flyers, the distant animal noises.

The clowns popping in and out, secretly shadowing people and making everyone laugh, all contributed to the rare atmosphere of the evening twitter.

To a loud fanfare, the Ringmaster entered, bowed to the seated two thousand paying guests and five hundred complimentary guests.

Is there anything like circus marching music? It pumps the blood and tingles the nerve ends. You look around like a child to see if mummy and daddy are there.

The show started with the big cats behind the safety nets just in front of the first row of VIP seats. Then the nets are spirited away with speed and efficiency as the clowns become a nuisance to them, to mask the scene change. Then the lovable seals flapped their way into the limelight doing their ball tricks.

The clowns ushered in the four Barbershop quartet singers to big

## 3. Career, Business and Family

ovation as the beloved personalities are recognised. They sang some old-time songs like *Underneath the Arches* and *My old Dutch*. They also told a few old Flanagan and Allen 'chestnuts', "Who was that lady I saw you with last night?" "That was no lady, that was my wife!" Ha Ha. They'd probably had a few because once going, they didn't really want to stop and did an encore.

Ringmaster, Maurice, had everything in hand and the next act of prancing ponies and their trick riders skipped into a different tune and a different mood in the audience.

Three Monday Clubbers, Di Valentine, Jos Fox and me, in our leggy fishnet outfits, nervously placed ourselves around the ring with hoops for the ponies to jump through. We got teased afterwards by fellow member husbands with fake propositions. The three were the same who appeared in the newspaper picture.

The Ringmaster had warned us that some of the acts required audience participation. We were so unsure of our audience that we had briefed some of our members and friends to stand by to take part if there were no real volunteers. Well, we had no need to worry on that score.

The Champagne was working. Hercules, the strong man, with his bare, well oiled, tattooed muscles did a few strong man flexes and tricks. He then called for ten volunteers. After a few tense seconds, there was a rush from the audience as prominent businessmen, doctors, lawyers and a mayoral councillor, ran down circus stairs and into the ring. We had an over-supply.

**Hercules** clasped both hands together and asked the ten heavily breathing formally dressed volunteers to link arms, five-a-side, and try to pull his arms apart. The tug of war was a sight to see. Of course, the sawdust didn't give them much traction, it was hilarious to see the elegant ten transform into competitive, rough little schoolboys determined to win, slipping and sliding and getting very dusty. After the match there was much shaking of hands and back slapping as they triumphantly climbed back to their sets amidst thunderous applause.

**Performer AWOL.** At this point, Adele, who was managing the Stars, whispered to me that they couldn't find the radio comedian Gabriel Bayman who was due in the ring in fifteen minutes. We knew he had arrived but had disappeared. The three of us went searching in all directions.

I soon found him in a circus caravan with one of the grounds men, happily slugging from a bottle of brandy and pretty well drunk. At first, he refused to come with me. I snatched the bottle and all five-foot-two of me pulled him to his feet and the groundsman and I pushed him across the lawn to the performers entrance. We forced coffee down him and could only hope that he would make it to the improvised mini stage with the microphone.

**Alright on the night.** Of course, like all pro's he staggered on stage like he was meant to and began his hilarious, perfect Cape Minstrel routine. Next problem, he was enjoying himself so much that he didn't want to stop and was drunk enough to ignore the Ringmaster. Adele, like the true pro she was, went into the ring, linked arms with him and, with distraction from the clowns, pulled him offstage. It didn't look as desperate as it was – just appeared to be part of the act, raising applause.

**Mrs. Wilke's birds.** Next was the highly professional and elegant Mrs. Wilke and her magical birds doing her bidding in and around the entranced audience.

The show was building towards the two main acts. The elephants and the trapeze. Dress suited Hugh Rouse was ready and waiting, as we were, in huge anticipation.

To the familiar Elephant Walk music, Hugh proudly waving, entered sitting forward with legs tucked in just behind the ears of the lead elephant. He acknowledged the roaring crowd and looked very pleased with himself. He was followed into the ring by three more elephants, trunks and tails linked. But we suddenly became aware that the lead elephant was very unhappy with its new man rider who had replaced the beautiful, sequined maiden usually on his back.

As the other elephant's broke links and formed up, side by side, we noticed that the lead elephant, with Hugh aboard, was flapping its ears and purposely bumping into elephant number two. We noticed a pained expression cross Hugh's face as his right leg was being squashed with every bump and stride.

**Elephant walk.** Suddenly the elephant turned and left the tent. He and Hugh, his terrified rider, swept out through the stage door and disappeared out of the tent, to the circus grounds, heading up the main Braamfontein road towards The Fort, the old disused prison at the top of the hill. This was serious. We'd lost a celebrity and an elephant. While the elephant act continued in the ring as if nothing had happened, other circus people and some Monday Club husbands gave chase in a car, on foot and on a bicycle.

Poor Hugh had lost much of his usual composure. He was helpless. He wasn't laughing. He was too high up to jump off. His leg was aching.

## 3. Career, Business and Family

When the rescuers arrived at the now still animal, the circus trainer ran up and tickled Elly's trunk and offered him an apple. Somehow, they managed to get Hugh down and driven off to get some medical care for his bruised leg and high-flying nerves.

A happy result. and the show went on. The elephant was led back home enjoying the snack, and not at all concerned. Hugh limped around SABC for about a week enjoying the attention. "It was an elephant that did it" he bragged. By the time they got back, the trapeze artists were flying and sensibly their joking invitation for volunteers fell on deaf ears.

All good things come to an end. Presided over by Adele, still wearing the Blue Angel outfit, there were many speeches and thanks.

The Monday Club had done it again. And everyone felt elated at such an amazing event and lifelong experience. A large amount of money had been raised for the new wing at Woodside Sanctuary.

**A&J Promotions Involvement** started for me, in 1967. When Adele Lucas asked if I would join her and Jenifer Williams in their brand-new Promotions business. It would be A.J.M. Promotions.

I decided to turn down the offer as my youngest child, Andrea, was only a year old. I said that I would work freelance with them from home and keep the arrangement flexible. A&J Promotions it was until years later when Jenifer and Adele parted company in business, whilst remaining close friends.

In retrospect, I remain happy with my decision.

Adele and Jenny were a top-notch selling machine. They could sell anything to anyone, but their project management and organizational skills, at that early time, were not great, mainly because it was not their primary interest. This was my strength, my interest and some limited experience.

I stepped in with A&J as a Freelance Associate, when they were involved with the early International Tennis tournaments at Ellis Park. Jenny's husband, Owen Williams, was making his name in the local and international tennis arena.

A&J helped him finance the tennis by a breakthrough arrangement with the local Tennis Association when they persuaded them to allow billboard advertising at the Ellis Park Tennis Stadium for the first time. A&J sold every possible visible square inch of space. Owen was rubbing his hands at the money generated. And the added value of it was that each sale of space had 'legs'. Annual contracts which only had to be renewed and topped up in future years. A&J commissions applied in perpetuity.

## My Life, a Roller Coaster Ride

There was also advertising in the programme.

Something called 'Sponsorships' for tournaments and players were suddenly becoming available and taken up. A&J took full advantage.

Owen's forte' was in getting the top international players to come to South Africa. No mean feat in those politically sensitive times soon after Sharpeville. He was an outstanding tournament organiser and had a talented team of people to make it happen. He took full advantage of his 6'3" height and was very autocratic in his dealings with people. He added to this image by smoking extra-long cigars.

Owen loved being 'the Boss'. "See me in my office". There were some who did. Others put up with it, and very few, like me, reacted and bounced it right back. A note of summons 'See me in my office' from him, would be returned from my office with 'See me in mine'. We got on well after these ground rules were set.

The very first time I was roped in to help with tennis was when Adele & Jenny with Owen had started what was known as 'The Tennis Patrons Club'. People who became courtside 'Box Holders'. The Press, Sponsors, Private Box Holders and special invited guests could also relax in the upper Club lounge in comfort in the informal atmosphere and watch the tennis through the panoramic windows, hear the commentary while drinking with their pals. This bar was also open to the seeded tennis players and international visitors who would all mingle with the local elite.

**Hugely successful.** It became socially the place to be at tennis time. Elegant clothes and even hats were the order of the day in the late sixties and seventies. It drew a whole new dimension into the game of tennis previously only enjoyed as a game for local tennis enthusiasts.

In the beginning, 1967 and 1968, we even did the catering ourselves for the Tennis Patrons Club. In amongst our other activities, we found ourselves cooking gammon and producing salads for lunch brought in from our homes in a motley variety of containers. The days before Tupperware, Gladwrap and Tin Foil.

**International tennis at Ellis Park.**

Is tennis just tennis? Well, yes, if it was just a game but Owen, Adele and Jenny turned it into SA's new entertainment medium and social scene. Our mini-Wimbledon enjoyed international and local excellence – combined with an atmosphere of social excitement.

Ellis Park was suddenly seeing faces usually only glimpsed in the social pages of magazines. It was before the advent of TV and therefore

## 3. Career, Business and Family

reliant for its life and growth through the interest in and participation of newspapers, magazines and radio for exposure and creating awareness.

Interesting sporting fashion developed in the Women's pages which guided the tennis fashion scene. Casual elegance. A good opportunity to wear sporty hats. A good excuse to enjoy gin and tonic at lunchtime – which sometimes lasted till dinnertime. It competed with the fashionable horse racing events of the time.

**VIP boxes (season tickets),** became a status symbol and were well used. Businesses used them as client entertainment and a good excuse to escape the office.

Although this is common practice these days, it was initiated by the innovative marketing genius of Adele Lucas in 1968 and avidly supported by Owen Williams. It was ahead of its time when the boxes were created and sold at a premium.

This was also practical and useful against the gamble of variable attendances dependent on weather and calibre of players in the early elimination stages of a tournament. It provided glamour and panache and gave energy to tennis occasions.

Because of the well-known S.A. hospitality and the carefully nurtured carnival atmosphere of the tennis staged by the three whizz kids, Adele, Jenny and Owen, it was never difficult to attract big names to the

'In the same vein of tennis and entertainment, seven years later, Megan staged 'Celebrity Tennis'. Seen conducting a Press Conference introducing stars, including Peter Lawford, Ringo Starr, Dino Martin Jr. ,The Three Degrees, Monkees.

## My Life, a Roller Coaster Ride

tournaments. The prize money was good because ZA R0.78 could buy one US dollar, and the calibre of our local players world class. Gordon Forbes, Abe Segal, Frew MacMillan, Bob Hewitt, and the charismatic, handsome Cliff Drysdale, were winning attractions.

The internationals were, the serious left hander, Rod Laver, handsome John Newcombe, straw-headed joker, Fred Stolle, chunky, cheerful Ken 'Muscles' Rosewall, gentlemanly Roy Emerson, cheeky, sometimes crude, Lew Hoad, shy and cool Bjorn Borg, reliable Stefan Edberg, wild and arrogant Jimmy Connors.

Sporty Billie Jean King, fiery John McInroe, temperamental Illie Nastase, flamboyant Pancho Gonzales, Matts Willander (Swedish who married the current SA beauty Queen Sonja Mulholland). Veterans Don Budge and Fred Perry came out to see and be seen. SA Tennis was the place to be.

**Teddy Tinling** was most famous for the lacy panties and short skirts of Gorgeous Gussy Moran. He came out regularly each year and was particularly memorable to me as I was asked to make sure he was looked after.

I enjoyed this friendly, gentle 6'4" giant of a man. He was not always part of the pack and more of a loner. I suppose in those days he would have been in his fifties. Still single for probably obvious reasons never discussed.

Teddy Tinling, the international tennis Couturier with Billie Jean King.

Always good humoured, funny and loaded with anecdotes, and very knowledgeable about tennis through the ages.

Teddy would not bow to pressure from the players to pursue the possibility of designing fashionable tennis clothes in colour for women or men. The most he would concede to was added stripes, ribbons, lace, bows, buttons, accessories. His reasons were sensible. In the days before breathable sports fabrics, coloured cotton, when wet, (underarms and back) became

## 3. Career, Business and Family

much darker and unattractive and therefore distasteful to see, photograph and wear. Sweat was not detectable on white.

I remember the day I invited Captain Chris Coldrey to join us in the VIP box on Ladies Day. He was the international Show Jumping Judge and Course Builder visiting SA from the UK, for the Rothmans Derby, which we were also promoting at the time. Two of the men players on court were building up a sweat, Chris said "If they were horses, I would be able to tell how the match would end from the pattern of sweat on their shirt backs". He said, "It would be easier to plot performance if they wore colours, not white". Teddy, who was sitting with us gave a satisfied chuckle.

All the tennis players knew and loved Teddy Tinling. He was always on call and ready to help and mentor. But he also loved getting into a corner with me to talk about homely and personal things and the SA way of life. He seemed a little lonely despite his popularity.

One day I had to beg off lunch with Teddy because it was my day to do Carole's school lift. He immediately announced that he would come along. I tried to discourage him from coming on this school run, more importantly because I had a nice new little VW Beetle suitable comfortably to carry two adults plus two passengers and their school bags. I would have to fit in Teddy and the three children of the lift club.

Picture Teddy's 6'4" frame jack knifed into the Beetle passenger seat and three scrunched up ten-year-olds and their satchels in the back. But he absolutely insisted. It was a magical journey.

Teddy, the middle-aged bachelor, held the three, and me, captivated by his stories, and imaginings and recipes for meringues and fudge. Teddy said it was one of the best days of his visit.

**Pucci.** The third year, the Ladies Day Judge was the very elegant Italian Couturier the Marquis Count Emilio Pucci. Better known simply as 'Pucci'. His designs featured his fabric designs.

The whole office was in high excitement about his visit. I was to host him at Ellis Park and make sure that his stay and his duties as judge went without a hitch.

We decided to assign our young nineteen-year-old blonde staffer, Victoria Cronwright, to accompany Pucci from the President Hotel to Tennis on Ladies Day. Vicky was an attractive and bright young woman. Her father being Guy Cronwright, Editor of the *Cape Times* and a good friend of my father.

I was at the hotel to meet Pucci and ensure he was briefed and dispatched

# My Life, a Roller Coaster Ride

on time. Vicky was waiting with the car at the Hotel front door. She stood back for him to get in. Instead, the gallant Count waved her ahead into the back seat. As she bent forward to get in, he gave her a hearty Italian pinch on her pretty little bottom, and she shot forward in such fright she almost flew straight through the far window. Blushing, she giggled helplessly, not knowing quite how to react to the Italian impulse or the mischievous twinkle in the eyes of the beautiful man. I am afraid I almost collapsed laughing at him behaving exactly as an Italian was expected to do.

In fact, having had his innocent bit of fun, he took his judging duties very seriously. Not easy, considering some of the very odd outfits which predictably always arrived on the Ladies Day scene, often more outlandish than elegant high fashion. In fact, the real fashion was not there for fashion judging but rather found sitting quietly in the boxes and in the Patrons Club where Count Pucci would hold real court after his public duty was done.

**Terry Flounders** was another regular visitor at tennis time. We became good pals as well as business associates. We were about the same age. He accompanied Lisa Beresford (wife of Max Robertson, BBC) and creator of *The Wombles of Wimbledon*. They were part of the tennis crowd, but Terry as a director of Wombles Inc, was introducing me to my new furry family of seven Wombles characters.

I had been given the promotional and merchandising rights to them in SA. Terry had hoped to license *The Wombles of Wimbledon* radio series

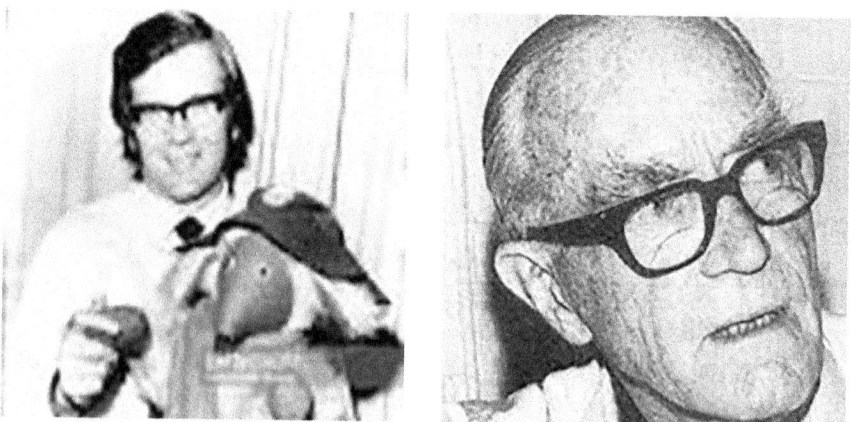

Left: Terry Flounders and Orinoco. Right: Capt. Mike Gibson, Wimbledon Tennis Referee. Mike came out for two consecutive years of the S.A. International tennis. Terry Flounders attended the tennis with Lisa Beresford, wife of BBC Tennis commentator and creator of The Wombles. Terry hoped to contract The Wombles Series to SABC as part of its Children's Radio programmes (before TV in South Africa). He had produced the BBC Radio and TV series, voiced over by Bernard Cribbins.

## 3. Career, Business and Family

to SABC as part of its Children's Radio programmes (before TV in South Africa). He had produced the BBC Radio and TV series, voiced over by Bernard Cribbins.

SABC turned him down. They said they produced their own characters, like *Wielie Walie.*

Terry and Lisa took time out to show me how the Wombles should behave in public, and the best props to show them off. They also encouraged the tennis champs to support me when press photos were needed.

**War of the Worlds.** Terry also had the rights to release H.G. Wells *The War of the Worlds*, a shattering Sci Fi film ahead of its time.

It so happened that I was in touch with Tom Geary who was the Curator of the Johannesburg Planetarium at that time.

Tom had asked me to think of a way to attract a broader public to visit the Planetarium. I had the idea that they could use *The War of the Worlds*, projected onto the 'Sky Dome' as a novel attraction. Terry agreed, Tom worked his magic, projecting the movie onto the high starry dome.

I then did a lively publicity programme to get feet through the doors. It was a sell-out. I did not charge a fee for the three-month event, which worked so well that Tom presented me with an interesting thank you gift. A Holographic eye framed in gold, linked on a chain to wear around my neck.

A hologram has its own mystery. Now it's here now it's gone at a twist of the wrist. It drew much curious attention every time I wore it as a jewellery piece.

The Sci Fi novel *War of the Worlds* written by H.G. Wells in 1898, had caused mass national panic on Halloween night, when broadcast on the radio in USA.

The actor and producer Orson Welles (no relation) had adapted the story for radio broadcast and, to promote the drama, had interrupted radio news broadcasts to say that the Martians had landed. Real panic followed.

It is on record that the people believed that Martians had invaded their country and ran out onto the streets, calling for the national guard to fight the alien invaders.

The author and the programme producer Wells and Welles became the good friends for life. Our Johannesburg Planetarium got a new lease of life. The Martians didn't make an appearance on the streets of Johannesburg that Halloween.

**Young tennis fans.** Carole Carr, Sarah Williams and Carolyn Lucas were regular faces at many tennis matches, delivered there by our driver straight

## My Life, a Roller Coaster Ride

from school.

They loved the tennis and social scene. The pretty little trio got much attention when dressed alike for a PR opportunity on Ladies Day. Adele, Jenny and I were happy mothers to have them around us as we worked.

**Chris Barnard.** It was at Ellis Park that tennis lover, Professor Chris Barnard, met and fell for his future young wife Barbara Zoellner. Barbara was frequently on duty at the Tennis and highly fancied by the Yugoslavian tennis player Niki Pilic.

Niki and Barbara made a habit of sitting incognito holding hands and whispering to each other high up in reserved seats in the main grandstand, to the utter frustration of the organisers who liked to keep tabs on the players before their games. We often had them followed to keep track of Niki before his matches. He was also just a kid.

**Chris and Barbara Barnard.** When Chris Barnard first saw the gorgeous 18-year old Barbara Zoellner, he followed her around Ellis Park like a puppy dog. He was incredibly beguiling, this forty-plus year old Casanova. She had no chance.

It was on Valentine's Day, less than a year later, that this beautiful couple got married and enjoyed what appeared to be a fairy-tale life in the glare of public spotlight.

**1969. A&J Promotions** rented offices in de Korte Street, Braamfontein. No small coincidence that Owen Williams had his Queen Anne Whisky

**Chris and Barbara Barnard.**

### 3. Career, Business and Family

Agency and Tennis Promotions business in the same building. Owen was smart enough to see the value of a closer business association with the talented duo Jenny and Adele.

**Décor.** With an eye for a good deal, Adele offered Ian and Des Calder, Interior Decorators, publicity for their business in return for designing and decorating the compact three-room open plan offices.

They did an amazing job transforming the dreary open space, with added value of semi-private areas, for each of the somewhat vocal all-female staff. The striking feature of the décor inside the entrance, was a pointed burnt orange Bedouin canopy, hiding the entire ceiling. Orange was the fashionable colour at the time.

## 18. 1969. Pivotal person, Sol Kerzner

**Sol** had moved to Johannesburg to start up Southern Sun Hotels. But what was missing was the love of his life, Shirley Bestbier. She was petite, with a perfect figure, tanned legs, auburn-brown hair and big brown eyes. Shirley had been a runner-up in a Miss South Africa pageant a few years back. She was bubbly, mischievous and was completely oblivious of anyone's celebrity status or importance.

Sol happened into the office one day and asked us if we could possibly give Shirley a job if he brought her to Johannesburg. And so, she became our receptionist. Hotel experienced and good for our reception shop window. We also discovered that she was a fair artist and so, with the thrifty multi-task inclinations of the directors, Shirley also did our artwork for programmes, invitations and anything else that needed visual help.

She was a born comedienne and kept us laughing and happy.

We welcomed the lovers' quarrels because a contrite and sheepish Sol would arrive at the office armed with a big bag of biltong – his and Shirley's

Left: Sol marries Anneline in 1980.
I, the press club and the public first saw them together, just before their marriage was announced, at the official opening of his Pilansberg Game Reserve in 1980.

Peter, my son, was sixteen. I took him along as my partner, in the press bus. That was the day we watched as they offloaded two rhinos into the park, and when the local population poured over the hills to help themselves to our spit-braai lunch.

favourite comfort snack – and the whole office would tuck in and share the booty.

Apparently, he made sure he always had a supply of South African biltong wherever he went in the world.

**Southern Sun.** Sol had invited Adele and me to a meeting to brainstorm a corporate name for his new hotel empire. He had already started building and had planned to name it Sun City. (He couldn't really call it 'Sol City') He simply wanted our endorsement and reassurance.

**A lesson in running conferences.** In 1969 Sol invited Adele and I to visit Beverly Hills to learn from the maestro himself, how to run the perfect business conference. He devoted two full days to this project taking us through business strategy and staff motivation, staff bonding and office communication.

He believed in the value of novelty, introducing a discomfort zone. Management's opportunity to assess staff behaviour, leadership ability, weaknesses and strengths.

Despite the specific business theme given to the conference, we were encouraged by Sol to design the event to give the client something extra incorporating many other factors.

**Good order.** The event should, first and foremost, be meticulously planned, set up and conducted. A perfectly set up conference room gives an air of order, and the delegates immediately relax and trust. Order manifests a feeling of wellbeing, causing the delegates to be receptive to what is presented.

**Good communication.** A full programme should be planned and pre delivered to participants to give them time to prepare the business side. But there should be open slots for mystery guest speakers and surprises. A complete change of tune can revive sleepy delegates, especially after lunch. Make them laugh and nail their sympathetic interest in the less palatable aspects of a tricky subject.

**Good notices.** Programmes and funny reminder notes can ensure fluidity and remove question marks and uncertainty from the programme. Calmly keep the wheels turning and no discomfort along the way. All executed to appear effortless.

**Example.** For a Cepacol Conference we organized at Beverly Hills, we had a life-sized stuffed ostrich made up and stood it in the foyer, 'The

# 3. Career, Business and Family

Cepacol Watchbird' was easy to spot. He stood there as the rallying point for the Cepacol delegates.

Welcome notice, Arrival Cocktails, the daily programmes and any special notices which needed display. The delegates knew exactly where to send and receive their business and interpersonal info. It was the meeting point, the talking point and the butt of many a joke. They all wanted to take him home with them. Someone did…Gone…Today this is all done online. Ho Hum.

**Sports days.** We always included at least a half day for sports and games.

Golf for most of the group. Tennis or bowls for the others. Also, for wives if they were attending.

Sport defuses tension, in and out of the office. It shows up personalities' strengths and weaknesses, team spirit and leadership.

Fun games show the same. Especially sportsmanship, tenacity, character and the willingness to stick their necks out. To laugh and be laughed at.

Sport was also a great leveller. It was mandatory that the games were played by every single member of the company present at the conference. The games were often purposely silly.

Imagine the MD having to race against the receptionist on a Kangaroo ball relay race across the lawn. Or a swimming gala obstacle race such as when the Atkinson Oates Motors conference swimming gala had staff playing an egg and spoon race with spark plugs and hub caps.

Very soon everyone got into the spirit of the moment. Pomposity had no chance. No inhibitions allowed at the coalface of the silly games. Team spirit was boosted as there were always team races. It also gave them something to take back to the office for common room chatter and the memory box.

**Surprise speakers.** In the middle of very heavy and intense product training, sales presentations, or budget forecasting, we would pop in talks on subjects as varied as Fashion Trends, Climbing Mount. Everest, Sporting greats on 'Winning' and top businessmen on 'Success'. I often used the Sedley Berger organisation on 'Building Self Image'. As well as giving self-confidence a boost, this would wake up and refresh the delegates for the following business sessions.

**Prestidigitation.** For a Seiko Watch Conference, I hired a local magician. He asked the audience of jewellers if anyone had a Rolex watch. Half the audience put up their hands. The magic man picked one of them and asked if he could '*borrow*' the Rolex. Waving the watch in the air as he trotted back on stage, he placed it on his table. He then took out a hammer and smashed the borrowed watch into smithereens.

There was a gasp from the mesmerised audience. Almost tears from the watch owner. Magic man then gaily said 'that's that'. Now for my next trick and continued with another trick as the audience eyes were still rivetted on the metal bits on the table. Taking pity, Magic man then told the watch owner to look in his top pocket. With spotlights shining on him, he pulled his watch out and triumphantly showed the audience. A good start to the evening's business. Conference dinners always involved speeches but rounded off with a comedy act.

**Using comedy.** I remember asking the comedy duo Hal Orlandini and Ian Lawrence to try to 'keep it clean'. This was very difficult for them, and they slipped into character from time to time to the delight of the audience, occasionally shocking some wives and some top brass. No real harm done.

I dare say the performers were sensitive to the audience expectations and didn't want to disappoint, having been paid in advance for the act.

**Biltong and Pot Roast.** Others used in the '70s were the comedians who burst onto the radio scene with their outrageous 'Biltong and Pot Roast' series with Brits and Locals vying for the weekly honours. The English side had such regulars as Ian Hamilton, Noel Glover, Dennis McLean, Paul Noble and in the SA team were Cyril Green, Hal Orlandini, Ian Lawrence, Mel Miller and Eddie Eckstein.

**Back to Sol and our conference education.** Sol practiced what he preached. Whilst giving us a crash course in effective conferencing, he made sure that Adele and I had fun. Sol was like a little boy when excited about something. What he taught us then, I value and use to this day.

**Pianist Sol.** I have memories of being treated like a VIP at his Beverly Hills hotel. We were entertained by our host at the piano. Sol was an accomplished musician. Passionate about music and all the good things in life. He seriously understood the hedonist in all of us.

This is what made him the success he was combined with his energy, drive and unerring eye for every detail, down to the hotel keys and 'Do not Disturb' door signs.

Obviously, we placed our first Conference at Beverly Hills. Part of Sol's ulterior motive in instructing us, was to secure our business loyalty because he saw A&J as a successful promotions company on the way up.

## 3. Career, Business and Family

He was smart enough to recognise in Adele Lucas, a genius marketing mind – and later appointed her as head of Marketing, PR and Promotions in his newly formed Southern Suns mega-organisation.

Sol and I continued to cooperate in other directions as my own business, soon after, took off independently and with different interests and services from those at A&J. Sol and I developed a kind of kinship and familiarity at that time which enabled me to count on Sol's co-operation five years later, when I brought out the film and music stars for Celebrity Tennis.

**1977. The Maharani.** He gave me a complimentary week for John Lawley and me, at the Elangeni Hotel in Durban to thank me for naming his new hotel 'The Maharani'.

Being of Indian Raj colonial design and situated on the Indian ocean, he thought of calling it 'The Mountbatten'. I was one of five asked to come up with a new name. He chose mine 'Maharani' Indian Princess.

The name of his first hotel 'Beverly Hills' said it all and was where his heart lay, near to Hollywood. He loved the entertainment business, and all who worked in it.

So, there was another connection to my Celebrities at the tennis.

**1975. Celebrity Tennis.** He set aside a full private floor of the Landdrost Hotel, with a lounge area, for my eleven movie and music stars for ten days at minimal cost.

**Boeing.** Because of the business relationship which evolved with Sol, many years later Sol lent me his Boeing to transport stars to Chobe where they stayed at no cost to me. He named the Honeymoon Suite at Chobe

Elangeni and Marharani Hotels along Durban beachfront.

# My Life, a Roller Coaster Ride

Percy Sledge on Tour – Press Farewell Party Percy Sledge, Soul Singer Carolyn Tew (A&J Promotions), Kay Starr (singer on the tour).

KWV Sherry Gang promotions.
My promotional girls and boys, all dressed in Sherry outfits and aprons, provided a party service with complimentary sherry from KWV.

## 3. Career, Business and Family

'The Elizabeth and Richard Burton Honeymoon Suite' which remains to this day 48 years later. The famous couple got married in Kasane, Botswana, second time around, and stayed as his guests at Chobe for their honeymoon. I was invited to the wedding but was unable to attend.

**Sun City.** Sol showed Adele and me the empty piece of ground two years before it would be transformed into Sun City and Lost City. He bounced ideas off us and implemented many of them. And we always had very definite opinions.

**Percy Sledge.** One of the earliest A&J celebrity promotions was to publicise the visit of soul singer, Percy Sledge. He became so popular and booked up with private gigs, that he was reluctant to leave at the end of his contract with impresario, Yango John.

Our next job was to get him to leave. He was outstaying his welcome with the impresario paying his overheads.

A&J delegated this job to me. I simply organised a 'Farewell Press Party' and invited all possible press with the Release Kit thanking him for his successful tour and local popularity, which was true.

**KWV** ran a campaign to promote their Sherries and make them fashionable cocktails.

Still as A&J Promotions Manager, I set up a service to any party givers who suited our campaign, to move sherry into the Bar Cocktail list.

Our Sherry Gang Service consisted of a basic supply of Sherry. Recipes for Sherry Cocktails, Barmen, dressed in Sherry Gang Aprons and straw bashers. They were trained by KWV to make bartending more fun.

Any business or charity group organizing a party or fundraiser could simply apply and would have the bar perfectly organised with the emphasis on Sherry.

**ARWA Parys Airfield launch.** ARWA had relocated its factory to Parys where there are very few earth tremors from mining and therefore fewer dropped stitches in the nylon pantyhose factory.

But it cost them in another way. The small Parys airfield could not handle Arwa MD, Hans Thierfelder's, private Boeing on its mini strip. So Arwa built a bigger runway and upgraded the facilities. Hence my contract to launch it.

I had an excellent P.A. at that time, Carol Windebank. She had been a British Ice-Skating champion before arriving to spend a year, working in South Africa.

## My Life, a Roller Coaster Ride

Together, with the cooperation of the Parys Airfield Management, we put on a full air show and entertainment with invited guests in three marquees.

**Three marquees.** One for the Retail Industry VIPs and Buyers. One for invited private pilots flying in from the whole of SA. (don't drink much!) One for the Press (drink a lot!) and local Mayor and dignitaries.

For PR purposes I had visiting international actress, Glynis Johns, Villagers actors, Gordon Mulholland and Clive Scott as novelty guests.

Dealing with the CAA, I worked with the airport managers to get all the aviation clearances and permissions required to stage an air show.

**Saturday Sabbath.** The local Parys community was largely Seventh Day Adventists with Saturday as their Sabbath. So, that was part of the audience not physically attending. Johannesburg was 120kms away, so that was partly out of play. The many invited guests and Arwa employees were the main audience for the air show.

**The best laid plans of mice and men 'Murphy's Law'.**
MD of ARWA, Hans Thierfelder, was once a friend of Adolph Hitler. They also shared an Astrologer. When settling on a date for the ARWA Parys Airfield Launch, there were a limited number of dates available. The Rand Easter Show was a major distraction. When I suggested the two options, Hans Thierfelder consulted his (and Hitler's) Astrologer, who advised him not to hold any event on either of the two Saturdays. The stars had spoken.

**Hotpants Skydivers.**
I had Skydivers with their own plane. Girls in Arwa red and white Hotpants and T-shirts wearing Arwa Pantyhose jumping out of their plane. Events included Skydiving stunt men freefalling. Stunt pilots doing their hammerheads and loops. Bands playing, local School Drum Majorettes and all the fun of the fair.

Right: Carol Windebank.

## 3. Career, Business and Family

**And the stars were right.**
We went ahead anyway. Record rainfall for 32 years starting the day before. The worst of the storm had petered out by Saturday leaving us with small windows of clear skies in between light showers. And a lot of mud.

Undaunted, we forged ahead with the full show. Skydivers, Hotpants girls, Marching Band and more. The noise of the rain on canvas was thunderous. The guest noise inside increased with the wine consumption.

Rain never stopped a good party.

The viewing public, arrived by car, remained in their cars and watched the full Air Show through their windscreens, occasionally with wipers at full blast. The Seventh Day Adventists praised the Lord for the rain and watched what they could from their covered stoeps. At least it was visible in the air.

**Bravely, as the weather was not too good** the Hotpants girls landed first, then Rod Murphy, Skydivers Captain, and the stunt skydivers performed a freefall and joined hands in a circle in the air before landing to the applause of an admiring audience, watching from the open-sided marquees.

**Mud mud glorious mud.** In my new Avo green couturier outfit, I had taken off my matching Avo green shoes and hat, and was wading ankle deep in mud, from marquee to marquee, directing operations.

**Hostages.** I had chartered a de Haviland 40-seater aircraft for the press and special guests from Johannesburg. Fortunately, the plane arrived before the worst rain deluge and landed safely.

**Problem.** The new Arwa Parys Airport managers had forgotten to acquire rolling steps for the passengers to alight.

I was called over the public address system to deal with it. Help! I dialled 911, as the trapped guests sipped their free drinks on board. I got the Fire Department to come and 'rescue' the passengers with their long ladder and gallant, uniformed. saviours. Best story, hot off the press.

# My Life, a Roller Coaster Ride

**Show verdict.** The entire atmosphere of the three marquee parties was jolly and noisy. The client and his wife, also with muddied shoes, spent time in each marquee.

After all the speeches and ribbon cutting, Herr Thierfelder thanked us and declared satisfaction with the show. Good publicity resulted and Arwa Parys Airfield had become the new stop for the Arwa Boeing and anyone else flying in to Parys.

My avocado green shoes and skirt hem didn't survive the mud.

Having met the Skydiver Team Captain, Rod Murphy, a real Irish character, we became good friends. Rod introduced Carole and I to the joys of The Okavango Delta.

## 1969. Indoor Horse Shows.

They ran under the A&J Promotions banner when I was Associate Events Organiser. I became involved with Horse Shows and the Show Jumping crowd. This is a very defined community which lives, breathes and exists in the world of horses and competition.

Our first big foray into this world was when Jack Shires, Marketing Director for Rothmans of Pall Mall, asked A&J Promotions to take on the organisation and promotion for the first Rothmans Indoor Horse Show. Everybody loved this elegant and talented Englishman.

A mammoth task never done before in South Africa.

We found a suitable pavilion at the Rand Show Grounds when it was still situated on Yale Road, Braamfontein, opposite the Planetarium. A brand new world was about to open to us. This large football field sized, grey metal structure standing empty was a daunting sight. My first job was to organise scaffolding-type seating on three sides of the horse arena.

Jenny Williams and Adele Lucas posing for a picture for the *Sunday Express*, the media sponsor, edited by Johnny Johnson.

# 3. Career, Business and Family

The arena floor had to be packed with deep peat and wood chips to protect the horses' limbs and hooves, allowing for scuffling and jumping. We also had to provide a Collecting Ring outside the horse entrance and an office, storerooms and catering corner.

The Equestrian Society of SA provided the gymkhana and course jumping paraphernalia.

With their help, we installed the Public VIP boxes, the Horse Society VIP boxes, Press Box and provision for the judging.

For each show, a specialist Course Builder would be invited from the UK. The two regulars were The Hon. Harry Llewellyn and Captain Chris Coldrey.

At that very time, Harry's son, Roddy, was dating Princess Margaret, having romantic trysts on the Island of Mystique – so the press never left him alone. How we danced around trying to shield him and give him some peace.

Chris Coldrey, whilst being a perfectionist on the course building job, and a walking encyclopaedia on equestrian matters, seemed helpless at other times and it became my job to mother him in and around the show office.

I remember, at the pavilion one day, sponsor, Jack Shires asked me, "Does he do anything for himself? I'm surprised you don't attend to him when he goes to the lavatory". At that very moment, Chris put his head round the door asking, "Meg, where's the loo paper?" Jack and I fell about, laughing.

Our show jumping stars at the time were Gonda Butters, Mickey Louw and the diminutive Janie Myburgh on her huge mount. Peter Levor was a bulky man on a bulky horse, who surprisingly broke the world high jump record. Over many hours, the tension in the hall, that memorable night, was palpable.

Apart from the show jumping, events such as the Lipizzaner's. The white horses of Vienna demonstrating Haute Ecole led by Col. George Iwanowsky.

For the younger ones, there were Barrel Racing and Gymkhana events. The South Africans competed equally with the invited international riders, representing their countries.

After becoming known for our successful Indoor Show events, we were in demand to promote other sporting events such as the Inanda Rothmans Derby, Ice Hockey and Pony Polo.

# My Life, a Roller Coaster Ride

Col. George Iwanowsky and the Lippizaners

**Time to say goodbye.** Owen Williams bothered me. I found his arrogant, bossy manner insupportable and, after a chat with Adele, I resigned as their freelance Promotions Organiser.

The three of them invited me to lunch, asking me to reconsider. I don't burn bridges and still enjoyed Adele and Jenny as good friends, so I simply told them I had decided to start out on my own as I had some good ideas to pursue, totally unrelated to A&J's current client base.

In fact, I had been having outside partnership offers, all of which I had turned down. I now felt ready to run my own show, my way.

**A critical decision.** No sooner had I left A&J, than I was again approached by likeable long time business friend Dawie Hoets, to join him as a full business partner in a massive national promotion for Shell and BP. He, too, was normally bossy, but not with me. I agreed to it on a trial basis. I never wanted to feel trapped again. And his proposition was a very attractive one. He had just resigned from the powerful PR company Group Editors.

We called ourselves 'Carr & Hoets Communications cc' Dawie was a brilliant ex-newspaper journalist and a creative writer and thinker. He had been entirely responsible for the high profile and successful, year-long, Milk Board Campaign which had just ended. Dawie and I had worked together on some aspects of it.

**BP and Shell.** As a result of his track record, Dawie had been offered the major corporate awareness campaign by Shell and BP. Dawie didn't feel he could manage the active on-site promotional side, which is why he

## 3. Career, Business and Family

asked me to join him. He would handle the PR. Dawie's highly efficient wife, Mary, was to run the office back-up and the books. We decided to set up offices in their house in Parkview.

The Shell – BP Marketing Equalisation Group (MEG) campaign was conceived to make the public aware of the splitting of the two brands.

Previously, they had worked together under the Shell banner. Now, they would divide the joint filling station portfolio down the middle and would thenceforth have separate identities. Shell would continue as before the split, so no promotion needed.

We would work on the BP new identity with new corporate image, green and yellow livery. All the BP identified petrol stations had, within a few weeks, been transformed with a brand-new appearance. They also opened excellent forecourt Convenience Shops. A new idea in the early seventies.

Our plan was to put two attractive BP liveried girls at each participating service station. They would talk to the motorists, engage their interest and ensure continued loyalty. Also, to introduce them to some of the products in the shops.

Of course, there were free balloons to attract the children. Always to be a BP ploy. Market Research had told us that children under eight could persuade their parents to do anything. Go anywhere.

**Kids like balloons,** so each participating Station always had bunches of balloons hanging at the pumps. One balloon per car. If a second or third child cried hard enough, they would also be handed one.

We hired 140 girls countrywide. I designed and produced double that number of outfits and had the headache of keeping tabs on these as, over time, the inevitable temp staff changes occurred.

**Dawie Hoets and BP girls.** They all wore the BP green blazer, hotpants suits with yellow T-shirts sporting the new logo. Green baseball caps and green knee-high boots which I had specially made in a range of sizes. To simplify our logistics, we decided to employ the girls in the size range of 32 – 36, and boots 4 – 7. Somehow it worked. Getting the girls was easy. Managing them was harder.

**Pocket money for students.** A perfect job for University and Post Matric students wanting to earn money. The hardest challenge was punctuality and transport.

# My Life, a Roller Coaster Ride

**Hulle smous met mooi meisies**

Mooi meisies is Dawie Hoets werk, en watter man sal hom nie loopbaan beny nie. Die vriende verkoopsters by Dawie is Kate I burn, Gedinka Bak en Andrea Ho

**Dawie Hoets and the BP girls.**

They didn't all have cars and some of the stations were not centrally located. So, I set up Supervisor / Transport-managers in each region and lift clubs, provided by those who had transport at an added fee. Duty hours were school lift times and business peak hours.

**Training.** I asked BP to organise training sessions for the girls in each centre. There is nothing worse than sales representatives who are not well informed about their product and, in this case, the rationale behind the promotion, the new BP Corporate Identity. In trying to retain the people loyal to Shell, we had to educate them that the BP fuel going into their vehicle tanks was the same as the Shell fuel that they had used all along. Just a new label for the fuel at their station. Men were more concerned than women.

I knew that, with training, the girls would gain confidence and project energy into their contact with motorists. The BP management was very 'pumped up' about this and devised training evenings which were entertaining, bonding and enlightening.

**Training evenings.** Welcome cocktails, sumptuous snacks in elegant auditoria. BP showed a specially produced documentary about the history

## 3. Career, Business and Family

of the company, the reason for the campaign and they even went into a simplified presentation on the workings of an internal combustion engine and the function of fuel and differences in fuel grades, the refining process and vision for the future. The girls were given printed information to back up what they had learnt and 'Frequently asked Questions and Answers' for reference.

At the training evenings, we revealed prototypes of the girl's proposed uniforms on dummy mannequins. The girls were very impressed. The BP men were excited. All raring to go.

The three-month MEG campaign was off to a good start. Incidentally, the MEG campaign was not named after me! The two oil companies, British and Dutch, had decided to operate separately instead of jointly hence this campaign was named.

**Future promo protocol.** Because this product training worked so positively in both morale building and practical common-sense usage and application, I adopted the product or service training idea, for use in all my future promotions to great effect. It provided Free Market Research for the client. Not just pretty faces which created a sense of pride in the job.

**Husband Peter Carr and some indications of his personality.**
He had his eccentricities, which didn't bother us. Even quite amusing.

A one-time Rally Driver, he would plot every journey by the mile and to the minute. He knew exactly the times between traffic light changes on the way to the office. On a long cross-country journey, he would make a list of the miles between towns and petrol stops and note down the ETAs, the 'E' meaning 'exact' and not 'estimated' time of arrival. The problem with this was that if he was running ahead of schedule, rather than be wrong, he would slow down to arrive on the dot – rather like the Swiss trains. Or drive like a maniac to make up lost time.

He bragged about the time he went into a hardware shop and asked the assistant, "Do you by chance have a very, very small screwdriver?" The assistant disappeared to the back of the shop and came back with a tiny watchmaker's screwdriver about the size of a pin and, with a smirk, asked, "will this be small enough, Sir?" Peter examined the screwdriver closely and, playing to the audience waiting for service, said "Not really, but I suppose I could grind it down".

That described him perfectly. To our mutual credit, we very rarely quarrelled. We spared ourselves and the children that. Our marriage wasn't awful or abusive. It just wasn't good enough to satisfy me for the next endless years. The real problem, for me, was possessiveness and control.

**The last straw in my marriage** came when, once too often, Peter found a way to prevent me attending a meeting. This time, a 6pm Horse Show meeting. He was happy to share the income I earned but didn't like to share me after 'office hours'.

Just as I was rushing off, I found him at my car with the bonnet up saying "I heard a funny noise in the engine. Just thought I would see if it is the tappets". I pulled the bonnet down and drove off to Inanda Club, running a little late.

On my return at about 8pm, still seething, I joined him in the study and announced that I had decided to divorce him. He was amazed, "but we're so happy", he said.

Andy was five and Peter was seven years old. Carole was fourteen, Tony sixteen when we divorced. Carole was delighted. Strangely, Tony was not. After Peter left, nothing really changed, except there was a feeling of relief and peace. No tiptoeing or anxiety.

**BP campaign over.** As soon as the BP campaign with Dawie Hoets, came to an end. I decided to follow my original plan and go into business on my own. My split with Dawie was practical. Too many miles to travel from Sandown to Parkview. His expertise was mainly in writing and journalism, so our joint association had served its purpose. We agreed to team up in future if a promotion called for it.

**Marriage over.** 29th February 1972 Leap Year. After leaving Court, now finally divorced, with full child custody, no Alimony or Child Support, I was floating on a nervous cloud of optimism about the future. Liberated and my own person. I positively felt that I had the momentum and capacity to support the five of us.

I headed for The President Hotel where Taubie Kushlik was rehearsing the upcoming musical *Jacques Brel*. Adele was doing the publicity and suggested I join them for coffee after divorce court.

I thought I had crept in quietly without disturbing the rehearsal, but Taubie didn't miss a thing. She stopped the singing, turned around to me and said, "Where have you been all morning?" "Getting divorced" I said. "Congratulations" said Taubie, clapping her heavily ringed hands, and got right on with the rehearsal. A good endorsement to my new life.

## 3. Career, Business and Family

### 19. 1971. The Wombles

**On BBC TV.** The Wombles of Wimbledon, would creep out of their holes in the Wimbledon Common and, gather up the debris left lying around by careless humans, put it into bags and into 'Wombles' bins. Lisa reported that one weekend, they found a group of children on the Common throwing out their bags of rubbish and waiting to see the Wombles arrive out of their holes to do a clean-up.

A talented entrepreneur, Terry was later a member of British Film Industry (BFI) and worked under his registered company Sproosser Innovations. His main business at that time was to contract out radio and film series from the BBC's massive libraries.

He lent me a delightful, animated movie, not yet released, *Butterfly Ball* in the hope that I could introduce him, and it, to one of our Media moguls, but that was early times for me, and I was not able to help him. However, my family loved the movie, except Tony who thought it more for girls. Understandable, as he was just fourteen at the time.

Lisa Beresford attended the tennis with her husband, BBC Tennis commentator Max Robertson, which is where we met. She brought the Great Uncle Bulgaria suit with her to promote The Wombles in S.A.

## The Star Tonight!

Friday August 29 1975

# Star glamour group for two-day SA visit

**BILL EDGSON**

A glamorous group of Hollywood stars, including Rod Steiger, Dyan Cannon, Peter Lawford, Elke Sommer and Jill St John, is expected in Johannesburg towards the end of September for a two-day visit that will include tennis exhibitions at Ellis Park … a banquet in the city.

Also expected to be in the party are two members of The Monkeys pop group, another group called Three Degrees and the United States astronaut Scott Carpenter.

All are members of an organisation called Celebrity Tennis, a group which was formed in 1970 and which has earned millions of dollars for charity in various parts of the world.

The party is being brought to South Africa by Megan Carr Promotions and the tennis exhibitions are scheduled to take place on September 28 and 29. They will also appear at a charity banquet.

Peter Lawford and Rod Steiger will be masters of ceremonies at the banquet and The Monkeys will entertain.

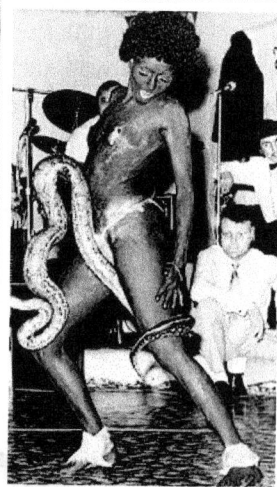

# Part 4
## Megan Carr Promotions

## 20. 1972. Megan divorces Peter

**Giant Leap.** That same day, my dear cousin, Dennis Westmorland, also my divorce and business Attorney, registered my new company Megan Carr Promotions (Pty) Ltd. (MCP). My new life had begun with a bang.

**Start of Megan Carr Promotions.** I was forty-one. I had met Graeme White the previous year. He and his partner Guy Todd owned an Advertising Agency Kenyon Wiles. He had asked me to join their agency as Promotions Director, but I had declined.

As soon as I mentioned that I had formed my own Promotions company, he immediately offered me office space and suggested MCP move into the prestige premises at a ridiculously low rental. The address was Bosman Building, Eloff Street, right in the centre of Johannesburg.

The first thing I did was phone Trisha Reunert. Dawie Hoets, my previous brief business partner, and I employed Trisha as a casual promotion's person, assisting me in the BP campaign. Although she was only eighteen, she was not only beautiful, but smart, sophisticated, sussed and energetic.

Left: I had a logo and letterhead designed, which served me well for thirty years.

**Miss Megan Carr and Trish Reunert (Megan Carr Promotions).**

## 4. Megan Carr Promotions

Trisha came from a prominent family and didn't really have to earn a living. Dawie always said "The best staff needs to be hungry". Sorry, Dawie, you are wrong. I have never seen anyone, so unhungry, so dedicated and hard working. In fact, Trisha was the ideal associate and alter ego for me in my brand-new little enterprise.

She had what you can't teach people. Trisha intuitively knew exactly what to do, how to handle people, how things should look and what would or would not work.

Trisha immediately accepted the job offer, and we were in business.

With the Kenyon Wiles spacious double office, furnished with two desks, typist chairs and phones, all we had to add was a filing cabinet, two typewriters, stationery, a table for client meetings, and a couple of casual chairs. We were in business. We even had the use of the K.W. switchboard with two dedicated MCP lines.

She was a very apt marketing and promotional aide, because she already had it in her genes. Her laugh was infectious. What happy days we had as a small team of two. I had a logo and letterhead designed, which served me well for thirty-five years.

**Instant business.** Better than just the offices, Graeme White already had a client lined up for MCP. It was Richardson Vick who had recently acquired the moisturising cosmetic Oil of Olay. Graeme was devising an advertising product launch and marketing campaign which included live promotions.

My specialty and experience was live promotions, exclusive to me in the South African marketplace at that time. We were soon established with a meaningful client and immediate media attention. Trisha and I got a thrill seeing our first letterheads and business cards. I also designed our first circular letter to businesses and Ad Agencies, advertising our unique brand of live promotional services.

In those days all mail went out by post in envelopes with stamps. The circular letter was in fact, in a circle, and needed a big envelope.

**Left: Graeme White, Managing Partner in Kenyon Wiles Ad Agency.**

# My Life, a Roller Coaster Ride

**The first 1968 seminar slogan impressed me.** On the opening page was a picture of a tortoise captioned:

'**Behold the Tortoise – It only progresses when it sticks it's neck out'.** I adopted it as a mantra for my life. Another valuable lesson was 'Time Management' is actually 'Self Management'.

**In this my life story,** I will include a selected few of the many promotions my company has conducted over thirty-five years.

The chosen few will be in some detail as an example of the intricate detail and creative thinking involved in a successful undertaking.

**Oil of Olay.** This first account was one of my most successful campaigns.

My thanks to Graeme White who had taken me under his wing. He also fancied me and seized the opportunity to score some points. Graeme and I were both newly divorced, so the timing was good.

Kenyon Wiles' big new client was Richardson Vick, of Vicks 'Vapo Rub' brand, which had recently purchased the home-grown South African moisturiser Oil of Olay. I was called into various development meetings and brainstorms to work out an innovative campaign which would be totally different from the usual cosmetic themes and incentives.

The aim was to develop and enlarge Olay's original success when their only advertising was on the last page endorsement adverts in The Readers' Digest. Even then Olay was surprisingly well known considering the narrow, simple advertising.

**The client.** The MD of Richardson Vick was a colourful, demanding character. He looked and talked like a typical Mafia boss. Slicked back black hair and natty clothes. I liked him. His staff feared and loved him.

**The Oil of Olay campaign.** The Oil of Olay Account Executive was a Portuguese South African. Not very outgoing and not hustler-typical marketing material. The Olay account was his chance to prove himself. His birthday was on the same day as mine. Two Taureans lining up for a brighter future.

Graeme White brought in his creative director Bennie du Toit, and we all brainstormed intensively and came up with something which got everyone very excited.

**The orchid campaign.** The Agency would take care of the new product image and advertising. Megan Carr Promotions would handle Promotions,

# 4. Megan Carr Promotions

PR and introductory sales.

My company had already made its name by having attractive girls, beautifully dressed in product livery for on the spot and In-Store promoting.

We were advised by the flower experts to use the Cymbidium orchid. This time the girls would have a dual function. To get a foot in the doors of 1 200 of the 1 750 Chemist shops around SA. Not an easy assignment. And then getting them to buy and stock Oil of Olay on their limited shelf space.

Getting the attention and interest of the busy and distracted chemists was the real challenge. The closest local cosmetic house rival at that time was 'Second Debut', which was ruling the roost with a cash back coupon for its moisturiser. Their incentive coupon was placed in the cap of every bottle for the customer to recoup at the till. An equal cash incentive for the chemist staff to recover on every bottle sold.

This was a nuisance for the chemists to administer.

**Soft Touch.** We decided to up the game with a very classy and romantic approach to building a strong awareness for Olay's re-launch into the SA market. We were dealing with women so the soft touch could work.

Our brainstorming came up with descriptive words with which to link the product such as 'exotic' 'velvety', 'silky', 'romantic', 'natural beauty', 'nature's gift'.

We then decided to link these to an exotic flower. We naturally came up with the orchid. In those days orchids were not as common as they are today. They were regarded with awe, mystique, yearning and love. Each pharmacy had an average of five shop assistants plus the chemist's wife.

**1 750 Chemist shops in the country.** We worked out that we could reasonably get to about 1 200 of them. The rest were contacted by phone about the advertising campaign to prepare them to order from the wholesalers. We could not take in the far rural areas but had to keep them in the loop. No computers, emails, social media or zoom. Just landline phones, posters, movie house and radio advertising. And MCP.

We calculated 1 200 chemists times six people per shop, equals 7 200 orchids plus spares would be needed.

I then had to learn more about these exotic flowers. Braak's nurseries in Pretoria were the biggest and most likely as the main source. The problem was how to get them all at our disposal within a promotion period of four weeks. Young Mr. Braak was very amused and intrigued at this unique challenge.

This quantity in a short time space was a first for him. He showed me

## My Life, a Roller Coaster Ride

around the orchid nursery and explained that he could probably supply about 5 000 in total over a four-week period. I would have to get the rest from other sources. As I looked across the undercover field of orchid plants, I did not spot one flower, with only a month to go. I contacted other orchid growers in Natal and Cape Town who contracted for the balance of 2 200 blooms at our wholesale price. And which would be used in their respective regions, making it practical for the MCP local organisers.

**Tough love.** Braak would force the orchids to bloom. They would have to be Cymbidium orchids and not the more exotic and less hardy Cattleya.

Braaks had to force them to bloom in phases and get them delivered, ready to handout, for easy transport and freshness, in padded, flat, shallow boxes containing 100 blooms per box. They sourced and supplied boxes for our account.

How does one force an orchid to bloom on demand? Make them feel endangered, apparently. Starve them of food and water and frighten them into producing offspring. A bit like people. Endangered communities have more babies to ensure survival of the species.

I selected seven of my best girls in Johannesburg. They were our best performers on the BP campaign. Beautiful, bright and good energy. I designed smart and trendy outfits for them to wear on their calls. Dusty pink, soft suede leather miniskirts and bomber jackets. Black and pink are the colours of the Oil of Olay logo. Zips were in fashion that year.

We launched Oil of Olay with beautiful promotion girls handing out fresh orchids to pharmacists and their staff. The unique promotion was so successful that it was used in UK and Australia. It also launched MCP with a bang.

## 4. Megan Carr Promotions

The jackets had bold zipped pockets. They wore black silky shirts, and medium heeled black patent shoes. The girls were bowled over by the stylish outfits. Very motivated and ready for action.

The girls all had their own cars (a condition of employment). They kept logbooks for reclaiming their costs. They were supplied with order books, planned visiting schedules and supplies of Olay product to sell.

Chemist shops rarely have more than five of any product on their limited shelves.

**Well trained.** Before hitting the roads, the girls had been thoroughly trained in product and packaging. They learned soft-selling and order taking techniques. The rather unique processes involved in getting to see the main men, the owners, of the chemist shops.

**Oil of Olay launch.** The lavish launch party was held at the M.D.'s rambling Linksfield home, with peacocks strutting the garden.

I had launched Scotchgard on the South African market in 1968. So, all the suede suits were Scotchgard-protected against mark damage and made easy to clean.

**Orchids, a hard act to follow.** The following year we decided to consolidate the promotion with a follow-up campaign. But how could we follow an orchid?

I had my dear friend, Dave Greig of Charles Greig Jewellers, make me 7 000 sterling silver bangles. Slim flat bands with 'Oil of Olay' imprinted on the inside. This meant that the chemist shop women could wear them without any advertising showing. Just an Olay reminder and a loyalty nudge. Classier than money vouchers and much more effective. No admin of money vouchers for the shops to bother with.

**Our Oil of Olay campaign was taken to many countries of the world.**

MCP. Another direct result of this campaign was that my little company was discovered and talked about. The business poured in, the first being Cacherel Perfumes, mainly Anais Anais (which day perfume I still use).

It shows the importance of a good launch and promotion, that they are still in high demand fifty years later.

## My Life, a Roller Coaster Ride

**Launch of the Eagle, fibreglass sports car.** Another of my very first MCP promotions. My friend and neighbour on the Vaal River was Bill Badesy, an inventor and entrepreneur. Bill had produced in his own factory a sexy fibreglass sports car and named it 'The Eagle'. He asked me to do the launch, even let me drive it.

It had a souped-up VW engine and light fibreglass body. What a creature it was!

**The Eagle launch.** Our guest of honour was the Minister of Transport, Dr. Piet Koornhof. For the Press launches around the country, I also brought in 1972 Miss South Africa, Stephanie Reineke.

In retrospect, what on earth was Cabinet Minister, Dr. Piet Koornhof thinking, gracing our modest launch with his august presence? I simply invited him, and he accepted. What a refreshing and gracious presence he was.

**1974. The next stage of MCP.** I pioneered In-Store promotions. I was one of twelve featured in 'The Year of the Woman' by the advertising journal, *The Clarion,* edited by Gerald Walford.

Within the first year, I had over 400 women promoters and 40 men and women supervisors signed up in the five main centres of the country.

For these we had to supply the girls with In-Store paraphernalia such

Launch of The Eagle, fibreglass sports car by Minister of Transport at the time, Dr Piet Koornhof. Posing on the right of the car is one of my promo girls, Zipporah Benn.

# 4. Megan Carr Promotions

as tables, cloths, plates, toothpicks, napkins, branded aprons and point of sale material.

We had to get them in place at hours to suit the stores.

**Hungry ones.** With food product promos, one of the hardest things was to prevent all the sample stock from being eaten by the store staff and the chancers who came into the stores to forage for food. We struggled, diplomatically, to keep them from cleaning the plate of little samples.

**Training and dramatics.** We had to teach the girls the value of market feed-back to the client. They kept daily notes on consumer opinion.

I meticulously monitored and checked the comments for objectivity. If not, we could get very biased and incorrect information.

Ninety-nine people would say "very nice" and warrant one line of comment, yet one dramatic person saying "I wouldn't feed it to my dog," would get the headlines and half a page in the report.

In this case monitoring was needed.

**Cabana Beach.** Early 1973. I was on a plane to Durban on Beverly Hills conference business, when I became aware of someone staring at me as we stood up to disembark. That person moved forward from his seat behind me to offer help lifting my bag down. 'What a gentleman', I thought, and thanked him. He insisted on carrying it off the plane and joined me walking to baggage collection. Once my case was retrieved and put on a trolley, he was back again and asked if I would like a lift to town. Such attention! I accepted and he dropped me at the Edward Hotel, where I was staying. We exchanged business cards and said we would keep in touch, as people do, thinking that was the end of it.

# My Life, a Roller Coaster Ride

That was the cautious start of a two-year romance, and an ongoing brilliant Anglo American PR and Promotion Account

The gallant gentleman was good looking Vic Wilson Taylor, Natal Regional Manager for Anglo American Properties and Chief Executive of the newly built Cabana Beach Resort Hotel.

The following day, of course, Vic phoned and invited me to lunch and to see Cabana Beach which was ready to be launched. I could only manage to be there late afternoon after my other business was done. He arrived to pick me up and after a tour of the hotel, we spent an intense evening together talking over dinner, discovering more about our work, about each other and our families.

He was long since divorced and had two adult children living in Johannesburg with their mother. A son, also Vic, at university and daughter, Noeline, in her late teens.

Vic was about my age, I was forty-one and had been happily divorced for a year. Tony was sixteen, Carole, just turned fifteen, Peter nine and Andy seven. So, the coast was clear for the inevitable relationship, which neither of us had been seeking. In fact, positively and actively avoiding at all costs.

Vic, in his capacity as Managing Director of Cabana Beach Hotel, was very interested in me as a PR and Promotions Consultant, owning my own company. Vic invited me to visit again the following day to talk business. I cancelled my flight and stayed over.

I gave him several references on my business. As time was of the essence, Vic followed these through and was satisfied that I fitted the bill to promote this avant-garde Resort.

Incidentally, one person on my reference list was Sol Kerzner, who gave me the thumbs up as I had run many seminars at Beverly Hills.

Vic explained that his urgent need was for me to manage the formal launch of Cabana Beach and ongoing PR and active promotions. What a spectacular account to undertake. Checking my business schedules and availability were just a formality, I decided that I would make it possible, with some client and office juggling.

Again, I changed my plane booking to complete the business briefing and meet the relevant personnel. This was the beginning of two and a half years of one of the most exciting accounts to date.

After orienting myself, I was bowled over by this magnificent and innovative hotel. Anglo had expected it to be rated a five-star resort. And

## 4. Megan Carr Promotions

rightly so. However, the Hotel Board, represented by Errol Reck, in its wisdom, would only grant four and a half stars because it did not conform. Each unit had a small kitchen. They relabelled them 'Apartments'. This label also precluded a liquor license for its restaurants. Big Brother calling the shots. It cost us many months finally to get a Wine and Malt license for the restaurants. And, further, in order to get this licence for Pablo's Restaurant, they made them carpet the restaurant, covering the stunning Spanish floor tiles. A very odd condition, with no reasonable rationale.

**Cabana Beach Hotel.** The hotel is Mediterranean Spanish Costa Smeralda in style. Everything was bright white with Spanish imported tiles in shades of rich jade green. Tall palm trees and rolling lawns completed the green and white theme. It had two swimming pools, in-house squash courts and Games and Creche facilities for children.

**Orientation of the units.** Penthouses on the top floor. Centre of the building was for four and six sleeper units. Ground floor for single studio apartments. Each sloping outer edge had duplex, eight sleepers, with a generous patio and braai facilities. Every unit had a sea view.

As the hotel was staffed and ready for business, in 1973, we organised a Guinea Pig weekend for senior Anglo and Cabana executives, Travel Agents and society leaders, to test the facilities. Reception, Porter service, Housekeeping, Restaurants, Squash courts and Kitchens to be assessed.

**No charge for the weekend.** Each guest had to complete an intensive questionnaire for use in assessing snags and fine polishing details and readiness for business. It was lots of fun and an excellent PR exercise as the word soon got around that this resort was different.

**Pablo's.** (Picasso) was the main restaurant. One of my first jobs was to produce a menu cover for the main restaurant. Roy Clucas, talented graphic designer with original ideas, came up with a stylised illustrated picture of Pablo Picasso with his fingers made of long bread rolls. I was nervous about presenting this odd idea, but the image was good, and it was accepted with hilarity and compliments.

**Visits.** I visited Cabana Beach from Johannesburg twice a month, always on a Thursday and occasionally stayed the weekend. On long weekends and school holidays, I took the children along and we would stay a weekend or a week. The four children would share a complimentary four bed unit and, by then I was shacked up with Vic in his duplex. That is to say that our romance took about six months to develop into a serious relationship.

My Life, a Roller Coaster Ride

# The year of the woman

*Megan Carr*

Megan Carr is managing director of a fast-growing promotions and public relations company in Sandton. She started the company in August, 1972, and concentrated mainly on in-store promotions, product launches, official openings and seminars.

Megan has a marketing and sales diploma and a sound knowledge of the South African market. She believes that the success of her promotional campaigns has been due to the application of this marketing knowledge to the company's projects.

Her company's attractive girls not only look good in product identifiable uniforms, but they know their product and its background and enter a promotion with the objective of moving it off store shelves *and* encouraging the stores themselves to continue to promote it after they leave. They also conduct mini surveys as they work and are able, on de-briefing, to give the client a fair, up-to-date report on the product's movements, the opposition product's comparative movements, and consumer opinion on quality, pack and so on.

As most campaigns are required on a national basis, Megan has appointed trained representatives in nine centres of the country to carry out her promotions with their own teams buyers for the collection in South Africa.

Until recently, Megan's company was an all-woman organisation with herself, four account executives and an administrative staff of three. In July, David Frost joined the company as a director and general manager to co-ordinate its activities and strengthen the administrative side.

All Megan's account execu-

**1973. Megan Carr, nominated by Clarion, the advertising newspaper, as the Woman of the Month in their Year of the Woman feature.**

# 4. Megan Carr Promotions

I fell in love with this man and the children adored him.

Imagine being a child having the run of the place in safety. They had signing rights at the Corrida Grill restaurant. I would settle the account as we left. Bathing in the Olympic size pool and the sea was safe for them, all good swimmers, but I did ask the beach lifesavers to keep an eye on them in the sea. For the second Christmas, we stayed a month and Tony managed to get a job assisting the handyman and made many friends as well as generous pocket money.

**Cabana Beach Promotions.**
My main brief was to launch the hotel and boost guest bookings. This started with strategic invitations to South African Travel Agents, Airline executives and Tourism offices starting with the 'Guinea Pig' complimentary weekend and later, Press and casual complimentary invitations to spread the word.

We also worked with Umhlanga Tourism to show off the attractive Umhlanga Village. Within four months, our simple starter promotions and publicity brought the bookings rolling in and word of mouth kept them coming.

Sol Kerzner, Southern Sun, acquired Cabana Beach from Anglo Properties in 1979. He was 44.

## My Life, a Roller Coaster Ride

**Miss Worlds.**

I approached theatre impresarios offering complimentary accommodation to selected famous visiting stars, which always attracted automatic publicity. We offered our Auditorium venue, with refreshments, for their Press Conferences.

This was my strength. In fact, I got three Miss Worlds, Penny Coelen, the 1958 Miss World, Australia and Miss World, Belinda Green 1972 and Anneline Kriel 1974, Miss World. Ballerina Margot Fonteyn and many interesting stars and business people stayed at our hotel.

I invited Penny Coelen to Cabana Beach to meet Anneline Kreil who would be arriving by military helicopter from Durban Airport. Penny lived nearby at Ballito. She agreed.

I had a double row of Lifesavers making an Arch of Honour, with their body boards to greet Anneline as she landed on the beach. Penny Coelen at the receiving end. This generated good publicity.

I travelled in the helicopter with Anneline. I have a lasting memory of beach umbrellas flying as the noisy army helicopter landed on a clearly marked landing spot.

Anneline told me afterwards that Penny had given her many valuable tips for her coming one-year reign. The main one being that the year would fly past, so she should make maximum use of every opportunity for her future after the reign ends. Also, to be reliable and punctual, which also suited us for the few days of her visit.

Above: Monica Fairall Miss S.A. 1968
Right: Belinda Green, Miss Australia and Miss World 1972.

## 4. Megan Carr Promotions

**Lion Park shower.** One of the fun amusements we laid on for Anneline's visit, was a trip to the Lion Park up the Natal North Coast. During the reign of a Miss World, it was a condition to have a chaperone in the party. This one was a middle-aged woman called Rita. Strong minded but fun company.

At the Lion Park, the magnificent beasts were kept in a very large fenced-in area, so the lions were easy to spot for tourists. On the day of our visit, four lions came up to the fence to check us out. As we stood around, Rita got so excited that she went right up to the fence and started very noisy baby talk to the big cats who were unimpressed and yawned at the 'Boo Booing' and 'Pretty baby' talk' from Rita as we stood around as amused by her as her other audience behind the fence.

Suddenly the Alpha male lion came nearer, turned around and sprayed Rita with a heavy territorial shower. Was he marking her for himself?

After the initial shock as the dripping Rita scurried away from the fence, we tried to help her but, honestly, the smell was horrific. We tried not to laugh. The gallant Ranger hosting the group, bundled her into his open Safari vehicle. We followed them to the office where the Park Management was hosing her down fully dressed. A futile exercise, as that reeking smell was detectable from fifty feet away. So, we drew lots to see in whose car she would not be travelling with her back to the hotel. The

Penny Coelen 1958 Miss World (left) Anneline Kriel 1974 Miss World (right)
I wonder who was the lucky man in the middle.

## My Life, a Roller Coaster Ride

shortest straw got the 'Eau de Lion' splashed Rita. We laughed all the way home, including the irrepressible Rita.

Back at Cabana Beach, even after two showers and hair washes, the odour lingered, and so did the giggles all round. What a good sport she was.

**Belinda Green, Miss Australia and Miss World 1972.** A healthy, smiling advert for both titles. No airs and graces, she was enchanted with South Africa, the friendly people and hospitality. "Just like home'" she said.

Belinda was our guest for only three days, but we got her what she wanted and missed – daily horse rides wearing very little make-up, in between her Miss World assignments.

We arranged a Champagne and Caviar party for Belinda to meet two finalists in the Miss Africa South (for blacks) Miss Sibyl Sibiya and Miss South Africa (for whites) Miss Beverley Macleod. Only the winner of Miss SA. (for whites) would enter the 1972 Miss World competition. Apartheid still at work.

**Monica Fairall, Miss South Africa 1971** highly intelligent and friendly. After her reign, Monica had become a Durban Broadcast Presenter and a celebrated musician, so was on our regular Press invitation list. We also became her source for interesting personalities to interview.

**Squash.** When the International Squash Championship was on circuit in S.A. in August 1973, we organised for the top eight players to stay at Cabana Beach where they could practice in relative privacy.

**Geoff Hunt.** Regarded as one of the best World Champions to this day, was number two in the world in 1973. Geoff was in Durban matched against Jonah Barrington, then World Number one champion, in an exhibition match.

It was an August long weekend, and I had taken the children along with me to Cabana Beach for a half-term break at the seaside.

**Left:** Geoff's book, a signed copy of which he sent to Peter, who still has it. No charge for Peter's lesson from the best.

# 4. Megan Carr Promotions

**The innocence of youth.** Young Peter Carr had taken up squash at St. Stithians, showing great promise. On this visit, he was ten. He never went to Cabana Beach without his squash racquet.

One morning he went down to the courts and saw a guy hitting up on his own. So, he asked the guy if he would like a game. The man happily accepted the (cheeky) invitation and the two enjoyed a rather one-sided game together. Then the kind man gave Peter some tips and some more practice. The man was Australian squash champion, Geoff Hunt.

**Later in the day** Geoff introduced Peter to Jonah Barrington and Egyptian champ Jahangir Khan.

Geoff Hunt became World Champion the following year 1974 and subsequently retained his world title for many years, winning 86 out of 180 world titles in his career. He received an MBE for his contribution to world sport in 1972 and the AM Australian Medal in 1982. He is in the World Squash Federated Hall of Fame and the Australian Hall of Fame.

**Mr. Ken Hovelmeier.** I met Ken Hovelmeier when Peter was at St. Stithians' College, mid seventies to early eighties.

Ken Hovelmeier had been a popular teacher at St. Stithians' Prep and a keen sports coach when he was diagnosed diabetic and, at the young age of thirty, he lost his sight completely, which happened almost overnight.

The Headmasters of St.Stithians' Prep and College consulted the School for the Blind in Rosettenville, to see what could be done for him. They advised that he could train to become a switchboard operator or a basket weaver. The two headmasters agreed that those would not be appropriate for Ken. They received the okay from the Governing Body to appoint him in the position of School Counsellor.

Ken could obviously not see who he was talking to, but he developed an uncanny ability to recognise people by voice and by scent.

He had been a good squash player and was appointed Squash Master at a time when squash had been regarded as one of the less recognised school sports activities. Within a few years, Ken managed to encourage some of the more athletic boys to frequent the squash courts, and in a short time he took St.Stithians' College to become the number one squash school in the country.

My son, Peter, was in the Squash team and, under the guidance and coaching of Ken, he received his Transvaal colours at the age of fourteen, and went on to captain the first team, which was unbeatable amongst participating schools.

# My Life, a Roller Coaster Ride

I would often go to watch Peter playing a match. Ken always somehow knew my voice, or would know by my perfume, who I was. He would greet me with a "Hello Mrs. Carr" and proceed to give me a summary of Peter's squash ability.

His coaching instincts were equal to any sighted person. I recall watching him guide and coach the boys as they played their matches. He could critique every shot that was being played on the court below.

Hovelmeier was later appointed Chairman of the Transvaal Squash Association. He was admired across the country for what he had achieved in transforming the game.

He never saw his blindness as dibilitating, and as such the boys admired and adored him, as did his staff colleagues.

Ken met his wife, Myrna at the school and they married. She was his other pair of eyes. They tore all over the place on their motor scooter. Myrna driving, and Ken sitting pillion, holding his walking stick, with a huge smile on his face as the boys greeted their arrival every morning at school.

It was a privilege to know him. He was a great role model for the boys. Peter ended up in the Transvaal Provincial team, and Squash Captain at 'Saints'.

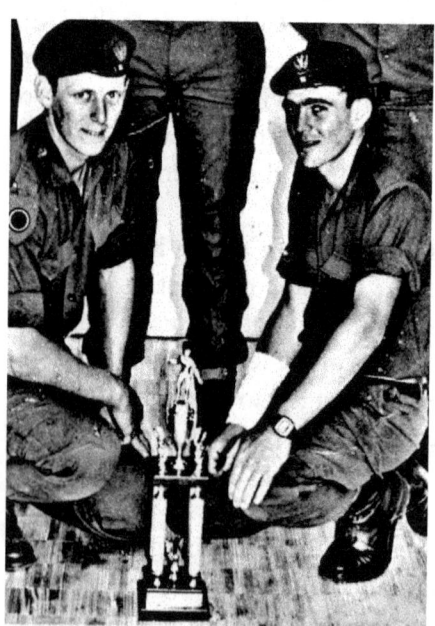
Andrew Hudson left Peter Carr right.

**In the Army.** At eighteen, Peter was stationed at Ladysmith, just four hours' drive from home. I once visited him there, and instead of greeting his 'guest' in army uniform, he strolled out of the squash court in whites to give me a big hug.

Peter recalls, "I did the first three months' Basic Training. During that time, I was co-opted into the four man army squash team which included the South African cricketer, Andrew Hudson. We won the Northern Natal Squash League trophy."

For the last half of his army life, Peter asked to be transferred

## 4. Megan Carr Promotions

to the army Film Unit in Pretoria doing what he intended to do as a career in Film and Video and still at it successfully, forty years later.

**1974. Time to promote Cabana Beach internationally.**
Vic Wilson Taylor had a meeting with the directors of Anglo Properties with a bold plan to open Cabana Beach to the wider international market. With their full backing the two of us set off in style for a four-week trip to France, Holland, Germany, England and America.

Anglo does everything in style, and we wanted to project our Resort in the best light. We were about to travel and live in great travelling comfort. By then, we were a serious romantic item, so we shared accommodation.

We engaged the help of SATOUR, our South African Tourist Association, who enthusiastically joined forces with us in the project. They devised and supplied lists of all Travel Agents in those countries and guidance in their singular likes and dislikes, seasonal trends and payment methods. No PayPal in those days. Better than that, through their international agents, Satour booked the venues and sent the invitations, in the name of Cabana Beach.

With bookings to make, audio visual to produce, door gifts to find and purchase, we had our work cut out to be ready in a month. And when I say 'work cut out' we also had our day jobs to reschedule, desks to clear and projects to delegate to keep the home show running.

Musgrove and Watson Travel Agency took care of all travel bookings with one briefing from us. Tiny (very tall) Musgrove gave it his personal attention.

Roy Clucas, graphic designer, and creative audio-visual producer came up with an ingenious fifteen-minute Carousel slide and sound show. No Power Point yet.

Door gifts had to be indigenous African pieces. Satour again introduced me to a curio authority who selected 2 000 Zulu bead items of jewellery. Head bands, necklaces, bangles, earrings, key chains, arm bands and ankle bands. Colourful, light and easy to transport to be set out on grass trays for the guests to view and choose from. A travel-safe, small and popular choice of trinket. Satour arranged for these to be delivered to each of the venues for us.

What SATOUR omitted to warn me about was the voracious appetite for gifts, of American travel agents. We learnt the hard way. Having managed perfectly with the well-mannered Europeans and English, who politely selected one each, the Americans were grabbing hands full, leaving some unlucky tardy one's gift less.

In fact, we only did four very big presentations in America. Seattle, L.A., Boston, winding up the entire trip in New York. A sophisticated, well-dressed audience with a strong showing from Pan Am Airlines. Happily, experienced by then, we had been careful in allocating our gift stash and had kept some in reserve after the well-turned-out grabbers had locusted the first trays.

We had an awkward experience in Los Angeles. We had booked the ballroom at the legendary Beverly Wilshire Hotel, then owned by film star, Gregory Peck.

I believe in early preparation and always do a pre-event rehearsal. I regard one mistake by me translates into three hundred mistakes heard in a 300 audience. I also live by the theory that if an audience comes into a perfectly organised and beautiful space, they automatically relax and trust the message.

The guests were invited for 6 o'clock. By 3 o'clock the stage and auditorium were ready to my satisfaction. Huge South African flower arrangements everywhere. Brochures on the chairs, Full size screen, lectern, light and sound connected to the Kodak Carousel projector and microphone.

A full bar was set up near the entrance where guests would be welcomed as Vic and I introduced ourselves. Waitresses would serve sparkling wine and snacks. Almost like Diplomatic events, the guests all tend to know each other.

I tested the equipment and ran through my presentation word for word including the sixty slide show with recorded blurb about Cabana Beach, Umhlanga Rocks and the magic of South Africa as a destination.

At 4.30 I returned to our room for a shower and cup of tea with Vic, changed into my cocktail dress and back to the ballroom by 5.30. I was always a little edgy before a presentation, but the full rehearsal helped me to relax.

6 o'clock on the dot they started arriving. Some looking aggressive, anti-South Africa, even rude. Some threatening to boycott anything South African. We soon discovered why. That morning, Helen Suzman had been interviewed on American TV with Albie Sachs, blasting the Nationalist Government and listing many Apartheid abuses which were rife at the time. (I marvel at the hypocrisy considering where the American Indians are today). But now we had to deal with the problem of the moment.

## 4. Megan Carr Promotions

Political diplomacy. Vic and I dashed out of site for a few moments to strategise and save the evening.

He simply stood up and asked for their attention. He explained that Anglo American, which owned Cabana Beach, fully and financially supported Helen Suzman's Progressive Party, fighting apartheid, remarking that Helen was the one and only Member of S.A. Parliament in opposition. We asked them to support our Progressive party by supporting us. Somehow, it worked, and we were back on track.

The party got noisier and after half an hour I asked them to be seated in the auditorium. I went up on stage and greeted the audience and made my speech.

I was ready for the slide show. I switched on the projector – and nothing happened. No pictures and no sound. Panic without showing it.

I had the Barman check all the switches. Still nothing. I called for the hotel engineer, who didn't appear in a flash. The audience was getting restless. In minutes, which seemed like hours, I simply had to apologise and stall for time till he arrived. I suggested they all get to the bar and collect a drink to bring to their seats. The barmen shifted into top gear and churned out the orders.

The engineer arrived. I gave him the useless mike as he loudly announced that the whole side wall of switches had tripped, and apologies on behalf of the hotel. Reprieve for me. I somehow dug out some South African stories.

Suddenly, they were on my side as they felt sorry for me. It took about twenty minutes to get the power fixed and the show went on to great applause. Sometimes bad things turn out well. I finally enjoyed a well-earned drink at the bar with Vic. A big success was recorded and proved by bookings which poured in.

### 1973. Our sixteen storey Christmas Tree. 320 West Street, Durban.

The Anglo-American Properties Office Block was nearing completion and already partly occupied on the lower office floors and shopping level. The Board agreed that the leasing programme was ready for a boost. They asked for ideas to promote the building. The team needed to do something dramatic to create the fast awareness they needed to coincide with an advertising campaign.

It was November, so a Christmas theme seemed obvious. I talked to the construction director and together we came up with something which, in most circumstances, would have been impossible. A massive Christmas

## My Life, a Roller Coaster Ride

Tree to be seen for ten kilometres in all directions.

The upper sixteen floors were constructed but unoccupied as the interiors were still unfinished. For the tree in the windows, thousands of metres, in rolls, of black, red and green crepe paper and broad Scotch tape had to be imported via fast courier. The construction manager set aside a couple of workers and hired students per vacant floor units to be cleaned and ready for action. Students were paid to work long hours each day to cut the rolls of paper according to window measurements for blackout surrounds, and red and green, for the red base and green uppers of the tree. They were making a 48-metre-high window tree. They had to stick the coloured paper to the windows. Sides of the tree blacked out.

We had a press launch at Cabana Beach with a model of the 320 West Street building, all electrified and treed up, for the miniature, remote, switching on of the lights, as we couldn't do it on site.

**Daily News.** Although we had little choice, using the model for the event, it was a bit of a fizzle, as the magnitude of the real thing didn't come across that impressively.

However, it told the story, and, after all, they could trot outside to see the Christmas tree itself which was awesome and worked as showstopper – or rather show starter.

This dramatic eye catcher was heavily backed by advertising and the retail space filled. They already had the magnet street level tenant of Pick 'n Pay operating.

**Below:** Anglo Properties Regional Manager, Vic Wilson Taylor and Mayor, Cllr Ron Williams with his finger on the switch, and 'Voila' there was a lighted tree.

## 4. Megan Carr Promotions

**Carole the Christmas Fairy.** My daughter, Carole, remembers that she was the Christmas Fairy on the retail forecourt of 320. They had installed a four metre Christmas tree and hired a Santa.

Carole had beautiful long, golden-brown hair. She was almost sixteen and paid for some highlights to look more like a fairy for this holiday job as Santa's assistant handing out gifts.

**1974. Brickhill Road Parkade launch.** Anglo had completed the construction of a multi-level Parking Garage in an area of high demand in Durban, near the Racecourse.

They asked me to organise the launch. The usual suspects were invited as guests. City Councillors, relevant to the area. Business Directors of the area, and the Press. What can you dream up to get the press to rave about a place to park a car?

**Launch party.** Getting the people there to listen to speeches and cutting a ribbon whilst fondling a cocktail and nibbling on canapes, was the easy part.

I then I had to be more creative to get it into the press and on radio. There had to be more. I contacted the local Vintage Car Club and invited

Maria Barnard (MCP), Vintage Bentley, pretty models,
Vic Wilson Taylor, Megan. I was wearing a red Ted Lapidus suit and red Bruno Magli shoes.

them to do a drive through and have their beautiful old cars on display.

Never to miss an opportunity to show off their oldies, they jumped at the chance. I rustled up a bunch of pretty girls to ride in the parade of old cars. And the press got its photo opportunities posing strategic VIPs in and around the impressive rally of old-time cars.

The publicity was massive, which backed up the commercial advertising.

**Transvaal House.** Another Anglo account followed. Tony Mason, director of Anglo Properties, asked me to take on the awareness campaign for their new Office Block in Pretoria which was slow in drawing business tenants.

At my briefing, I discovered that Transvaal House was one block outside the main CBD and that Pretoria businessmen did not easily stray from the usual city centre blocks, even though only one street outside. Hence the slow occupancy rate.

Our target market was already renting premises in the main area. My aim was to lure them a block away to our building. I decided on a two-pronged approach.

**Publicity and a market survey.** Obviously, I would opt for the usual ongoing awareness attention-getters in the press.

In addition, this time, using my Oil of Olay campaign technique of door-to-door calls by well-informed attractive women carrying out a 'Survey'.

I had a good team of promotional temps based in Pretoria and called on them to reserve two weeks, maybe more, for a very aggressive sales campaign. I dressed them in smart business suits with Anglo Properties name badges, and armed with business cards and Questionnaires on clipboards, looking both professional and unthreatening.

Transvall House. Mercedes Kornfeld, top model, posing for the *Pretoria News*.

## 4. Megan Carr Promotions

I had segmented out the main CBD into manageable call areas and assigned the girls their turf. Two consecutive calls were planned.

**1.** To get an idea of current leases and expiry times. Also to discover the pros and cons of their present premises. People love to complain, so this ammunition was like gold in our next phase.

**2.** The girls' second visit was only to the most promising selection of their previous calls. This time, giving out info about the advantages of Transvaal House over their current leases. They explained Anglo leasing policy and incentives for them to transfer across as their current leases expired.

By this time, Anglo had produced very attractive brochures for distribution.

**Spotting a gap.** This Market Survey also got the leasing management to put their heads together for new ideas. They were probably the first to set aside a single floor for small businesses which could lease a single office or small suite of offices, sharing central reception and telephone board.

...I need to feel successful

MEGAN CARR of Megan Carr Promotions is a highly successful, imaginative woman who learnt her trade in the hardest school of all: the Johannesburg charity scene. 'I was vice-chairman of the Monday Club and I did things like organising a banquet for 300 people. I've catered for Africa. Before I married I was a shorthand typist, but after my first two children were born I had to go out to work. I wanted to do something interesting. I became an underground hostess for the Chamber of Mines. It wasn't just a matter of looking pretty and showing people around. We really had to know about mining. We had to handle journalists, mining engineers from other countries.

This unique facility would save small businesses money and provide professional responses to calls if the offices were closed for the day, or the single owner was out on calls. It gave our girls an added facility to sell.

They worked on a good retainer plus commission on successful leads when followed up by Anglo Sales Reps. We realised that some signed leases would take time to move in but had value as guaranteed future tenants. It worked well. The stylish modern building was fully rented out within eight months and the novel promotion was hailed as a complete success.

While the active selling was in progress, I realised that I needed to run a three-month active press promotion to keep the pot boiling.

# My Life, a Roller Coaster Ride

Chatting to the architect, we came up with an idea to fit in with the final stages of building completion.

**Sculpture competition.** Transvaal House had planned to place a three-metre high sculpture in the central courtyard. What a timely opportunity for me. I suggested we get high profile sculptors to present a miniature maquette version of a sculpture, with a view to Anglo commissioning the winning artist to produce the full-size courtyard figure. The five aspirant sculptors had two months in which to submit their work.

Winning entry is seen extreme right in pic below, sculpted by Hungarian-South African Zoltan Borbereki.

The three-metre-high winning sculpture was placed in the Transvaal House courtyard a year later to much fanfare. *Pretoria News* and *Die Transvaler* were Press Sponsors for the event.

**1974. Group Editors.** I was approached by Aubrey Sussens, CEO of Groupe Editors (GE), the largest PR company in the country, to link up with them as they expanded their Marketing arm.

We had often worked together on projects, such as The Milk Board campaign, so it seemed a natural progression for both of us.

Terms were agreed upon and they placed this quarter page advert in the *Sunday Times*.

Shockingly, to both Aubrey and me, this caused a mini rebellion in Group Editors as their current Promotions team threatened to walk out. Our merger never got off the ground. We parted with the understanding all

# 4. Megan Carr Promotions

round that my company would be called in as an associate when situations called for it.

To seal the deal, I was invited into the GE legendary Pub for a celebration, to be declared an Honorary Member of the GE Pub. An honour indeed, which I enjoyed at many a Friday evening in the lively company of good friends.

**1973. Fair Lady feature The Moneyspinners.** From February 1972 to September 1973, with a bare minimum of capital to start, my small company, with a staff of two had blossomed to four office staff and hundreds of promotional girls and supervisors around the country.

The client list was growing beyond my wildest dreams. It was also the time when my children needed attention. Much juggling of time was the order of each day.

I moved out of the Kenyon Wiles offices in the town centre to office premises nearer home in Sandton City. I had moved house from Katherine Street to Kambula Flats a block away from Sandton City. I had almost moved over to Group Editors and then had to unplan that move. No time or need for a local social life currently. My relationship with Vic was confined to Durban.

# My Life, a Roller Coaster Ride

## FAIR LADY
### September 1973

### ...I need to feel successful

MEGAN CARR of Megan Carr Promotions is a highly successful, imaginative woman who learnt her trade in the hardest school of all: the Johannesburg charity scene. 'I was vice-chairman of the Monday Club and I did things like organising a banquet for 300 people. I've catered for Africa. Before I married I was a shorthand typist, but after my first two children were born I had to go out to work. I wanted to do something interesting. I became an underground hostess for the Chamber of Mines. It wasn't just a matter of looking pretty and showing people around. We really had to know about mining. We had to handle journalists, mining engineers from other countries, students, all sorts of people who asked penetrating questions. We also had to organise aboveground events — sports meetings, dinners. I learnt about protocol, catering and, most difficult, keeping people happy. When A & J Promotions started I joined Adele Lucas and Jenny Williams — in fact our first office was in my house — and we did very well. When that partnership dissolved I decided to go on my own.' Megan Carr Promotions was started in August 1972 and by the end of that year Megan had paid out R16 000 in salaries and had a turnover that surprised even her.

'I really don't know what motivates me. Perhaps I inherited a business sense from my father. He is chairman of Evelyn Haddon, semi-retired now. I always had to work, my husband was the sort of person who would have a boat but not enough money to pay the telephone bill. I discovered housework was easy, it took no longer than an hour and a half a day, and I had to have something to fill my time. My marriage wasn't happy but I don't think that was a motivating factor.' She was divorced early last year and claimed no

*FAIR LADY, SEPTEMBER 5, 1973*

child support or alimony. She and her husband are still friends but she feels nothing but relief that a marriage which 'never really got off the ground' has ended.

'I could stop work now, I've made some fantastic investments, but I don't want to. All night, all work is an escape. From what? I can't sit around and do nothing. When I relax I really relax, but I need to feel successful. I know I'm not saying what motivates me but I'm doing my best.

'As a kid I was a nothing. I was shy and it wasn't until my adolescence that I began to blossom. I was a dead average student. But I had a very happy childhood. I have three younger brothers and we are very close to each other and to our parents.

'When I think about marriage I realise I should marry three different men to get all I want out of it — but then to make a success of it I'd have to be three different kinds of women. Maybe that is what marriage is all about. I have a very good time now. Men seem to find the combination of attractiveness and a business head very desirable. Even men who say "I would never let my wife work" find business women interesting. It is rather sad. A lot of men don't allow their wives to develop and then they wonder why they grow apart.

'I know I made an unintelligent marriage — says me, with four children — and I certainly wouldn't rush into marriage again. But I'm surprised at how many available men there are.' Megan has a boy and a girl in their teens, and a boy and a girl of primary-school age.

'I'm not getting any closer to explaining what motivates me, am I?' The truth is, Megan doesn't know. She doesn't feel that she has to prove herself. She is dynamic, full of enthusiasm, and if she were a man people would see her success as a natural outcome of her abilities. She finds her business endlessly challenging and puts the same quality of enthusiasm into a promotion for whisky as for perfume, into organising an airshow as into promoting health foods.

Megan spends her money well. Three of her four children are at private schools, the fourth will be going to Kingsmead soon. She has a 'super big flat, very lived-in with the dog jumping on the leather chairs' in exclusive Sandown. 'I can't live in a house. Then I would need a man. I have a fantastic maid, too, and we have lots of visitors. Sometimes the place is like a teenage coffee bar. I don't mind that, I encourage it because teenage trends worry me and I like my children to bring their friends home. We hire movies and there are always records.'

She runs an Alfa Romeo 'Spider' — 'vastly impractical, I can't even get all my children into it' and a Kombi for business and more sedate family occasions.

Her real extravagance is a weekend cottage on the Vaal, a power boat and a small sailing boat. 'I do most of my entertaining down at the river — I spend masses on Cape estate wines — and although my cottage is an extravagance I need the river for relaxation. Business, however attractive, can be very tiring.'

I admired the black, sportily-cut trouser suit she was wearing with a white, high-necked sweater and platform shoes. 'I'm glad you like it. I bought it at Derbers. I nearly always buy French clothes. The cut is right for me.' Megan is petite. 'And I buy Italian shoes. I'm not saying they are better than South African shoes but they are so much more stylish. Leather is my extravagance. I love leather coats, shoes, bags, even furniture.

'Money gives me the freedom not to have to budget stringently. In my 17 years of marriage I always had to budget so I'm not likely to go wild, but things are very expensive. Even the children's pocket money comes to a lot. Imagine, they have to pay R1.50 for a cinema seat. My older son gets R25 a month and that seems hardly enough.

*FAIR LADY, SEPTEMBER 5, 1973*

## THE MONEYSPINNERS

*If we're so smart why aren't we rich? Some of us are — and self-made too. Some very unusual tycoons... apart from anything else, they're all female*

FAIR LADY salutes

## 4. Megan Carr Promotions

Sanity was saved by our Vaal River most weekends, where permitted, and the huge help of my amazing mother, stepping in with lifts and caring when she could.

**The Money-Spinners.** *Fair Lady* decided to do a story about three successful women titled 'The Money-Spinners' subtitled 'The Girls who earn big money'. I was not happy with the story which didn't come across as I thought I had told it.

**Platinum and diamonds.** February 1974 It was just a normal Tuesday when I was called to a meeting by Johannesburg Consolidated Investments (JCI) and Sterns Jewellers to discuss an urgent promotion. I was there within an hour and briefed. Instead of having the luxury of a week to come up with something special, they wanted my proposal by the end of the day. Off I rushed and had the full staff of four, drop everything to brainstorm and research.

The brief was to promote platinum to be used in jewellery manufacture. Sterns was brought in because, as diamond jewellery retailers, this would work for them as a joint project. They had a huge diamond to sell. The 85 carat Sterns Star and its satellites. (Carat size quoted according to the owner Syd Barnett.)

## My Life, a Roller Coaster Ride

My rushed presentation, at the end of that day, recommended that we bring in the newly crowned 1974 Miss World, the South African beauty, Anneline Kriel. I had established by phone that she was available, and we could have her for three months. My proposal was accepted in full.

I quickly checked my passport and booked myself to London two days later. I was met at Heathrow by the Miss World manager, John Osborne. We drove straight to the Miss World offices and started the negotiations where I formalised and signed the contract with a phone acceptance by my clients In South Africa.

The Miss World CEOs Julia and Eric Morley were out of London at that time, which suited me, as John Osborne was business-like and easy to work with.

That settled, I had to stay over in London for the weekend to tie up loose ends, and to meet Anneline on Monday. This gave me time for some London treats as I waited.

Saturday, John Osborne got me an invitation to a fashion show presented by *Harper's Bazaar* Magazine.

He suggested I might find suitable evening gowns for Anneline to wear at our jewellery shows.

Anneline. Sterns Star (arrowed) at her throat is wearing a crepe, softly draped, elegant white Yuki gown.

**Harper's Bazaar.** Apart from meeting the influential magazine's fashion editor, Pam Suthern, and the film star Gail Hunnicutt, I met the currently favoured Japanese couturier, Yuki.

John Osborne then, knowing Anneline, advised me on suitable evening wear for our events.

I bought a deep coral gown for alternate appearances. This one was inherited by Carole, much to her delight.

John said he thought Anneline would carry off the swaying silky fabrics with grace and charm. No plunging neckline as we wanted people to focus on the jewellery!

## 4. Megan Carr Promotions

**Pulling strings.** Having done my job for the moment, as I passed the weekend waiting for my meeting with Anneline, Miss World, on Monday, I took myself off to two amazing shows the same day, at Shaftesbury Theatre. *West Side Story* and *Jesus Christ Superstar*. As they were fully booked for months ahead, John Osborne showed the power of the Miss the World organisation and wangled me my two single seats five rows from the front.

**Monday.** John had arranged for me to meet Anneline, to brief her on the South African Platinum and Diamonds tour at which she would model around the country.

**Briefing.** The JCI objective was to promote the use of platinum as a valuable metal base in the manufacture of jewellery as an option to gold and silver. After her official tour, she would be free for other private bookings and holiday time. Typically South African, she'd been homesick and was very excited at her luck, getting this first assignment in South Africa.

My job was to get the client message across as Anneline was not yet sufficiently familiar with her role in the project. Her English was not fluent, although her soft Afrikaans accent added a charming South African flavour to the message.

Anneline and Megan at the press reception at Jan Smuts Airport.(MCP Photographer).

## My Life, a Roller Coaster Ride

Itsy-Bitsy, Teeny-Weeny R7 500 (scratchy) Platinum Bikini.

## 4. Megan Carr Promotions

JCI had spun platinum into fine thread and 'fabric' and created the Bikini for a *Sunday Times* front page picture. It shredded her pantyhose at the bikini fitting.

**The Sterns Star.** Equally brilliant, was the set of diamonds she wore for media photos.

The 'Sterns Star' Pendant, set in platinum, was 85 carats and larger in diameter and much deeper than the old R5 coin.

Satellite diamonds, set in rings and earrings, made up the dazzling array which sparkled all around the country at press parties and at retail appearances in shopping centres which had Sterns shops.

Syd Barnett, MD of Sterns, hoped to find a buyer for the Sterns Star at this time. Valued at R1 million in 1974.

All the contracted Platinum and Diamond events around the country met, and even surpassed all expectations. The clients were supremely happy.

Mission accomplished. Anneline was then free to take on personal paying assignments. Which is where I came in. Again.

The first one happened to be Cabana Beach which was her sponsored holiday time, combined with several press conferences and meeting the other South African 1958 Miss World, Penny Coelen.

**MCP offices, Sandton City.** MCP Reception backed by a wallpaper forest of trees. The eleven staff had their specialities. Trisha Reunert was my Deputy, Sylvia Holder, writer and advertising liaison, Diana Anderson, press liaison. Lindsay Swan, Manager, The Wombles and other characters, Sally Ann Hotson, client and press liaison, Caz Steyn, the perfect secretary and continuity person, David Frost, Accountant and Client Manager (the lone man in this mini universe of women.)

**Gail Lieberz,** my P.A. and alter ego. She could step in and do everything I needed done. She almost morphed into me. She even started to sound like me on the phone. She could turn her hand to anything. Sheilagh Gilbert, Bookkeeper and in charge of the driver. Carole Carr and her friend, Pippa Bell temped after school and in the holidays.

**Megan Carr Promotions chronology.** Impossible to put things in date order as so many events and ongoing contracts overlapped. Many of our Promotions ran concurrently, sometimes four or five at a time. For example, some were permanently ongoing like nine years Pick 'n Pay, two or three Expos per year, for eight years, of John Thomson Exhibitions, two years

# My Life, a Roller Coaster Ride

of Cabana Beach and ten years of The Wombles and other characters. Nine years with two Alpha Mind Power seminars per year. The single events such as launches, Seminars, Awards Receptions, all needed setting up and mopping up time. These were fitted in between the regulars.

**Semiprivate Cubicles.** Each staff member had her/his semiprivate office cubicle, with ceramic bird tiles at their entrances bearing their names.

Lindsay Swan (seated right) oversaw the Wombles and other characters. A big job involving the student part-timers and their training, briefing, transport and costume maintenance.

An extraordinary well-oiled team of eleven in a busy office. Many happy years on the 15th floor of Sandton City with its view across the North, all the way to Pretoria. And only a five-minute walk from my home in Kambula. I drove to the office, of course, because I always needed my car handy. I never used the driver for my own appointments. We all had reserved parking spots in the garage basement.

**Below:** Carole Carr (standing) could be relied on to step in when extra back-up was needed.

## 4. Megan Carr Promotions

**Lindsay Swan.** In July 2023 I received this Facebook notification from Lindsay.

Exactly 45 years ago today I sailed for Cape Town on the RMS *Pendennis Castle*, one of its last ever crossings. Life changed forever for me. I met Sylvia Holder in Johannesburg. We and Sally Ann Hotson Page worked for **Megan Carr whose PR agency was one of the hottest tickets in town**. We launched the *Wombles* – they lived in mine dumps instead of Wimbledon Common – I played every single one of them. And we found ourselves organising the first **SA Celebrity Tennis** tournament with **Ringo Starr**, the **Monkees**, **Peter Lawford**, the **Three Degrees** and **Dino Martin**. **Elizabeth Taylor** and **Richard Burton** were the (non-playing) icing on the cake, who seized the moment to get married again.
Back in London, Sylvia and I ran **Holder Swan** PR, which, even though I say so myself, was seriously cool (we were back in the northern hemisphere by now).
And then Sylvia set up **The Venkat Trust** and so it all goes on.

(A delightful surprise 'notification' for me, and still to be on her short list of friends).

**Rowland Emett and Chitty Chitty Bang Bang.** One of the most magical people it has ever been my privilege to know.

In 1975 Rowland and his wife, Mary, had heard of me and approached me from their home in Sussex to consider showing Rowland's amazing, quirky, Chitty Chitty Bang Bang machines for exhibition and promotion in SA.

He had also created the Choo Choo steam train which was a special feature of the Festival of Britain in 1952 as it transported people around the show.

Rowland had been commissioned to produce his crazy machines for the Chitty Chitty Bang Bang film, based on the story *The Magical Car* written by Ian Fleming (creator of James Bond).

Others in his stable - his Silly Working Sweet Factory machine, his Robot Moon Landing Craft. The Playboy Special comes with twirling Martini Glass steering. The shows were attended and enjoyed as much by adults as children.

**Sponsorship.** Looking for a sponsor, it was pounced upon by the first prospect I approached, Basil Landau, when he was CEO of Leyland Motors. He planned to move the exhibition around the country to publicise Jaguar and Triumph latest models and feature the collection in their Showrooms.

# My Life, a Roller Coaster Ride

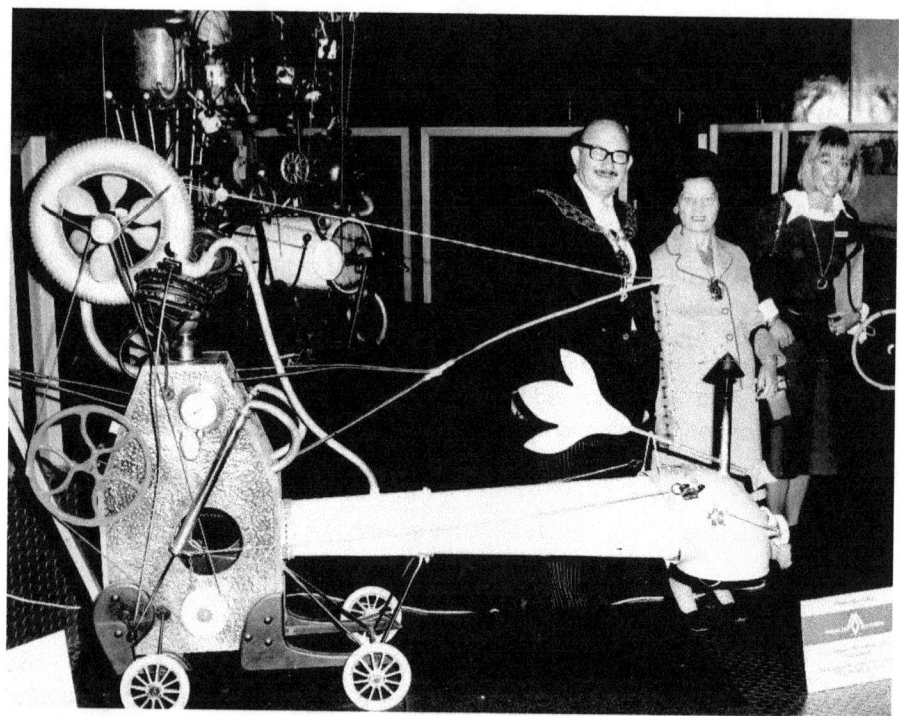

Famous *Punch* cartoonist and creator of the 'Chitty Chitty Bang Bang' machines, Moonwalker, and many other humanoid creations. Many of these are displayed at the Smithsonian Institute in Washington, DC. Megan Carr Promotions brought Rowland and these machines to promote Leylands' Jaguar and Triumph cars in showrooms nationwide.

Megan, Mary and Rowland Emett. Rowland, then getting on in years, was a legend in UK and known for his cartoons and caricatures in *Punch* Magazine.

# 4. Megan Carr Promotions

**Launch.** Invitees to the pre-public opening were agents, fleet owners, favoured customers, and the press. The event had the added credibility that Rowland and Mary owned a pale blue Jaguar in UK and had owned a string of Jaguars over many years.

**Invitation to the factory in Sussex.** At the end of their visit, they invited me to visit their Chitty Chitty Bang Bang factory the 400-year-old 'Forge' and be their guest in their home in Sussex.

Rowland collected me from the train station in the now famous pale blue Jaguar and showed me around the old Forge building near their house.

That is where there was an ongoing production line of crazy machines all made up of gardening and household odds and ends, implements and bits and pieces from charity shops and miscellaneous gifts from the fans.

The workmen in the 'factory' were all hobbyists, giving of their spare time to work on the silly nonsense machines, all perfectly constructed, and precision engineered. All in perfect working order, ready for exhibitions booked in many countries of the world.

After my two-day visit, the Emetts lent me their studio flat in Sloane Square which enabled me explore London and to see a few shows before returning home. Mary Emett and I corresponded for five years.

Sadly, years later, I heard that both Mary and Rowland Emett had died. The machines are now housed in museums in the UK, France and in the Smithsonian Institute, Washington for the enjoyment of the public both young and old. Mary said they had fetched high prices. They sold some individually and not as a collection.

Typical of the Rowland Emett sense of humour. At the Durban Airport we had to hurry to the car in a heavy downpour. Our luggage was drenched. He cheerfully remarked (of his pigskin luggage) "thank heavens pigs are waterproof".

**Ponte Tower.** Megan Carr Promotions and the Grand Opening March 1975. The Property Director, Mr. Ivan Bloch, contacted me to organise the launch.

Never missing an opportunity…and perfect timing, after the Leyland promotion was over and before the Emett's returned to the UK, I contracted the 'Chitty Chitty Bang Bang' Collection to be on exhibition at the launch of the Cylindrical Ponte Tower building in Hillbrow, Johannesburg.

The machines went on display to attract visitors to create an awareness of apartments for sale and shops to let. The Exhibition and Official Opening of Ponte was attended by Mayor, Cllr. Max Neppe and Mayoress of Johannesburg.

An engineering wonder, Ponte was built on a foundation of solid rock. It was designed in its round shape to deal with the strong winds blowing up the valley from the East. It actually sways in strong winds. It is 174 metres tall, fifty-four storeys.

Chen Sam, later that year, left MCP to join Elizabeth Taylor as her P.A. in USA. Later it was known as the ideal and convenient departure point for suicides down the central open core of the building.

The apartments were minimal and practical inside with panoramic views and easy access to the city centre, which was still vibrant at that time

Forty-eight years later. Ponte remains the tallest residential apartment building in Africa. It now attracts respectable and high-profile business and residential tenants from all over the world.

Vodacom spoils the Johannesburg skyline view of Ponte with its distasteful signage (in my opinion a shameful topping).

Mayoress of Johannesburg, Mrs. Neppe, Sally Ann Hotson (MCP), Megan, David Frost (MCP) Trisha Reunert (MCP) Chen Sam (MCP) Mayor Cllr Max Neppe, Pippa Bell (MCP) and in front Andy Carr (8) who presented flowers to the Mayoress.

## 4. Megan Carr Promotions

**1972 – 1978. The Carr Family** were living in the Kambula apartment, a block away from the Sandton City offices.

**Tony (18)** had gone into his Army Service in the Signals Corps and doing well with his mathematical ability and excellent memory. He had been transferred to the Cyphers and Coding Unit and in charge of the sophisticated decoding equipment. When his friend Charles Greig visited him in the Namibian Rundu Camp, he reported to me that Tony strolled out in shorts, army T-shirt and a monkey on his shoulder.

**Carole (16)** having left Kingsmead, where she was not happy, was doing her Matric at Damelin College, which she enjoyed. She was mature in her thinking and highly capable, having participated in many of our business promotions.

It was 1975, the year of the floods and my year-end financial collapse.

**Carole recalls...**
I matriculated at 16 and at 17 my friend Carolyn and I persuaded our mothers to pay for us to go to *Cap d'Ail* near Monte Carlo to the *Centre d'Etudees Francais*, a type of Youth Club Med and French language school, for six weeks.

My Mum was running a massive Celebrity Tennis event in Joburg with Elizabeth Taylor, Richard Burton, Ringo Starr, and other movie and music stars.

**From the South of France** Carolyn and I went to Paris with friends for a few weeks, then on to Twickenham in the UK to stay with her aunt. Then to pick grapes in Vertus, Champagne. Back to Paris with new friends, on to Baker Street lodgings in London, a brief job in Westminster Theatre, then on to Essex to work as maids for regular people (an interesting experience for two girls who had always had maids in SA), but it was that or sleep on park benches).

Back to SA after five months away. We spoke to our parents on random collect calls from public pay phones. They'd had no idea where we were after leaving *Cap d'Ail* and we'd known from the first day that we needed

## My Life, a Roller Coaster Ride

to take care of ourselves, which we did.

When we returned to SA we were more empathetic of our maids and cleaned up after ourselves more. We hired a Madame Carriere to talk to us in French when we returned.

**Peter (10)** was at St. Stithian's Prep School. The Jaffee's did the morning and some afternoon lifts. No public transport between Sandown and Randburg. In his last two years Peter rode to and from school on a motorised bicycle.

**Andy (8)** was at Sandown Primary school, near home, where we had a good lift club. In Standards four and five she rode to school on her bicycle.

**Hail Hitler.** I employed a driver, named Hitler, for my kombi. Having Hitler, helped a lot with occasional afternoon school drives. My Secretary, Caz Steyn, sometimes had to fill in when my diary wouldn't stretch, or I was away on business. My mother was a gem and was always there for us in family emergencies.

Andrea Carr and Richard Greig modelling at the Waterless Wonder Cookware launch Circa 1974. Andy and Richard both enjoyed being models until the stylist smeared chocolate on their faces and new clothes.

# 4. Megan Carr Promotions

Hitler worked for me for two years until I caught him running a private taxi service in the Kombi and filling up cans of petrol on the business account. He made his passengers duck out of sight if he saw me or a friend approaching on the road. But got caught with a bus full as he was spied, in Rosebank, by a friend and reported. I felt somewhat betrayed and sadly fired him.

**Amazing Grace.** I was fortunate to have a highly competent Cook-Housekeeper, Gracie, a mother of a son and two daughters, living on the premises. She was warm and funny with a wise quote for all occasions. Her favourite surprise expression was 'Gee-Whizz'. She was a superb cook. She would stand no nonsense from the young, energetic Pete and Andy. Lunch sandwiches always made and schoolbags ready, including swimming costumes on Wednesdays and pocket money on Fridays. Our housekeeper and 'other mother'. She was with us for twelve years, till I took a year's sabbatical at the Vaal house, and she didn't fancy living so far from her home near Pretoria. Donald Greig snapped her up for his housekeeping.

When we returned to the Sandown house in 1979, from time to time, I allowed Gracie to have her adult, but mentally challenged son, Cedric, to stay with his mother in our double staff quarters, for a few months at a time. She insisted that he do chores around the garden for this favour.

We grew to be rather fond of this simple person and enjoyed his idiosyncrasies. For example, I once asked him why he hadn't watered the garden. He, dramatically bumped his forehead with the heel of his hand, so hard that he fell over backwards, and asked, lying there, "Haven't you heard of soil erosion?" Hard not to laugh.

**Critical decisions.** This chapter, all by itself, marks several critical decisions and events which changed my life in every way.

**Mid 1975.** I was 43. My children were 19, 17, 11 and 9. I was at the top of my game, financially on a high with a 'Dream Team' of eleven staff and all the children doing well.

My current escort was a gentle man, a surgeon not yet divorced from his wife. I was just recovering from the Vaal River floods and still at the mopping up stage.

Having made a name for myself in high visibility projects, it was a natural progression to get interesting, if strange, offers involving celebrity events.

I'd previously been offered world champions in Kick Boxing and Sumo Wrestling. Exhibition Tennis in the form of show-off player, Bobby Riggs and champion Billy Jean King. This had been passed on to me by the incumbent BBC Tennis commentator Max Robertson, husband of Lisa Beresford, writer and creator of The Wombles which franchise she had offered me. All very incestuous connections.

Sensibly, I turned them all down except for The Wombles.

Above: John, Megan and Andy (10), Christmas dinner 1976.

Left: Megan relaxing on a Vaal weekend.

Below: Peter, in bowler hat and Guy in straw basher, aboard my quadracycle.

# 4. Megan Carr Promotions

## 21. Celebrity Tennis

**June 1975.** I received a phone call from Los Angeles asking if I would like to stage their annual charity event called Celebrity Tennis. An event whereby the entertainment community raises funds for its International Actors Benevolent Fund which helps those 'resting' out of work actors and musicians. In fact, those who have fallen on hard times.

They explained that it was a good business opportunity for the organiser.

It sounded worth considering and I asked them to send a list of which actors would participate to assess if they would be attractive to South African audiences.

I doubted if the more notable actors would even come to our shores considering the Equity ban on them at that Apartheid time.

A major consideration for me was, as always seemed to happen in South Africa in those dark political days, I would end up with the has-beens or unknown opportunists trying to get on a bandwagon however small the wagon was. Free travel. Free publicity. A moment of recognition with a less than entertained audience.

The first offering included 10 names I'd never heard of plus Aretha Franklin and Dyann Cannon. A start. I told them to jettison the unknowns (in SA) and come up with a few others. For them it became easier to 'sell' knowing I could be interested.

The Three Degrees

The next offering was more exciting. The Three Degrees (their hit *When will I see you again*) very hot at that time, The Monkees (*I'm a Believer*), John Marley (horse's head in his bed in *The Godfather* and also the father in *Love Story*), Rod Steiger, (Mr. Joyboy in *The Loved One*) Peter Lawford, and Bond girl Jill St. John. I was encouraged. Then later came Elke Sommer and Dino Martin Jnr.

Once I had provisionally booked Ellis Park Stadium, I then decided to try and get sponsorships. Coca Cola and Ster

# My Life, a Roller Coaster Ride

## 4. Megan Carr Promotions

Kinekor agreed, in principle. They would cover the airfares which would be two first class tickets from LA, New York or wherever to South Africa, for each of the stars and the organisers. I also did a deal with SAA on special discounts.

The one thing my gut feel warned me about, was the unreliability of agent promises, especially when it was an unsigned variable agreement.

The people agreeing to come were meant to be keen amateur tennis players who would come for the charity benefit. However, they were entitled to cancel if they were made professional contractual offers or required for promotional appearances at home. I would have to agree to accept any available replacement if anyone cancelled.

Each player was to receive two first class air tickets, full hotel, board and drinks, Security and transport.

The entertainment industry in the seventies was uncertain, if not volatile, when it came to international stars. Two famous stars who had recently changed their minds at the last minute, were guitarist, Jose` Feliciano and actress, Connie Francis. They didn't pitch up. Bookings and money were taken from star-starved public and not refunded. There was very little public trust in impresarios and promoters for good reason.

We held an emergency meeting in the office to weigh the pros and cons. I made the realistic decision to pull out. I told the agents that it was too risky for the high costs and not quite enough heavyweights in the mix. A huge relief.

**The universe plays its tricks.** Later that same day my arguments were blown away when the agents informed me that, Beatle, Ringo Starr, would come. The next day Elizabeth Taylor and Richard Burton agreed to come from Gstaad, Switzerland.

**Dilemma.** How do you turn down Taylor and Burton – even though, like Ringo, they didn't play tennis? Like a dog with a bone, the agents wouldn't let go. I capitulated.

When I spoke to my father about it, he was discouraging and trotted out one of his famous quotes 'Cobbler, stick to your last', reminding me that I should stick to my known business, which was certainly not Show Business.

**Celebrity sport cc.** I had been advised by my father and friends to register a separate company and run the whole event as a separate business enterprise. But due to extreme tardiness of the top legal firm based in Sandton City, it didn't happen in time, which I lived to regret, financially.

# My Life, a Roller Coaster Ride

My father, Alf Steer, a seasoned business 'man, relaxed only when I told him which attorneys were handling this matter. Little did we know how hopelessly slow they would be in this instance.

**Critical choice.** The project seemed to be viable. I signed them up. This turned out to be a very fateful and critical choice and a defining moment in my life. Mainly because it became a serious gamble. Nobody to blame but myself.

Fate? I could not possibly have considered some unforeseen, even freaky, turns of fate which would cost me a lot. Even almost everything.

The biggest freak event was, in July '1975, the rand devalued. The as yet unsigned sponsors changed their minds about getting involved. So, no airfares paid for. Our biggest expense.

It was leaked to us from an insider, that various jealous rivals were out to sabotage me by tampering with the booking process. Suddenly only expensive box tickets were 'available'.

The weather looked like rain. Last minute withdrawals of some participants, Rod Steiger, Jill St. John and Elke Sommer. The suspicion factor in the public, waiting to see if the stars would materialise.

Back to work, I was delighted to get my friend Henry (Sir Henry Grattan-Bellew) to be the Event Host and Manager. I knew that, with his Show Jumping and Equestrian eventing experience he would be the perfect host for the job. He agreed instantly and proved to be the very best choice I could have made. Because it was half charity and half business,

**Taylor and Burton, mobbed on arrival.**

## 4. Megan Carr Promotions

and my overheads budget was limited, we drew up a feasibility study and spent carefully.

MCP Accountant, David Frost, was a valuable support and calmly kept everything under control.

Because it was a very glamorous charitable event, funded and underwritten by me, I was able to tempt many people to donate their talents, facilities and time, to become involved. I had a good name for reliability in the promotions business.

I had seats to spare in exchange for favours which was a huge saving.

**Venue.** We naturally elected to hold the event at the 3 000 seat Ellis Park Tennis stadium. The Tennis Club Committee was excited and most cooperative. Full use of the Club facilities. Tennis officials were jostling to be Linesmen, Umpires and Ball Boys. (only boys in 1975).

Sylvia Holder, my talented and quirky writer, prepared a brilliant advertising campaign. Roy Clucas, head of his new Ad Agency, designed and placed the ads.

SAA was alerted and seats reserved. Sol, dear Sol Kerzner, allocated us the whole of the 4th floor of the Landdrost Hotel at a very nominal rate. He was excited about it.

All of this was put in place before Celebrity Sport cc was registered by the tardy legal firm. So, all bookings were contracted under my company name. Before we took anything further, it was time to make an announcement to the press before it was leaked. This was also a final act of commitment.

Sir Henry Grattan Bellew, on court with Ringo, Liz and Mickey Dolenz.

## My Life, a Roller Coaster Ride

**Announcement.** I phoned Ron Anderson, News Editor of *The Star*. I told him that Elizabeth Taylor, Richard Burton, Ringo Starr and ten film and music stars would be coming to South Africa to take part in Celebrity Tennis.

Silence on the other end of the line. Then: "If I publish this announcement today, Stop Press, and it turns out to be not true, you will live to regret it all your business life". He published Stop Press front page and appreciated getting the Scoop.

Then our lives became almost a nightmare of media jostling for every little snippet of information. Many of the papers contacted the stars and their agents direct. Not that easy in those days of telegrams and booked trunk calls. No fax machines or cell phones.

Just when we were run off our feet. The above story appeared in *Die Transvaaler*.

In September 1975, just before Celebrity Tennis, I was summoned to appear before a Government Commission of Inquiry, investigating charity organisations and charity events. It was a phone message for me to appear at short notice. I was not available to attend at that time. When I did not appear exactly on time, they phoned my office and were informed by my secretary that I was not available right then, I could only be there some time later. They informed my secretary that if I did not appear, they would have to subpoena me to appear when they reconvened in Pretoria.

**Airmailed photos of Richard and Elizabeth arrived within three days.**

## 4. Megan Carr Promotions

I later attended, and must have satisfied them, because I heard no more.

However, I noted from *Die Transvaler* article that I was in good company. My friend Alan Tiley, Boys' Town, Family Planning Society, The Christian Institute and Lions International had also been summoned to appear.

They seemed concerned about money laundering and charity money leaving the country. Fair enough. I was happy to cooperate.

**Mischievous article.** The collateral damage that this type of article causes, directly affected me. Mud sticks. Both the *Sunday Times* and the *Rand Daily Mail* picked it up. Both printed articles speculating as to whether I would be paying the funds to the charity. The Ass in Assumption.

For this reason, I challenged the *Sunday Times* and the RDM to cover the handing over of the cheque to United Artists of South Africa after the event. The *Sunday Times* did me proud with a prominent photo and article. The *Rand Daily Mail* picked a tiny spot near 'Obituaries' to apologise in ten lines.

Once the Press had milked the positive information on the stars, dry as a bone, they then ferreted out negative snippets to fire up items of news. Once the media door was open, it was a hungry beast. A period of frenzied public and media attention engulfed us. The MCP air was electric.

## Megan Carr te ‚besig' vir kommissie

MEV MEGAN CARR, eienares van 'n promosie-agentskap wat die Burtons en verskeie ander rolprentsterre vir 'n tennistoernooi na Suid-Afrika gebring het, was nie gister betyds om voor die Kommissie van Ondersoek na die Insameling van Vrywillige Geldelike Bydraes te getuig nie.

Nadat die kommissie, wat in Johannesburg sit, vyftien minute op mev. Carr gewag het, is na 'n onderneming gebel om te hoor waar sy is. Mev. Carr was glo te besig om te kom en die woordvoerder van die skakel het gesê dat mev. Carr eers 'n halfuur later beskikbaar sou wees.

Die kommissie het verdaag nadat die voorsittter, prof. I. J. J. van Rooyen, gesê het dat mev. Carr vandag om twaalfuur voor die kommissie moet verskyn. Indien sy nie opdaag nie, sal die kommissie genoodsaak wees om mev. Carr te verplig om later na Pretoria te kom om voor die kommissie te verskyn.

Die Nasionale Welsynraad het onder meer gister verskyn. Dr. R. McLaghlan het namens die raad aan die kommissie gesê dat nuwe probleme onder die Nasionale Welsynraad se aandag gekom het:

Daar kan vra gevra word oor wat van die geld word wat sekere welsynorganisasies insamel. Al die organisasies wil hulle by die welsynraad registreer, maar die vraag ontstaan of al die geld in Suid-Afrika bly en hoeveel verlaat die land.

Ander organisasies wat gister verskyn het, was: Die Gesinsbeplanningvereniging, Boys Town en die Heilsleër.

Vandag verskyn mnr. A Tiley, eerw. B. Brown van die Christelike Instituut, die Nasionale Instituut vir Aftrede, Lions International en mev. Megan Carr.

# My Life, a Roller Coaster Ride

**Staff assignments.** I appointed my staffers Diane Anderson and Sally Ann Hotson to handle the stars and the press full time. Trisha Reunert was assigned to local celebrity and VIP involvement. David Frost and Shelagh Gilbert juggled the money. Gail Lieberz was at my side taking loads of detail work off my shoulders and keeping me in the loop of each activity. She was my ears and eyes. English Rose, Lindsay Swan, manned the crazy switchboard with firmness and diplomacy. Caz Steyn, my secretary kept all communications on track. Chen Sam came in exclusively, to look after Liz and Richard and manage their borrowed Rolls and student driver.

**Promotional history.** The bright, modern suite of MCP offices, occupying half of the 15th floor of Sandton City (shared with *To the Point*, a political publication), was a hive of excitement and industry. Everyone displayed superhuman energy and high good spirits. Ten women and one man worked as a well-oiled machine. No histrionics or tantrums. There prevailed an infinite sense of promotional history in the making.

It was so all-consuming that our regular accounts were asked for their patience and left simmering on temporary hold. This helped us cope with the multifaceted event organisation. To compensate the faithful clients, we rewarded them with complimentary tickets in the Main Stand at the Tennis, together with our promotion's friends, Gordon Mulholland, Des and Dawn Lindberg, Hal Orlandini and Ian Lawrence.

The financial implications, the tennis protocol, officials, security, traffic, guest ticket requests and demands and, of course, the frenzy of publicity, consumed us. Everybody we knew or even didn't know, wanted in on the act. Meanwhile, all service accounts opened by me had to be paid by me from personal resources and income from the event. It had all the prospects of making a fair profit for us and the charities.

The Charities were, the International United Artists (USA) and the Local Artists' Union, which was managed by the very able Irene Menell.

**The U.S. business deal.** All profits from the Ellis Park Friday and Saturday tennis event, would accrue to Megan Carr Promotions. Fortunately for me, at that time, one USD equalled 0.75 ZAR.

A Celebrity Banquet on Sunday night. Profit after costs go to the United Artist charities. This would include the income from the charity auction.

The two accounts were run independently and accounted for in separate accounts. I always retained a separate special personal account for home and schools which was never used for the business.

# 4. Megan Carr Promotions

**The charity 'Banquet with the Stars'** was held at the new and fashionable Carlton Hotel.

None of the stars were required to do stage performances but would take part in the banquet fundraising auction of personal items which would accrue to the fund. All would appear at the tennis event both days and the banquet. All would cooperate with media, except for Taylor/Burton, who would offer only one press interview but would allow all photographs at public appearances.

**The US package.** The Three Degrees: Fayette Pinkney, Sheila Holiday and Valerie Ferguson, who would be the named Star Act and who were accompanied by their manager Brian Turner. Their current hit at that time was *When will I see you again*.

The Monkees, Mickey Dolenz and Davey Jones. Current hit *I'm a Believer*. John Marley, the father in *Love Story* and in *The Godfather* (horse's head in his bed).

Peter Lawford, aging screen star and member of the 'Rat Pack', married to Pat Kennedy. All of whom arrived as contracted. Dino Martin Jnr, handsome singing son of Dean Martin also arrived with the group. A few years later, sadly killed when piloting his plane, he hit a mountain.

Bond girl Jill St. John. Swedish bombshell Elke Sommer, Dyan Cannon, Oscar winner Rod Steiger, Mr. Joyboy in *The Loved One*, none of whom arrived.

Megan's introductions. Mayor, Cllr. Max Neppe, Liz Taylor, State President The Hon. Nico Diederichs, Mrs. Diederichs, Richard Burton.

# My Life, a Roller Coaster Ride

Elizabeth Taylor on stage at the 'Banquet with the Stars', auctioning off her pewter 'Liz' beer mug. Richard then auctioned off his 'Hiz" mug. Businessman Gerry McCullough bought both.

The gorgeous Dino Martin Jnr and Ringo performing on stage at the Celebrity Tennis banquet.

On stage at the charity banquet and auction. Sally Ann Hotson with a pair of pewter beer tankards on a tray ready for auction engraved 'Liz' and 'Hiz'.

# 4. Megan Carr Promotions

**Security.** I had to supply security which was thought to be necessary for the wellbeing of the visitors.

**Insurance.** I only took out personal liability and accident cover for my company. The tennis stadium and the two hotels were covered for public liability.

**Game Reserve visit.** I accepted Sol Kerzner's invitation for them to visit the newly opened Chobe Game Lodge just across the SA border in Botswana and very near to the Victoria Falls. All at no cost to me. Adele Lucas was then Sol's Marketing Manager, facilitating arrangements between us which made our lives easier.

**Ticket prices.** In those days, people were accustomed to paying about R8 for a ticket to live events. We decided to charge between R8 and R15 per ticket. R15 being the VIP boxed area around the stars. It seems ludicrous today when we now pay in the region of R1 000 to be near Pavarotti and Robbie Williams.

One of the group got hold of the air tickets of the no-shows. After a tip-off from one of the others, Gail found them in his bedroom closet and reclaimed them for refund. He never reported the loss!

**Doubting public.** The public feeling was one of scepticism that 15 celebrities would actually set foot in this equity-boycotted country. Also, the gamble of high calibre of the names visiting this pariah of international countries because of apartheid. Bookings did not take off like a rocket as I had naturally assumed.

**Event management.** What few people out of the promotions and event management business can possibly realise, is that it is not straightforward management. One has to attend to many unplanned and unforeseen snags, which waste precious time.

**Her doggie.** Elizabeth Taylor wanted to bring her little 'doggie' along. I put her off by saying that the poor little darling would have to languish in quarantine for the whole length of her 14-day stay. Settled. The Animal Rights groups wanted an interview with Elizabeth Taylor to get her to voice her thoughts on 'Beauty without Cruelty'. I simply turned them down for 'security' reasons.

The Welsh community wanted Richard Burton to do an evening of Dylan Thomas poetry. This one we set up. Richard enjoyed it.

The Rugby Players wanted to talk to Richard about his rugby passion. I set this up with the delightful Syd Nomis and they had a very raucous get-together. A week after the tennis, they ceremoniously presented Richard with a Springbok tie in public view at the Pretoria Rugby Stadium. It was one of the highlights of Richard's visit to South Africa. He found tennis very boring. ( See pic on page 184).

**S.A. versus the visitors.** There was an extra element to the Tennis event. One which would have been a huge promotion in itself. Local tennis and show business celebrities to play against the visiting celebrities.

Getting these became a question of who we would allow to play. The volunteers were legion. The local Tennis Federation helped here. They could not afford trampled feelings in their midst.

**The South African team** Gordon Forbes and Abe Segal (Abe pretended he was doing me a favour). Gordon was charming and fun. He said. "Wild horses wouldn't keep Abe and me from playing". Several other top tennis names took part.

**1975.** Miss South Africa Vera Johns played a very good game.1974 Miss World Anneline Kriel and singer - producer Richard Loring, who were dating at that time, offered to play for SA at least, they appeared on court and knocked a few balls at the side. The court had become a stage.

**Sir Henry,** our tennis organiser and Master of Ceremonies, was the very eloquent and elegant. Sir Henry Grattan Bellew, who had a gift for drama and the right words. He was well informed, funny and charismatic. (The title was also very useful, he always said).

**Gifts.** Many companies and organisations were on the phones wanting to get a piece of the Celebrity action. Oudtshoorn sent through a magnificent ostrich feather full length cape which enchanted Elizabeth. She immediately paraded for us through the Celebrity lounge, like a Ziegfield girl.

The Landdrost fielded dozens of parcels, letters, cards, wines, which we had to collect, sort out and deliver at our discretion. All had to be acknowledged. We didn't return any gifts – it would have burdened our office and the Post Office.

We simply accepted them and sent glowing letters of thanks and distributed them amongst the visitors in their lounge. It created a festive atmosphere.

But I get ahead of myself.

The hardest condition of the Taylor-Burton contract was that they would only grant a single formal press interview. It almost damaged my business future as the press excluded, blamed me, personally.

## 4. Megan Carr Promotions

The other celebrities were happy enough to face the press. But once the Burton Taylor names were published, they overshadowed the rest for press demand. Even the funny, restless and irrepressible Ringo.

**Press.** The main body of nine stars arrived three days before the event. The first full press event at the Landdrost was for these stars. ( See pic on page 155). Sir Henry was the MC. I welcomed them all. The stars dutifully answered all the Press questions – many dug out of the woodwork of gossip publications.

It certainly provided lots of padding for the events to follow and enough photographs to paper the walls of the hotel. Taylor and Burton had not yet arrived.

Those last few days, we were faced with many dilemmas and quick decisions. People clamouring, press demanding, VIPs and socialites crawling out of every crack wanting to invite them to every function real or improvised for the occasion. Lindsay Swan, at the switchboard in our office, and someone at the Landdrost office worked full time to field them and record them for our attention.

**Glitterati.** Then there was the thin line of crème de la crème of Johannesburg society who pretended that they were not at all interested in the show business stars.

I had the lesson of my life in human behaviour ranging from pure expertise offered and genuine kindness, to people on the make with lies and promises which all had to be assessed and dealt with.

Our biggest worry two days before the tennis event – the bookings had been impeded and only started picking up as the stars arrived. Credibility factor. 3 000 seats to fill. Only about 1 100 booked and two days to go.

**Sabotage suspected.** The bungled bookings information told buyers that the regular seats were all sold out. To our horror, we had only been alerted to this very late, when tipped off by a sympathetic friend in the know, who suggested we test the system as she had reason to believe that things were 'not right'. My entire staff and some friends all went out on a 'mystery shopping' expedition to buy tickets. and sure enough 'sold out' except for the expensive seats. When I confronted, and threatened, the party concerned, he said the staff had made a 'mistake' and would correct it – which they did – but really almost too late because the weather was turning, and it looked like rain.

Happily, the first big press presentation, with real live stars, especially

## My Life, a Roller Coaster Ride

Ringo Starr, brought in extra interest. (See photo page 101). But we urgently needed more. And in a hurry. Three days to go. Would the arrival of Burton and Taylor next day do the trick?

Two days before the Tennis event, I saw the sensation that the Taylor Burton announcement was creating. I realised that their own single security person, Gavin de Becker, would not be enough. I engaged the best VIP security firm in the country. They had four security men on roster, on 24-hour duty.

**Airport duty.** I asked the airport police to assist for the arrival They put 100 police officers on duty and six mounted traffic officers as motor escort. It was a mob scene. I had a convertible Rolls Royce Silver Cloud waiting outside and went in to welcome them. There must have been thousands waiting for them.

Elbows locked, ten of the policemen circled the five of us and walked us out to the car. The surge of people squeezed us into a tight little moving ball in the middle and at one stage I was being propelled along without my feet touching the floor.

**Mounted escort.** We got into the Rolls and drove away with a very impressive mounted escort. After driving a short distance, in self-defence,

Richard Burton  Megan Carr  Liz Taylor
they appeared in Arnold Benjamin's Annual publication
'And now for the Good News'
'A very unofficial record of 1975'

Still the whole thing had a surprise fairy-tale ending – if you like fairy-tales

For our next trick we could get married again

With me, surely one boob is enough?

## 4. Megan Carr Promotions

and to save Elizabeth's hair, we had to put up the soft top. Guiding us out of the airport, our escort of rotating wingmen hovered. One ahead to stop other traffic – even at traffic lights – two each side and one in the rear taking rotating turns so that one was always ahead to stop traffic at the lights and intersections. We ran many red lights in this manner.

Holding hands, Liz and Richard loved it once sanity prevailed. Their Security man, Gavin de Becker, always looked anxious.

We arrived at the Landdrost to much bowing and scraping. Richard Burton was always at Elizabeth's side – to protect the enormous tear-shaped 33 carat diamond ring which she always wore. This diamond had been given to Liz by Richard after filming *Cleopatra* and their first marriage. It had previously been owned by the ex-wife of a Nazi War criminal, Alfred Krupp.

Having given them time to settle in, open some gifts, and to rest a little, hairdresser, Carlton's Jean Meyer, was on standby to work his casual no-fuss charm and magic.

I had organised a Taylor-Burton exclusive press interview at 5pm and had been allowed to invite two journalists only. Better than the original single reporter in the contract, and with their consent.

**One and only press interview.** Because of the slow bookings, and closing weather dilemma, and no TV in those days, we selected two radio people -

Elizabeth is persuaded to flash her (Krupp) 33.18 carat diamond for the press. A gift from Richard Burton in 1968 for which he paid US$308 000. They married after co-starring in the film *Cleopatra*. They divorced in 1974 and remarried in Botswana in 1975 a few weeks after appearing at Celebrity Tennis.

## My Life, a Roller Coaster Ride

Bea Reed (morning radio) and Willy Camillieri (same evening radio news, as they could get their ten minute pieces across fast and get millions of listeners excited enough to get impulse bookings by next day, the day ahead of the first of the two day Friday-Saturday tennis event.

It went very well. Both of our veteran broadcasters were slightly nervous but came out of the interview elated with a career scoop. As we left, Bea then told me she needed to test her tape recorder to make sure it had recorded. (It was too late to fix in any case!) She pressed the button. Nothing. Again, and again. Nothing. She looked aghast and embarrassed. I suggested she sit down, have a glass of water and relax. She then tried it again – and, of course, it worked – somehow. Even the best of pros can get an attack of nerves. A superb ten-minute interview with the famous pair was broadcast twice next morning at drive time. Willy managed to get his out on the same evening's 7pm, 8pm news and little extra pieces on the following morning news services.

The print press was furious that they were not invited. They then started to vent their anger on me personally and often turned favourable items into negatives. Even nasty. I suppose bad news sells newspapers. It also worked for me, drawing attention to the event.

One frustrated paper resorted to dressing up a reporter as a waiter and almost managed to get past security. This happened several times. I praised them for their tenacity and wished that they had succeeded.

All the playing Stars went to the courts early to 'practice'. Sir Henry, assisted by some of my staff, took charge of these informal rehearsals. Some hamming it up for the crowds.

Henry was good at organising horse shows – so no problem for him.

**Friday.** The people started arriving early at the gates and the rain kindly held off as requested. The stadium, though, never filled beyond two thirds. However, it was sufficiently spread out to make it look packed, noisy and a buzzy atmosphere of excitement which was almost tangible. The early crowds had excellent value just watching all the antics of people born to entertain.

**Preparing for the event. Chen Sam.** I had assigned and carefully briefed, exotic looking MCP staffer, Chen Sam, to be personal attendant and 'runner' to take care of Liz and Richard, making sure they kept to their schedule and times and to liaise with our office, Security and Rolls driver to get them where they needed to be. They had all been given printed schedules of their commitments.

## 4. Megan Carr Promotions

Local VIP tennis players arrived to meet international stars on court. Gordon and Abe were gracious hosts on the courts and gave the visitors a few tips, for example, for some new players. how to hold a tennis racquet and aim to hit the ball across the net. In this case, Ringo and Three Degrees. They were ably assisted by Star tennis players Peter Lawford, Dino Martin, John Marley, Mickey Dolenz and Davey Jones who played a very good game.

We had to get the national anthems on tape for the various countries represented. South Africa, England (The Monkees), Wales (Richard Burton) and USA for the rest. The Welsh anthem proved a difficult mission. Eventually we borrowed a copy from the SABC library. After the Anthems and short speeches of welcome, the tennis re-started.

**Sabotage again.** Sir Henry, as Master of Ceremonies, arrived early to check out the programme for the day and test the Public Address equipment which had been professionally set up and tested the previous day.

Henry called me urgently to say, "The PA system is dead". Fortunately, as always, we had set up a standby technician who discovered that wires had been cut.

**Missing.** Everyone was in place, briefed and awaiting the guests of honour, the SA State President. No sign of Taylor and Burton. Phone calls back and forward. They had got the times wrong and were still asleep at midday. And where was Chen Sam? The State President was due at any moment.

I received a reply from the Rolls driver to say 'they' had instructed him to pick them up in two hours. It would take them that time to get ready. With a few strong words, I dispatched Chen Sam, whose job it was to collect them as fast and diplomatically as possible. A tricky job.

The presidential guests of honour chose that moment to arrive exactly on time. Friday 12 noon. I met them personally and escorted them into the Clubhouse where refreshments were waiting. 12.30 was court appearance time. Could we work a miracle with Taylor-Burton?

I put the dilemma to Diederichs and asked if we could make the opening appearance at 12.30 as scheduled and bring in the two stars when they arrived? He answered, "Certainly not – it's against protocol". So, with 10 minute updates and the crowd getting restless – we started the tennis programme on schedule and announced that the official State President opening would happen after lunch.

I ordered lunch early to buy some time. Sadly, this meant us missing

## My Life, a Roller Coaster Ride

some fun matches whilst dancing attendance and hosting our honoured guests and keeping tabs on the tardy ones. Fortunately, 'Their Honours' were very understanding and gracious about the rudeness of our stars. (Who later said they thought it was not that important to be on time!) Strange coming from people who should know better.

**Official opening by the State President.** I had invited the State President formally to open the Celebrity Tennis Event.

The acceptance was immediate and graciously handled by his office. Conditions were that I provide parking and seating for his entourage and to meet them personally. It was also important to know that they would not enter the public area until all the Celebrities were present and ready to participate. So, we set it up with all the players present and ready in good time.

**Rugby.** In chatting to the State President (plenty of time to do this), he said that he would be going to the big international rugby match Lions vs SA at Bloemfontein next day and thought he would invite Richard Burton to accompany him as his guest. I was shocked and asked if he realised that Richard's obligation and contract was to be present full time at the Tennis. I suggested he didn't even mention it to Richard who would clearly have preferred the rugby. Later in the VIP box I heard him whispering to Richard an invitation to go with him to the rugby. Richard then asked me – and I had to, very firmly, say "No". However, Richard and Liz did attend

**Richard Burton receiving a Springbok Rugby tie From Syd Nomis on behalf of the Springboks who were due to play in Bloemfontein on the same day as the Tennis. He was upset he couldn't go as the invited guest of the State President and the Rugby team.**

## 4. Megan Carr Promotions

a Provincial match with Syd Nomis the following weekend, where the Springbok Rugby tie was presented to him.

**Success.** Two glorious days of excellent tennis and some fooling around followed to rave reviews. Even the Umpires, Lines people and Ball boys got in the mood and kept up the festive atmosphere, carried across with Henry's light-hearted commentary. Improvised entertainment at its best.

Behind the scenes, the tennis side turned out to be something of a challenge for Henry to work out. Four who had never played, all the rest were really good players. So, we had some 'foreplay' where they just fooled around the court and made everyone laugh.

Our Miss South Africa, Vera Johns acquitted herself well. Anneline just looked gorgeous and wandered around waving a racquet with Richard Loring looking adoringly at her, occasionally hitting a ball.

No wonder the press labelled the event Megan's Tennis Circus. I was very proud of this label and played it up.

Ringo had previously said that he needed oxygen because of the altitude. We had given him some aerosols for this. A born comic, his court routine consisted of sniffing oxygen and then playing a very slow-motion moon-walk parody of a very serious tennis game. That alone was worth the gate money.

The two days of tennis, interspersed with light misty showers of rain, went very well – but I knew the worst. Not nearly enough gate money was realised to cover the cost of the event. I had to keep this information strictly between myself and David, the accountant. We put on a brave face.

**Cover up.** An incident happened at lunch which gave me a slight reprieve. The very daunting Mrs. Diederichs spilt some gravy on to her jacket lapel and was distraught. She and I went to the cloakroom, did our best with towel and soap – but a small stain was immovable. So, I went to the dining room, found some flowers and made up a small corsage which I pinned over the offending mark. Friends for life after that!

When the two tardy stars finally arrived after 2pm, they turned on the charm and had the Diederichs under their spell in no time, and instantly forgiven. The Diederichs sent them and me each huge a bunch of long-stemmed red roses the day after, thanking them for coming to South Africa, and me for hosting them.

**The Krupp diamond.** At all times it was noted that Elizabeth wore her 33 carat diamond Only once was she persuaded to flash it for the press. Some tennis purists asked, "who would want to see bad tennis?"

## My Life, a Roller Coaster Ride

Some of them even stayed away. Those who came, entered the spirit of the event and went home happy with a day's entertainment and even some excellent tennis.

**Event success.** I still had the Sunday night banquet to run at the Carlton with capacity 600 guests paying high plate cost. Drinks not included except at the top table.

**Financial loss.** However, with high costs, loss of air ticket sponsors and less than full capacity stadium, there were questions about the financial outcome.

Fair enough.

The *Sunday Times* of the previous week had speculated that the Tennis Circus would run at a loss. The headline read, 'All Star Tennis Promotor shrugs off big loss'. Good acting on my part. Nobody understood that the charity funds would come from the banquet and not the tennis.

**Banquet profit.** The charity banquet made an excellent profit, every penny of which went to the charity after physical costs of food and orchestra were paid. The rumours caused the Arthur Murray orchestra and the Carlton Hotel to demand payment in advance. They got it. Every banquet invoice was paid in full.

The then editor of the *Sunday Times* had done the expected. Milking the event positively then negatively for some sensation throughout the event.

**Cheque handover.**

The *Sunday Times* had the good grace to print, and to syndicat a photo of me handing over a cheque to Irene Menell, representing the charities. The cheque was for the full 600 person ticket income less cost of the orchestra and the hotel restaurant account.

The donation amount was R14 000. It seems a pittance, today, until you remember that you could

## 4. Megan Carr Promotions

buy a nice house in Sandton for R50 000 in 1975.

I threatened to sue the Editor of the *Rand Daily Mail* for printing a spurious story saying that 'Megan Carr will not be able to pay out the charities'. With bad grace, he later printed a very tiny three-line apology hidden in the classified back pages of the Mail. One of my newspaper heroes, as it turned out, had feet of clay.

Arnold Benjamin featured the Tennis event in his 'Now for the Good News' annual review of 1975.

The Friday – Saturday Tennis was done. I still had a banquet to run Sunday night. Fortunately, I'd bought a beautiful gown to wear. I'd written and rehearsed my speech for that night. My hair? No time for a hairdresser.

**When a stranger becomes a saviour.** In the middle of all this, on Sunday morning, I had a phone call from someone I had never met. Len Hack. A businessman with a furniture shop near Ellis Park, crazy about the film stars, who said to me that, with rumours of financial difficulties, I should know the basics of how to handle it to avoid legal damage. He would brief me on how to handle it.

Here was I, with only a Sunday morning available to attend to this critical matter, I humbly and gratefully accepted. I couldn't go to my father.

The Carlton and MCP staff had the banquet arrangements well in hand.

Mr. and Mrs Hack collected me from my flat and took me to their house in Bramley. She was a hairdresser and did my hair and nails. He, meanwhile, lectured me on exactly what to do to avoid possible insolvency through impatient creditors.

I received the best advice I could have had from this guardian angel out of the blue. I try not to take my good luck for granted. My thanks to them was a very well positioned table for two, squeezed in front of the star-studded main table at the banquet.

Len Hack's sound advice served me well then, and ever since.

I got ready for the banquet and was collected early by my escort Ian Pepper who whisked me to the Carlton. He was a doctor, so no trouble parking. I sat him down at the best table in the room, together with my family, then rushed off into the frenzy of last-minute banquet activity.

The interesting part of this banquet was the people. The cream of society who had sworn not to be there, were there in full force in amongst an eclectic mixture of all layers of society. At an unheard of R150 per person per ticket (R3 000 today).

We were sold out. I Could have sold out several times over. In those days no one had ever heard of such a high price for a banquet place.

We heard stories of shop assistants and out of work actors scraping together enough money to pay for a single ticket.

This strange singles dining booking pattern turned into a nightmare for seating ones and twos and not only tables of ten. When they did arrive, they simply swopped places to be with their friends and were immovable. The table seating plan, pinned up at the entrance became almost redundant, except for the full group tables. Brief chaos reigned but was soon sorted out by my trusty staff.

Another strange phenomenon was, no matter where people were seated around the banquet hall, and despite security guards posted in front of the banquet top table, people streamed past the raised main table and unashamedly gawked at the stars. I was host at that top table and marvelled at the sight of this strange parade, greeting those I knew – and didn't know. Like royalty.

Meanwhile, there were other side issues going on. I suddenly remembered that Richard was on the wagon and there was to be litchis marinated in gin for the starter course. I rushed to the kitchen and got some fresh litchis into a bowl and personally checked that these were placed in front of him.

Richard, naughty boy, was caught by Liz drooling down the décolletage of a staff member and got a sharp rebuke for it. As host, I had seated myself between Ringo Starr and Richard Burton. Ringo was pouring brandy into his red wine and getting merrier by the minute. Richard bravely sipping on Soda.

**Restless Ringo,** couldn't resist the stage and kept taking the mike and doing an added hilarious commentary on absolutely everything. And a surprise comedy show on stage with Dino Martin Jr.

I was very relieved that I would not have to pay realistic fees for such stunning stage appearances by world renowned artists. The evening was a resounding success both financially and show business at its rousing best.

Unexpectedly, the two of them took to the stage in an impromptu comic singing act. Dino sounded much like his famous dad. I asked myself 'Am I dreaming?'

What a sparkling dinner companion was Ringo. Chatty, funny and sometimes a little pensive when talking about his family. I mentioned that my daughter, Carole was in London. He immediately said he would take her to lunch when he got home. He scribbled his number on a napkin.

## 4. Megan Carr Promotions

When I phoned Carole to tell her about Ringo's invitation, she just laughed and said, "don't joke" and refused to call him on his private number.

**Ringo the Starr,** was my favourite of all the visitors although all of them were pleasant and friendly.

**Auction.** The main event of the evening was the charity auction. Each of the International and local stars and tennis players donated, and personally presented on stage, a personal item for auction. After my welcoming speech and some fun remarks by Henry – the auction began.

Cherry and Gerry McCulloch bought the, engraved 'Liz' and 'Hiz' beer mugs. Ringo gave a diamante lapel star which fetched a fat sum.

Twenty personal items were all presented on stage for auction by Sir Henry. Anneline sashayed onto the stage wearing a Feather Boa to be auctioned.

**The day after the night before.** The event was not yet over. Outstanding money was not exactly pouring in. We still had to look after the starry guests and get some of them to Chobe Game Lodge for their promised holiday. The staff would easily manage that.

The previous week, I'd had to find a way to get them to Chobe bearing in mind the financial constraints. I couldn't spend any more on air tickets. It was taking time to get eight first class refunds for the no-shows. It was almost as expensive to get to Chobe as to London. What did I have to offer in barter? Who had an aircraft for ten of them? Louis Luyt and Sol Kerzner.

I decided that Sol had helped enough – so on the Sunday morning, the week before the Tennis, I phoned Louis Luyt at home. About 11am – surely up by now. No Sunday Rugby to attend. Mrs. Luyt answered the phone and said Louis was unavailable. "Please phone later". 12 noon, still unavailable. 1pm, he was "having his lunch. Phone later". 2pm – "phone later". 3pm, he finally took the call. He listened to my story and promptly said "No".

My proposal was not a bad one. He and Mrs. Luyt would fly with the stars, stay at Chobe Lodge and be my, and Sol's guests for three nights before returning with them all to Johannesburg when, except for Taylor-Burton, they would be departing for home.

**Then I thought ... Maybe I should call Sol!**
Who immediately said "Yes" and wasted no time setting it up. Sol had

such vision and was so very generous about it all. Of course, it was also good business for him in using the opportunity to promote the new Chobe Lodge.

Sol named the main Chobe Lodge luxury suite 'The Elizabeth Taylor Suite'.

**Mevrou Carr.** What about Louis Luyt? Monday morning's *Die Transvaler* Newspaper ran an article with bold headline 'Mevrou Carr (translated) 'bothers Louis Luyt on his Sabbath'. I was shocked as one phone call could have settled the matter, instead of being fobbed off hourly for five hours. I was furious but decided that Louis probably needed every opportunity to score points by looking pious on his Sabbath, when he could simply, sanctimoniously, have switched off his phone on his Sabbath. I took it from whence it came. But it didn't end there as you will discover later.

**Kindness and favours.** This second half year in 1975, has memories of much kindness and many aircraft.

**Toothache.** In the thick of pre-Celebrity Tennis organisation, I got an abscess in a premolar tooth. I had the best dentist, the blond, green-eyed Italian dentist Dario Ferri. In between the open-mouthed fiddling with my teeth, he dragged out of me, stories about all the goings-on in the promotions business up the road in Sandton City.

**Abscess treatment.** The abscess immediate treatment was a pin, a crown and regular appointments at a time when I didn't have a minute to spare.

**Fatigue treatment.** The afternoon of the final polishing of the tooth, a few days before the tennis, Dario had noticed my extreme fatigue. He told his receptionist to inform my office that I would be late back at the office. I protested, but he wouldn't listen. He spirited me out of the surgery and into his sports car and out to Grand Central where his Cessna aircraft was waiting, ready for us to fly too nowhere in particular.

Once in the air he said 'what would you like to see as we cruise around and de-stress you?' We overflew my house on the Vaal River and explored the winding ribbon of water at low altitude. After a dreamy while in the air – we returned, and I was dropped at my car feeling amazingly relaxed and de-compressed – and only a little over two hours spent in a very good cause. I felt re-energised, comforted and back in full control of my life and my business.

I also need to say that after 19 years, I still had that gold-filled crown anchored on its little pin till it was knocked out by a burglar in 1994. That

## 4. Megan Carr Promotions

story follows later. I love to reward people for their kindness which is given from the heart and without any expectations. I had Dario and his friend, Sharon, sitting near to Liz and Richard in the VIP stand at the tennis.

**Winding up.** After the banquet I had much mopping up to do whilst also caring for my last few visitors. Creditors to be managed. Ongoing entertainment for the last of the celebrity visitors. Liz and Richard, The Monkees and several others.

**Big Brother.** Then suddenly a request from Government which complained bitterly that the VIPs were visiting Chobe and not our own Kruger Game Reserve.

### Minister of Tourism Marais Steyn and the Kruger Park.

I explained to the Ministry of Tourism that the accommodation at Kruger Park was too basic and just not good enough. Very few private luxury game reserves were in operation in those days and they were too expensive for me and my crowd of guests. The Department of Tourism then offered me the Diplomatic Bungalows at Skukuza. They were not too good either, but better than the public rondavels. Liz and Richard were so happy at Chobe and so in love again, that they didn't want to move.

Ringo and Peter Lawford had left to go home. The Three Degrees were hating every minute of bush life. The rest were very amenable to any arrangements we made. And the US show agents were there to mobilise them.

**Protocol.** I got Liz and Richard to agree to a two day visit as guests of the SA Minister of Tourism, Marais Steyn and his wife. And because I said that they were actually obliged to agree to this invitation from our government. The others followed. I booked this lot onto the government plane which landed at the Skukuza airstrip.

Meanwhile, as the plane from Botswana was about to arrive, I received a call from the Minister's office to say that he couldn't make it after all as he had laryngitis. I lost it and demanded that he get out of his sickbed and into his car or a helicopter without delay and fulfil his diplomatic obligation.

The Three Degees donated one of their stage dresses all wispy, size 0, and very sexy. Fayette, Sheila and Valerie.

# My Life, a Roller Coaster Ride

I had gone to huge trouble to get the visitors there as his guests and insisted that he be there to dine with them that same night. They got the message! The Marais Steyns arrived by car from Pretoria that same afternoon.

**Skukuza.** We, the hosts, had all arrived by helicopter early that day and had the best game viewing from the air.

**Emergency.** As Richard Burton stepped down from the aircraft, he dropped the newspaper he was carrying. As he stooped to retrieve it, his pants split. He whispered to me "Help!".

With the newspaper guarding his rear, I shuffled him off to one of the bungalows, gave him a towel to protect his modesty, he stripped off his pants and handed them over to me. In my profession, I always carried a set of tools in my handbag. Swiss Army knife and sewing kit. So, out with my needle and thread and cobbled up the offending seam. It all happened so quickly that no one realised what had happened. It remained Richard's and my private joke. Till now!

**Helicopter game viewing.** The helicopters gave game viewing rides for the visitors. Not ideal because of the noise, but they were all enchanted with what they saw, especially remarking on the families of warthogs running in fright, tails in the air.

CELEBRITY TENNIS Stars arriving at Game Reserve
Adele Lucas, Liz Taylor, Megan Carr, Richard Burton

## 4. Megan Carr Promotions

The Rangers were dressed in their very smartest uniforms and were good hosts, quite unphased by the big names, and proud to show off their animal treasures.

They took the stars to the baby animal orphanage and allowed them to feed the little ones with milk in big two litre coke bottles with teats on. Lion cubs and giraffe calves being at their most endearing. In fact, their day of game viewing was a winner and by the time it came for the evening braai round the fire that night, it was one big happy family in mellow mood and high spirits.

**Minister Marais Steyn** made a speech and asked Liz and Richard if they would re-marry. He said that he and his wife had divorced and re-married and it was much better second time around. Loving looks between them confirmed this. Richard jumped up and said that he intended to take this advice seriously. He later used the advice by re marrying Liz a week later in Kasane, Botswana. He also said that he felt that South Africa was a wonderful, friendly place and he would tell this to everyone he met. Good PR for the country. Much verbal back slapping followed that night around the campfire.

Next morning at breakfast time, Liz and Richard were 'sleeping late'. Richard had been through to ask me for a glass of Vodka and guava juice for Liz.

**Chutzpah?** Marais Steyn came and parked himself next to me at the long breakfast table and said "Megan, you've got real chutzpah demanding that I get out of my sickbed to keep this appointment." My answer was a question "Do you regret it?" He laughed and said it was the most fun he'd had in a long time, and I deserved a big 'thank you' maybe even a medal. Which never happened. I wasn't holding my breath.

The stars who were the most fun were Ringo Starr, Mickey Dolenz and Davy Jones. So funny with their Brit humour, they had everyone in stitches. Mickey was meant to play some funny tennis with his rubber (bendy) tennis racquet. But forgot it at home.

Eventually they were all gone except for Liz and Richard who had been invited by Sol to stay on at Chobe. I had them delivered, by the same Government plane, safely back to Chobe with Liz's two trunks of clothes.

She had brought on the South African trip, six trunks, including 120 T-shirts. She kept one filing box listing their contents and one for her three jewellery boxes, kept in the hotel safe. I was amazed at her efficiency and discipline, keeping tabs on each item like an office filing system. She also

## My Life, a Roller Coaster Ride

kept a file of what she wore and when, to avoid the society sin of wearing the same outfit twice to the same audience.

A few days later, I received a phone request from Richard in Botswana for a set of Encyclopaedia Brittanica. I doubt if I sent all ten volumes. Then an invitation by phone to join them at Kasane where they would be married. Sadly, I had to refuse. I couldn't make it as I was too busy putting out financial fires. I regret my decision.

It would have been fitting end to an amazing two month experience of a lifetime.

**About the event.** I was impressed that Liz and Richard were kind and considerate to our staff and the hotel staff. Called them all by name and asked about their lives and families.

Having spent huge amounts of money on four full time security men, I was shocked and amused to find out that these highly visible celebrities enjoyed devising a cunning plan to escape from their suites, one night, and went down the Landdrost fire escape and took a taxi to Hillbrow where they gorged themselves on Hamburgers and Kentucky Fried Chicken. Unrecognised.

One of the visitors I welcomed to the Celebrity VIP room was impresario, Brian Mills who knew them all. He had created various singing stars such as Engelbert Humperdink and Gilbert O'Sullivan. A wonderfully warm and amusing man. He was valuable to us in keeping them all amused and in line.

When I was informed by the Landdrost manager that Liz and Richard were ordering (at my expense) Dom Perignon champagne for the VIP lounge, I instructed the hotel to deliver Here XV11 SA sparkling wine instead. They did this and received no complaints.

It was quite hard to keep up the image I presented knowing that the cash flow was getting tighter by the second. But the SA honour amongst the visiting VIP's went undamaged to the end.

In the long waiting time at the official opening, I had the opportunity to get acquainted with State President Nico Diederichs. He mentioned that he was interested in buying a holiday property on the Vaal River. I had mentioned that I had a house the Vaal on the sought-after 'Bend' which is precisely where he wanted to invest.

I later did a little research, found a few houses which I thought suitable and connected the State President with my friend, Estate Agent, Tony Chase to take the deal through. Within a few months Diederichs bought

## 4. Megan Carr Promotions

the property and wrote thanking me for my trouble.

A few weeks later in November 1975, I received an invitation from him, personally notated and signed, inviting me to his presentation, receiving the Freedom of the City of Johannesburg. I regretfully had to decline because I was going at Sol's invitation, to Mauritius for the opening of the St. Geran hotel. I did weigh up the two options for a few moments!

**20-20 Hindsight vision after Celebrity Tennis.** It was an ambitious notion to tackle this event. I had a staff of eleven. All good at their promotion and PR jobs, but proved themselves exceptional in managing this giant of an undertaking, with flair, intelligence and high good spirits. I suppose that the opportunity could be considered exceptional in anyone's lifetime. They all proved to me, and to themselves, how one can stretch to meet any occasion. I was proud of every one of them.

**The Sunday Afrikaans Newspaper *Rapport*,** made a very nice gesture after it was all over. They felt that the press, whilst benefiting from boosted readership, had given me a hard time and wanted to make amends. They admitted that they, too, had milked the event and star cast dry and had circulation numbers to prove it. Everyone in South Africa seemed to know all the details of the dual celebrity event.

I ended up with nine fat albums of press clippings. The two renegade air ticket sponsors told me they regretted not being on this bandwagon of unprecedented intense press coverage. They wished that they had shared the attention. Strangers asked me for my autograph.

**October 1975.** *Rapport* Sunday Newspaper published a full page devoted to the event covering me and my magnificent staff. They sent reporter Eddie Botha and photographer Hoffie Hofmeister to our Sandton City offices to report the story. ( See page 196).

I am very proud of this press story and kept the pictures they took of my staff beavering away with mopping up details whilst knowing that I would have to make drastic cuts to the business in my reduced financial circumstances. They were fabulous and many still keep contact to this day and talk about the surreal two months of Celebrity Tennis.

The one big thing they all remember was the good times and camaraderie of our office family.

**Business rescue.** Picking up the pieces after Celebrity Tennis. December 1975, I gathered the staff together and broke the news that the company was almost bankrupt and that I would have to do a Business Rescue to

# My Life, a Roller Coaster Ride

## All-star tennis promoter shrugs off big loss

By RAY SMUTS

MRS MEGAN CARR, the Johannesburg public relations executive

*SUNDAY TIMES Vaal Regional, October 12, 1975*

**Expenses**

On Tuesday she handed a cheque for R14 340 to Mrs Felicia Kentridge, chairman of Union Artists, the Black theatrical organisation.

Only the hotel accounts for the stars, the local agent's fee and newspaper advertising remained to be paid.

Mrs Carr said her original expenses, discounting the gala banquet which raised the money for Union Artists, had been calculated at R100 000, but the sum was now considerably less.

Four stars — Rod Steiger, Elke Sommer, Jill St John and Dyan Cannon — did not arrive giving a saving of about R12 000. A further saving was effected because Peter Lawford and Micky Dulenz, two of the stars at the tournament did not bring partners with them.

"The outstanding accounts should be settled within a month, and I think it will take me three months to recover my losses," she said.

**Investment**

Referring to poor attendances on the first day of the tennis at Ellis Park she said: "If one does not make total money at the gate it does not mean that something was a flop or a fiasco.

"The loss was a good investment. It has drawn more attention to me."

She had received several approaches from companies offering money for the stars to appear at various promotions.

Mrs Carr said she knew nothing of reports that actor Peter Lawford left a liquor bill of R450 behind and explained that a hospitality suite had been open 24 hours a day...

Mrs Megan Carr: "Another tournament probably next year."

# THE FIGHTING SPIRIT

This era of political uncertainty, financial anxiety and personal insecurity has claimed more than the usual quota of victims. CHLOE ROLFES talks to three potential losers who have all survived

PHOTOGRAPHS: STRUAN ROBERTSON

## DIÉ AGT MEISIES HET SWA GEKOU AAN TAYLOR-SIRI

ELIZABETH Taylor-sirkus het Carr en haar sewe mooi dippe laat sweet. Daar is on haar span hap te groot, ile het gehou en gekou ile dit kon insluk. Hier is meisies wat vir so baie aien het: Pippa Bell, Gail Shelagh Gilbert, Megan ndsay Swan, Sally-Ann Sylvia Holder en Patricia Reunert.

Deu EDDIE B Foto's: H HOFMEI

Pippa Bell, Gail Lieberz, Shelagh Gilbert, Lindsay Swan, Sally Ann Hotson, Sylvia Holder, Trisha Reunert, Me at my desk. Missing: Di Anderson, David Frost, Chen Sam, Caz Steyn.

## 4. Megan Carr Promotions

save complete collapse. We all hoped that MCP would soon resume and carry on as before. Wishful thinking.

That farewell was one of the hardest days I can remember in my life. All the harder because each one was so generous and understanding. Some even offered to stay on working for a while, at no salary. But it was almost Christmas. We all needed a rest and fresh ideas for the future.

Before closing-up shop for four weeks and trying not to feel sorry for myself. I did accept the help of Shelagh and David to sort out the accounting and who to pay what in which order. They banked outstanding fees, including from three current permanent clients, who, thankfully, continued with me.

I had been well advised by Mr. Len Hack, to pay the 'little guys' immediately, and in full, and negotiate the debts of the ones who could afford to compromise being paid immediately 50 cents in the Rand or settle in full over 12 months. We had the funds for this plan. It worked and I was saved. If it had been done through Celebrity Sport cc, I could have simply walked away. And shame on me. My clear conscience came at a price for me and the children.

And 'I told you so' from my father. We had to pull in our belts and soldier on. Carole later commented that she remembered seeing only a litre of milk in the fridge, usually fully stocked.

One anxious creditor sent a Sheriff of the Court to attach my leather lounge suite to pay quite a small debt. I paid him and got it back same day, but not before the children returned from school. It was very embarrassing

**1975. 14 October.** Following a month of highs and lows, I received a letter from Councillor John Tyers, Mayor of Cape Town, which read.

> *Firstly, may I congratulate you on your enterprise in arranging for the stars to visit South Africa. My wife and I were pleased to have the opportunity of meeting Miss Taylor and Mr. Burton.*

He went on to say he would like to invite them to visit Cape Town in the future and to keep him, posted on this possibility.

I later received an invitation to visit him in Cape Town, which I did.

I was presented with a desktop medallion. Size 6cm in diameter by 1cm deep, heavy in its little box. Presented as a token of Cape Town's recognition for bringing eleven international film and music stars to South Africa despite the universal Equity Ban on all Show Business professionals visiting South Africa. He said that It was just what the country needed at

# My Life, a Roller Coaster Ride

that pessimistic political time.

I was honoured and very moved by this thoughtful gesture. I accepted with somewhat emotional thanks. It was exactly what I needed at that time.

The medallion made a decorative paperweight to show off on my desk.

( see Appendix for full letter)

**Invitation to Mauritius.** In November, Sol invited 150 special guests to the opening of his new St. Geran Hotel in Mauritius. I was honoured to be included in this exclusive mix. Dirk Mudge still important in Southwest Africa, Lucas Mangope – associated with Sol in Bophutatswana and Sun City, bankers, theatre and sports personalities, and a large contingent of press.

When a cancellation came up at the last minute, Adele asked me if I knew anyone suitable to fill the last-minute gap. It was my absolute pleasure to offer it to my Italian dentist Dario Ferri and partner. The one who took me for an air flip when my tooth abscess was hurting. Dario accepted, cancelled a week's dental appointments, and blended nicely into the elegant crowd.

The event was superbly organised by Adele Lucas. It was a sumptuous four-day holiday with rounds of non-stop entertainment.

The timing was right for me, ready to relax after running my exhausting two-month Celebrity Tennis.

When I went to settle my account on leaving – all I had to pay for was my skiing lesson with Dierdre Barnard who helped fulfil my waterskiing desire to jump off on one ski out of knee-deep water – which had always eluded me.

**Gotcha.** Anyway – back to Louis Luyt, also Sol's guest at the St. Geran, whom I had gladly written out of my life.

Sitting at lunch with press friends Stephen Mulholland, Kate and Marshall Lee, Adele and Bob Lucas and others, we noticed an awkward looking man approaching across the open terrace. He addressed me in Afrikaans. "Mevrou Carr, Louis Luyt wil et jou praat" I replied, "Jammer, nie, ek eet my kos". The poor man, everyone watching, sloped off back to his master. Soon, the poor guy re-sloped back and said, "Louis Luyt would very much like you to join him for a liqueur after your lunch".

By then we were all curious. I replied, "Thank you, yes I will join

## 4. Megan Carr Promotions

him". When I did eventually join Louis, his first words were, "You don't like me do you?"

I then suggested that an apology would be in order as a good start to help set things right.

To his credit he did so very sincerely, and it put a band-aid on the old niggling *Die Transvaler* incident which was quickly set aside in all the merriment of the moment.

Mauritius measured up to all the hype and advertising. What a delightful place to visit with its turquoise warm, calm sea and interesting islands.

**Fair Lady.** November 1975. A month later, Chloe Rolfes did a story, 'The Fighting Spirit' about three businesswomen who had survived difficult times in their personal and business lives. They recognised my overcoming the severe bump in my business journey (See page 196).

Now, in 2024, looking at the Chloe Rolfes caption – nothing much has changed in politics and peoples' circumstances forty-eight years later.

**1975 Creative Circle and the Loeries.** Much of my business was linked with advertising and marketing campaigns. I was therefore asked to sit on the Steering Committee for the Creative Circle. My Secretary Kathy Stelling attended as Committee Secretary.

More than creative interaction. the aim was to inspire creativity and relevance in brand communication.in the advertising industry. The Creative Circle Steering Committee proposed to set up an annual Advertising Excellence Award. Originally 'The Occay Awards'

**The Loeries.** The objective of Creative Circle was to integrate the industry to keep up to speed with local and world trends. At this time, it is carried throughout Africa. To this end we would have monthly events, workshops and theme get-togethers, cross referencing and sharing ideas and ideals. Each monthly meeting would have a specialist guest speaker or visiting entertainer.

Two of the many notable entertainers were the BBC Quiz panellist and Comedian (*My Word* and *My Music*), Frank Muir, who was visiting South Africa with his wife, Polly, on a book-signing tour. Another was the famous comedienne, Joyce Grenfell.

One year we created a workshop competition. We set up twelve teams of four mixing top creative directors, copywriters, photographers and designers – each from a different agency per team. The challenge was to design an advert for a charity.

# My Life, a Roller Coaster Ride

I presented them with a list of twenty charities to choose from. I also had the job of securing the free ad space from one of the newspapers. This was easy, as good for the chosen newspaper. They were always happy to ingratiate themselves with Advertising Agencies, their main source of revenue.

The resulting entries were wildly creative and unusual. Some licence taken because they were not working for a paying client or representing their own Agency as the team members were simply demonstrating their own personal talents, well out of their comfort zones.

**The winner.** A tabloid sized Charity Advert. A parrot's cage with a 'dead' parrot lying on its back, feet in the air, next to a frail old woman, in a sparsely furnished room, weeping into her large white handkerchief as she gazes out of a window with a dismal grey view (a dismal view picture stuck onto the inward facing side of the glass). The Caption 'I lost my best friend today'. The charity was 'The Senior Citizens Benevolent Fund'. Bold charity banking details displayed underneath.

**The production.** The winning team had us in stitches as they regaled us, at our next monthly luncheon, with a description of their antics, setting up the 'dead parrot'.

CREATIVE CIRCLE STEERING COMMITTEE. The start of what is now The Loerie Awards For Advertising Excellence

## 4. Megan Carr Promotions

Firstly, they rented a parrot in a cage. They then consulted a Vet to find out how to sedate the poor thing without harming it. They drew straws for who would handle this as none of the team wanted the job. Whilst the two shortest straws were attending to this, the other two set up the bleak-looking room and weeping woman.

They had approached the local Retirement Village for the elderly 'model' dressed in her own homely clothes. (They paid a modelling fee). There were many volunteers for this.

Once the bedroom scene was set, the other two administered the bird sedative and set the snoozing bird on its back on a blob of Press Stick on the floor of the cage.

They couldn't get the legs to stay up in the air to their styling requirements, so they shortened two kebab sticks and glued them to the legs, now facing nicely upwards as required. The kebab sticks were camouflaged, and the lot pressed into the Press Stick on the cage floor, hidden under the wing feathers. They had to work fast before the bird woke up. Hasty photos taken and developed. The ad was ready. The groggy bird was returned to the Pet Shop with the agreed fee. The elderly model was paid her fee and returned home to her envious friends and a good story to tell.

The tear-jerking professional advert was duly seen by thousands of *Sunday Times* readers and the money poured into the Senior Citizens Benevolent fund.

**Our first awards were held at the Carlton Hotel.** We brought out the famous advertising personality, Bill Bernbach, to be Judge. Bill made his name using innovative ideas such as the AVIS message 'We Try Harder', the Rye bread ad 'You don't have to be Jewish' (to enjoy rye bread). Almost challenging, to give them a try.

**A scare.** In the middle of the Awards Banquet, I was called to the phone by the Carlton hotel Desk Clerk.

My heart dropped as I had been worried by reports that several South African soldiers had been injured in an attack on 'The Border' where Tony was based. I picked up the phone and a stranger asked, 'Will you take a reverse charge call?' Relief was instant as I knew that bad news would not come in a reversed charge call.

Tony, knowing I would be worried, was there on the line.

## 22. 1976. Pivotal Person: John Lawley

October of that year: "There is someone you just have to meet" she said. "No Diane, I'm far too busy to start dating. And I'm over relationships. Maybe some other time, in the new year. Maybe?"

"Actually, you don't have a choice. You will meet him when you come over for dinner on Friday. It's not a date, just a dinner guest. There will be eight of us. If he doesn't appeal to you, or you to him, nothing is lost, or gained, and nobody will be any the wiser. That's final."

After the usual frenetic business week, Friday arrived. Till then, I hadn't given it another thought. However, getting dressed for dinner, I found myself taking extra care with my hair and makeup and pondered between the black or pink dress and even feeling a little apprehensive.

I had only dated two men seriously since my divorce. Vic and Ian.

When I arrived at dinner, I counted only seven of us and felt relieved, thinking that Di and Brian had respected my wish not to be saddled with a blind date.

And then it happened. The door opened and in walked a six foot three blond blue-eyed bundle of energy, who was introduced to us all as 'John'

After introductions all round, he walked right over to take my hand and give me a little peck on the cheek. I managed to recover somewhat and joined in the dinner banter, all the while conscious of this handsome creature sitting right next to me. He was noisy and funny and perfect. I'd never felt anything like this before. Maybe my heartthrob cricketer, Denis Compton, in my teens.

The dinner party was a good one and went on for hours and hours. Guests started leaving. Di and Brian went off and made coffee. Eventually they went off to bed. John and I, still at the table, didn't want the evening to end. By then we were holding hands.

I was reminded of a song, 'Two sleepy people at dawn's early light and too much in love to say good night'. It was love at first sight.

At six in the morning, we crept out of Di and Brian's house. John followed me to my place for coffee and toast. It was Saturday and

## 4. Megan Carr Promotions

the children were still fast asleep. John then left as he had a business appointment at nine. We made plans for dinner that night. He had to go to his meeting unshaven, in his dinner suit of the night before.

That was early October. We saw each other every single day after that. Both John's and my businesses were time consuming with year-end craziness. Peter and Andy, still at school, had upcoming exams and activities to programme in. But we managed it all, somehow.

John's two children were in boarding schools and spent the holidays with him as his divorce was pending and his wife had already returned to Scotland.

As was our family custom, we spent weekdays in the Kambula home and weekends at the Vaal River house. John would join us there at the weekends. My children liked John. He was easy going and lots of fun. My children and John's two got on well. Life was good.

My mother reserved judgement as she said I shouldn't trust a Scotsman and he was far too good looking. She was a Scot. We all laughed at her joke.

John loved his music and had a big collection of LP records, as I did. When the children were safely tucked up in bed, we would put on a record and dance and enjoy a glass of wine. He liked Nina Simone and Francoise Hardy. I liked Perry Como and Ella Fitzgerald. But we both liked almost everything musical from classics to jazz. Not heavy metal.

Both in our early forties, we felt young and carefree and decided that after his divorce became final, we would marry. It was as simple as that.

**Boxing.** Surprisingly John had been the boxing light heavyweight champion of Scotland before coming to South Africa in 1967. It was his chosen sport and had a crooked nose to prove it. He was also a sought-after retailing boffin in his day job.

He was determined that I should get to know and enjoy boxing. I had my doubts, but love can make strange things happen.

There was a big fight coming up. Gerry Coetzee and *TapTap* Makathini. It would be outdoors at the Rand Stadium. The weather was still cool in the November evenings. John and his friend, Bill, came to pick me up. When we arrived at the stadium, John unloaded from the boot of his Mercedes, a huge suitcase and a four-litre vacuum flask which had a carrying handle. Bill carried a basket of party snacks and cokes.

I asked, "What on earth is in the suitcase. Surely, we aren't staying the night?" John laughed and said: "Wait and see". We were shown to very good seats near the ring. John had reserved a block of twenty seats in two rows of ten. Seventeen of his friends and colleagues were already there with us sitting in the centre seats of the front ten.

He introduced me to those I didn't already know, and the party began. John brushed aside the teasing as he opened the suitcase, bringing out two fat cushions and a warm tartan rug. Many hoots of laughter to be heard. On my seat he put the two cushions, one on the seat and one at my back and covered my knees to keep me warm from the cool evening breeze. I loved the care and attention and went all soppy at his thoughtfulness and complete lack of inhibition in front of his men friends.

Next, out of the basket, came twenty plastic Coke cups which were then filled with the contents of the air flask and some coca cola to camouflage the Gin.

The activity in the ring started with everyone standing to sing *Die Stem*. John's voice was the loudest among the loud in our group. The fighters were announced with the familiar "Ladeees and Gennelmen" and the fight began.

I was delegated to be *bookie* for our group. Given pen and paper already prepared with twenty names and a paper snack-bowl to collect the bets.

For me, the best part of the evening was the interaction of the audience heckling and cheering with many a smart or funny remark heard above the general hum.

Gerry Coetzee won after a good fight. The bets were worked out and paid and we packed up and left the stadium to go directly to the Vaal River house for the weekend.

The romance blossomed over the next two months despite both of us having heavy year-end work commitments. Then off to the Vaal with my children and John's children for the Christmas holidays. John and I commuting to Johannesburg for business.

We had a very good Stereo sound system and took along our collection of LP's, so the house was always filled with music to satisfy the two generations. John often arrived home with a new LP. Tony had been fanatical about music since a very young age. He adored the music-loving John and they vied with each other *ad infinitum* on the merits or otherwise of the current artists and groups. The other five children joined in, and the music played on.

The only thing to upset the blissful applecart was John's occasional migraines. At these times, the music was kept to relaxing and quiet tones.

Just before Christmas, I had a call from one of John's colleagues telling

## 4. Megan Carr Promotions

me that John had had a hyperventilation episode at the office and had to get treatment at hospital Emergency, where he was admitted for observation.

John had listed me as his next of kin. I was asked to visit the hospital doctor looking after him. He showed me an ultrasound plate which showed that John had a serious Hiatus Hernia in his upper digestive system which would require surgery.

It was hard to think of this healthy, energetic giant of a man having any health problem. I knew he always had Eno's handy after rich food which didn't agree with him, but this seemed extreme.

The Doctor and John agreed that surgery could wait until after Christmas but not after New Year. Surgery was scheduled for 27th December.

Christmas was a jolly affair with all our families, including my parents also in residence at their middle house.

My father was Father Christmas by family tradition and the children seemed unconcerned by the prospect of John going in for surgery. He looked so healthy; he would surely be fine.

Our whirlwind romance was almost three months old. Our engagement was private and only known to our families.

The time for reality came. The four children stayed at the Vaal house with my mother caring for them. I moved back to Sandown to be there for John in hospital.

The surgery for this procedure is brutal. Side ribs opened and spread open for front upper chest access to the hernia. After surgery I walked John and his draining contraption on wheels up and down the corridors which seemed cruel punishment after such serious surgery. We would joke about his interesting rear view with the back-tied backside-revealing gown.

After a few days I noticed John starting to drag his left foot. I reported this to the surgeon who thought it might just be post operative trauma. I persisted and they agreed to check it.

New Year had come and gone. I was called in for a meeting with two senior physicians. I was shown two MRI pictures. These were of John's head. It revealed a brain tumour. Not sure if it was benign or malignant which would require close monitoring. Meanwhile he had to recover from his hernia surgery.

After a month they scheduled a left-brain biopsy. No warnings of what this entailed except that it would be invasive, investigative brain surgery. 'It will take just a few hours' they said.

A friend, Dave Marcus, came to visit me on a business project, and then sat with me at home while I waited, and waited. It was the longest six hours I can remember.

During surgery they had decided to remove the entire tumour. He was in Milpark intensive care for a week.

I took John to my home to nurse him back to health. Being a left-brain procedure, he had lost his power of speech, and we had to make notes to communicate. Soon he was walking again and having speech and physical therapy. We both found it very frustrating trying to cope with one-sided conversation.

In February, I had to return to the office. All the children were back at school. I had my housekeeper, Gracie, take care of John and help him if he fumbled with small things like holding a cup of tea or playing his beloved records. He couldn't concentrate long enough to read.

One day I received a call from Gracie. She said John had gone missing from the house and she couldn't find him. I told her to go up the road and wait outside Sandton City in case he had gone shopping. He couldn't talk and might get lost. I told her to keep out of his sight, but not let him out of her sight. He had to feel independent.

Sure enough, John, still dragging his left foot, came shambling out of Sandton City with a package under his arm. Gracie didn't let him see her and followed him home.

When I arrived home that evening, John welcomed me with a hug and kiss. Less handsome, with his shaven head, stapled left side C wound

Melanie Lawley.

Crystal and Danny Lawley 2019.

## 4. Megan Carr Promotions

covered with a transparent plaster, but with that irresistible, naughty smile. Perry Como had no chance. Proudly, he handed me a beautifully wrapped gift for our fourth month anniversary. I opened it to find the face of my favourite Perry Como smiling at me. The title of his new album was *And I Love You So*. We played it and held hands after a candle-lit dinner. For us, music was the food of love...playing on.

Late in February, when John started getting headaches again, further tests revealed that the cancerous tumour was back and that it had metastasised from the kidneys. The medical team debated the merits of removing one kidney. I asked them the big question – would he recover? Probably not, they thought. The speed at which the tumour had returned told the dreaded story.

John's children were aware of how ill their father was and accepted that he had to be in care and near to medical help. I contacted John's brother, Joe, in Scotland and put the kidney surgery question to him. We both agreed – no more surgery.

Within a week, John had slipped into a semi coma lying right there in my flat. When the convulsions started, I called the ambulance and got him back into Milpark Medi Clinic. It was March. His friend, John Irving, visited daily.

We were both with John when he died on Easter Sunday afternoon. I dreaded telling Daniel and Melanie.

Their mother, and John's family were in Scotland so I, the single mother of four, suddenly became the single mother of six. And running the business. The Scotland family agreed that Danny and Mel could remain with me in South Africa and finish their schooling. I made the necessary funeral arrangements followed by John's Memorial for family and friends at my house.

Dozens of people, many unknown to me, arrived to pay respects. Raymond Ackerman and three Pick 'n Pay directors flew in from Cape Town for the memorial and to meet and console Dan and Mel. And to meet me. John's children stayed in South Africa for a further two years till Danny matriculated at Woodridge College where he did very well in Matric and even acted in a stage production of *Twelve Angry Men*. I made a special flying visit, to applaud him.

That was forty-four years ago. They have both been highly successful in their careers and kept in touch with us all. In fact, Danny and his wife Crystal decided to return from Hong Kong to retire in South Africa. Melanie

## My Life, a Roller Coaster Ride

has visited twice from her home in Scotland. They call me their Stepmom.

They still have their Scottish accents peppered with South Africanisms. Danny and Crystal travelled to Hermanus to attend my 90th birthday party in April 2022.

**Carole Carr and Tony Webber.** In the busy year of 1977, Carole (19), was invited to sail to Montevideo, Uruguay on a raft built on oil drums, by Tony Webber, self-styled 'doctor' of Anthropology. A man with a big dream. He had been inspired by Thor Heyerdahl's Kon Tiki expedition, which had drifted across the Pacific, in 1947. Tony Webber wanted to be Thor Heyerdahl, leader of the raft crew. In the press, Tony Webber was later called the 'Walter Mitty of the *Apelila* saga'.

He was a good salesman. Secretary, Carole Carr, had joined him for admin support. They secured many sponsorships in cash and kind. Tony built a huge raft with two sails, basic living accommodation and essential equipment. Carole was invited to join the expedition as crew. She had been introduced to him by my previous associate, Jimmy Thomas.

**Sailor Tony and Walter Mitty.** The aim was to 'drift' across the Atlantic to Montevideo, Uruguay, South America.

After months of work and before sailing date, Carole was becoming disturbed by frightening tales of 100-foot waves along the route, and Tony's limited seagoing experience. She wisely decided to withdraw from

The *Sunday Times* reporter, Ric Wilson, interviewed and photographed Carole Carr (above) About the *Apelila* Expedition. 1978.

## 4. Megan Carr Promotions

the expedition. Tony, however, was confident that it was perfectly feasible and finally launched from Walvis Bay and headed out to sea.

*Sunday Times* reported, 'Tony Webber was besotted with Kon Tiki and obsessed by becoming famous in a similar attempt'.

Finally The *Apelila* foundered 200 kilometres from Walvis Bay, off the Skeleton Coast, and had to be towed back into harbour, at considerable expense, by an SAR&H Tug.

The big dream was washed up, as was his bank balance. He left the country. Carole returned to her career in film.

**1976. Green Oaks.** Robin Binckes invited me to become an Associate in his Promotions and PR company, Green Oaks. I was still suffering from my tennis losses and given up my Sandton City 15th floor offices. I retained a skeleton staff on the 4th floor of Sandton City to service my few regular clients. My joining up with Robin gave me a steady retainer income to carry on with

Green Oaks' biggest client was Ian Munro, MD of OK Hyperamas. A handsome and charming man on a mission. He knew exactly what he wanted. He had the added gift of trusting us to get on with the job of drawing people into his O.K. Hyperamas. His only Hyper at that time in Edenvale.

Green Oaks MD, Robin Binckes was a gifted promoter and Public Relations Consultant. We liked and respected each other and worked well together. In addition, he had never once complained about my absences for John's illness and death. I owed him for this and plunged into the work at hand.

Robin had come up with the concept of Hyperama Heydays with amazing promotions and price specials. He was a born showman and entertainer, and he injected this into his clients' promotions. Sometimes, a little over the top. The client always played along with Robin, and the Heydays promotion was good enough in visibility and turnover to carry on for 43 years through many company transitions through House and Home and Checkers Superstores.

The Hypermarket situation at that time was that Pick 'n Pay had SA's first Hypermarket in Boksburg and the OK had followed with one Hyperama in Durban. The competition between the two business competitors, was tangible.

Another interesting Green Oaks client was the Parker Brothers' Monopoly board game client, which he handed over to me to promote.

## My Life, a Roller Coaster Ride

**Monopoly.** How to promote a board game? Get some prominent people to play it in public. I had been working with Sol Kerzner, Ian Munro and just met Raymond Ackerman.

I set up a Monopoly Challenge Match with the three of them plus the new Wits Rag Queen, in the foyer of The Llandrost Hotel, with Sol's usual cooperation and the *Sunday Times* as exclusive media sponsor. I also asked actor, Bruce Miller, to do the game commentary for the invited audience, watching from scaffold seating in the small auditorium.

I was amazed at the fierce competitive spirit which pervaded the game. It had become a personal vendetta between the three. Personal honour and reputations were at stake. In the end, it didn't matter who won as it became a wild overplaying and show-off affair, keeping the audience amused with smart heckling and repartee.

Prominent *Sunday Times* exposure gave the Monopoly client his product boost and the three men taken back to their youth, playing an ordinary home game. The Rag Queen easily kept up with the three business tycoons – not just a pretty face.

**Awards parties.** I learned from Robin that there is a time to be conservative and a time to be risqué. OK Hyperama had annual staff parties and prize giving's for rewarding staff performance.

Robin was in his element. Wives were always invited. A grand venue was mandatory. Everyone dressed up. Robin's wife always attended these occasions to help with the prize giving. Their marriage was one of those love stories that everyone admires.

The highly anticipated cabaret was always kept secret to the very last moment. The build-up to the cabaret was presented by Robin. Scantily dressed girls dancing and singing songs with staff names sprinkled in amongst the words.

One of the acts involved male staff members who could volunteer to come up on stage for a dare. Each man had to reduce his name to the first four letters. Peter would become e.g. Pete. Robin would be Robi.

Five bikini clad dancers positioned themselves in a circle facing outwards mid stage. The five men would be given a red lipstick. The music started, the girls performed sensuous, undulating dance moves and the men would then have to write their names anywhere on the girls' bodies.

The only rules were – they may not lift any bikini part, and their written names had to be legible. Not just random letters. Well – the hilarity ensuing was raucous because the undulating girls weren't that easy to reach. Some

## 4. Megan Carr Promotions

of the eager staffers fell flat on their faces as the girls moved away. After about ten minutes, one would finally get his name written and win a fabulous prize of a weekend holiday for two.

After this in-house cabaret and finger supper, the dancing started. Live band. Lots of champagne.

Suddenly there was an eerie quietness in the room. Chatter had ceased and everyone's eyes were on a couple smooching in a dark corner of the dance floor. It was Robin and Glenda Kemp the famous stripper, wearing a thong and two stars. Shock as Mr. Faithful Husband was 'doing the dirty' on his much-loved wife. Some of the secretaries tried to lure *Mrs. B* away on some pretext to spare her embarrassment.

**Robin was shameless.** His hands were all over Glenda. The Hyperama MD Ian Monro looked very annoyed and agitated and eventually sent a minion onto the dance floor to drag Robin away.

At this moment, on cue, the band struck up and Glenda Kemp, now dressed, came back onto the stage and did her famous Strip act with her pet python 'Oupa'. Relief was tangible that practical joker Robin was having us on. Glenda played it up and kept making a move on him as he gathered his wife into his arms, and they all laughed at the joke.

**Back to MCP.** My eighteen months with Robin at Green Oaks were an interesting, and timely, interlude in my life. But I soon found I needed to move on. I was accustomed to my own space and own way of doing things and decided to reopen MCP. Instead of returning to Sandton City offices, I converted rooms in my Sandown house, reclaimed from Jimmy Thomas, into two offices and set up with my marvellous new secretary Jane Evans.

**1979. The Fiat Mirafiori.** At this right moment for me, Jimmy Thomas, ex Journalist and ex Manager of Group Editors invited me to join him and his partner Vic Hanna in the grand launch of the Fiat Mirafiori. For this event, Fiat had invited the Italian film star Gina Lollobrigida to S.A. to open the show. My job was to organise the launch, invite the press and special guests, and to 'manage' the star. This time I did not handle the publicity. That was Jimmy and Vic's portfolio.

It started off with a bump. I had booked Gina and her party into the President Hotel. I knew the Hotel manager, Bruno Corte, from Cabana Beach Hotel. In fact, I knew him better than he liked when I heard that he had organised a Press Conference to be held a few hours later in the hotel foyer on Gina's arrival.

# My Life, a Roller Coaster Ride

**Scooper scooped.** This was unprofessional as his press would have scooped the Fiat press conference scheduled for a few hours later after they had settled in their suites and freshened up. I have my sources as a press friend phoned me from the airport and warned me about Bruno Corte's plan.

Instead of the car carrying Gina and her cousin/companion Guido Lollobrigida, pulling up outside the main entrance to the hotel, I had someone guide the driver to the garage entrance and stop at the second-floor garage lift, where they sneaked Gina to her suite skipping the party ready waiting downstairs. Gina thought it was great fun. Bruno was furious.

Although Gina regarded herself as something of a princess, she was professional and was also friendly and helpful behind the scenes. She took her obligations seriously and made herself available for all press interviews including a TV interview on SATV, only two years old as a full service, at that time, and falling over themselves to have this famous star to interview.

The Apartheid Equity ban had us starved for international film celebrities.

Getting her to Broadcast house in Auckland Park, Carole (21) kindly assisted me, driving us to the door to save the parking walk. Gina tapped Carole on the shoulder and said "It should be you having this interview,

**The M.D of Fiat, S.A. and I look on as Gina is interviewed by SABC's Willy Camillieri.**

## 4. Megan Carr Promotions

you are beautiful". I was touched and impressed, Carole blushed, and then the 'princess' and I stepped out of the car and she royal *highnessed* to the studio to do her rehearsed Mirafiori punt. In this promotion she was also representing Italy.

Incidentally, Jimmy had organised a lunch party with one of the Afrikaans newspapers. She was all dressed up, they had arrived in safari outfits, not quite combs in their socks, so to speak. She took one look at them joking around the bar, smoking and with beers in their hands. She turned on her heel and demanded that Jimmy take her back to her hotel. Still the princess, we felt she was not wrong to let them know they had disrespected her and who she represented. The editor offered an embarrassed apology.

Gina's hobby was photography. And very good at it. I spoke to Adele about setting up an exhibition for her collection which she did. Gina was like a child with excitement. Although there were only about 30 framed photos on show, the elegant crowd showed their appreciation and Gina's thanks were sincere in very excellent Italian-English. After all, she had become famous for her starring role in the English film *Buona Sera Mrs. Campbell*.

**Back alley car art.** A funny thing happened which impacted my young ones in the school lift.

Fiat had organised a car-art competition. The winning artist's theme painted all over a brand-new Fiat Mirafiori, was a back alley in Hillbrow. Rubbish boxes with dirt spilling out, rats climbing all over them. Really disgusting.

As part of the promotion, I had the use of this painted up car at that time. The children made me unload them well away from the school gate to save them embarrassment and teasing.

# My Life, a Roller Coaster Ride

## 23. Pivotal Person Raymond Ackerman

Because of John Lawley's earlier association on the main Board of Pick 'n Pay, Raymond Ackerman and a few directors had flown to Johannesburg for John's memorial service.

Raymond asked me many questions about my business, and I told him of my association with Green Oaks and the OK Hyperama. When I mentioned the 'Hyperama Heydays' promotions, he said that it was hurting Pick 'n Pay and immediately invited me to join his company. I turned him down as it was not appropriate at that time in my life.

I also said that I did not wish to join any big company but would consider acting as Promotions Consultant when the time was right for me. He said that when that time came, I should call him.

I didn't have to. Raymond called me regularly almost weekly to enquire after John's two children and always asked if I was ready to consult for his new Hypermarkets which were almost ready to expand from one only in Boksburg and which, by the way, John Lawley had been instrumental in developing.

Later that year, 1977, after leaving Green Oaks, I told him I was ready to consider his offer.

Raymond's secretary, Diana, booked an airflight to Cape Town and accommodation for my visit to attend the opening of his second Hypermarket in Brackenfell, Cape.

Raymond Ackerman. Pivotal person in my life 1977 – 1988. Pick 'n Pay.

## 4. Megan Carr Promotions

Next morning, we met in his office where he outlined the job of Promotions Consultant for Brackenfell Hyper and the launch of two more Hypers in Bloemfontein and Durban in the final stages of completion. He was very charming and very persuasive. My arm was easily twisted as I was now free and ready for it. He signed me up and doubled the fee I suggested as he said I didn't understand how much I would be letting myself in for.

He was right – as he always was. For the following ten years I spent alternate weeks on flying visits to various Hypers.

**The Pick 'n Pay association all started for me with John Lawley.**
John's brain tumour had reappeared, and he was lying, semiconscious, in my Kambula flat in Sandown, when I received a call from Raymond Ackerman asking to speak to John. When I explained that John could no longer speak, he asked me to give him a message. Please tell him, "Raymond would like to thank him for all he had done in getting Pick 'n Pay established. His energy and commitment were implicit in its early success". Raymond then asked me to keep him informed on John's condition.

When I passed on the exact message to John, he broke out in a big smile which stayed on his face as he lapsed back, semiconscious.

Less than a week later, on Easter Sunday, he died. His good friend, John Irving, and I were with him, and we had to lean on each other for comfort at the sad loss of this high energy special man, friend and life partner. I phoned Raymond to tell him.

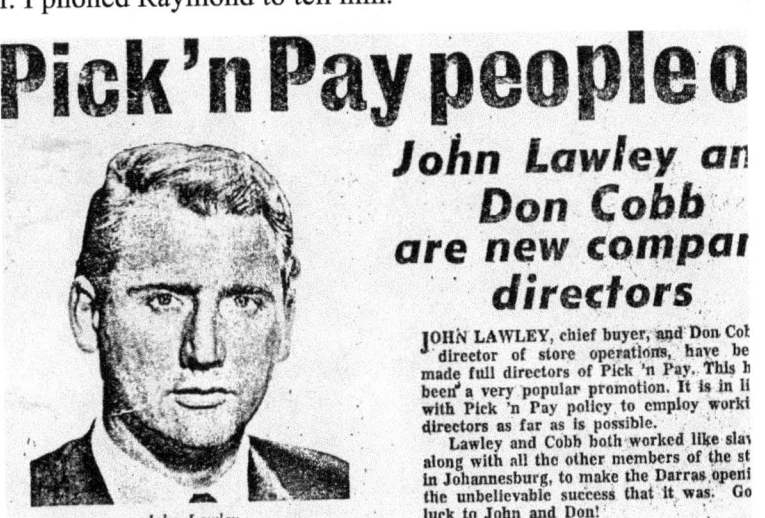

Pick 'n Pay people o

John Lawley an
Don Cobb
are new compar
directors

JOHN LAWLEY, chief buyer, and Don Cob director of store operations, have be made full directors of Pick 'n Pay. This h been a very popular promotion. It is in li with Pick 'n Pay policy to employ worki directors as far as is possible.
Lawley and Cobb both worked like sla\ along with all the other members of the st in Johannesburg, to make the Darras openi the unbelievable success that it was. Go luck to John and Don!

John Lawley

## My Life, a Roller Coaster Ride

John had been a full director on the Board of Pick 'n Pay and been responsible for instituting its Buying Policy from 1967 when four Pick 'n Pay stores were first acquired from Jack Goldin, who later started Clicks.

However, by the time he died, ten years later, he had moved on.

Not only did I land this outstanding retail account, but it led me into the deeper side of the retail trade. For the next nine years. I joined in the fortnightly promotion meetings, with all Hyper heads and Department Managers, learning about buying, selling, pricing, product placement and incentive policies.

How independently run were grocery marketing and promotion from hard products such as Clothing, DIY, Sporting Goods and Appliances.

By the end of 1978, I was thrown into planning the openings of the next two Hypers in Bloemfontein and Durban. I was given a free hand in how I implemented these. They liked novel ideas – my forté.

No such old gimmicks as throwing thousands of one Rand notes from helicopters causing chaos and injuries in the ensuing bunfights.

**The Villagers.** For initial crowd-pulling promotions, I brought in regular visits from favourite cast members of the TV Series, *The Villagers*, all the rage at the time.

Gordon Mulholland who played Hilton McRae mine manager, Stuart Brown who played Chesa Labuschagne, the cheeky barman.

Many people were so invested in the TV Villagers characters, that they seemed real. For example, when we were promoting a health week, we set

Clive Scott who played the comical fool, Ted Dixon.

## 4. Megan Carr Promotions

up a gym area highlighting exercise equipment. We had Gordon Mulholland signing autographs as he peddled an exercise cycle on its stand. One woman rushed up to him begging him, "Mr. McRae, don't pedal so fast. You might have another heart attack," as had happened to him on TV.

**Bloemfontein Hypermarket.** My first Hyper launch, Bloemfontein Hyper, was somewhat different for me. It was 90% Afrikaans in staffing, signage and shopper profile. In everything we did, I felt it important that the printed message was always accurate. I engaged the services of a Professor of languages at the Bloemfontein University to approve all signage and launch press releases.

One traffic sign which amused me 'Speed Humps' on the roads 'Vaarthoeppels'!

Driving them to the Bloemfontein airport after a two-day promotion, we had stopped at a red robot when a car drew up alongside us and the driver shouted to Clive "Hey Ted, what happened to the baby tortoise?" (on TV the week before). His quick answer was "I ate it, I thought it was a meat pie". Probably ruined her day.

**Durban Hypermarket opening.** A month after Bloemfontein opening, the Hypermarket team and Raymond Ackerman, called me into a special planning meeting. This time I had to come up with something extra special for the Durban Hypermarket.

Clive Scott (Ted Dixon of The Villagers) Aubrey Zelinsky, GM of the Durban Hyper.

Why special? Durban had stiff competition from the new OK Hyperama, Game Stores and their own Regional Super Stores, run by the dynamic Alan Gardiner.

I already knew Alan socially as he was John Lawley's good friend, and we had visited the Gardiners in Natal for a few days en route to our holiday weekend at the Elangeni Hotel.

I held a brainstorming session with colleagues Jimmy Thomas and Vic Hanna. We came up with the idea of giving the proposed Hyper a character of its own. 'The Hyper by the Sea'.

# My Life, a Roller Coaster Ride

Above: Martin Rosin, Buyer, Aubrey Zelinsky Hyper by the Sea General Manager), Raymond Ackerman and (behind Raymond) is (tall) René de Wet.

Left: No posters allowed in Randburg, so we made walking smiley posters.

Right: Unique advertising in the 70's. The sails of the tourist yacht sang out the Hypermarket message.

Below: Article and Invite.

# 4. Megan Carr Promotions

Up to that date, Hypermarkets were simply massive soulless grey warehouses with 42 000 items at mass marketing ultra-low prices. We went wild with dozens of ideas, as Think Tanks do, tempering them down to a captivating Nautical theme.

Once approved by management, and working with Dave Buirski, the Hyper Ad Agency G.M, our novel nautical theme was well executed by the talented advertising team.

We put a naval captain's cap on the H of Hypermarket. We dressed the staff in sailor collars on their T-shirts. They cut a fishing boat in half and put it against the fish counter to display the fish on ice. Staff quarters became 'Crew Quarters'. Flags in the parking lot all featured the new branding, The ceiling banners and streamers were variations on the nautical theme.

No regular store was allowed to have prices lower than the Hypers.

My job was to get feet through the doors on opening day and thereafter. The advertising, promotions and creative merchandising did the rest.

On launch day and thereafter, in Durban, I had organised for the *SS Impala* Tourist sailing boat to wear new sails with our signage 'Hyper by the Sea', which we'd had manufactured in Hong Kong. This pleasure boat sailed up and down the coast with tourists.

The afternoon before the public opening, I had the Press and special guests, partying on that boat, sailing around the Durban Harbour.

Raymond, his directors and managers all wore 'Hyper by the Sea' T shirts. The Press Kit hand-outs comprised Hyper T shirts, kids' plastic life belts, Alka Seltzer as a hangover remedy, energy bar, and of course the Press Release with a photo of Raymond Ackerman with his 'Welcome Aboard' message, all in a bag labelled 'Hyper by the Sea Survival Kit.'

Carole accompanied the photographer in a helicopter taking pictures of the Press Party on the yacht.

## My Life, a Roller Coaster Ride

The nautical theme injected such new energy into the entire company that they decided, in future, to use apt themes for all their Hypers.

In following years, The Vanderbijlpark Hyper became the 'Hyper by the River' with a boating theme, The Norwood Hyper in Gardens, became 'Hyper in the Gardens' with a flower theme.

However, the real public drawcard was always price, a massive selection of products and bargains.

With a few thousand people waiting to get in as the doors opened, the front page of the *Daily News* cartoonist Bob Connolly, next day read, 'Tidal Wave at Hyper by the Sea'.

The *Daily News* front page picture, with the boat and group photo, and headline read 'We do like to be beside the seaside'

Launching Durban's Hyper by the Sea aboard the good ship 'Impala' as it sailed past, loaded with spectators. The General Manager Aubrey Zelinsky drew the line at being called 'Captain Zee'. I don't know why as he was a mischievous G.M.

**Naughty boy.** Once, in a Board Meeting, Aubrey managed to sneak under the boardroom table, and tied everyone's shoelaces together, causing chaos at tea break when they all tried to stand up.

**Special supplement on Hypermarkets in the *Financial Mail*.** In this special feature, Ackerman stressed the importance of Promotions in creating excitement and fun for all ages for those shopping at the Hypers.

Although the real drawcard was the low prices and regular food specials. I was especially delighted when Ackerman stated that he regarded 'Carr as an extension of myself teaching GMs to be Promotion Conscious'.

Amongst other things, he explained how Rex and I were despatched to Argentina to maximise the shopping experience of the influx of Argentinians which was taking place at that time of 1979.

**Carole.** Then twenty-one, helped me with this huge project. She was indispensable and my rock in those hectic days. As she is right now in my retirement. She was also very popular with the Pick 'n Pay management. René de Wet (pictured in the group), Raymond's righthand man, took Carole up in his helicopter to show her the overflowing parking lot and long queues waiting patiently for their turn to enter the Hyper as the controllers only allowed a certain volume of traffic inside.

**Record opening.** Over 15 000 people were counted through the Hyper that day. By 1979, I had become involved with Pick 'n Pay on a corporate

## 4. Megan Carr Promotions

Nutricare: June Andrews, Consumer Director, Raymond Ackerman, Professor Dr. Harry Seftel.

level with special reference to PR, TV appearance panel discussions for Raymond's participation.

MCP helped with a new store opening in Randburg, which was off the main road, and needed public attention. Street posters were banned in Randburg, so I produced Sandwich Boards (see page 318) with shop directions worn by students wearing yellow. Smiley Faces wandering a round town. That one got us some local publicity. The students earned easy pocket money.

Ackerman wrote me a special 'thank you'.for the Pinelands store. ( see letters in Appendix), saying that the Pinelands opening had gone so well that they would, in future, be continuing with similar promotions in all their store openings.

## 24. Promotions

**Nutricare** was a massive national promotion to announce Pick 'n Pay's breakthrough consumer-based health policy to label all foods with ingredient and calorie contents. This became a national policy on all foods in all grocery stores.

Professor Dr. Harry Seftel was delighted to assist with the development of Nutricare as he thought it very important for people to know what they were consuming in their daily diets.

Letter received from June Andrews thanking me and my various regional managers for our assistance in the Nutricare national programme.

# My Life, a Roller Coaster Ride

She said, We both know that your help was essential and that we could not have managed it without you. We especially enjoyed Dr. Harry Seftel.

I trained up a Promotions Manager for every Hyper and set a programme of events for them to follow. These events were both seasonal and according to special brand offers and current entertainment on TV and in sport.

I have dozens of such letters in my file which tell the story of an effective working relationship over ten years. Raymond was always meticulous with his thank-you letters, dictated on his pocket mini recorder for secretary Diane to type and post.

### As a family aside. Chris Steer, my brother

The *Financial Mail* covers were designed and processed by my brother Chris Steer for 26 years from 1973 to 1999. The FM team would liaise with him, present the theme for the week, photo or image, heading and subtitle for him to pull together and put through the photo lithographic process, ready for printing. The FM Editor at the time was Nigel Bruce.

**Argentina.** In 1978 there was a flood of Argentinians shopping at the Hypermarkets buying mostly outdoor furniture, sporting goods, clothing and hardware. They arrived in the country in chartered Boeings which left the country loaded with the mass purchases.

In August 1978, Raymond and the directors were intrigued, and called me up to ask if I would consider going to Argentina to assess the situation. I was booked to leave a few days later on the Friday flight. I got my passport and visa in order.

*Financial Mail.* My brother, Chris Steer was the photo lithographer for the *Financial Mail* covers for 27 years. The word Game refers to its new competition to Game Stores.

## 4. Megan Carr Promotions

**Up, up and away.** Of course, at our morning exercises, I mentioned to Adele that Pick 'n Pay had booked me to Argentina that Friday, so I would miss the following two week's workouts. She was happy for me and said "Now, I'm in the mood to travel, you lucky thing!" I may have mentioned that Adele was impulsive and sometimes preoccupied when her mind was buzzing. She is after all, a 10th December Sagittarian.

Next morning, I arrived for exercises. I knocked and knocked and finally Harriet came to the door and said "Mrs. Adele is not here". Just then Bob strolled out and said "Dalie's gone to Florida, USA, Gregory Brown booked her on a flight last night to go and watch the Mohammed Ali – Leon Spinks fight.".

Adele didn't like boxing, but an adventure was irresistible. She was able to manifest things at will. She had forgotten to phone me with the news. I exercised by myself that morning and took the rest of the week off. Bob took it all in his stride after so many years with this mercurial woman.

So off I trotted on an eight-hour flight Johannesburg – Cape Town - Buenos Aires. The S.A. Tourism Association had given Rex all the contacts and booked us into a top hotel for our nine days stay.

That country was suffering massive 110% inflation and short of everything.

The city was Parisian in appearance and atmosphere, but the pavements were broken and the cars old. Sophistication long gone, except in the elite circles. We were honoured to be invited to a few private homes where the late afternoon teas were feasts with waiters hovering. I silently thanked my mother and grandmother who were sticklers for old fashioned good manners.

In the evenings after 'work' Rex and I went to night clubs to watch Argentinian Tango over a few cocktails and dinner and take in the scene. One night I couldn't get to sleep and took a taxi to a movie at 2am. I saw the newly released *Saturday Night Fever*.

It was perfectly safe to wander around at night as the law was so strict that criminals received long and cruel sentences which deterred crime. (Any lessons here?)

Mid mornings we would find a pavement Café. The Turkish coffee was strong in small cups accompanied with a tiny liqueur sized glass of cognac.

It was while we were sitting drinking our coffee, one morning, that there was a big noise in the streets and a car whizzed by with a banner announcing '*il Papa Muerto*'.

'O God, I thought, the Pope has been murdered'. Then someone explained that 'Muerto' means 'dead'. Pope John Paul had died mysteriously in his

## My Life, a Roller Coaster Ride

bed after only 33 days in office.

My other observation was the constant hooting of every vehicle all the time. What a noise. I noticed my taxi's hooter button was absolutely worn away on the left side.

A wonderful trip and a good deal of business in the making for our Hypers, knowing what to stock for these visitors who refused to pay overweight 'baggage' in the chartered flights for their stash of, for example, 500 hockey sticks. 200 deck chairs, a pinball table, 1000 camping tents.

I remember we paid R0.76 for one US dollar. Their paper money was a joke. Almost worthless. I took wads of it to buy a cup of coffee. But they always begged for dollars

Raymond's note after our return.

> Dear Meg, I have heard from Rex what a wonderful and successful trip you had (in Argentina) and I hope that a lot will flow from it.

Another letter reading as follows:

> Dear Meg, I was very impressed to hear about The Boys on the Border baking Contest held at Norwood yesterday and the TV coverage we got. They are sending me down all details but I would like you to communicate the whole promotion to all Hypers and let them know about it because this is a very warm sensitive area which we could work on. As you were working on the idea of messages to the boys on the border – is there any news on that? Please let me know.
>
> Kindest regards,
> Raymond.

General Webster was our contact for all our promotions supporting The Boys on the Border.

## 4. Megan Carr Promotions

**Prue Leith.** Raymond also wrote thanking me for bringing Prue Leith to the Hyper's for cooking demonstrations.

Prue was already well known in SA before going on to greater heights in UK, catering for Princess Margaret and then taking on the Orient Express and judging *The Great British Bake-off* with Paul Hollywood.

**Boys on the Border.** Jannie Botha, General Manager of the Norwood Hyper, and the person who was Promotions Coordinator for all Hyper promotions, planned at our fortnightly meetings.

### 1979. The Pick 'n Pay Great American Air Circus.

Pick 'n Pay's M.D. Hugh Herman, a top attorney in his other life, may have been bored in the board room. He decided to spice up everyone's lives by signing up The Great American Air Circus to visit South Africa over three months to stage Stunt Air Shows with a South African Circus Trapeze act for entertainment on the ground.

My job was Publicity and Promotions to bring in audiences at ten different airfields around the country. Friday and Saturday afternoons. Wednesday Press previews prior to each weekend show. This made it 30 shows in all. Some place names are listed below.

Baragwanath Johannesburg, Wonderboom Military Air Base in Pretoria, Vanderbijlpark Airfield, Springs Airfield East Rand, Tempe Civil Airfield in Bloemfontein, Oribi Airfield in Pietermaritzburg, Welkom Airfield, Free State, Uitenhage Airfield Port Elizabeth, Old Airport, George, Garden Route, Ysterplaat Civil Airport, Cape Town.

Wednesday Press Reviews were not full shows. Just joy rides. Press Kit handouts and refreshments catered by the local Pick 'n Pay. Some stunt rides left some of them a little green about the gills.

**See Appendix for larger version.**

# My Life, a Roller Coaster Ride

Lindsay Hess 'Cutting the Ribbon', five metres above the runway, upside down in The Pitts Special.

# 4. Megan Carr Promotions

Every Press show yielded good press stories, radio interviews and photos. Note gate ticket prices. R3 for adults and R1 for scholars. The trick was that they could be purchased at a discount for R2.75 if purchased at Pick 'n Pay. (A disturbing reminder of how our ZAR has devalued).

There was no formal seating. People brought their own garden chairs as the space appeared infinite. The nature of the shows was live outdoor family entertainment including Trapeze Acts with a Clown for the young ones – but enjoyed by all ages.

Bob and Cassie Edie owned and presented the shows with a strong public address system with speakers up on poles playing ground-to-pilot live commentary.

There were four stunt pilots from USA and our own Scully Levine from SA. The Americans were Opera Singer and lead Stunt Pilot Lindsay Hess, piloting the Pitts Specials and the Piper Cub. Comedy Stunt Pilot Grace the Ace in the 1937 Piper Cub, and stunt pilots, Bob Porter and Susan Gearhart in their Pitts Specials. We sourced all the planes in South Africa and applied our Hypermarket decals on all of them.

Sculloy Levine, S.A. Stunt Pilot.

**Upside down.** We staged this pic at a nearby field, for the *Cape Times* front page. Lindsay Hess flew upside down in the Pitts Special, cutting a crepe paper ribbon with his propeller just five metres above ground. You can see the bits of ribbon flying in the air to the left.

The classical air stunts were awesome in the hands of the outstanding air aces. Lindsay Hess preferred the amazingly aerodynamic Pitts Special biplane, designed that they were safely flying at any angle and not just upside or downside as was, for example, the single engine 1937 Piper Cub piloted mainly by Grace the Ace which could fly inverted, but not flying sides up-down.

**A fun stunt.** During the Cape Town air show they called for a volunteer. It just happened to be me. I was strapped into the front seat of the 1937 Piper Cub and headed for Table Mountain. Flipping upside down for me to view the top of Table Mountain up close, Lindsay Hess then flipped the plane right side up and glided back to the airfield with the engine stopped.

## My Life, a Roller Coaster Ride

### THRILLS APLENTY AS AIR ACES WILL DEF

**MAIL REPORTER**

THRILLS aplenty, with spectacular stunts and death-defying dives, will be provided by the touring Great American Air Circus at Pietermaritzburg's Oribi Aerodrome on Saturday and Sunday, May 5 and 6.

Aerobatics is the name of the game — among the most dangerous of all.

The Pick 'n Pay group has sponsored a national tour of the two-men-and-two-women team of American stunt fliers, who will not perform in Durban because of the lack of a suitable venue.

So, folks, this is your once-in-a-lifetime chance. Don't forget your cameras.

See Grace "the Ace" Page burst a flour bag on the ground with her wing tip. Watch Lindsay Hess cut a ribbon six metres off the ground with his propeller at 200 km/h — upside down.

Look out for Snoopy doing his dogged utmost to outmanoeuvre the Red Baron.

There will be all of this to see — and a lot more.

Tickets may be bought at the aerodrome or at your local Pick 'n Pay store — but if you move fast, you won't have to pay.

The first eight adults who ring the Highway Mail on 72-4415 from noon on Friday, April 27 will each receive a R

*Bursting a flour bag tied to a wing tip is routine for Grace "the Ace" Page (left) of the Great American Air Circus.*

**Grace the Ace, Lindsay Hess on his head Susan Gearheart peaking through his legs. Always good sports, thinking up stunts for press pics.**

## 4. Megan Carr Promotions

Bob Edie, speaking to Lindsay, ground to air, and on the loudspeakers at the airfield, warns Lindsay to be careful not to stall the plane, as it would not be possible to tweak the propeller to start it again. Lindsay pretends to mis-hear and says, "OK Bob, engine's off and the propeller stopped" The audience held its breath as the plane had gone quiet. Lindsay, sounding nervous, then announced that he would try to glide back to base, eight kilometres away.

The audience cheered as we appeared in the sky, landing perfectly in front of them, coasting to a stop exactly on the take-off mark. All excitedly commentated on the loudspeakers, by Bob Edie.

Although not on my bucket list, for me, it was one of those exhilarating life experiences. One of the perks of the job. For Lindsay, it was just another day at the office.

In the press picture (left), it shows precision flying in the 1937 Piper Cub as Grace's wing tip bursts a packet of flour on the ground as she leans out, waving to the crowd. None of the crowd would have argued against the description of her act as 'The craziest, comedy act in the world'.

With over 20 000 hours of instructing on her record, Grace's acts were pure comedy as she bounced in and out of sight of the onlookers pretending to be a passenger in the rear seat, and the plane out of control. She would hang out of the rear cockpit, talking on her intercom, or waving both arms, shouting for help at close to ground level, whilst piloting with her knees and feet.

Chief stunt pilot, Lindsay Hess, did all the classical stunt moves like the Hammerheads straight up then U-turn down, pulling out at maximum G-Force in the nick of time not to hit the ground.

He almost crashed at the Vanderbijlpark Show as he had not sufficiently calculated the high altitude and thin air. It was close. Very dramatic. Only he and we at the office realised what had almost happened. The audience simply thought it excellent risky piloting – which it was.

Lindsay told me that his air stunting friend Richard Bach, author of *Jonathan Livingston Seagull,* almost crashed doing the same stunt that same year. He managed to pull out just a few metres from the ground.

**Surprise Wedding.** Halfway through the shows, fifty-three-year-old Grace had met 38-year-old Derek Tinsley, a member of the ground crew. They fell in love and married. I was privileged to be Matron of Honour at the small private church wedding.

Derek joined Grace when they returned to America where she continued

# My Life, a Roller Coaster Ride

Left:
Tommy the Clown and the High-Flying Wrights Team.

Chief pilot and opera singer, Lindsay Hess, comedy pilot, Grace the Ace, Megan, sponsor, Raymond Ackerman.

## 4. Megan Carr Promotions

to wow audiences, and he became her manager.

Other precision flying and daring stunts would fill out the programme with our Scully Levine and the two US pilots doing duet flying tricks.

**Tommy the Clown.** In between air acts, Tommy the Clown would appear and tease the trapeze artists. They were The Flying Wrights. A triple act. Without doubt an excellent afternoon's entertainment. And as usual in South Africa, in late summer, the weather was perfect.

For the family and me, it was one of the fun things the job brought to our lives. The show lived up to its Circus theme. A full circus trapeze was set up near the air strip.

A shack 'toilet' was placed nearby so that Tommy the Clown would rush out screaming and pulling up his pants when it was 'bombed' with powder bags (mealie meal), by Grace the Ace.

Tommy, looking very drunk, staggered to the trapeze and interrupted the act to much laughter and applause.

As we travelled from airport to airport by road, I threw my brand-new Ford Cortina, into the carpool and transported Lindsay and Bonnie, the show's bookkeeper, between shows all around the country.

As I had a tow hitch on my car, I also helped tow the planes from the hangars to their starting spots on the runway.

Every evening during the two months, the whole team got together for dining and entertainment. We, the staff, enjoyed our wine, whilst the pilots did not drink the night before shows, but made up for it on Sundays and Mondays.

When the Americans first arrived, we called a press conference to announce the Great American Air Circus and its programme of events.

The first two weeks allowed the pilots to acclimatise to the high altitude, do some practicing and get familiar with the aircraft, all of which were supplied by us with the help of our own stunt pilot. Scully Levine. Grace the Ace never flew any unfamiliar plane without taking it to pieces and putting it together again with her own fair hands.

So, we allocated her a private hangar at the Springs airfield, in which the 1937 Piper Cub awaited her attention.

Raymond Ackerman flew in from Cape Town and expressed the wish to meet the pilots. The first was Grace, so I drove him to the Springs airfield where we found Grace in greasy overalls and bits of aircraft spread all over the floor.

Now, Raymond Ackerman is a formal dresser, always in his dark suit

## My Life, a Roller Coaster Ride

Two members of South Africa's Flying Wrights trapeze team yesterday had a unusual wedding. Both dressed in trapeze suits and white satin cloaks trimmed gold braid, Terry Delport and her high-flying partner, Lloyd Sanderson, were ma before 8 000 spectators at the start of the Great American Air Circus at Ysterplaa Force Base. As they took their final vows, one of the show's pilots, Lindsay H swooped low over the couple, executing victory rolls in a Pitts S Special from w trailed streamers. And before the couple left on their honeymoon, they gave the cr the trapeze act for which they are world famous.

Flying at an angle with one wheel on the ground, the American queen of the s "Grace the Ace", thrilled 8 000 spectators at Ysterplaat yesterday with her comic dare-devil antics.

**Top Right:** Terry Delport and her high flying partner, Lloyd Sanderson, were married before the 8 000 spectators at the start of the Great American Air Circus, Ysterplaat Air Force Base.

## 4. Megan Carr Promotions

and Pick 'n Pay company tie. I called out to Grace to come and meet the sponsor. She rushed over and, with a naughty expression on her face, held out her grease-blackened hand to greet Raymond as she was introduced. To his gentlemanly credit, he too held out his hand and was relieved when Grace let him off the hook and stepped back, laughing. A happy start to a memorable three months.

**The *Cape Times* article 1979 reads as follows:**

A blanket of cloud parted over the Cape Peninsula yesterday, allowing the world's greatest aerial spectacular to get off the ground at Ysterplaat. And the four pilots of The Great American Air Circus with the dare devil imaginations of more than 8 000 spectators. Two and a half hours of breathtaking aerobatics – at times only a few metres above the ground – held the huge crowd spellbound. It was unlike any other show staged in South Africa. The performance was funny, chilling – and just downright amazing.

The climax came in a blasting wind when the lead pilot, Lindsay Hess, swooped in upside down in his Pitts Special, and cut a ribbon suspended just five metres above the ground with his propeller. Although he could not hear it, the applause was deafening.

He did the slowest slow roll in the world, lasting 35 seconds. Trailing smoke, he did the world's only performance of the inverted flat spin.

The crowd held its breath when he cut his engine at about 1 000 metres, going through his 'dead stick' ballet to land silently without even a bump. A former opera singer, Hess has 16 000 flying hours behind him. He is married and has two children. He does about eighty shows a year in America. The darling of the show, the legendary Grace the Ace, holds the world record for 81 flat spins from 3 700 metres. She also holds a master's degree in English literature.

**Here comes another bride.**

At the start of the final Saturday show, we had a surprise for the crowd.

A Trapeze wedding! Another real romance. What a grand finale it made to the two months of 21 air shows. The whole show began with a trapeze act by the South African Three Flying Wrights. One of which was Tommy the Clown.

Two members of the South African Flying Wrights trapeze team had a most unusual wedding. Dressed in trapeze suits and white satin cloaks trimmed with gold braid, Terry Delport and her high flying partner, Lloyd

# My Life, a Roller Coaster Ride

Sanderson, were married before the 8 000 spectators at the start of the Great American Air Circus, Ysterplaat Air Force Base.

Bob Edie, the true professional, popped it into his show script to make good memories for Terry and Lloyd and the spectators.

As they took their final vows, head pilot, Lindsay Hess swooped low over the couple, executing Victory Rolls in a Pitts Special from which trailed smoke streamers. And before the couple left on their honeymoon, they gave the crowd the trapeze act for which they were famous.

As Public Relations Consultant I was over the moon. I couldn't have organised the grand finale better if I'd had the power to do so.

## 4. Megan Carr Promotions

**A memory.** In 1980, a year later, I happened to be in Orlando, Florida, and wondered if I should pop in to visit my stunt pilot pal, Lindsay Hess and his wife, Carolyn.

He sounded delighted and told me to get myself to the Atlanta airport and he would pick me up next day and they would then fly me with them to Barbados for the weekend. He also asked if I had a suitable British Visa. I phoned around to try and arrange it but, with Apartheid in full swing, there was no chance a South African was welcome. I had to turn down his kind invitation.

He phoned back in minutes and said they had cancelled Barbados and would pick me up next day in Atlanta. He brought his two sons along for the ride in his Beechcraft Baron 58 six-seater plane.

I stayed with the family for two days before moving on back home. In those two days he and Keith, his young son, flew me, sightseeing all over North Carolina.

Lindsay Hess owned the Salisbury Airport, Charlotte, N.C., so he used a selection of his small aircraft to suit our mini trips, one of which was to get me back to the Atlanta Airport.

Unfortunately, the day he was to get me up for a wing walk flight – standing on the wing tied to an upright pole, in flight, the weather turned rainy, and we had to abort.

This had been a long time dare since his visit to South Africa, now crossed off the list. I was told it is no big deal to wing walk. Perfectly safe to do – in good weather. I was in my late forties – and game for it.

Fifteen years later a male friend and I booked ourselves on a Bungy Jump off the Storms River Bridge on the Garden Route. This too, was aborted because he woke up with a bad headache that day!

I was comforted by a friend who said that sometimes a Bungy Jump can cause a detached retina. Saved again.

**1979. Kyalami Race Track Western Flyer sports cycle promotion.**
The Hyper Director, Ig Ferreira (Yelling on right of centre picture left) asked me to shine some light on one of his new Hyper products. The Western Flyer Sport cycle. So, I looked around for a prominent event.

As it happened, Formula One was about to run at Kyalami. So, I approached the organisers who agreed to allow me to have a lunch interval Cycle Relay Race with well-known personalities.

Among my Western Flyer personalities were: Charlie Weir, champion boxer, Mercedes Kornfeld, top model, John Berks, SABC Morning Radio

# My Life, a Roller Coaster Ride

host, Barry Richards, cricketer, my friend Adele Lucas, A&J Promotions and three Pick 'n Pay Managers.

This was the historic day that South African Jody Scheckter won the main F1 event in front of his proud home crowd. The record crowd now had a fun event to watch whilst awaiting the main F1 attraction at 3pm.

Much cheering as the two teams of four cyclists passed on batons as they raced around the track for half an hour. Ig Ferreira provided the trophy and medals to present to the two sweating teams. This event was enjoyed by all personalities involved as well as the spectators chewing on their picnic lunches.

John Berks spoke about it on Radio Today for a whole week, he was so excited. Pick 'n Pay got their publicity.

I also happened to own a four-wheel quadracycle. So, I used this as a novelty marshalling vehicle during the race. Four wheels, two sets of pedals, one wide seat and a single central steering stick. And a square canopy with relevant signwriting and advertising. It had its own personality and novelty factor with two men peddling like crazy and yet not going fast.

**Dr. M Scott Peck.** When Dr. M Scott Peck visited South Africa, I was asked to set up a series of public lectures for him to talk about and discuss his bestselling book, *The Road Less Travelled* (published 1978), selling millions. It later evolved into a trilogy with *The Road Less Travelled and Beyond*.

At the end of each lecture, he was mobbed by people asking questions. They couldn't get enough of him. His patience was exemplary as he shared and inspired. My client was Penguin books.

M. Scott Peck was a modest person. His book was inspiring, depicting lessons he had learned in his life as a psychiatrist. This person and his teachings were amongst some of the inspiring lessons which have enhanced my life.

## 4. Megan Carr Promotions

**Penguin books.** To promote Penguin paper-backs for the client, I had two life-sized Penguin characters made up to ride my trusty quadracycle around shopping centres with major book shops. I had to ensure that the flappy feet could also peddle the cycle. A cushy job for two students. They were not expected to answer questions because Penguins can't speak - or read.

**1980 Easter.** We all looked forward to spending the Easter Weekend together at The Vaal. Mattie and Alfie already in residence in their middle house. John, Margie, Leanne and Grant, Milton, Debbie, Gavin and Beverley, and me and my family. We had come a few days before Good Friday. Chris came for a day visit.

**Another shocking Easter Sunday.**
Just Three years after John Lawley's Easter Sunday death my brother Milton and family had come to the river for Easter weekend.

Milton.

On the Thursday before leaving home, Milton had been having severe chest pains and visited his doctor. All we know is that the doctor, Milton's 'friend', told him to go to the Vaal and rest and come back on Tuesday to decide on treatment. It was Easter, after all.

On Easter Sunday afternoon, the pains were so bad, he decided to motor back to Johannesburg. He drove himself and the children safely

**Brothers Chris and John.**

# My Life, a Roller Coaster Ride

Marine Jahan, the dancer in *Flashdance*, was brought out by Roche to make the Jane Fonda-type exercise video for their Fat Off diet product. She spent a weekend with Megan and family at The Vaal.

back home. Milton then collapsed and died right there in the kitchen. He was forty-seven'.

This kind, handsome, funny family man, died a multi-millionaire, running his printing and packaging company, 'Britepak'.

Milton's death came as a huge shock to the family. We all got together for comfort and to help Nan and his children, Mattie and Alfie, and each other.

Soon after this, my parents decided to sell the property as the memories were too hard to bear.

**Milton's client and Berocca:** Roche Pharmaceuticals had just introduced *Berocca* to the market. Milton brought me a dozen packs and said, 'use it'. And I have been for forty-four years.

**Roche.** I was destined to work with Roche a year later, when they introduced slimming product 'Fat Off'. By then I was marketing director of Chroma TV, contracted to make their exercise video. For which they brought out a dancing film star, Marine Jahan (*Flashdance*), to do a Jane Fonda-type exercise video.

When the 'Fat Off' video wrapped, after celebrating, I drove her to the Vaal for the weekend. When she asked young Peter (16) to take her for a

## 4. Megan Carr Promotions

ski (bikini top back on), he was thrilled.

Then, while expertly skiing, hanging on with one hand, she took off her bikini top and waved it in the air with naughty laughter.

Blushing young Pete got such a shock he almost fell out of the boat.

Marine was mischievous. As she was leaving, she sent me this photo of her stuffing herself with food, and a pillow stuffed under the Fat-Off Tee shirt. Her message read:

*Megan, To an amazing gal on the River Vaal ! You've been lovely.*
*Cheers. Marine*

**Big Foot.** In the early 80's my company's biggest client was Pick 'n Pay, with special focus on the emerging Hypermarkets. I had to source fun activities for the marketing managers to feature in their advertising and promotions.

Children's amusements were in big demand, so I secured the agencies for many famous film and TV children's characters. These giant character costumes were animated by trained students earning pocket money.

The first characters I used with human inners were The Wombles of Wimbledon. Then came The Rescuers. The Muppets and Paddington Bear. Finally, after tough negotiations, I managed, briefly, to get the famous Disney favourites, Mickey Mouse, Minnie Mouse, Donald Duck and Goofy and Pluto. Like all the other characters they were huge in size. In fact, they frightened most of the smaller children who ran blubbing to Mommy.

The after school and Saturday morning promotions were perfect job opportunities for students. I was never short of volunteers. The characters are very strictly quality controlled, so extra care had to be taken with costume fittings and a strict behaviour code. The students were not allowed to speak to the children for very good reason. The Mommies' little darlings would sometimes bring a pin and stick it into the behind of a furry fella. Or nastily twist the nose of a Womble, sometimes provoking naughty cuss words. Swearing, kicking or slapping the mini customers was strictly prohibited. But there were times when the exuberant young students were not controllable and caused me some grief. And some chuckles.

Sixteen year-old Peter Henderson, dressed as Goofy, was dared by his friend Willie Gubb, who was Pluto, to play a trick on one of the Hyper satellite shops. Now, Goofy had very big feet and shoes.

After his Goofy appearance time was up, Peter changed back into his School uniform, but was still wearing Goofy's size 18 shoes. He went into Cuthberts Shoe Shop and asked the saleswoman for size 18 shoes, 'in black'. Willie, as Pluto, kept watch through the window, outside.

Looking at this teenage boy with huge feet, the poor saleswoman looked puzzled, but her training snapped in and was anxious to please. She regretted that she was out of size 18, in black, but obligingly started calling her other branches to try and find them. This was too much for the two jokers and they got the giggles and ran off.

She realized she had been fooled and ran out of the shop shouting at them and making a scene.

I received a formal complaint about my students. I had to haul them over the coals, whilst trying to keep a straight face. Obviously, Peter and Willy had to apologise, and present her with a bunch of flowers paid for out of their earnings.

**Donald Duck.** Andy reminded me that she was Donald Duck because he, like her, was quite small. Kermit the Frog also fitted. She was about fifteen and wore a size two shoe.

She remembered that the duck head was big with a heavy beak, hard to manage. Also, that the tennis shoes inside the feet were bigger than hers so we had to pad them out with socks. If a child accidentally stepped on her webbed foot, she lost her balance. My child team earning pocket money again.

They had fun doing these jobs except for the times when brats would pull the tail or stick fingers in the eye holes.

**Andrea 'Andy' Carr.** Andy was the Make-up Artist on Jamie Uys's film *The Gods Must be Crazy*. Penny wise, Jamie expected multi-tasking from his crew. She once found herself clinging on frantically as she hung from a high tree branch, making like a stuntman, as they filmed some action around her. She was young and fit, and game for it.

Andy was with Jamie and 'Gods Must be Crazy' filming for about eighteen months, travelling around the country. Lena Ferugia starred in the film. She and Andy became close friends for over thirty years.

Andy later became Production Coordinator on *The Adventures of Sinbad* made in the Cape, which took about two years. Visiting their studio in Pinelands, she showed me around, pointing to huge drums overflowing with broken arms and legs covered in 'blood' and other gruesome items. They built the sailing ship, visible from the main road, lying in the grounds of the Cape Film Studios, on the way to Somerset West. Almost a landmark and since used by other film companies.

# 4. Megan Carr Promotions

**Carole** was the first of my children to work in the film industry. At nineteen, she moved on from professional photographer Dudley Lawrence's P.A, into TV commercial production, and was a Producer for over 20 years until she moved to the country with her two young children.

**Peter.** After he matriculated, and before going into the army, Carole told him there was a gap for a person finding locations and supplying props. So, he and friend Guy Drummond, started 'Spots and Props', which kept him busy for six months till he entered compulsory army service.

In the army, as well as playing in the Squash Team, he was drafted to the Film Unit in Pretoria, and that was the beginning of his successful film and TV production career.

Executive Producer for 'Velocity Films' for twenty years. Velocity specialised in Commercials. After Velocity Films closed, he continued producing commercials under his own name, and still at it today, enjoying forty years in the film industry.

**Family.** All four of them helped in the family business from time to time, making up badges, selling programmes, morphing into furry characters, fetching and carrying. And, importantly, later in MCP office management.

They also got to attend sporting promotions and shows. Those were the perks for them and my perk, having them nearby.

Tony started off, after the army, as a qualitied Photolithographer, like my brother Chris Steer, who did the *Financial Mail* cover for twenty-seven years.

Photolithography became redundant with the advent of electronics and Computer Graphics. So, Tony ended up in the motor industry and later in Real Estate as he was a good salesman. He earned a certificate as Salesman of the Year.

Peter was the entrepreneur at an early age. At St. Stithian's he asked me to buy him twenty pairs of dark mirror glasses from the Oriental Plaza. Best prices there.

He would pay me back when they were sold. The following weeks, thirty pairs, sixty pairs, eighty pairs. They were selling like hotcakes.

Doing the school lift, I was sitting in the car at the gates when the boys started pouring out, every second boy was wearing the dark mirror glasses. 'It could be mistaken for a school for the blind, I thought.'

Peter made enough money to buy a very nice stereo sound system.

## 25. 1980. Fun and Fundraising for the Wildlife Society

Again, I felt I was walking the daily treadmill. I needed a fresh challenge. Tony and Carole, at that time, were independent in their twenties. Peter was sixteen and Andy fourteen. As Peter senior was now paying for Andy's school fees at DSG, Grahamstown, and I only had the St. Stithian's fees and extra murals to cover, I felt free enough to take on something of a gamble and completely fresh.

I had been told that The Wildlife Society of SA was looking for a fundraiser. I approached John Fowkes, CEO of the Society and offered my services to fundraise on a commission basis. No salary or retainer, I presented him with my idea.

In 1972, eight years earlier, I had worked closely with Shell and BP on their national Marketing Equalisation Group ( MEG) campaign, which had worked well for them. I therefore approached my Shell contact, Patrick Erleigh, with a joint promotion idea in association with the Wildlife Society of South Africa.

Shell was always looking for ideas to bring the public into their

Andy Carr, Miss Piggy, Grant Steer, Kermit the Frog, Leanne Steer, Studying the 'Collect to Protect' sticker Album to be available at selected Shell Service Stations throughout S.A. for a three-month campaign.

## 4. Megan Carr Promotions

service stations and convenience shops. Wildlife Society, whilst needing to raise funds, was always on the lookout for conservation educational opportunities for the public. We put our heads together and came up with 'Collect to Protect'.

For a nominal price, Shell would distribute informative sticker albums in their Forecourt Convenience Shops and sell mini packs of five stickers to match the numbered blank spaces. These mini packs would be sold in carefully spaced-out batches to extend the promotion over three months.

John Fowkes, Head of WSSA, and Mike Nicol, the Wildlife PR and Publicist, together constructed an album filled with educational snippets of information set out as questions in blank boxes on pages to be filled with correspondingly numbered stickers which could be bought at the participating Shell shops. Much sticker swopping happened at schools, creating extra energy and competition.

Income from each pack of five stickers represented 50% for production costs and 50% to Wildlife's 'Collect to Protect' programme. Thousands of packs were sold.

**The album.** An example of how the album and stickers worked. Blank album space for sticker with question beneath example 'Why does a crocodile swallow stones?' Answer on the sticker, 'For ballast to help it go deeper underwater'.

**Campaign launch event.** To launch the Shell 'Collect to Protect' campaign, we ran a parallel donor Fundraising Campaign to initiate the junior Wildlife magazine 'Toktokkie' to be devised and edited by Mike Nicol (currently, a lecturer at UCT and bestselling crime author).

We launched it with a party at the beautiful Johannesburg Zoo Elephant House. Willie Labuschagne, the Zoo Director was excited about the unique occasion and the publicity it would attract for the Zoo.

Our guest list, limited to one hundred, comprised known Wildlife supporters, Shell personnel, City Councillors and the usual list of generous business and society people.

Other famous guests were The Muppets, Miss Piggy and Kermit the Frog. (My characters) posing with Andy Carr and her cousins Leanne and Grant Steer.

I had invited the Johannesburg Parks Department to help with decorating the magnificent building as the two elephants were escorted outside with some goodies to keep them happy.

'Parks' transformed the Elephant House into a mini jungle with bushes

# My Life, a Roller Coaster Ride

Carole awaiting the arrival of guests with 'Welcome' cocktails. Zoo Ranger, David, keeping cool with a wrap-around python. Neither seems concerned about the python.

Guests arriving at the Elephant House in the Zoo passenger trailer. Their arrival was delayed fifteen minutes as they stopped to watch an Eland giving birth.

## 4. Megan Carr Promotions

and using mounted railway sleepers as bar counters.

I went to Carnival Novelty and bought some animal masks and hid these in and around the bushes. I also bought some tiny torches which I switched on, so that the masks showed night eyes – like rabbits in the headlights. I also found, in the Wildlife library, a tape of bushveld animal noises which, with the lights dimmed gave an amazing outdoor bushveld atmosphere.

All this, shamelessly, to help sharpen the emotions and cheque writing enthusiasm of the visitors. We met the VIP guests at the Zoo parking gate and transported them to the Elephant House on trolleys. This tour excited our guests with tender memories of childhood.

The trolleys were delayed fifteen minutes as they watched an Eland giving birth. This event brought us excellent publicity and the funds rolled in. We exceeded what we needed for Toktokkie Magazine with a handsome amount to spare for Conservation and Shell was delighted with the three-month Forecourt high energy campaign.

My year with Wildlife Society brought me a satisfying commission based on a percentage of the funds raised. Win-Win-Win.

I had also hoped that my sojourn at the Society would get me some interesting excursions into the wild. This side was slightly disappointing, as Wildlife office work – and my own business, kept me too busy for the luxury of trips into the bush.

However, I was invited to join a four-day group visiting Timbavati Private Nature Reserve and Lodge. I was fortunately able to take Peter and Andy along.

**A walk in the bush.** Andy still vividly remembers it. Memories hard for us all to forget. We joined a Game Walk with two armed Rangers and a Tracker. The tracker far ahead of us, one Ranger in front and one at the rear of the walking line of ten.

We all stopped as we heard baboon screams followed by a lion's roar. My two precious offspring were front of the line, I was further back. Suddenly a baboon ran towards us, so we knew the lion was not far behind. The baboon saw us and stopped in its tracks.

Andy remembers the lioness appearing suddenly, just metres away from her. The hunting big cat stopped when she heard the two rifles click. She turned and ran off.

The most dreadful feeling came over me. 'What was I thinking, bringing my children into danger?' However, the lion was smart and experienced.

# My Life, a Roller Coaster Ride

When she heard the rifles being cocked, and her prey parked near us, she veered off and away. The baboon found a nearby tree, and safety. A very long two minutes.

I had a favourite purple track suit which came with me on this trip. When the day cooled in early evening, I changed into my snug tracksuit as we all sat around the Boma for supper. The rangers said that they had heard the noises of a kill nearby.

One of the Rangers had the talent of making realistic lion roars to frighten us. We snuggled nearer the fire for safety.

It was a merry party with other guests. A Ranger then came in and whispered to me "There is a Zebra kill reported nearby, would you like to come with me and have a look?"

**A bird in the bush.** Of course, I jumped at this singular privilege. I checked that he had his rifle, but he assured me that I would be a less tasty dinner for the lions, as zebra and baboon were preferred items on the menu. He warned me to walk lightly and not to speak. 'Just creep along softly' as we approach. It was almost dark. He had switched off his shaded torch. And there, in the moonlight, the kill and three lions could be seen about fifty yards away.

Just my luck, as we crept closer, a Francolin ran onto the pathway at my feet. I let out a scream of fright. The lions took no notice and munched on.

Double amputee, James (Jumper) Wide (left) and his pet Baboon, Signalman Jack, standing like a human, on the right.

## 4. Megan Carr Promotions

For the next two days I became laughingly known in the camp, in birding terms, as 'The Purple Breasted Shriek'. Even the kids laughed and wished they had been there to see it. And the kill.

**The magazine.** After the Elephant House fundraiser, Mike Nicol developed the Children's magazine, *Toktokkie*. One of the first stories told in the Magazine was about Jack, a famous working Baboon.

**True story.** Uitenhage Railway Signalman, James (Jumper) Wide earned the nickname 'Jumper' because he fooled around jumping between carriages of moving trains, until the inevitable accident happened and had both his legs amputated.

In 1881, James, no longer the 'Jumper', bought a pet Chacma baboon, whom he named 'Jack; and taught him to assist him work the railway signals.

When concerned observers noticed a baboon changing the signals, they reported it to the railway authorities. A committee of officials arrived to observe and assess the situation.

They were so impressed with the excellence of Jack's work that they employed him at a salary of twenty cents a day and a bottle of beer a week.

He worked the signals till he died of TB, nine years later, in 1890.

In those nine years Jack never once made a mistake.

His skull is on display at the Albany Museum in Grahamstown.

**1975. Vaal floods and The Old Lady.** Part of the property package was an elegant cruiser boat which we simply called 'The Old Lady'. She had an inboard Volvo Penta motor which chugged along faithfully and never gave trouble over 35 years.

She had many seats and a sliding cabin roof to sit on. She could carry 14 people at a squeeze. Her paintwork was a basic white with a broad navy-blue stripe at water level topped with a thin gold and thin blue stripe. A kind of naval look.

**1975 March.** Mattie and Alf had arrived at the Vaal for the weekend. Mattie noticed the river running very fast and rising. Being very efficient and always pro-active, she called the Barrage office and spoke to the person in charge saying

"You had better open the water gates as the river is rising fast". He seemed impatient and said, "I have had no instructions to do that, and we are knocking off for the weekend". Bad mistake.

She noticed that, not only was the river rising in front of the house, but that it was also doubling back as it sped round the bend and flowed back

## My Life, a Roller Coaster Ride

VAAL FLOODS: March 1975 Torrential rain caused the 350 metre wide Vaal river to flood, because the barrage gates, down river, were not opened in time. The water rose so high that two of our houses haged a metre of water inside. We boated up the driveway to get to our cars.

## 4. Megan Carr Promotions

into the farm's lowland. The two of them started collecting their valuables and stacking them high up. They were alone on the farm and couldn't manage the other two houses.

Next day, the rest of the family arrived. By then, they had to park their cars on the Marlbank road and wade through the muddy water down the driveway to get to their houses. The middle house was on high ground and a few inches safe from the flood, but the other two already had a few feet of water inside. It was not possible to open the doors. The Barn had a stable door, so we were able to open the top half of the orange painted door above the water level and paddle the canoe over the lower half to tie it halfway up the stairs. We made several trips in the little boat, laden with important articles from each of the houses to store in dry safety upstairs.

We estimated about one metre of water in the Barn and the cottage had water halfway up the windows.

The flooding river was a sight to behold. Whole islands with trees rushed by. One even had a terrified sheep standing on the approximately 3 x 3 metre floating island.

It was too dangerous to try and rescue it, or stop logs, drums and every kind of debris as it flew past on the relentless surge.

The rain stopped and it took a few days for the water to drop, but the river silt was slimy and each one of us, at some stage, went slipping and sliding in the mud all over the place.

One lasting strange memory still comes to mind. In the Barn, the gently rising water slowly lifted almost everything off shelves to float around the house. When the river subsided, the water in the Barn flowed slowly back out under the stable door. The gentle movement carried all the floating objects with it. Glasses, bowls, wooden tray of cutlery, bread board, pots and pans, vases, and a cut glass punch bowl.

When we went to open-up to inspect the inevitable devastation, expecting everything to be broken, we were amazed to find dozens of items deposited safely on the floor inside the door. It

**Tony skiing past the Old Lady.**

looked like a family of imprisoned household goods trying to escape. Of course, we were less lucky with the bed linen, cushions and bottom of the curtains all mud-soaked and most had to be discarded and replaced.

Carole remembers, when we were getting back to normal and used the kitchen toaster, a mud caked dead mouse popped out.

The walls of the houses were so waterlogged that it was many months before they dried out ready for paint and habitation.

The timely insurance payout paid for Carole to travel to the French language school in *Cap de Ail*, France, as well as repairs to The Barn.

**Buying the Marlbank property from my parents.** After 16 beautiful family years, the 'old folks' decided to sell the property. Milton, 47, had just died very suddenly of a heart attack.

Selling was unthinkable to my family. The Vaal had become such a part of our weekend and holiday lives that I decided to put together a syndicate to buy it from my parents. An amount was set and agreed to.

**Syndicate.** No advertising was needed. The best kind of syndicate emerged by word of mouth. Megan knew Alan Gardiner and Errol Cohn, good friends of the late, John Lawley. Alan and Errol knew Neil Malan through their various associations with Pick 'n Pay and the Malan's egg business. Libby Gardiner's cousin was Brian Murdock. Rose Murdock was friends with Janine and Jos Lalieu. And so, the six shares were filled by osmosis.

It worked like this: Three houses - six partners with equal votes. Each share value differed according to position, size and condition of the buildings. We made fair rules of sharing to ensure good friendships.

**1982 – 1992. After two years** when the Lalieus and Murdocks wanted out, I bought their share. We moved across from the back of the barn to the West Cottage.

It was during one of my lengthy sabbatical escapes to The Vaal that I decided to make some additions to the cottage. I decided to add two more bedroom-suites and some lounge space. Also to add a storeroom for the boating equipment, and to spruce up the caravan for overflow. I had some building 'experience' when the haphazard builder of our Athol house conversion had gone bankrupt, and I took over the project management.

**D.I.Y. at Marlbank.** With no budget for the luxury of a professional architect, I got some draft paper and a ruler (a wise start), drew up a simple design which I thought I could manage. Two 4x4 double bedrooms, each with a shower and loo. Adding a dressing room to one, and a small necessary

## 4. Megan Carr Promotions

storeroom for skis, petrol, life jackets, etc. I also added to the original lounge to expand the communal area. The two new suites would meet up at right angles to three metres short of the cottage, leaving a covered connecting open patio. On checking the drawings, I even remembered to include a plan for electrical conduits, plugs and water pipes.

**Highly 'meganised' DIY building.** Defying all the sceptics on this project, I barged ahead and contacted a local bricklayer/builder named Jacob, who had done good building odd jobs for neighbours. To avoid the job being dragged out forever on a weekly paid basis, I asked him for a quote based on my drawing.

Megan's entire new building additions.

# My Life, a Roller Coaster Ride

New lounge looking onto the garden and enclosed garden courtyard.

Original lounge-dining area. John's cat 'Boots' loved that chair.
On the wall - Flying Geese painting - which got coloured in by Brandon Busuttil and his pals!
I had to get it professionally restored. They were just kids doing me a big favour.

## 4. Megan Carr Promotions

He gave me a labour cost and timeline to work to. I divided the money by the weeks and paid him a weekly draw. Also, a 5% bonus was promised if the work was completed on time.

All deadlines and soft standards were achieved and the bonus happily paid.

**2006. Next Vaal generation.** When Barbara and Neil Malan retired from Vaal life, their son, Jacques, took over the middle house. He later sold a half-share to Peter and Leanne Carr.

They scrapped the old house and built a magnificent new one, with a new boathouse and a swimming pool. This compatible partnership of old friends lasted four years till Peter's boys' sports activities prevented their regular weekend visits and suited their plans to move to the coast.

Alan Busuttil bought 50 percent of Megan's West cottage share in 1990 and Alan and Karen Busuttil bought the other 50 percent in 1992, owning the full share when Megan moved to Cape Town.

My Porshe was one of the casualties of my sabbatical-living at the river. When I moved to the river for a year in mid 80's, I still had to commute to Johannesburg a few days a week to service some of my regular PR clients. The Marlbank road didn't agree with my precious little car as the corrugations were rattling it to pieces. So, I sensibly decided to sell it, and regretted it ever since.

**Tony Buzan.** This attractive, dynamic young Oxford Professor came into my orbit in 1982 exactly when I needed him!

I set up a series of one day seminars where he introduced his new concept of Mind Mapping. A two-dimensional method of note taking and memory guiding.

Tony Buzan was more than that, his practical ideas and observations on life hit the spot with students and business-people alike.

One observation which surprised me. When out driving, your mind is more alert and takes in more detail when driving fast than if you trundle along slowly. Tony also developed the technique of Speed Reading.

I subsequently ran two special seminars on Speed Reading. Like reading a 3D picture with eyes squinted, you run your eyes and index

# My Life, a Roller Coaster Ride

finger down the centre line between left and right pages and scroll down. The peripheral vision takes in information from both sides. Guiness Book speed reader is Howard 'Speedy' Berg who can read 80 pages a minute. (I had to trust Google on this one). The speed reader gets a fair impression of the contents. Not recommended for those needing fine detail. Berg now runs seminars on more advanced techniques using skimming and scanning for different study and business purposes.

**Matric help.** The timing was perfect for me. Both Raymond Ackerman and I had sons writing matric and both were having problems focusing on their schoolwork at that critical time.

After Tony's first lecture, I called Raymond, in Cape Town, to explain Tony's concept. His response was to put young Jonathan on a plane to Johannesburg to attend a lecture and mind mapping demonstration.

Both Peter Carr and Jonathan Ackerman enthusiastically adapted Mind Mapping into their school and personal lives. Both easily passed matric and have used this process in their successful business lives ever since, as we all do in the family.

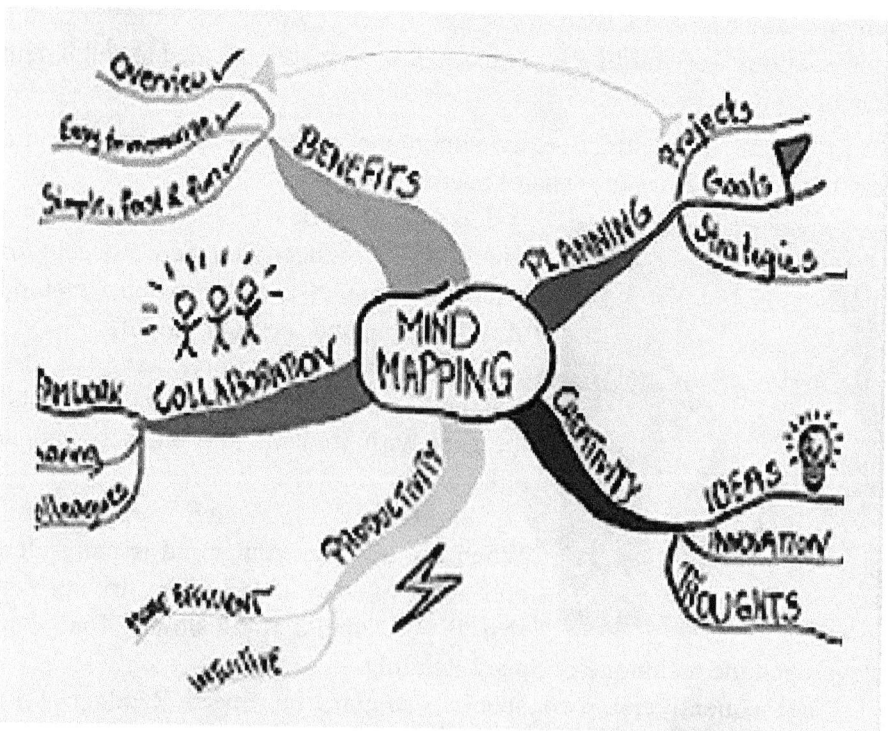

**Mind Mapping gives you the tools to organse your thoughts and ideas effectively.**

## 4. Megan Carr Promotions

**The Fair Lady Who's Who of South African Women** was sponsored by Barclays Bank from 1980 to 1984. This sponsorship ended with the first rumblings from the UK about disinvesting in Barclays South Africa. Barclays Bank became First National Bank in 1987.

The Who's Who of South African Women ran for five-years. It started out as the *Top 100 Women's Club* which met monthly for discussions, invited speakers and held workshops. The women members were Professionals in a vast variety of expertise and profession. All top of their game. Membership selection was by a professional committee, and by invitation only.

I and my friends Adele Lucas, Carole Charlewood and Margaret Essberger were all included in the five years of publication (1980-1984).

When I moved to Cape Town, in 1992, I automatically became a member of the Cape branch of the Top 100 Women's Club which had continued meeting after the exit of the bank sponsorship and the end of the annual Who's Who.

I was also invited to become a member of the Cape Town Press Club.

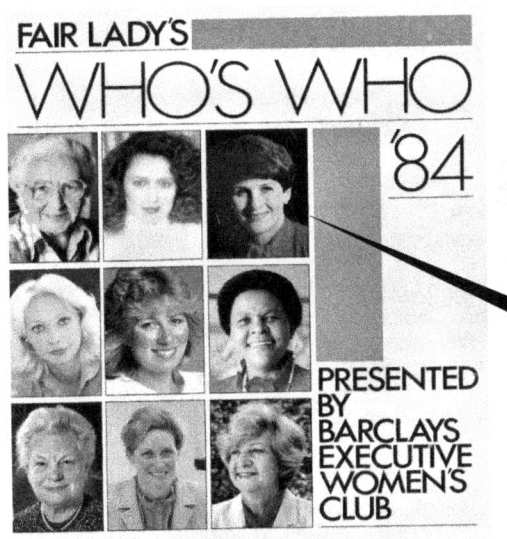

Fair Lady's Who's Who 1984.

Schoolfriend, Carole Charlewood on cover. Megan Carr and Adele Lucas also featured in the five years of the 'Who's Who of S.A. Women' campaign.
My daughter, Carole, was named after Carole.

## My Life, a Roller Coaster Ride

**1982. Megan Carr heads Mortimer Tiley (MT) Promotions.** Mortimer Tiley has taken over Megan Carr Promotions (Pty) Ltd to form a separate company Mortimer Tiley Promotions, which, with Megan at the head, will operate from the Oxford Park premises in Sandton.

**Mortimer Tiley (MT) Takeover.** By the late seventies, MCP had recovered from the Celebrity Tennis financial losses and rebuilt itself to a healthy Promotions and PR company.

Enlightened men were starting to accept that women had a brain and could be useful in the business world. Alan Tiley was one of them. Ad Agencies were including live promotions in their advertising mix. I was approached by Alan Tiley, head of MT Agency, to sell him a controlling share in MCP and to work within his advertising agency, managing PR and Promotions.

Alan 'Big Al' was a giant of a man, physically and in personality. I got persuaded, partly because I liked his thinking and his client base. Announcements were made in the Press. I had the use of a suite of offices in his building. I related well with the MT staff and clients, except for one. The very capable 'Janine', who had been in line to start up MT's Promotions Division before I came on the scene.

### Megan Carr heads MT Promotions

MORTIMER Tiley has taken over Megan Carr Promotions (Pty) Limited, to form a separate Company — Mortimer Tiley Promotions — which, with Megan Carr at the head, will operate from the agency's Oxford Park premises in Sandton.

Megan has a wealth of promotions experience behind her. After completing her Marketing Diploma (ICTI) in 1967, she became a founder member of the Institute of Sales Promotion. She is also a full member of the Public Relations Institute of South Africa.

She founded Megan Carr Promotions in 1972, specialising in product promotions and launches, in-store promotions, the organisation of seminars, conferences and exhibitions, shopping centre and hypermarket promotions as well as public relations programmes. She also spent a year promoting and fund-raising for the Wildlife Society of South Africa.

She also obtained — and still has — the promotional rights to The Wombles, Paddington Bear and other children's characters.

●Alan Tiley and promotions girls Maureen Spiro and Carla Morton, welcome Megan Carr, right, on her joining the agency earlier this month.

With her staff of five, she will now handle promotions for all Mortimer Tiley clients as well as for outside companies. Radio fundi, Robin Alexander, will contribute on a part-time basis for specific MC-type work.

According to agency MD, Alan Tiley, promotions are now playing "a big part" in the below-the-line activities of ad agencies resulting from the increasing number of clients who are becoming more "results-orientated."

"And in harder economic times, promotions become even more of an integral part of the marketing mix."

## 4. Megan Carr Promotions

Naturally, she was upset and blocked me at every turn. I did my best to work through the obstacles. I decided it was time to confront Alan with the problem. Meanwhile…

**Peter Maxwell.** At that same time, I was enjoying a very active social life. I had met the visiting British entertainer, Peter Maxwell, at a private party. He invited me to dinner at the top of the new Carlton Hotel's *El Gaucho* restaurant where he had a contract playing piano performing his sparkling musical comedy hour-long show every evening.

**David Munton.** After a glass of wine together, when it came time for Peter's show, he introduced me to his English friend, David Munton, and asked him to 'look after me' during his show. Afterwards, David asked us to join him for dinner. Peter laughed saying "Certainly not". And off we went to a late dinner. However, when this happened a couple of nights in a row, David was always there to 'look after me' as Peter performed. David and I enjoyed chatting and became casual friends.

When Peter returned to the UK, we kept up correspondence, pending his next SA contract. No romance involved. Just pals. He explained how lonely it could be away from home and never a familiar face. I loved his amusing and gentle company.

When running one of the Advertising Creative Circle lunches, I had a last-minute cancellation so, to fill the empty chair, I called up David Munton and invited him to a free lunch with Joyce Grenfell entertaining. I owed David for many a glass of wine at *El Gaucho*. He jumped at the invitation. By then I had known him a couple of months.

**Big Question.** After seeing off all the lunch guests, David had lingered behind and invited me to join him at the top of the nearby Hillbrow Tower, for coffee. I accepted and there we sat and chatted. Suddenly he jumped up, fell to his knees, and proposed marriage to me. No ring in his hand. Just a sweet soppy look on his anxious face. Shock and bewilderment on mine. This was out of the blue, and out of the question. I thanked him for the compliment, but suggested we should not rush into such things, and that I would give it some serious thought.

It was not an impetuous flash in the pan. He phoned me every day after that, to say he was dead serious about his proposal. I enjoyed his company but would need to be 'in love'. I had other things on my mind at that time, like trouble at the Mortimer Tiley offices with the rival who was making my life uncomfortable.

# My Life, a Roller Coaster Ride

## 26. Chroma Television

The following week, David invited me to lunch on Saturday. I accepted. He said he would pick me up at 10.30. I thought it a little early for lunch, but he explained that he would be flying us, in his Cessna, to Tzaneen for lunch in a Game Reserve. What can you say to such an invitation? If he wanted to impress me, he did.

Now, it became quite sneaky. He had a plan, this eccentric and very smart young millionaire. When whizzing through the skies, plugged in to each other's earphones and mikes, it became very personal. Like his brain plugged into my brain.

This time, he didn't talk romance. He enthused about the new company he had created and was about to launch in Wynberg, Johannesburg. David was an Electronic Engineer and in love with TV and show business and everything electronic which made them work.

Chroma Television was a state-of-the-art TV Post-Production company. His staff comprised a bunch of young *whizz kids* in their special electronic fields covering all aspects of TV and Video production. I was interested, as three of my children were in various aspects of Film and TV Production.

Over lunch, he showed me a photo of the Chroma Office Building and his vision for the future. Passionate stuff. I was drawn to his excitement and energy. I had been vaguely aware of David's plans, but only in casual conversation.

Source: Clarion Newspaper

## 4. Megan Carr Promotions

He then proposed to me a second time. Not on his knees. This one was to invite me to join the Board of Director's in his company as Marketing Director.

**Awkward.** I had only been with Mortimer Tiley for six months. They owned 51% of my company. I explained this to David. But he would not let go. All the way back to Rand Airport, his voice was in my ears and into my head. I could name my price. What perks he could offer, like a brand-new car of my choice, handsome salary. No interference from himself or the other directors.

**Fate takes a hand.** He persisted offering 'The freedom, within reason', to semi-manage MCP's few solid regular clients like Pick 'n Pay, now being handled by my capable account managers, but still under my personal eye. I was weakening! I said I would discuss the matter with Alan Tiley and seriously consider the compelling offer.

Just as we landed at Grand Central, he shot a question at me asking,

"What would be the tipping point?" I jokingly replied. "I've always wanted a Porsche Sports. Ha-Ha." His instant reply was, "You've got it as soon as you join us. And you can own it in your name."

I set up a meeting with Alan Tiley, which I had earlier warned him about, and told him of the unhappy situation between 'Janine' and me. He would have to choose between us. I mentioned that I'd had this amazing offer and would prefer to leave and save any unpleasantness. 'Janine' was under contract with a year to run.

We agreed to part company in business. It also saved our personal friendship which our two families have enjoyed for many years.

Alan's son, Bruce, was friendly with Peter. They were twenty. I attended his marriage to Sue at Granny Mouse House in Nottingham Road. They are now proud grandparents of two. Bruce never forgets my birthday. Alan Tiley's oldest son, Craig Tiley, is the CEO of Tennis, Australia.

**1982. Chroma Television.** David's and my almost-romance fizzled from one-sided to zero, but our friendship and business association was healthy, and fun-filled. David remained single for the rest of time.
A condition of this position was that I would work from Chroma offices. I now lived in Louise Terrace, Rivonia, so conveniently nearby.

My job at Chroma was to introduce this new company to Film, TV and Video producers and the Advertising community, which I knew well. I sent out invitations to the launch Cocktail Party and enjoyed a healthy response.

# My Life, a Roller Coaster Ride

• Alan Tiley and promotions girls Maureen Spiro and Carla Morton, welcome Megan Carr, right, on her joining the agency earlier this month.

Right:
My stunning bronze gold, with black trim, Porsche 911 Carrera Targa.

**POST PRODUCTION**
Edit your commercials, documentaries, in living room comfort, using Chroma's ultra modern "state of the art" equipment.

Our Grass Valley 300, 3 mix effects 24 channel video mixer integrated with the GVG two channel digital video effects unit is the ultimate in digital picture manipulation.

Five dedicated MARCONI MR2B 1"C Format VTR's with stereo dolby sound coupled to our Datatron ST5 SMPTE TIMECODE edit controller provide frame accurate edits.

Aston 3 creates full colour electronic captions, or use our caption consoles for artwork input into the GVG 300 and DVE MKII.

Our professional, conscientious editors are ready to use their expertise on your next post production edit.

## 4. Megan Carr Promotions

Our main rival at that time was Trillion, which had enjoyed a near-monopoly till then. So, our State-of-the-Art Postproduction, competition and innovation was welcomed by most clients.

The remarkable aspect is that David allowed me to continue servicing my regular clients with the help of skeleton-staff from my MCP office at home, the main client being Pick 'n Pay.

My Vaal River syndicate partner and friend Errol Cohn found me a stunning bronze gold, with black trim, Porsche 911 Carrera Targa, which was almost new.

I would have to learn to manage the left-hand drive.

My feet barely reached the pedals, so a fat sheepskin seat cover was found. Timing was perfect as I no longer had any school lifts.

**The launch party** was held at the Chroma offices and included working demonstrations on the state-of-the-art equipment.

The guest list included Advertising Agency relevant representatives, Film and TV producers, Commercial photographers and the press.

Of course, several personal invitations happened like our staff's significant others including my parents and my best client Raymond Ackerman, who also became a Chroma client. No surprise!

From that time onwards, I invited target-clients, after office hours, to visit our studios for cocktails and to play with creative ideas and experimentation with our experts in a casual setting.

**Alf Steer, Megan, Mattie Steer at the launch of Chroma Television.**

## My Life, a Roller Coaster Ride

I decided to make our progressive company enjoyable and user friendly.

The personal touch was our watchword. We made many friends, and our prices were competitive. Our own staff of Nerds enjoyed showing off their toys. The business rolled-in, and our competitors became anxious and adjusted their fees.

**Hazel Feldman, Southern Sun,** was bringing in top entertainment from Hollywood and the UK. South Africa had been starved of visiting stars because of Apartheid and the Equity bans.

As Sun City was based in Bophuthatswana, a Homeland, it was a loophole for stars to evade the Equity bans. So, I also included this exciting new element into my PR client building exercise as a reward for their business. Each time a new star arrived, I would book a block of seats, hire a bus for an evening of dinner and show, two-hours out of Johannesburg. I would call Hazel Feldman, Southern Sun's Entertainment Manager to advance block out the best seats before bookings opened to the public.

**Double act.** This happened with stars Rod Stewart and Elton John. Other stars were Shirley Bassey, Linda Ronstadt and many more. One night, our client group, and my family, had a special treat. Rod Stewart was on stage doing his thing with his husky voice. Off stage, at the side, Elton John, in plain sight of the audience, was mimicking Rod's performance and getting some laughs, which baffled Rod. Then Elton ran onto the stage, and we got a unique clowning musical duet, which went on for an hour.

Hazel Feldman had confided in me that temperamental Rod Stewart had a reputation for throwing tantrums. Once, at a different venue, he had thrown a piano crashing out over the balcony. She wrote into his contract, a clause forbidding damage to property, which he signed without a fuss and behaved himself.

**Video production.** I started a side business for Chroma, making private documentaries and training videos. My client Pick 'n Pay made a D.I.Y. video for sale in its Hypers. Pick 'n Pay also made a quarterly filmed Newsletter.

Raymond's letter reads:

*'Dear Megan, I would like to thank you for your excellent idea of putting our Open Letter on video and for the excellent way it was executed. It has been very well received and I'm sure much benefit will derive from this. Thanks once again.*

*Kindest regards. Raymond'*

## 4. Megan Carr Promotions

**'Fat Off' exercise video for Roche** Pharmaceuticals who brought out the dancing star from Flash Dance, Marine Jahan for this highly successful Jane Fonda-type Exercise video.

**Farewell to Chroma.** After three years, discontent started to manifest amongst the senior staff. They complained that David's arrogant interference with their work was unacceptable. Chroma had three major co-investors in the business, so the discontented staff persuaded the two non-executive directors on the board, to ask David to resign. With two to one vote against him, David was bought out and left the company. David saw his dream crash out.

As far as I was concerned, it was David's vision and leadership which had created Chroma in the first place. I was on his side and thought he had been badly treated.

I, resigned in disgust. The company was, by then, highly successful and only three years old. It was later sold to a competitive company and sadly lost its identity. The original staff all dispersed back to the UK or found other jobs. A sad end to a magnificent dream.

I am reminded of something a little bitchy. Accountant, Allan Appel, the family man with a sensible family car, was always a little jealous of my Porsche 911. He must have been approaching his midlife crisis because, one morning, appearing on the company notice board was a fat arrow pointing to a press clipping from the *Financial Mail*'s 'Have you heard' back page of funnies. 'What is a middle-aged woman driving a Porsche called? A Meno Porsche'. I asked myself what to do? Leave it unchallenged? Certainly not. But neither to be touchy nor equally bitchy.

I live with convenient timely synchronicities. The right thing pops up just when I need it. At that very time, Coca Cola was running a slogan in its advertising 'The Pause that Refreshes'. I cut out the Coke ad and changed one word. 'The Porsche that Refreshes' which went up next to the Meno Porsche on the notice board.

Everyone got it and a red-faced Alan came clean about what he'd done and apologised. All was forgiven and my Porsche continued to refresh.

**Ferris Bueller's Day Off.** Another memory about the Porsche. I told my twenty-year-old son, Peter, that he was never to drive the Porsche unless I was with him. Years later, he confessed that he'd had a spare key made, and when I was away on business, he and his pals would drive it the 120kms to the Vaal River house at high speed.

# My Life, a Roller Coaster Ride

**Bye bye Porsche.** Driving the last two kilometres to the Vaal house could only be done at crawling speed because the road corrugations were rattling the sports car to pieces. When I took leave to live at the Vaal for a year, I reluctantly decided to sell it.

Friend and regular Vaal visitor Radio 702's Stan Katz had asked me to give him first refusal if I ever decided to sell it. He bought it and managed to crash it in his home driveway on his first run. No injuries to himself, only to the car.

## First Grandchild

Tony and Lee introduced us to Sean Carr on 19th June 1983.

Sean Carr, 6, got his picture (bottom left) on the Port Elizabeth *Daily News* front page, titled *Dreaming of Beaches,* on the first day of school.

In 2024, with a Bachelor of Business Science degree from UCT under his belt, he married his beautiful school sweetheart and talented artist, Nicole Cronje. They have a daughter, my great granddaughter, Beatrix Kate.

They emigrated to Canada in 2020. Sean is now Deputy CEO of a Financial Investment company in Ottawa, Canada.

**1983. Carole,** a film producer, had met and married Sam Michel. Carole was wearing an off-the-shoulder Laura Ashley gown. A crown of rosebuds in her hair. Sister Andy was her bridesmaid in pink and rosebuds.

The marriage lasted two years. No children. The wedding was held in a marquee in Adele and Bob's Garden.

Sean, dreaming of beaches.                                    Tara, Sam, Carole, Andy.

## 4. Megan Carr Promotions

**Mattie's farewell.** Her cancer was in its last stages. The pain and awful radiation treatment was taking its toll. In December 1985, Mattie was admitted to Sandton Clinic and had difficulty walking. The family conspired to bring her to the Vaal for Christmas and a family gathering one last time. I picked her up at Sandton Clinic and drove her to the Vaal middle house, where they had lived.

Chris met us at the house, we got Mattie out of the car and into her old familiar chair on the stoep. She was looking remarkably good with her pink satin sprigged dressing gown, fresh make-up and Chanel 5 perfume. Not to mention massive medication keeping her comfortable.

When John brought Alfie onto the stoep and he saw his beloved Mattie sitting in her old familiar chair, he said, "Aah Ma, you came" and stretched toward her for a gentle kiss. Even the men shed a tear at this moving moment, forever in our memories.

That early evening, we put them both into padded seats in the 'Old Lady' boat and took them for a cruise. They sat holding hands like teenagers.

Christmas day was a family celebration and a kind of farewell to Mattie, the family matriarch.

**1986. A sad year.** Mattie died peacefully at home at 'The Lodge' late January. Alfie's eulogy at her Memorial was a tearjerker. He talked of having lived a life of friendly bickering and enjoying a whisky together at the end of each day, Mattie was greatly missed leaving a gap in his life. Alf seemed lost without her after fifty-six years together.

At the retirement Lodge, with the departure of Mattie, his days of scones and roses began. Not even the eager single women at The Lodge bringing him cookies and scones could fill the void. Even the old, retired Admiral popping in to fill his own loneliness helped much, although he persuaded Alf to join him in inviting the ladies and other pals to a Sundowner Party, which ended in dancing.

We all laughed when our anxious father phoned to ask how to order a tray of snacks for the party. He was quite capable of ordering the drinks.

Mattie had a rose garden on the front terrace. Alf would go out each Friday and snip off a long-stemmed rose and lovingly place it in a single rose vase on Mattie's dressing table, paying homage to their life journey.

To make him feel loved and not so alone, John, Chris and I and our families, all set up a schedule of visits at Sundowner hour for one or more of us to be with him. As time passed, the tots got bigger - and there was nothing wrong with his eyesight.

# My Life, a Roller Coaster Ride

I took Gracie every morning at 8.30, to make the bed, tidy the house, do the laundry and make sure he had delicious home cooked food ready. I would arrive at 12.30 pm to pick her up. He always insisted I join him for a G&T. Fortunately, there was a handsome indoor Palm tree just inside the lounge behind the sofas. No wonder it faded and died after a while. Where else could I pour my man-sized G&T without being noticed? I had to drive home and still do an afternoon's work.

In August that year, my dad phoned me, at the river, to say that he had just put the last rose of summer on Matties dressing table. Monday morning, I got the call that he had died in the night, Sunday 25th August. Tony's thirtieth birthday.

Coincidentally, twenty-seven years later, Tony died on Sean's thirtieth birthday. 19th June 2013.

## 1986 and 1987

**Sabbatical.** I had been devastated by Mattie's death and decided to wind down my business and start writing. I had the Smith Murder story ready to go. I sold my Louise Terrace house and bought a lock-up-and-go flat in Parkmore. 'The Villa'. Living the easy life at the river house was a luxury after many years of full-time work and parenting. The children now aged 20 to 30, were all independent and working. Daniel and Melanie had long since returned to Scotland. I had emptied the cup – now how to fill it?

**New Toy.** I bought myself a Phillips Video Writer to replace my faithful Olivetti portable typewriter. No personal computers then. It was a glorified typewriter with a box screen and used flat square 'floppy discs. I kept each subject on separately labelled discs.

The subject of my first book was all about a true crime which had happened in 1982. I had been fascinated by the ridiculous incompetence of the husband-murderer. I had registered the crime with my Press Clipping Service, so I had a file of newspaper cuttings ready for reference. My working title was 'Comedy of Errors'.

The question was, 'should I write it as a true crime story or as a film script?' I started writing up the Smith Murder Story as a TV script. With three of my family in films, it seemed a good idea.

When it was done, I asked Carole to check it out. She gave me the best honest advice, as she always does. "Rather write it as a story and then script it". It didn't flow well, scripted with the scene setting in amongst the story line.

## 4. Megan Carr Promotions

I set it aside for future action. I didn't try script writing again. Thirty-three years passed before I picked it up again. I finally wrote and published *Shopping for a Killer* in 2021.

**1987. Three months in the UK.** Using some of my inheritance, John Harvey and I decided to take a three-month holiday in the UK where John had been born and educated. He had many relatives and friends there. Adele Lucas was also visiting the UK, so we had many opportunities to meet and socialise.

**Canal long boats.** I had always wanted to try the canals on the gypsy-like longboats. The first one we hired for a week, travelling from Oxford to Banbury and back.

Left: Canal long boats.

One of our first UK visits was to John's farmer friends Andrew and Jacqui at their farm in Taunton, Somerset. We had stopped at the historic Stonehenge and Salisbury Cathedral en route.

**Awesome Glastonbury.** While in Taunton, we were introduced to a retired Trappist Monk, Olaf Engerdal, who offered to show us around Glastonbury and other local tourist highlights. I had loved King Arthur and the Round table stories, Olaf brought the history alive for us.

Left: Megan at King Arthur and Guinivere's burial site.

## My Life, a Roller Coaster Ride

Then we took a casual trip along the Cornish coast down to Penzance.

**Scotland:** I then took off on my own to visit the place of my mother's birth Kirkcaldy, in Scotland. Then Edinburgh and the Isle of Arran where I hired a bicycle and toured all on my own.

I missed contact with Melanie Lawley, as she was an Air Stewardess and away.

Megan and John in Somerset.

**Norfolk.** We took another boating holiday week on the Norfolk Broads where I remember watching the 1987 electioneering on a tiny defective TV on the boat. We could only see the lower half of anyone on screen. Conservatives won by 6%.

**Back home in South Africa.** We arrived in June, as winter was setting in. Living at the Vaal house was a perfect way to come back to reality. Warm days and icy nights and almost no neighbours around.

**1987. John Harvey.** Our ongoing problem was that John wanted marriage (number three). At the very mention of the M-word I wanted to run a mile. "Marriage is not necessary" I said, "We are quite perfect as we are".

Importantly, into the equation, was the fact that he was fifteen years younger than me. I looked younger, he looked older, so we did not look like 'The Odd Couple'. We left it at that for eight enjoyable and companionable years together.

Before our UK trip, I had moved to the river house for a year. On our return from the UK, John had to find a new job. I suggested he live at The Villa in Sandton.to seek employment, which he did. He was an outstanding salesman, so no problem there.

He then looked up an old girlfriend. We mutually agreed to part company. It was time. He married Sonja and they were together for thirty years till she died in 2021.

John and I are still good friends and remain in touch, as we always have.

## 4. Megan Carr Promotions

**Maggie Thatcher.** July 1988, when I saw this cartoon in *The Star*, I was so amused that I decided to send it to Maggie Thatcher.

In May 1988, the UK elections had been held in Britain. Maggie's Conservatives won at 39% and Neil Kinnock's Labour party lost at 33%. The Liberals took the rest. Neil Kinnock was Leader of the Opposition, Labour Party.

Soon after, in July, flying to Zimbabwe at the invitation of Robert Mugabe, Neil Kinnock's plane mistakenly landed at the wrong airport. A military airport 60 kms short of the Civilian Harare Airport. Neil and Glenys Kinnock were forced out of the plane and held captive at gunpoint.

**Robert Mugabe** and the reception party awaiting them at Harare Airport were alerted to the problem and they were soon released. It was pilot error. Apologies all round saved a Diplomatic meltdown.

With a reply, thanking me for 'Your letter and enclosure, which was of interest to Mrs. Thatcher. Mrs Thatcher sends you her personal good wishes.'

**1987. Conflict and the press.** I was living at the River House after our UK trip, when I received a phone call from Adele Lucas. Not to welcome me back, but to ask me to get back to Johannesburg fast, to help with a very important Conference. I was ready for it and returned to The Villa next day.

Adele Lucas Promotions was working with *The Star* on its 100th Centennial Conference. Her good friend, Robin Courage was her event organiser. She had employed a pretty, young trainee to manage the impending invasion of visiting editors. The trainee felt out of her depth and preferred to step away from the full responsibility. Hence Adele's call to me to step in.

The event was a Conference of forty-five top international Editors and 200 eminent South Africans. Press, Business and Academic professionals debating the subject 'Conflict and the Press'.

In essence, 'How did the presence of the press affects the cause and outcomes of conflict situations?' A full discussion on Press Freedom and Press Responsibilities.

**Harvey Tyson,** Managing Editor of *The Star*, and Adele were handling the sticky problem of a government which did not want this conference with forty-five international editors and associates, snooping on the Apartheid situation.

When showing the impressive list of almost three hundred local and international delegates, Harvey Tyson asked Pik Botha, Minister of Foreign Affairs, for his assurance that not one of the visitors would be refused admission to the country. Pik was reluctant to commit himself, but got involved, eventually recommending a blanket Visa for the forty-five Editors who had to be individually named and designated.

Harvey Tyson, Katherine Graham, Lord McGregor    Photo courtesy of Harvey Tyson.

## 4. Megan Carr Promotions

He specified that once the blanket Visa was granted, no changes would be allowed. A loophole for themselves which they played. Pik made it clear that if the travel and entry matters were not 100% in order, they would all be turned away on arrival at the airport. He had a finger pointing Prime Minister, P.W. Botha, to answer to.

Alarmed at this, Adele and Harvey decided to set up Plan B in case the unthinkable happened. They travelled to Gaborone in Botswana and planned for a Marquee to be set up outside the local hotel, which would also accommodate the international visitors. They kept this Ace up their sleeves, not to frighten anyone off, but also as a bargaining chip, when the chips were down. So to speak.

Of course, in the nature of things, names got switched and changed over the build-up to the conference. For each change, Home Affairs would cancel the block visa and make a big fuss.

Finally, the Wednesday before due date, Adele talked to Pik Botha directly with her own ultimatum demanding a blanket open visa for a set number of editors. He refused. Adele then said, "If I don't have your agreement by twelve noon Friday, Harvey and I will switch the entire conference to Botswana. We are just one call away from making it happen." Adele was out of the office at noon on Friday, so I took the call from Pretoria. It was Pik, himself, in his inimitable voice saying "You've got it. It's on its way right now".

**Lord Oliver McGregor.**

**Paul Johnson.**

## My Life, a Roller Coaster Ride

We were battling with forty-five international publication offices, and national offices across South Africa and Namibia, using the telex method of text communication.

I went to Adele and said, "I've heard of a new way of communication called a *Fax* It is a machine using our own telephone. Why not buy one to streamline our interface with all the delegates. I'm assuming that, being in the communication business, a fair percentage of them already used them.

Now, Adele was known to be thrifty and didn't splash out easily. She said, "It sounds expensive". I had done my homework and assured her it would save money and time, which also has value. And just think how impressive we will be, keeping up with technology. That did it. We got our first fax machine with its rolls of waxy paper (which faded in time). No good for the archives, but we only discovered this later.

One other problem, which Robin and Adele had to deal with, was those 'important' businesspeople who missed the cut being included on the list of South African delegates invited to participate in the Conference. The list had been compiled by *The Star* Business Editor and Adele.

Because of the prestige of the event, there were many noses out of joint. I was relieved that it was not my problem.

My assignment was a pleasure and delight. To look after the visiting contingent of editors and associates, and make sure they were informed, comfortable, transported and connected. I also had the young trainee to do the running.

As a PR consultant, I was honoured to meet many legends in the publishing world, such as Katherine Graham of the *Washington Post*, Andreas Smith, *The Independent* and Donald Trelford, *The Observer*, all of whom played prominent roles in our event.

For me, the best of all was the diminutive, irrepressible Lord Oliver McGregor of Durris, attending our conference in his capacity as Chairman of the UK Advertising Standards Authority and as Chairman of the Conflict and the Press Conference.

As he was my responsibility – and his wheels, we became friends. Sometimes, we skipped some of the conference lectures and, over many hours of relaxing chats and cups of coffee, he filled me in on his life and work.

Humble beginnings and a stint as a gunner during WW2, he went on to graduate with honours in Social Studies and become a university Professor. He was recognised and rewarded for his work with a CBE and Baronetcy bestowed on him.

# 4. Megan Carr Promotions

Lord McGregor, "Call me Mac" introduced me to his good friend, historian and author, Paul Johnson.

**Paul Johnson, author historian, editor, book reviewer** was a delegate at our conference, so the three of us took off on a few occasions for lunch or sundowners. A humbling thought to be in the company of two such legends of the literary world.

I didn't kid myself about being in their intellectual league, but I was the key to their mobility and Mac's brief escapes from his conference duties. We had fun and a British sense of humour in common.

Paul, apart from being the Author of *The History of the American People, History of the Jews, History of Christianity*. He also wrote the controversial *The Intellectuals* quoting Marx, Tolstoy, Sartre, Chomsky using their fame to further their beliefs and theories. He also wrote literary Reviews for *The Spectator* and *The Literary Review*. He was Editor of the *British New Stateman*. His resume is too long to relate, but worth a Google.

Over our many hours together, Paul didn't flog all this, just a very lively and pleasant companion. Like many others have said, travel can be a lonely life. This prolific genius died in 2023 at the age of ninety-four.

During the 2½ days, I sat in many of the lectures including some hot debates. One thing I noticed, from my seat at the back of the hall, was *Sunday Times* Editor, Tertius Myburgh, also sitting in the back row, arms folded, as he indulged the hosts with his presence.

**The Opening Banquet.** This was a working tool to set the scene for the Conference.

**At the Closing Night Banquet** 'The Evaluation' was eloquently presented by the engaging Donald Trelford, Editor of *The Observer*.

The proceedings closed with Harvey Tyson at his combination of serious and light-hearted, best.

On the last evening, I was lucky enough to be seated next to *Star* Columnist, James Clark, who kept the whole table entertained in between the speeches.

I became friends with Harvey Tyson and Rex Gibson in business and socially. We all retired to Hermanus, and the stories continued. Rex kindly offered to pre-edit my true SA crime story *Shopping for a Killer*. He also suggested the title.

James Clark wrote a hilarious book about five aging-editors taking their bicycles to Europe and peddling through English and European country

## My Life, a Roller Coaster Ride

sides. Its title *Blazing Saddles*. Rex muttered to us at a dinner party "More like 'Blazing Bums' ".

Rex Gibson co-wrote a book *Conflict and the Press* covering the conference.

Rex was Deputy Managing Editor to Harvey at the time of this conference. He was once editor of the liberal *Rand Daily Mail* when it was sensationally closed down due to current politics. His book *The Final Deadline* tells the shocking story.

**1987. New health product Cerebos EggMix.**

I was approached by Doug McKinnon Smith, Marketing Manager for Cerebos, to introduce a brand-new health product to the general public and the retail grocery trade.

At that time, cholesterol in eggs was considered a serious heart hazard. Since my father's heart attack in 1970, he had only been allowed one egg a year on his birthday.

## Eggs without cholesterol

GOOD news for all those who on medical advice are cutting down on egg consumption or even trying to do without eggs completely.

Cholesterol-free eggs will be on sale in Port Elizabeth later this month.

Before you get over excited at the thought of eating a cholesterol-free fried, poached, boiled, or even coddled egg, relax. You will only be able to eat the new eggs scrambled or as an omelette, but they do make excellent French toast and are super for baking, puddings and crumbing.

It is an egg mix from which the cholesterol is missing because the egg yolk is missing.

The egg whites and the nutrients in the mix once reconstituted are similar to that of a medium-size egg but the fat content amounts to only a two hundredth part of a fresh egg. For this reason the egg mix is also most suitable as a diet food.

Mrs Megan Carr of Johannesburg, who was in my office to tell me about it, also pointed out the advantages other than medical of this new exciting product. It is a fine convenience food for campers and for those who have no refrigeration facilities. The egg mix has a shelf life of up to two years.

Samples sent to the United States were well received and were judged superior to similar products marketed there.

In appearance the egg mix is a remarkably light-weight powder. Packed in plastic tubs of 100 grams, the yellow and black pack is the equivalent of 25 medium eggs and compares well in price. It is reconstituted with skim milk or water or a mixture of both and from then on is handled like ordinary eggs. It is

MRS MEGAN Carr of Johannesburg who is thrilled the response to the cholesterol-free low fat eggs sh promoting. The egg mix is available in Johannes and on the Reef and will be in Port Elizabeth su markets within two weeks.

egg mix — Megan gave me a sample — I was so carried away that I forgot to add any form of fat. It stuck only a little bit to the bottom of the enamelled saucepan I used.

## 4. Megan Carr Promotions

Cholesterol is only in the yolk, so Cerebos researchers had come up with a solution for people like my father. 'EggMix'. This product was a powder made of egg whites, albumin, which could replace eggs in cooking and baking. Good for breakfast as fluffy light omelettes, but not scrambled or fried. It was completely cholesterol free. and tasted like egg. Certainly nothing like the wartime egg powder which was slimy and unpleasant.

My Spitfire pilot husband preferred not to have his hen's eggs whisked to smoothness as it reminded him of his wartime breakfasts.

**The Cerebos launch breakfasts.** Presenters Jane Evans and Gordon Mulholland seen below demonstrating 'EggMix' at the first launch Tasting Breakfast. I set up a Launch Breakfast with demonstrations in each centre of the country.

My secretary at the time was Jane Evans, who kindly agreed to don an 'EggMix' apron and chef hat and demonstrate how easy it was to have delicious breakfast egg without the dangerous cholesterol.

Actor Gordon Mulholland did the running commentary for the demo as the press and opinion leaders, like Housewives League, Woman's Institute, Professor Harry Seftel, retail buyers and media, enjoyed their EggMix breakfast omelettes.

Of course, the Chief Sub Editors had a field day with their captions and headlines. Mostly 'Eggcellent'. This unusual promotion worked well for years, until the medical profession calmed down and real hens' egg's crept back into daily use.

### Childline

In the mid 1980s I volunteered a day a week working the Childline emergency phones. Childline was introduced for emergency telephone help to provide a capable channel for children and parents to talk through their troubles and get guidance to professional help.

I responded to a call for volunteers to join the newly formed Childline starting up in Johannesburg. They had over 600 replies from people offering their time.

The University of the Witwatersrand (Wits) Medical Faculty of Psychiatry set the parameters for the initial selection to ensure the suitability of volunteers taking on this sensitive task. We all attended several weeding out group meetings until there were only 50 in the pool.

We had to commit one full day a week for a minimum of a year, to sit in their offices and 'man' the phones on their toll-free number. There were always two of us in the office together, which was a learning curve, as each one I met had some kind of interesting history and reason to be there.

**Commitment.** This one day a week was tricky for me, still running my business, but I was fully committed and had to make a plan to be absent from the office every Wednesday, office hours, for at least a year.

The semi-final group of fifty was then called in for further fine assessment by the head of Wits Psychiatry Faculty through two group meetings where test cases were presented for each of us to 'handle' as we saw fit. It felt like back to school as our answers were recorded and taken away for assessment. I made it into the final remaining 27 who were all deemed fit for the job. I felt ridiculously proud of myself and very privileged to be selected.

I then discovered that the primary requirement was not to be judgmental or to be tempted give free personal advice, but to listen, privately assess the situation and then refer them to the appropriate professionals or institutions, qualified to assist. These professionals had already been introduced to us for referral.

**Filtering.** Immediately discarded were those potential volunteers who, when asked what they would do, faced with an abuser of a child?

If the answer was. "I would beat them to within an inch of their lives", they would be excused and not taken on. Non-judgmental was the watchword. Not our job to deliver justice, only to listen and refer to the professionals.

I chose to work Wednesdays and there I went for almost two years. Once chosen we had further intensive training weekly for six-weeks.

**Intrusion.** One interesting exercise was when, sitting in two circles of fourteen volunteers and a group director, the Wits Professor told us to take

## 4. Megan Carr Promotions

up our handbags and wallets. He then told us to pass them to the person sitting on our right.

Each one registering shock and horror as we were instructed to rummage around inside to find what was in them. At first no one moved, so odious and intrusive did this act seem, but he insisted. Uncomfortably, we duly rummaged, and then he let us off the hook as he explained that the very nature of our job was to delve into the private lives of strangers, and to remember that they had invited us in, therefore, never to feel guilty or reluctant. It was simply part of the job.

**Sage advice.** He instructed us never to take the cases home with us. Not easy. After twenty-one months, I resigned after both my parents died. I decided to take one-year sabbatical to live and run my curtailed business remotely from the river house.

**1981. Norscot Manor.** Believe it or not, I made an offer to buy Norscot Manor, a rambling vacant manor house, which had been iconic in its day but left badly neglected by the family.

It had been built and owned by Ernst Eriksen and his wife, Ethel, in 1935. They named it Norscot Manor, after their countries of birth Norway and Scotland.

### My idea of a Social Etiquette Academy

Whilst I was a director at Chroma Television, I had decided to make up a documentary programme of individual videos on social etiquette for young men about to enter the business world and who would benefit from some polish in their professional lives.

I found interested sponsors for ten aspects to be covered such as Table Manners, (Diners Club), Wines and how to serve them (SFW), Forms of address for example, a Judge, a Bishop, a Mayor. a University Chancellor. (FNB) Society manners. Invitations, Business meetings. Speech-making and Toasts.

I then decided to create a Social Etiquette Academy where they could practice what they were learning on video, I would have to find a suitable venue for the Academy.

**How I found it?** I was driving around scouting, when I spotted a faded 'FOR SALE' sign almost hidden behind a hedge and a large building hiding behind it. I phoned the Agent's number on the sign. He came and showed me the property. I was bowled over by what I saw. A magnificent rambling manor house, in sadly run down condition.

# My Life, a Roller Coaster Ride

Although it was far from tenable as it stood, the quality of the original edifice, fixtures and fittings made me realise that spit and polish and lots of TLC would bring it back to its obviously former glory. I did ask myself, though, why it hadn't been snapped up already.

Asking the price, I was shocked at the ridiculously low figure he quoted. The family was anxious to get rid of their 'millstone'. I had to have it.

I rushed off to Charles Dearlove, my aptly named, wonderful Sandton Barclays Bank Manager, who had supported me through some trying financial turmoil, but who also had seen me back on my feet again. And currently on a fat salary at Chroma. He met me at Norscot Manor to make the assessment for granting a mortgage bond.

He offered me a 75% bond. I had the 25% deposit, and the offer was made and accepted 'in principle'. Charles was satisfied with this marvellous collateral.

I thought I had it in the bag. But it was not to be.

When the Peri Urban Counsel heard about it, they woke up, had a meeting, and put a proposal to the public to turn Norscot Manor into a Public Recreation Centre. They must have bettered my offer and pulled rank, and mine was turned down.

The new Sandton Recreation Centre opened a year later, in 1982.

And what happened to the Academy for Social Etiquette?

It was at that time that there was an internal rebellion starting at Chroma against David Munton who was forced out. I resigned in sympathy, as it was David's concept and dream. I didn't like the disloyalty and ugliness of those he had nurtured in the business.

It also ended my production of the Social Etiquette programmes.

In later years, Norscot Manor became a Heritage sight and it is now an elegant guest house.

# Part 5
## The Move to Cape Town

# My Life, a Roller Coaster Ride

## 27. The Move to Cape Town

**1992. November.** When I first moved from Sandton to Cape Town with my puppy dog, Rosebud, I decided to settle in Simonstown. Being ignorant of the logistics of travel and transport in that area, I rented a house in Froggy Farm for a test period of three months. I loved Simonstown and all the people I met there.

My daughter, Andy, lived in Wynberg and so it was good to be near enough to visit each other.

I had sold my *Witkoppen* house because of three burglaries. After the third break-in and already two replacements of all my electronics, the hardest decision of all, was to sell my beloved weekend house on the Vaal River, having enjoyed it with my growing family for twenty-eight years.

Living alone in the Johannesburg area seemed just too dangerous. In fact, my Insurance Assessor and I were getting to know each other. So concerned was she about my safety, that on her third visit, she brought me a gift of a Boerbull/Mastiff puppy for my protection in the future. She was a pretty-little-thing. I called her 'Rosebud'.

**Ready to Roll.** I was driving a new white two door sporty Nissan Sentra. Items piled high on the roof rack, inside stuffed to the gills with suitcases and pulling a trailer full of everything I felt I needed for my new life in a furnished rental house. I made a nest on the passenger seat for the six-month-old Rosebud and lots of towels in case of puppy 'accidents'.

Along the road on the 1 600 km journey, I stopped every 300 kms to

Peter talking to his Maltese Poodle 'Charlie Girl'. 1982 I gave him a puppy to encourage him to stay home and swot for Matric. He passed his matric and Charlie was part of the family for 14 years.

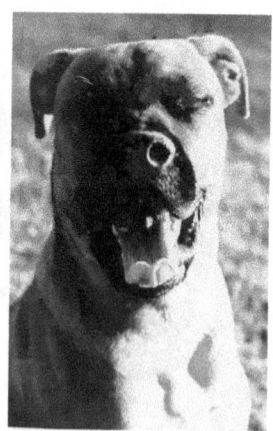

Disney.

## 5. The Move to Cape Town

let Rosebud out for water, walk and wee. She drank the water but simply refused to relieve herself.

Eventually, we arrived at Andy's Wynberg house, our first overnight stop. Andy threw open her front door when she heard the car arrive. Rosebud was so pleased to see her that she ran into the house and let loose what she had been saving up for 16 hours.

Talk about a tsunami in the passage! Welcome to Cape Town.

**The Froggy Farm rental** had a beautiful view and looked straight down a steep hill to the sea below. At last, I could consider myself in retirement. Lots of books, walks with Rosebud and greeting the friendly neighbours.

Rosebud was so friendly that, the minute the house door was open, she would run out onto the quiet road and follow anyone who happened to pass. Every day I would run around the neighbourhood calling her name until she emerged. It was too much to control. It gave me much exercise running after her, but also acquainted me with all the nearby neighbours.

Nothing like walking a dog or baby to make friends.

Feeling perfectly safe away from the dangers of Johannesburg, I phoned my son Peter and asked if he fancied having my little Rosebud as his pet as I simply couldn't manage her in a house without a fence. He wanted her and she flew SAA, mildly sedated, to Johannesburg in a little cage, with her toys, to her new master.

Peter didn't feel good about the Rosebud name, a macho thing. Being in the film industry he renamed her Disney, bonded instantly and they were best pals for many years until she died. This was Pete's second dog. I got him a puppy when he was writing matric to keep him home and focused. It also worked. We shared Charlie Girl twelve years.

**Cape Town welcome.** In addition to be living near Andy, I was fortunate to be made welcome in Cape Town by my friend Ann Wallis Brown.

Ann had been my Cape Town business manager when one of my major clients had been Defy. So good was she at the Defy promotion that I was approached by the Defy Marketing Manager, Barry Drain, asking me to release Ann to take on the fulltime job of marketing Defy for them. Of course, I agreed, happy for her to create her own company to take on Defy. She went on to become a PR and Marketing force in her own right

When I moved to Cape Town in 1993, Ann set about introducing me socially and in business to all the right people in her orbit. She found me office premises in Loop Street, Central Cape Town and signed me up to the Cape Top 100 Women's Club and the local Press Club. I met influential people such as Aaron and Adele Searle and the diminutive powerhouse Ina Paarman. Ann's personal friendship and hospitality made for happy times in my new life.

Through the Top 100 Club, I enjoyed many light and serious lectures, talks and seminars. Interesting speakers such as Terry Pratchett, Carl Bernstein (*Washington Post*) and writer-poet, Rod McKuen. I attended seminars such as 'Time Management' (Self-Management) and Phillip Crosby's 'Quality Management' (Do 100% of what is possible).

As a member of the Press Club, I met all the local editors and journalists like Kosie Viviers and John Scott, (*Cape Times)*. I already knew Jonathan Hobday and others.

Through the Cape Town Press Club, I was privileged to meet Nelson Mandela at two press functions. The second being at a Press Breakfast at the Kenilworth Racecourse where we shook hands, gently, fingertip to fingertip, as he walked through the room. Gently, to save those fragile aging hands which were said to shake hundreds of hands each week. That famous smile, always welcoming. His very presence, palpable.

**November 1992. Back to work.** No sooner had I settled into my life of leisure than, after only a month, I got a call from Adele Lucas to ask if would take on the job of running one of her big Cape projects. An Anglo-American Properties Development promotion. The Welgedacht Homes Show, a large housing development near Durbanville.

I accepted. I had to start immediately. I still had over a month to go on my Simonstown rental and found the daily run to the offices in Gardens in Cape Town and further, to the Durbanville vicinity of the Show, a huge traffic monster to face every day. I thought I had kissed the traffic jams of Johannesburg goodbye forever.

**Fisherman's Quay.** I decided to move nearer town. Having given up my beautiful river house in the Transvaal, I hunted for something next to water and found it in Fisherman's Quay, Marina da Gama near Muizenberg. A quaint two bedroomed cottage right on the water's edge.

I got the furniture out of storage and cosied up in my new home. I bought a paddle boat. My neighbours on the water were ducks and coots.

**The Welgedacht Homes Show.** The awareness campaign for the 450 erf Estate development was to be a three weekend Homes Show. A three-month undertaking involving the preparations, publicity and activities for drawing in the public to see the five spec show houses, the overall

# 5. The Move to Cape Town

development and have an enjoyable family day out.

It needed an intensive publicity programme. The organisation involved contracting entertainment, catering, general management and supervision of the events.

One of the many events we presented was an afternoon of music by the Stellenbosch Symphony Orchestra under an open-sided marquee as the visitors sat on rugs and in their garden chairs on the sloping lawns.

Another attraction for the children and their dads, was a Kite flying demonstration and competition.

The *Weekend Argus* was the media sponsor of the Welgedacht Homes Show. Thereby hangs a different tale, which had a big influence on my future in Cape Town. The five magnificent spec-built showhouses, individually architect-designed, decorated, furnished and landscaped, were an attraction all on their own.

**Opening party.** The night before the show opened to the public, we organised a launch party in the huge marquee destined to be the show restaurant. It had a smaller attached tent for the kitchen, complete with stoves, fridges and stocked for public dining.

The evening party for about eighty guests representing the top Anglo American personnel, the Mayor, the Press, the five House builders, their architects and decorators. The party ended at 10pm.

Adele had flown in from Johannesburg. Then the unthinkable happened. A huge wind and rainstorm in the night blew down the marquee. Adele and I rushed there to help the catering staff and the marquee people to get it all back together in time for the public arrival.

We found ourselves cleaning up mess and picking up things which had been scattered everywhere. Then setting tables and finding flowers for the reception area. By 11 am, somehow it was done and ready for business.

Over the three weekends of the campaign, the Anglo sales staff were kept busy signing up sales. One of the show houses sold on the first weekend and the other four within a month.

**1994. Near death experience.** There is a sting in the tail to my reason for moving to the Cape. To be safer and away from crime in Johannesburg.

I had been living in Marina da Gama for about a year. It was early April 1994 just before the iconic Democratic elections. I had been out to dinner with some Press Club friends and returned home late evening.

Hours later, I awoke with sharp pains in my head and face and blood everywhere. In the reflected moonlight off the water, I saw a young man standing at the foot of my bed, looking down at me and fiddling with his zip.

I didn't scream. Intuitively, I realised that it would empower him if I did. His intentions were plain to see, so I talked quietly and soothingly about his mother and grandmother watching him. I asked him if they would like to see what he was doing. How very old I was just like his grandmother.

Next thing, he pulled back the bedclothes and my underwear and crawled on top of me. I kept calm, talking softly. With my voice in his ear, he tried his best to be the macho man, but thankfully couldn't perform. Maybe the image of his grandmother under him saved me. His downfall – so to speak. He shouted "You must help".

**A terrifying situation for me.** I kept up the mantra of mother and grandmother. And guess what? He slowed his pathetic activities and fell asleep right there on top of me. His head next to mine. He smelt of chemicals probably drugs. Certainly not fresh and clean.

Sometimes I make light of it when telling the story. I wonder if I should be insulted at someone falling asleep at such a moment! I'm a typical Taurus – according to Linda Goodman's Star Signs, a Taurus would joke on the way to the gallows.

In fact, I was slowly regaining full aching consciousness from concussion as I realised that he had come into the house earlier and beaten me unconscious with a bottle as I slept. He thought he had killed me and wandered around the cottage helping himself to food from the fridge and cash from my handbag and the contents of the petty cash box.

**Lying there,** pinned down by this sleeping intruder, my dilemma was what to do next? I had seen the bottle weapon still in his hand and thought that perhaps I could reach down and get it and beat him up with it. Still groggy,

## 5. The Move to Cape Town

it was not sound reasoning. As I stretched down the bed for the bottle, he woke up and got vicious, telling me to leave his bottle or he would kill me. I then firmly said to him "You must leave – now".

And tamely, like a sleepwalker, he got up, hitched up the pants around his ankles and left through the forced open French doors saying, "if you follow me, I will come back and kill you". Then ran off.

I immediately grabbed my dressing gown and wobbled, partly undressed, into the lounge through the bedroom door and locked it. I threw on the dressing gown and phoned the Marine Patrol who came within five minutes and took a statement.

They called the police who also arrived quickly. My description was good enough in the reflected moonlight, they knew exactly who he was.

They did their best to tend to my smashed face and head, still bleeding. The detective took me in his car, to the hospital. The Police photographed the bedroom scene and bagged my two left back molar teeth and underwear lying on the floor.

**Forensics, False Bay Hospital and fromage.** After the necessary forensics, I was treated in surgery. I had 35 stitches above my left ear, broken cheekbone, broken jaw, concussion and was very shaken by the traumatic experience. They kept me in hospital for five days. A month later, a Maxillofacial Surgeon repaired the cheek and jawbone.

Meanwhile, immediately after the attack, the police waited for Sammy Kitcher, the villain, at his shack in the Vryegrond squatter camp nearby. When Sammy casually strolled up shortly afterwards, they searched him, found my Megan Carr Promotions petty cash slips, money and a large piece of good french cheese in his pocket. Then cuffed him and took him to the Police Station to charge him, then the forensics and police cells.

The cops cheered me up in hospital, next day, when they visited for a more a coherent statement. Apparently, Sammy and two friends had been doing the rounds in Marina da Gama that afternoon with some shopping trolleys doing some opportunistic breaking and entering.

Sammy then went to the police to claim a reward by reporting his two co-robbers, who were then arrested.

**Rewards.** That same night, when the cops arrived at the Station with Sammy, they put him into the same cell as the other two and mentioned that he had claimed a reward by reporting them. The cops had to stop the resulting onslaught before a death occurred. Sammy was placed in a different cell to save his life.

## My Life, a Roller Coaster Ride

**What's New?** Of course, the forensic samples 'got lost' between Cape Town and Pretoria. A few weeks later I was asked to give a new set of blood and DNA. The familiar detective came to pick me up in his car to take me to the hospital.

As I got into the car, I immediately jumped out again. I said. "he's been in this car, I can smell him!". The officer admitted that he had just taken Sammy from jail to the hospital for his forensics.

**Trial.** When the case finally came to court almost a year later, Sammy was found guilty of attempted murder and attempted rape and got sentenced to 22 years, probably to serve 15 years if he behaved himself. He would be 38 by that time.

So much for coming to a place safer than Sandton, Johannesburg.

**1994. Cape Town.** After the successful Welgedacht Homes Show, the *Weekend Argus* media sponsor, editor Jonathan Hobday, recommended me to John Thomson MD of Exhibition Management Services, to publicise his upcoming Cape exhibitions.

And then came the violent attack on me in my home.

With my face still a mess, Jon Hobday arranged for me to meet John Thomson. Because of Hobday's endorsement, Thomson bravely invited me to manage the publicity for his Exhibitions about to launch in Cape Town.

**John Thomson.** The *Weekend Argus* would also Media Sponsor John's Exhibitions. We had worked seamlessly and productively together, so it made sense.

John Thomson is a very imposing man who tries to be a little intimidating on first meeting. That doesn't work with me, so we sorted that one out and got on well thereafter.

Having said that, John is highly talented and successful in creating and managing commercial exhibitions.
A field which was also familiar to me.

**Culemborg Exhibition Centre.**
John's first step was to acquire Culemborg, a disused railway terminal, and convert it into his personal venue which he leased, long-term, and converted for all his future exhibitions. Also to rent out for other commercial events.

# 5. The Move to Cape Town

For events outside John's company, he appointed me as letting agent. I worked in conjunction with John's local manager, handing him prospects to be signed up and managed.

Like all smart executives, John Thomson had employed an outstanding Cape Town organiser and salesman, Johnny Malherbe, a happy, smiling soul with loads of energy, hiding an inner steel. We all loved Johnny which made our partnership all the happier. throughout the 1990's, after which John retired from the Cape Town scene and into semi-retirement.

1994. The first, and typical, exhibition was The Cape Media and Marketing Exhibition.

My job was to liaise with The *Weekend Argus* sponsor, with its substantial readership, firstly to attract exhibitors and then to get the right feet through the doors.

I always booked a four-page tabloid pull-out supplement, then assisted the *Argus* sales team to sell ads from the exhibitors list to pay for two thirds of the space. The remaining third was for free editorial, supplied by me, to generate interest in the expo, including the grand opening by a VIP media or political personality.

Once a show was open to the public, I fed stories to the general media. I would then produce a report and feature story for the second *Weekend Argus* edition to attract visitors to the second weekend of the show.

Between us we would decide who to invite to open the shows. Usually a Politician, a Mayor or an appropriate well known business person. Controversial politician Peter Mokaba was the CABI opener.

# My Life, a Roller Coaster Ride

Jonathan Hobday handing the portrait to Peter Mokaba.

The 1995 award went, unanimously to Raymond Ackerman for his Summer Olympic Bid Campaign.

**Left:**
**Culemborg Exhibition Centre.**
Before the empty space before installation of stands.

## 5. The Move to Cape Town

**Peter Mokaba.** Opened the CABI Cape Business and Industrial Expo. He had been a firebrand ANC Youth Leader in his earlier life but rather less fiery in later politics. At that time, he was Minister of Sport and Recreation.

I commissioned an artist to paint a portrait of him as a thank you gift. Peter was thrilled with it as you can see by the big smile, perfectly matching the portrait. Sadly, he died just a few years later. This portrait was displayed at his coffin in the TV coverage at his state funeral.

**Olympic bid.** In 1995, I was still connected to Raymond Ackerman on his Cape Town Summer Olympic Bid campaign. On the Bid Committee were Deputy Minister of Sport, Ngconde Balfour, Clive Keegan and Chris Ball.

Raymond was determined to get the Summer Olympics for his beloved Cape Town. Sadly, we missed out to Atlanta, Georgia which won the 1996 Summer Games.

Taking advantage, for both the Expo publicity and the Olympic Bid drive, I suggested to John and Jon that we create a 'Marketing Person of the Year' award. His award was a framed caricature of him and the Olympic story, by the *Argus* cartoonist.

The following year we voted Maureen Thompson 'The Marketing Person of the Year'.

**Maureen Thompson,** Promotions and PR Manager for the Cape Town Waterfront Centre as it was launched the previous year. Jonathan Hobday, always smiling, Media Sponsor for many of our Promotions in the Cape.

**Old railway station.** Imagine a 220m x 40m wide warehouse-type building with a sunken railway line down the middle. They partly filled in the railway passageway to make a magnificent 9 200 square metre expanse to divide up into modules to lease out as show stands and relevant offices and utilities.

**Coffee Shop.** Another convenient aspect for me. I asked John Thomson if my son Tony Carr and his wife, Lee, could run a Coffee Shop at the show. He jumped at the idea. It became a popular gathering point at the show, and at all future shows.

# My Life, a Roller Coaster Ride

**Telesales.** Lee Carr then offered her services as a telesales person, selling exhibition stands. She could sell anything to anybody over the phone. Working with Johnny Malherbe, Lee became their best salesperson, earning handsome commission income over the years. Tony, in support, dealt with the contract signatures and advertising materials. Only fax then available to make selling easier. This was a lucrative side business for them and enjoyed by this nepotistic mother.

**Stand Judging.** One pleasant side aspect was to appoint suitable, independent people to judge the stands on the opening day. Regulars over the years were Gorry Bowes-Taylor, The *Weekend Argus* Woman's Page Editor (married to Doug Bowes-Taylor, *Argus* Chief Photographer) which was all good for the show publicity.

MCP : 50% PARTNER & PROMOTER - 1995
LEISURE, PLEASURE & TRAVEL EXPO

Below: Andy Carr waving atop the Topless Bus.

Left:
Hot Air Balloon. To get further attention, we advertised the show with a Hot Air Balloon anchored near the main road.

# 5. The Move to Cape Town

**Peter Cazulet** was another regular Judge over the years. He was the brilliant and charismatic Stage Designer for Artscape theatre complex. So enjoyable with this arrangement were they, that they never allowed me to let them off the hook when I worried that I was imposing on them. They took their judging responsibilities seriously and were respected by the exhibitors as being unbiased and fair.

**Exhibition Regulars.** Annual or biennial shows which followed were, the Media Marketing Expo, CABI, Cape Business and Industrial Trade Show, Fish Africa Expo, Refrigeration Africa Show.

**This Expo** was suggested to Thomson by me. Andy and I became John's 50 percent partners in this with great success. We had the Cape Town Mayor open this one as it boosted Tourism.

**Leisure, Pleasure and Travel Show.** Topless Bus Commandeered to advertise the show through the streets.

**Family Art.** In 2010 Lee Carr persuaded John, for the Fish Africa Show, to place Carole's display of fish at the reception to the show. Carole did it as an opportunity to show her work. After the publicity received in the Argus, Koi Restaurants commissioned Carole to produce a fish wall-display for their Rosebank restaurant. This was so admired, that they commissioned one for their Pretoria Koi Restaurant.

This display of fish publicity led to the commission of further fish installation at two Koi restaurants in Jhb and Pretoria.

# My Life, a Roller Coaster Ride

**An Alpha Seminar in progress.**

**Alpha Seminars. At regular breaks delegates would stand and rub each others' backs to the tune of 'Don't Worry, Be Happy'.**

# 5. The Move to Cape Town

## 28. Alpha Mind Power Seminars
## Peter Heibloem, a pivotal person in my life

The Alpha Seminars became, not only a highly profitable part of our business, but what we learnt from them was like getting a toolbox for life.

Better than that, they were life enhancing.

It was mid 1993 when I received a phone call from Brisbane, Australia. The very Ozzie voice introduced himself as Peter Heibloem. He said he would be visiting South Africa to attend a Cycad conference.

He then mentioned that he would like to introduce his Alpha Dynamic seminars to South Africa. He said he had asked around and been given my contact details as the recommended person to run his Cape Town seminars, if I was interested.

He mentioned that he would be working with Adele Lucas for the Johannesburg seminars. He had done his homework from Australia. I was impressed.

I was particularly interested when learning the content of the seminars. Just as he had checked me out, I checked out his reputation in Australia which was faultless. Even exciting. However, introducing new and somewhat esoteric seminars was risky and expensive. Was South Africa ready for it?

Carole and Andy were living in Cape Town at that time and the three of us decided to accept the challenge. I say 'challenge' because there was a competing and popular Life Coach doing the rounds at that time, John Kehoe, whose theory for self-confidence and success in life, was based on affirmations and self-image. They worked well enough, but on a conscious level, as opposed to Peter Heibloem's more superconscious levels based on brain rhythms and relaxation.

Andy had attended a John Kehoe seminar. The good thing about Kehoe was that he had done a lot of solid groundwork work persuading people, especially those in business or having life problems, that their lives could be better. Part of the work was done for us. Our job was to persuade the public that ours was different and better.

The Alpha Mind Power theory had evolved and developed from the proven teachings of Jose` Silva, called *The Silva Method*. He wrote a book of his teachings and successes endorsed as 'The World's Leading Personal Development System'.

The Silva Book sub-title: 'Tapping the Secrets of your Mind for Total Self-Mastery' with the challenges 'Turn your Desires into Reality', 'Reach

# My Life, a Roller Coaster Ride

New Goals', 'Improve your Health', 'Solve Business and Relationship Problems', and 'Lead a Happier and More Fulfilling Life'.

Silva's proven method teaches you to function at the inner-conscious level - the Alpha brain frequency – and to use your right brain hemisphere for enhanced intuition, creativity, problem solving' and more. 'Whatever you can visualise, you can actualise'.

**Richard Bach,** the author of *Jonathan Livingston Seagull* (also a stunt pilot), says that this method of living has become an important part of his daily life.

Peter Heibloem, was a Mr. Bean look-alike. A Chartered Accountant in his other life, he had developed a failproof formula for attracting people to his intensive 32-hour seminars.

People love the promise of self-improvement. They also like something for nothing. Heibloem acknowledged that people selling 'life enhancement' were two-a-penny. Our job was to set up two or three free lectures before each main seminar, to explain, not only how to be 'more successful' but, closer to home, to show proof of how it improves short-term memory.

He tempts with easy weight loss, stop smoking and how to get into 'the zone' to be more creative and confident at your office meetings. Better sleep habits. Better energy. All daily life problems which are real. Not something seemingly out of reach.

We three Carr women discussed how to approach the advertising and PR to best attract attention to the Free Lectures, and ultimately, the main thirty-two hour seminar.

Each of the fourteen sessions was different, inter-active and thought provoking. Each was a revelation and a lesson, digging deeper and deeper each day. Profoundly life changing.

Andy was pregnant with Alex at that time and bounding with energy. Carole was briefly between film projects and was available to join us in getting the Alpha seminars going. I had not yet started up my new Cape Town business was still trying to retire.

To promote our Alpha Mind Power Free Lectures, I approached Stan Katz, of Cape Talk 567 Radio with a proposition.

If he would grant us a half hour live interview when Peter arrived in Cape Town, we would back it up with a series of paid 30 second spots ahead of the live interview and Free Lectures. Stan happily agreed to this and even offered a discount for the radio spots as we were friends.

His bright and chatty Morning Programme Host, Lisa Chait interviewed

## 5. The Move to Cape Town

Peter for this first seminar, which was so well received that she adopted us and remained our radio interview friend and Alpha supporter for many years. TV was too expensive and therefore out of our reach. It would have to be Radio, leaflets and posters.

Fortunately for us, Peter Heibloem was a radio natural. He was very amusing and persuasive on the air. He had the audiences in the palm of his hand at the free lectures. He provided excellent four-page brochures which made people drool with the expectations of what they could achieve, especially as the Australian graduate endorsements on the brochures seemed, and were, genuine. It helped that, on the radio, we only talked about our Free Lectures, which looked less commercial.

Our Free Lectures were booked out within a week of every radio broadcast, supported by the radio commercials and printed street posters. At the first Free Lectures, we had to play it by ear as we had no idea what to expect.

Carole and Andy sat taking Seminar bookings at the end of the first two lectures. 274 people booked for the first paid four-day Seminar, at what was considered a steep price for the 32 hours. Most paid immediately, others sent in or delivered their cheques to our new offices, 19 Loop Street, in central Cape Town

The first Cape Town seminar at the Arthur's Seat Hotel in Sea Point, delivered such amazing personal results that we realised we would have to plan a follow-up event without delay as word of mouth had gone viral and we had a list of hopeful bookings even before we had announced the next seminar date. Johannesburg was having an equally good turnout.

The second Seminar took place a few weeks later at the Municipal Dromedaris Hall in Cape Town. The main seminars ran 6pm - 9pm Friday and Monday and 8am - 9am Saturday and Sunday. An intense 32 hours in total.

The beauty of the seminars is that they transcended all beliefs, religions, ethnicities and ages. People were helped with self-image and health issues and general upliftment.

Graham, a student, had not been able to make his own phone booking, but had a friend book for him because he stuttered so badly. He phoned me a year later to prove he was still speaking perfectly normally without his stutter. A hundred percent life changing success.

Susan cured herself of M.E. (the chronic energy-sapping 'flu'). The disease had cost Susan her job at her Ad Agency. The Agency had booked eight of their staff and asked us if we would sponsor Susan. We did. We gave her small jobs to do at session intervals, to make her feel she was earning her fee. (I believe freebees are valued at what they cost). Within a month, she was back to good health, and in a short time, back to work in a top job.

Many delegates would return for a second seminar, simply to reconnect with the amazing energy and joy of the weekend. Some became 'helpers' and attended at half price. Also useful to us as they knew the drill by then, straightening chairs at breaks, tidying, serving Rooibos tea and selling subliminal tapes.

Their presence reassured hesitant first timers and took some pressure off our shoulders running the show.

Carole and Andy played a critical part in making the first two Alpha seminars the phenomenal success they were. They set Alpha up to become a part of the newly revived MCP in the Cape.

Over the following nine years, Andy organised most of the 17 seminars and facilitated the Follow-on Workshops, which ran for 8 weeks after Peter had departed for Brisbane.

Many delegates called on Andy for further counselling, which later inspired her to become a Life-Line Counseller and a Hypnotherapist. (Currently in Johannesburg).

At each of the Free Lectures, the most convincing live test was to put an Alpha graduate on stage to be memory tested to prove the relaxed brain

Andy Carr.

## 5. The Move to Cape Town

rhythm theory for good memory. It was a risk because if this didn't work, the bookings would show it.

An 'Alpha Graduate' would be called to the stage, sitting on a chair, back to the several hundred person audiences, and Peter, front stage with his flip chart facing the audience. The audience was invited to say their name and call out items to be written up, 1-20 on the Flip Chart.

Because of the risk of embarrassing failure, it was not easy to persuade any graduate do the test.

I tested myself and found that I was able to do the memory test, using memory pegs and a relaxed mind, as we had discovered in the Alpha seminars.

So, in the absence of volunteers, I became that reliable memory volunteer on stage, on a regular basis over the years.

The clue callers always tried to be smart, challenging the volunteer to fail and themselves to triumph. Things like 'A three legged dog called Charlie', 'My car registration CA 236 768', A bottle of 1997 Sauvignon Blanc', 'Cell phone 083 555 8765', 'My watch time reading is 19.46', 'A 1966 Blue VW Beetle' and so on till 20 clues were on the chart.

Peter always gave me a second between clues to digest them.

Then he would question me on the clues in order as they appeared on the chart. I almost always got all twenty right. Never less than eighteen. Then he would pretend to trick me asking "what number on the chart is the VW Beetle"? "What time was on the watch", "What was the cell phone number"? "What was number 19"?

In my later sixties, Peter mentioned my age which attracted many older people concerned with failing memories.

How did I do it? I would take myself off to a quiet place to relax my busy mind before going on stage. Although all Alpha graduates were able to do this, performing before hundreds in the audience is another story and I was the only one who was prepared to risk it and somehow did it, and feel I could still do it today in my nineties I simply follow what he taught us.

One funny person in the audience, instead of delivering a memory clue, called out 'where did you get those nice shoes? I told her and it raised a laugh. One disbeliever came on stage to test that I couldn't see the flip chart in mirrors or picture glass on the walls. She also checked my ears. I then challenged her to test me, but she stomped off, a little embarrassed in front of the audience.

I was always satisfied that, once people attended the main seminar, they would get a hundred times more value than what they thought they were buying.

To relax between sessions, we stood in lines and rubbed each other's backs as we all sang to the music *Don't Worry, Be Happy*. Peter in blue suit always joined in.

Off the Cape Town base, we ran two seminars in Port Elizabeth and later four seminars in Windhoek. The demand was generated through word-of-mouth.

By then radio stations were also eager to interview the, now a well-known celebrity, Peter Heibloem. The Windhoek seminars were sell-outs because the German community went wild about the Alpha brain rhythm concept. These were also followed by four Firewalks a year or two later. Peter Heibloem senior used our seminars to train up his twenty-year-old son,

**Peter junior.** A tall, blond blue-eyed beach boy, hunk of a man. He was allowed to run two or three of the sessions over the weekend. In later years he completely took over the seminars from his father and was equally competent and very much admired by all.

Over the nine years of running the Alpha seminars, more than 6 000 people had attended.

As our Rand devalued and young Peter's family in Australia, grew, the South African seminars ended in the early 2000's.

## 5. The Move to Cape Town

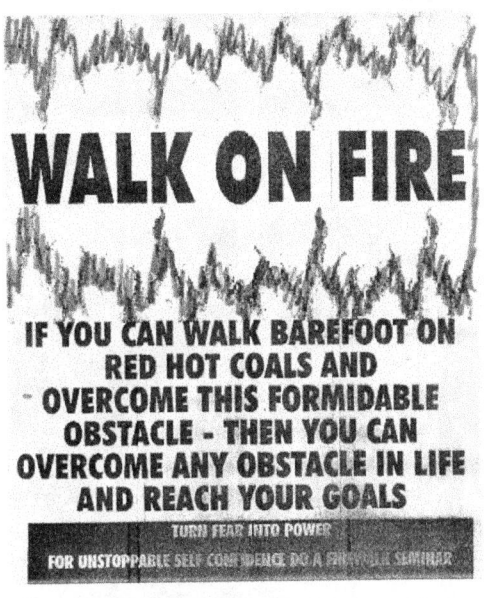

**Fire-walking.**

In one of our later Alpha seminars, Peter Heibloem told us of how he and his wife, Clare, had attended a Personal Growth Seminar conducted by the renowned American Anthony Robbins when he visited Sydney. They had taken along their seven-year-old boy, Stephen.

Anthony Robbins is spellbinding in his delivery. Strong, handsome, funny and highly credible having had, and advertised, hundreds of success stories resulting from his work. His (name dropping) endorsements include Bill Clinton and Andre Agassi.

At the Robbins seminar in Sydney, Anthony started off the weekend Seminar with a two-hour indoctrination lecture and a mass fire walk, just to get things going.

How do you persuade over a thousand people, in a Stadium, that they can walk on fire? Especially when Fire Walking was not the primary reason they had signed up. A lecture – and trust in the facilitator.

The Firewalking hot coals covered an area the size of a tennis court with dozens of groups walking across *en masse*.

Anthony Robbins teaches his version of NLP - Neuro Linguistic Programming. A method of changing the frequency at which the brain operates by changing 'aural perception'. The result is a total change in perceived reality which, in many cases, convinces people of their inherent, often latent, capabilities.

NLP was perfected at Harvard University in the 1960s and developed by the CIA and US Military.

**Tony Robbins NAC.** He developed and enhanced this capability to his own model NAC Neuro Associative Conditioning, which he has been using for decades to change perceptions of reality in his seminars and life's work. In simple terms, he gives insights into using the unrealised or under-utilised capability of the mind. Many say most people only use

# My Life, a Roller Coaster Ride

**Setting the example Left Megan Right Andy.**

Alex Carr (6) asked if she could also walk. She did.
Now, aged 31, when facing a challenge, tells herself, "I can do it. I walked on fire."

## 5. The Move to Cape Town

about 10% of their brain's potential. With that as a base and example, he introduced fire walking as living proof that it worked.

Nothing new in Fire Walking, the spiritual Indians have done it for centuries.

**Family surprise.** Halfway across the Robbins fire walk, Peter and Clare were shocked to see little barefooted Stephen following them. He hadn't had the benefit of the introductory seminar but, trusting his parents, he assumed it would be alright. And it was. The family of three finished the fire walk together.

Having told us this story, Peter Heibloem then recommended that we organise such an event for our Alpha graduates in Cape Town. We sounded out our current group of 320 Alpha delegates in the room. They were excited by the idea. Many wanted to book on the spot.

Nothing ventured, nothing gained, we set about finding a South African Fire Walking Guru. He was Mervyn Niland, a hyperactive smallish man with an engaging personality and lots of confidence. He produced many letters of endorsement from companies such as Coca Cola, who used Firewalking as a motivational and self-enhancing tool for its senior staff.

Mervyn's practical approach and shared business deal were all Andy, and I needed to get going. Equal partners in costs and profits and so confident that neither of us even thought of signing a contract or taking out injury insurance – if we could get it.

**MCP'S first iconic fire-walk.** July 1999, Organised by Andy Carr under the banner of Megan Carr Promotions.

As Fire Walk Organiser, Andy selected the River Club Sports Club as the venue in Observatory for our first event. It had a big enough ballroom for the seminar and attractive grounds to set up our bonfires, the five metre fire walk pathway of hot coals and refreshment tables.

Mervyn Nyland's leaflet. The obscured lower message reads 'TURN FEAR INTO POWER For unstoppable self-confidence, do a Fire Walk Seminar. This will change your life forever'.

I elected to go shopping for the correct 4"x 4" wood blocks from the Timber Mill in Retreat. Two bakkie loads were ordered (They checked them for having no nails) to be delivered the day prior to the event. One bakkie load per hundred walkers.

We phoned our list of graduates from previous seminars. Our first event attracted 129 people of varying ages and backgrounds.

Andy arranged for the building of the two-metre-high bonfires. To

## My Life, a Roller Coaster Ride

add to the drama, I bought two gallons of paraffin and a couple of plastic watering cans. Two volunteers poured a trickle of paraffin each side of the path of hot coals, creating a knee-high passage of flames for dramatic effect and to keep the coals hot.

We asked Tony and his son Sean to manage the coals, to keep them hot and ready. He agreed "As long as you don't expect us to walk on fire".

Mervyn instructed Tony and Sean to throw fresh burning coals on the pathway after every third walker. About one minute per person. taking about 90 minutes for 129 walkers. It was a family affair, with Tony's wife Lee helping Andy at reception and their daughter Camilla helping.

**The day arrived,** we were very nervous at this new leap of faith. Our business reputation was on the line if it didn't work. A new experience for us as well as for the 129 who put their trust in us.

Daughter, Andrea, the function organiser, was there to work – and to walk. She brought her daughter Alex (6).

Mervyn was the Facilitator and entertainer. His excited audience was seated in a double circle around him. Mervyn played little games. He put many questions to the audience to keep them on their toes and to assess their receptiveness. For a correct answer, just for fun, he would throw that person a small packet of Smarties.

Young Alex (6) was riding her tricycle outside the open French doors and found that she knew some of the answers. Being a keen bird watcher, she shouted out the correct answer to a question on bird flight formations. She got her Smarties and happily peddled off to enjoy them.

Mervyn has always had the audience riveted to the many amazing tales of seemingly impossible acts of mind power manifestation. How a woman, seeing her child trapped under the wheel of a runaway car, single handed, lifted the car and its wheel off the child and dragged him out.

And how the quickness of the hand deceived the eye and mind, when a man, seeing a red-hot coin lifted out of burning coals and dropped onto the back of his hand, shrieked in pain with an image of the coin branded onto his skin. Meanwhile, the coin had been smartly switched for a cold coin. So, his expectation of heat made the scorching actually happen.

**Self-limiting beliefs.** After 90 lively minutes, when Mervyn felt the audience was ready, we passed out slips of A5 paper and pencils. He instructed the delegates to write down their self-limiting beliefs that were holding them back from their life purpose and goals. The room went silent

## 5. The Move to Cape Town

as they got stuck into the task, writing furiously. Some asked for more paper.

At this stage, Andy went outside to get the first two bonfires lit. After about 10 minutes, Mervyn led everyone out, clutching their papers with their innermost revelations. They filed out to the bonfires, flinging their most private self-limiting belief confessions into the blazing flames. "Gone forever" Mervyn sang out and they joyfully joined in the chorus.

**Practice run.** While this was going on outside, our team transformed the ballroom into a virtual Fire Walk surrounded by the circles of chairs. There, across the centre of the room, the delegates returned to see a five-meter red passage carpet runner with a small blue plastic basin with a puddle of water at one end.

Settled back in the room, shoes off, the rehearsal started. One person walking every minute with Mervyn observing their body language. Any sign of nerves and he put them at the back of the line to try again.

Clearly audible was the sound of each new person chanting with audience echoing. "Can I do it? Yes, I can." "Will I do it? Yes I will." "Here I go Yes. Yes. Yes. Go. Go. Go" . then stomping firmly over the carpet to the puddle of water in the basin at the end. No tiptoeing allowed.

The audience chanted in time to the walker's war cries and clapped to encourage him or her. They were ready.I, proud grandmother, snapped away with my camera. The entire group cheered her on.

Before 6 pm, the late winter afternoon was darkening. Timing was good for the special effects of the bonfire flames and the coals fanning red in the evening breeze.

Mervyn then challenged each person to walk the hot coals. 129 people at ninety second intervals, which took almost three hours to process, including quick breaks.

**Outside, shoes off.** The symbolic removing of the shoes and rolling up of pants' legs was even a little emotional. The atmosphere was electric, the group was on fire – so to speak.

What happened? I discovered that Tony and Sean had also joined in the practice walk inside. Was I seeing things? They had been determined not to walk. I didn't try to persuade them. Something had changed. It was a very personal decision, like the reliable workers they were, having passed the test, Tony and Sean returned outside to start shovelling the coals from the base of the bonfires, on to the walk path. They were ready, and more than that, they decided to surprise us and were the first two to tread the

# My Life, a Roller Coaster Ride

coals which they had just spread.

The depth of the coal is about eight centimetres to start with, then, after every third person, more coals are added. They appear grey after a few minutes, but the least breath of wind fans them red. With Tony and Sean doing sterling work with the shovels, another two volunteers paraded up and down the pathway spewing a thin stream of paraffin each side to keep the edge lines of flames going.

Meeting 'walkers' at the end of the walk were two people. Mervin Nyland and our photographer, to get the right angle to include feet, rolled-up pants and facial expression. He had two cameras and an assistant to do quick camera swops to change the film.

Of course, as organisers of the event and enthusiastic Alpha Mind Power people the family all participated in the fire walk.

**Alex Carr (6).** When she saw what was going on, asked me, her grandmother, if she could also walk, My reply was, "Ask your mother".

She did, and Andy then consulted Mervyn.

Mervyn took Alex to the carpet trial run and put her through her paces. She knew exactly what to do and say.

Mervyn gave her the nod and told Andy, "She will easily do it". And she did, as the family and the entire group, gathered around and cheered.

**Camilla Carr (10).** On the other hand her cousin, Camilla, Tony's daughter, was displaying doubts as she heard someone say "She will not

**WE DID IT!** Andy Carr, Alex Carr Megan, Mervyn Nyland.

## 5. The Move to Cape Town

do it" as she was about to walk. Mervyn noticed her sudden doubts and would not allow her to walk, and she sadly missed the experience.

The family, and the entire group, gathered around, at this momentous thing about to happen.

At the fire path start, Alex chanted "I can do it, I will do it, Yes, yes, yes, go.go go", and with a big smile marched across the coals.

I, proud grandmother, snapped away with my camera. The entire group cheered her on.

This little girl, with her bright copper curls, had captured the hearts of all present. Later, in her teens and adult years, she said that whenever anything looks scary or difficult, she tells herself "I can do it, I walked on fire.".

**The Proof.** An important aspect of the Fire Walk is the bragging rights. The evidence. The proof positive to satisfy the cynics and non-believers and useful in a CV.

It is the rare gift of a journalistic photographer to get each person captured in the act. Once in the middle of the walk and once arriving safely, mostly with an expression of wonder and achievement on their faces. It must be captured in the instant.

Our talented photographer was Elton, who never missed a beat over three solid hours of accurate, inspired photography. You can't exactly ask a person to walk again if he misses the shot.

**Follow up. Ready for framing and showing off.** Almost as much fun, and hearing more personal insights and revelations, was when, a week later, Andy organised an informal get together. This time with wine and snacks, when the delegates could pick up their photos, signed Fire Walking Certificates and the opportunity to share what the experience had meant to them. Also, to pick up sundry items such as jackets, spare shirts and even a pair of takkies left behind at the Club.

We ran three Cape Town and three Windhoek Fire Walks over two years with never a hint of a burn or blister. Over 1200 people altogether. With, maybe, a little less leg hair on some!

**Jurgen Wolff on Writing.** In 1994, the American Jurgen Wolff, was visiting South Africa. He had written and created the American series 'Family Ties', 'Benson', 'The Relic Hunters' and many more Sitcoms. He also conducted workshops on Commercial and Creative writing.

I joined Jurgen's four-day Writing Workshops in 1994, in Cape Town. A day each on 'How to write a Novel',' A Successful Sitcom for Radio and

# My Life, a Roller Coaster Ride

TV', (Sitcom writers, he tantalised, could earn US$ 16 000 per half hour). 'Professional Scripting' and one day devoted to life enhancement, 'How to Focus and be Successful'.

An expensive and valuable investment. Four days and money well spent. My creative writing came years later when I had moved to Hermanus.

**Potto House, Uitsig Peninsula.** After the attack on my life in Fisherman's Quay, I decided to move house and found an available rental in Uitsig Peninsula, Marina da Gama. The owners had moved to Darling.

My new rented house was a two and a half storey, spacious residence right on the water and facing North. Andy and Alex moved in with me.

Our house-help and nanny was a delightful young woman called Thelma who became Alexi's best friend and who crept into our lives as part of the family.

Andy and I used the ground floor study as the office. Alpha Mind Power, The Leisure Pleasure Travel Show, and the Rugby World Cup Shows were the main activities around that time.

Later that year, Andy had a fulltime job as Film Coordinator for *The Adventures of Sinbad* at their studio in Pinelands. She worked long hours, so it came in handy that I was at home with Alexi as we developed a close relationship which we enjoy to this day.

I lived on the top floor with a magnificent view over the Marina. Andy and Alexi occupied the Mezzanine level. Ground floor was divided into the recreational and MCP offices.

I bought paddle boat which was moored just footsteps from the front patio. With a small two-year-old and the water nearby, I had a metre high metal vertical bar fence installed to keep her safe. I thought. No sooner was the fence in place than we were shocked to see Alex carrying two buckets, park them at the fence and climb right over. A preview of the determined and innovative person she was to become.

It was from there that I got my grandchild nickname. Alexi climbed the stairs to my room each morning. She knocked on the door with her tiny fist. I called 'Morning' and she would climb into my bed for a chat. Today, at the age of thirty, she still calls me 'Morning' as does her fiancé Olli, and Cousin Matthew.

For Alex and me, our daily pleasure was to go for early walks along the water's edge and in the park at the end of the road. I started to teach her to identify birds and bought along mini binoculars on our walks. She had a list of over 40 birds she could identify.

## 5. The Move to Cape Town

**Alex aged three.** When my bird and wildlife-fundi brother, Chris, visited and said to her "look at the pretty ducks, Alex", she casually pointed out to him,"Those are Egyptian Geese, Chris".

**Robin and Lavinia Boyd.** Robin was an adventurer and had travelled the world, mostly on sailing boats. Eton educated and a military man. Robin published his book about his adventures 'The Seven Seas'.

As their neighbour and (single) friend, I was invited to many of their dinner parties and included in their picnics at outdoor music concerts in and around Cape Town.

**1995. Rugby World Cup.** The promotions we ran from that house were the Alpha seminars, the Leisure, Pleasure, Travel Exhibition, and planned two special viewings of the Rugby World Cup semifinal and the final games.

Rugby frenzy had hit South Africa. All tickets were sold out.

Andy and I decided to use our Culemborg Expo Centre to set up 500 chairs and two $3m^2$ screens with Public Address speakers to show the semifinals and finals.

**Judy Blaine, Deon Duvenage, Andy Carr and our World Cup Banner.**

# My Life, a Roller Coaster Ride

## Meet the fitness guru of the mind

Neurologist Carla Hannaford is in the city demonstrating why children's [minds need] a proper exercise regime just as the body does in order to stay on t[rack]

**THERESA SMITH**
**Education Reporter**

WHILE lecturing on human biology and physiology at the University of Hawaii in the 1980s, Dr Carla Hannaford became involved in counselling pupils from Grade 5 to Grade 9 who were getting low marks.

She heard about brain gym from a parent and liked the idea so much she incorporated it into her sessions.

It involves a series of movements that are aimed at making brain function more effective – a kind of fitness regime for the mind.

A neurophysiologist and educational specialist, Hannaford is in Cape Town presenting seminars on brain gym and alternatives to drug treatments for children with learning disabilities.

Since the brain gym work was a pilot project and she had never done anything like it before, Hannaford did not bother to read the children's files, she explained in an interview.

"So I had no preconceived notions about what to expect," she said. But she suspected one of her pupils, Jessie, was older than the rest.

"He said he wanted to work on his reading and that he liked motorcycles."

A keen motorcyclist herself, Hannaford unearthed some biking magazines and they worked on his reading skills, starting with brain gym exercises before each lesson.

After three sessions, his usual English teacher approached Hannaford in amazement.

### What is brain gym?

Brain gym is a set of 26 movements designed to integrate the brain's functioning. These range from unfurling your ears – using your fingers – to help your hearing, to a balancing act involving legs, hands and the tip of your tongue – good for calming the adrenalin flow when you're under stress.

The brain gym theory is that successful brain functioning requires efficient connections across neural pathways located throughout the brain. Stress inhibits these connections, but brain gym seeks to stimulate the flow of information along these networks, restoring the ability to think and learn.

Integration between the left and right sides of the brain is important f[or being able to move] and think a[...]

The back [...] need to w[...] blend co[...] understa[...] previous[...]

Child[ren with] disorder[...]

"She [...] read i[...] know [...]

It tu[...] but s[...] phas[...] beca[...] read[...] stud[...] him[...]

deficit hyperactivity disorder (ADHD) have problems with this ability.

Integrating the upper and lower structures of your brain harmonises emotion with rational thought – which is why stress leaves you tense and out of sorts.

Paul Dennison developed the idea of lateral repatterning (movement to integrate the brain) in California in the 1970s and set up a series of learning centres.

The international brain gym foundation was founded in 1982 and it has 54 international trainers working in 34 countries across the world.

In fact, movement – described as educational kinesiology – is an essential part of the national education curriculum for the foundation phase: grades 1, 2 and 3. [...] Western Cape

the interm[...] time with [...] and I was [...] university [...] Hannaford [...]

Since the [...] her PhD i[...] physiology [...] national ed[...] and publish[...] about the v[...] gym exerci[...]

Her theor[...] what has b[...] deficit diso[...] deficit hyp[...] (ADHD) an[...] lems such [...] stantly und[...]

Although [...] a measure o[...] normal circ[...] reacts in a [...] basic respon[...] of the non-d[...] brain shuts [...] works on th[...]

"You becom[...] you can't re[...] on," Hannaf[...]

She believe[...] experience [...] have domin[...] if the left s[...] mostly dorm[...] tions it is n[...] for are really[...]

Introducin[...] forces the en[...] (deliberately [...] your balance [...] of your brain [...] up the dorm[...] brain.

"As soon a[...] grated move[...] adrenalin-ba[...] response sto[...]

"That's wh[...] when they're [...] actually thin[...]

308

### 5. The Move to Cape Town

When the World Cup organisers realised the extent of the many people doing what we planned, they upped the showing rights fees so high that we sensibly decided to abort the mission.

**World Cup.** We watched that thrilling, winning final at the Cape Town Waterfront screening in one of the big halls.

## 29. Brain Gym Seminars

I was drawn into something of particular interest to me. I had become aware of the misuse by some parents, doctors and some of the school communities, of Ritalin to calm lively scholars. There was a new convenient label applied; 'hyperactive' children had 'A.D.D. Attention Deficit Disorder'.

Disorders have to have labels so that the pharmaceutical companies can then produce so-called (chemical) remedies for them, instead of finding natural and healthy ways to manage the exuberance and hyper energy of children. Or checking on their unhealthy sugar and TV habits.

I was approached by Rita, a teacher and Brain Gym practitioner in the Western Cape, to join her in bringing out a Brain Gym teacher from USA, Neurologist, Dr. Carla Hannaford. She was President Bill Clinton's personal advisor on Education in America.

We set up a series of seminars at a nominal fee, to draw in the educators and parents to introduce them to the practical and healthy practice of Brain Gym in preference to drugs. Ritalin is a Schedule 2 drug.

Rita and I worked *Pro Bono*. We thought this would be an easy one. We hadn't counted on the persuasive power of the pharmaceutical industry and their relentless brainwashing and fearmongering as opposed to the healthy, effective and drug free option. Brain Gym and a healthy diet.

**Left. Dr. Carla Hannaford (USA).** We ran ten seminars in Cape Town and Johannesburg. Some schools sponsored a representative teacher to attend from as far afield as Natal and Eastern Cape.

We, ourselves, participated in the fascinating and physically active seminars. We also learned the simple classroom left and right brain exercises which the students should do at the beginning of each day and sometimes the start of a class. Just a few minutes needed to get the left and right brains working in sync.

When Carla discovered from Rita that I was working pro bono, she sent me a generous cheque and bunch of yellow roses with a charming thank you note.

# My Life, a Roller Coaster Ride

After all that, we were surprised that several private schools clearly declined to send a representative to learn more about Brain Gym from this world authority in education, child behaviour and the dangers of Ritalin.

They must have preferred teaching zombies, chemically controlled to make their own teaching lives easier.

I have been happy to discover, through grandchildren. twenty years later, that the practice of Brain Gym is commonly applied in the classrooms of some private schools.

**Three house moves.** The owners decided to sell 'Potto' house and I moved across the road to Zee Close.

It had a Jacuzzi in the garden. The lawn sloped down to the waterfront where I parked the paddle boat.

With my friend and neighbour, Robin Boyd, now across the road and (singer) Nick Taylor, my new neighbour next door, life was good.

Andy and Alex had moved away.

Zee Close Jacuzzi, popular with the grandchildren.

**In the picture below** Sean, Camilla, Lee, Andy, Dusty, Carolyn Alex, Megan, Carole. A year later, when the owner decided to sell, I moved to The Tides. This time I bought the property.

After two years living at The Tides, I bought two North facing Bonnie Brook units at favourable prices. They had been standing vacant as

## 5. The Move to Cape Town

the owners had emigrated to Australia in 1994 just before the Mandela government came into power. They were a fantastic investment and tripled in value after I had converted the old block to sectional title. The flats overlooked the public park and Lagoon.

**Wiso Mhlango** was the resident housekeeper at The Tides. When I sold my Tides apart-ment and moved across the Lagoon to Bonny Brook, Wiso offered to help me with the short move, packing my rented trailer with everything to be trailed across behind my Hyundai Sonata.

In my storeroom I had a Mountain Bike, bought in a New Year's resolution moment, which I never got around to using. It was huge. My feet hardly reached the pedals.

We were about to pack the bike onto the trailer when I saw Wiso looking at it with longing in his eyes. I asked him if he would like to have it. You can see from the photo, the brilliant smile with which he rewarded me.

From then on, every day he would cycle past Bonnie Brook and I would hear 'Megaan!' as he cycled by, waving.

A month later, he knocked on my door and asked me how he could enter The *Argus* Cycle Race which was coming up. I phoned around and

**The south-facing view from The Tides.**

## My Life, a Roller Coaster Ride

sent him off to a Cycle Shop in Fishhoek which took entries for the 112 km race. I heard no more about it, but he continued calling to me as he cycled past.

A few weeks later, I had another knock on my door. This time, it was a beaming Wiso with his Argus Cycle Race medal hanging from a red ribbon round his neck. He had completed the course in the allocated time.

I was close to tears and filled with humility and pride in this man's vision, tenacity and achievement. It also told me how such a simple impromptu gift could make a difference to someone's life. To his life and to mine.

**The Bonny Brook Block.** This was simply an investment opportunity, in a block built in 1948 comprising eight, three-bedroom apartments. Four units per floor. Mine were the two, one above the other on the near corner in the photo, representing a quarter of the entire building. They had huge front windows overlooked the park and lagoon.

Once I had redecorated them and rented one out, I wondered what to do next.

**Sectional title.** I wondered if I had a notice on my forehead saying, 'Ask this one to do it'. I was approached by the board members of our complex to become the Chairman of the Tenants Committee. No big deal – only eight of us. Four permanently resident. A big frog in a small pond.

I found myself persuaded to take over the job of getting the eight units Sectional Titled. A new field of expertise for me and more laborious than I had anticipated, with the complication of some owners now resident in Australia. That mission was successfully completed in a year, which immediately tripled the values, as Share Block was difficult to sell.

After 2 years at sea facing 'The Tides', I moved to Bonnie Brook overlooking the park and lagoon. My two flats front right, one above the other, representing one quarter of the block of eight flats.

# 5. The Move to Cape Town

The nuisance side of the job, dealing with tenant problems and complaints and supervising the staff, was when I knew I had taken a wrong direction.

I was also on three other committees, Brain Gym for Children hooked on Ritalin, Local Seniors' ARP&P and fundraising for the DA, I realised that I was on an unchallenging treadmill.

However, something good always turns up. And sure enough, it did.

**D.A. Southern Cape fundraiser.** I was approached by Ed Coombe and Dimitri Qually, representing our local Progressive Party (now D.A.), then headed by Tony Leon. They needed funds. I had a one-person (me) brainstorm and came up with an idea.

**Mary (Oppenheimer) Slack's house.** The magnificent historic, Herbert Baker house was the only one sited on the Maritime-owned side of the main road. This single residential dispensation had been granted to the Oppenheimer's by Princess Alice in 1899 when the British Navy still had servitude rights on the country's shoreline. The adjacent beach is known as 'Alice Beach'.

As a matter of fact, for years I had thought it was 'Ellis Beach' when told the name by our Cape Malay gardener.

DA was known, in those days, as The Progressive Party – shortened to 'Progs'. I suggested to the committee that I ask Mary if we could use her house to hold a Cocktail Party as a fundraising venue. Being strongly 'Prog', Mary immediately, and graciously, agreed, and dispatched her property manager from Johannesburg to assist with the arrangements.

**Visible across the lagoon from the windows of my Bonnie Brook apartment.**

# My Life, a Roller Coaster Ride

Mary (Oppenheimer) Slacks (Herbert Baker) house. venue for the Progressive Party (Now DA) Fundraiser.

**Singer, Nick Taylor's artist son, Kim,** agreed to do a sketch of the historic house for the invitation.

We decided we could accommodate 120 at a squeeze. Dimitri Qually, Ed Coombe and I compiled a list to invite. When word got out, there was no problem attracting the guests. The house was something of a mystery in the Cape. Everyone was dying to see inside.

Some even demanded an invitation. Every single invitee accepted. Many more were 'insulted' not to be invited. You can't win them all.

When I asked Mary's manager what would happen if someone spilt red wine on the all-white upholstered chairs, he replied, "So, we will just have them cleaned".

I got the wine sponsored. The D.A. Committee women produced trays of snacks. We set up a full bar run by Prog volunteer barmen. A P.A. system and technician, was loaned from a local company.

Tony Leon, Chairman of the Progs, arrived from Johannesburg to host the evening. Ed Coombe acted as Master of Ceremonies.

Best surprise of all, Mary Slack and some friends arrived from Johannesburg, and enthusiastically headed the bidding for donations.

Everyone was well behaved and didn't spill a drop of red wine on the couches. The evening was a satisfying success.

One thing leads to another –

## 5. The Move to Cape Town

**The St. Francis Adult Education Centre.** Ed Coombe was also on the Committee of the St. Francis Adult Education Centre in Langa, Cape Town.

Its 25th Anniversary was coming up and it was decided to make a celebration of it to draw interest and support for the Centre.

The Adult school uses the Lange High school building after school hours for its adult classes.

Something binding these together, left alone At the same time, they ran a week- long Careers Expo leading up to the Anniversary, which, with some heavy hints from Ed, I volunteered to publicise for them.

St. Francis Adult Education Centre conducts full schooling for adults who have not had the opportunity to finish their schooling.

This project excited me so, as always, I searched around for something which would arouse publicity to gain public support.

I had read that, the then, Prince Charles would be coming to South Africa to visit the Isandlwana historical site in Natal and would spend a few days in Cape Town. It so happened that he was due to be in Cape Town exactly when I needed him.

# My Life, a Roller Coaster Ride

**Prince Charles and St. James Palace.**
Nothing ventured, nothing gained, I sent a letter, care of the British Ambassador in Cape Town, to Prince Charles, inviting him to visit the Centre for the 25th Anniversary Celebration.

I received a reply from The Palace of St. James, signed by Prince Charles' Private Secretary Nicholas Archer, who has since 1997 gone on to become HM Ambassador to Denmark and various countries thereafter. (See Appendix)

I wondered if his dad was author and politician Jeffrey Archer?

*Dear Miss Carr,*
*Thank you for your letter of 30th June to the Prince of Wales, inviting him to visit the St. Francis Adult Education Centre.*

*His Royal Highness was interested to read about your Centre. Sadly, however, the programme for the Prince of Wales visit to South Africa does not allow the time for him to see the Centre for himself.*

*His Royal Highness has asked me to send you his warmest best wishes.*

*Yours sincerely, (signed) Nicholas Archer.*

**Meeting Prince Charles.** Having put the Prince Charles idea out of my mind, out of the blue, I received an invitation from Miss Maeve Fort, British High Commissioner, requesting the pleasure of my company (love that), at a Buffet Reception in the presence of HRH Prince of Wales on 5th November 1997, at the South African Museum, Queen Victoria Street, Cape Town. I was amused to note the time, 11.45 am to 1.45 pm.

It was a cool, dry day. I decided to dress in a formal soft green and white sprigged dress with a flared hem. White accessories. Spring was in the air. 'No hats' was specified, when I tested the dress code (which was 'lounge suit').

The 200 or so guests were dignitaries and the usual social regulars. I knew many of them. Always a relief to have friends to chat to at such times.

Once there, I asked where HRH was, and was told he was checking the Museum exhibits upstairs. Or rather, up ramp. I figured he would come down the ramp to join the party, so I parked myself near the bottom, along with many others. He eventually descended at exactly 11.45. As he

## 5. The Move to Cape Town

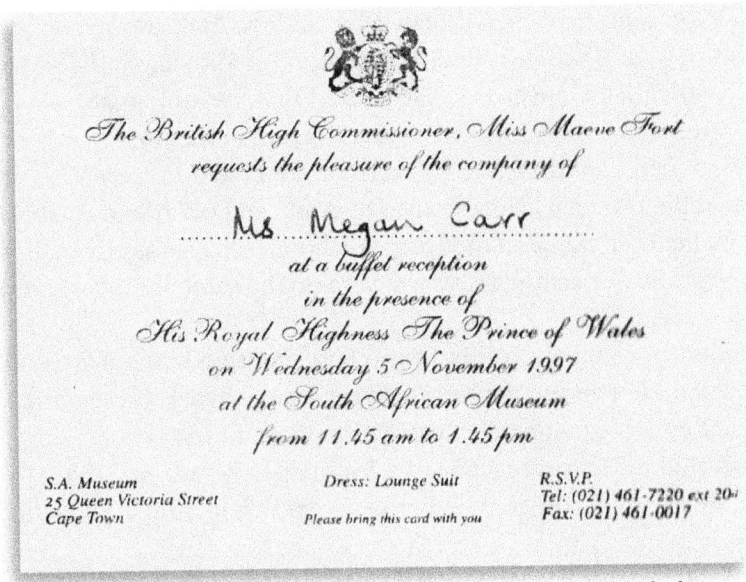

**I received an invitation from Miss Maeve Fort, British High Commissioner.**

approached, I said, Welcome to Cape Town your Highness'. Being a well brought-up man, he stopped and thanked me. Having his brief attention, I then asked him if he had managed to get some painting done at Isandlwana. He brightened and said, "Sadly, no time, but my friend had done some painting, and I hope to return to do so".

Lunch with HRH was a Grand Buffet with no seating. I can't remember if there was wine. I think not, as we had to hold our small plates. However, a day to remember. There was a sense of excitement. No speeches.

As I'd had to park near town and taxi in because of roads cordoned off, I managed to hitch a ride in a pre-ordered taxi with friends.

**St. Francis 25th Anniversary.** On the day of the Anniversary Celebration, the Guest of Honour was the Minister of Education, Sibusisu Bengu. A very imposing and gracious man. Before becoming the Minister of Education, he had been Vice Chancellor of the University of Fort Worth.

A measure of the importance of adult education to those taking advantage of the school, is illustrated by two examples which spring to mind. A twenty-four-year-old woman who had given birth to her first child at the Seapoint hospital in the middle of the night, rushed by train to Langa school, next morning, to write a Matric exam at 9am.

A woman who passed her Matric at the age of sixty-five.

Both were mentioned in the *Cape Times*.

## My Life, a Roller Coaster Ride

**David Icke.** I have been fascinated by the original, even revolutionary, philosophies on The Universe, Alternative medicine, Self-Healing and even the so-called Conspiracy Theories of this dynamic man.

I admit I was uncomfortable with the reptilian theory.

1998. When David visited Cape Town, I booked to attend his one-day seminar at the Baxter Theatre, joined by Andy and her friend Dusty Bristol.

We had earlier attended the Deepak Chopra seminar and, of course, our Alpha Mind Power seminars, so we were on the same journey, and wanted to learn more.

Blonde, longish hair, in his fifties, and shooting straight from the hip, he had the audience riveted to his unorthodox, casual, presentation style, illustrated by a professional Power Point presentation.

He started off by saying. "I am a Journalist. What I am about to say is a result of my own research, experience, and deductions. You can take it or leave it".

I bought into most of his theories, but with some reservations to test for myself. I was comfortable with his anti-establishment opinions and almost all his political observations, supported by the many known facts, many of which he illustrated on the $2m^2$ metre screen.

David, like me, had a political distrust and pet aversion to one political figure in particular. Henry Kissinger. He knew how to take his revenge.

MCP Office and Stand at the Careers Expo. The organisers kindly offered me a complimentary stand on their exhibition. This turned out to be a convenient base to work from, as well as good exposure for my company.

# 5. The Move to Cape Town

Just before the lunch break, he pointed out the dangers of certain kinds of politician and listed the many questionable decisions Henry had made, using his power and influence over the American public, and world affairs. Up popped the full screen face of Henry, with his finger up his nose. As David continued with examples which he regarded as dictatorial and offensive.

Just as he was about to expound further, he said, "I really shouldn't put up the next image". He waited theatrically, as if hesitating, then said "Sod it. Here it is", and up went another full screen photo of Henry with the same finger in his mouth.

David said no more and left it mellowing in our minds as we walked out for lunch. A lively talking point over our buffet meal.

The 665 people in the capacity audience were back in their seats with time to spare. We couldn't get enough of David.

Next day, Andy and I were raving about the Icke Seminar, when Tony arrived and lamented that he had missed it. He was about to have his 42nd birthday, so I said that, as a birthday present, I would book him to attend the Icke Seminar in Knysna the following weekend. And off we went. No hardship for me to see him a second time, and I was equally impressed.

After the full house audience at The Baxter, I was surprised at the modest four hundred capacity hall in Knysna and the ease with which I was able to buy two places. It was not nearly full.

Asking about this with the organiser, she said that there was a militant demonstration, partly religious, in opposition to the Icke theories. They even did an Anti-Icke march with placards. They tore down all the street posters.

Tony and I had arrived early, having driven four hours from Cape Town, and were seated near the front. As David arrived on stage, with his arms overloaded with his presentation material, he stumbled, and his papers went flying. I rushed up on stage and helped him pick them up and set up his worktable. When done, we chatted for a bit before the show started.

I asked him why he had chosen Knysna for his seminar. His answer was a surprise, which made me like him even more. He said he loved steam trains and had heard of the Vintage Rovos Rail Express train and booked himself on it. The seminar was what he called an 'add-on' to his programme.

David had been a professional football player but had to give it up because of his chronic arthritis. He then became a BBC Sports Presenter. He gave that up to be spokesman for the Green Party. It was the search for

## My Life, a Roller Coaster Ride

an alternative remedial cure for his arthritis which led him to go to natural healers and deeper insights, which became his life mission to share with the world.

Born in 1962, David has written over twenty books. Twice married and has four children. Currently, there has been a new surge of interest in David Icke's work.

Carole, Andy and I remain keen followers of Icke. Anthony Cuerden, the designer of this book, thinks otherwise.

**March 1999. Peter Carr marries Leanne Mooney.** The grand country weekend wedding was in Dullstroom, amongst family and friends arriving from all over the country. The hotel and every guesthouse in the little town were taken over by the wedding guests. Peter wrote a beautiful poem describing the wedding.

November 1999 Sebastian Carr born. October 2001 Nicholas Carr born. Carole, in the wedding picture was expecting Matthew, born October 1999.

In 2000, Carole divorced Anthony and moved to The Wilderness with the two children. There she started a lighting company, Divali Natural Lighting.

Andy and Alex, Peter Snr, Carole, Megan, Bridegroom Peter, Bride Leanne, Mavis and Wally Rodd, Leanne's parents, Shelley Beer, Leanne's sister.

## 5. The Move to Cape Town

**It was April 2002 when I first felt the lump.** I couldn't believe it. Refused to believe it. However, it was diagnosed malignant. I went and bought the Brandon Bays' audio tapes *The Journey* and Deepak Chopra's book, *Journey into Healing*, Carolyn Myss' *Anatomy of the Spirit*. I dug into my bookshelf and found Louise Hay's *You can Heal Yourself*. I made up a five-day mind programme and got to work.

I found a book in a Health Shop *The 10 Day Cleanout Plan* and bought the appropriate fresh fruit, vegetables and salads – and a new liquidiser.

To cut a long story short, I tried everything alternative from checking into a Health Spa, to meditation and positive thinking, without immediate success.

I finally checked in to the Medi Clinic at midday the day before surgery. When the surgeon visited me in the ward, he asked. "How did you spend your morning?" I replied, "I did my Canadian 11 BX exercises and swam 20 lengths". He said, "I wish all my patients would do that".

Surgery went well and I was discharged five days later with the instruction not to drive for ten days. I drove myself to the movies four days later. I would not let this define my life.

Whilst recovering after surgery, I had several visits from recovered breast cancer volunteers, whose mission was to reassure and help with adjusting to the new me. They brought a little bag of birdseed to weigh down my bra cup. Now who would have thought of that? They gave me the contact number for a bra prosthesis shop and told me which exercises would keep me flexible. Good kind people.

I had to return to the Cancer Specialist for six-monthly checkups. I did it for a year and then decided I would never go there again.

I was wrong! Déjà vu.

**Another scare.** In 2012, exactly ten years later. I was living at Leumann House, I woke up with a sharp pain exactly on the scar. I thought 'Oh God, it's back'. I made an urgent appointment with the same Cancer Specialist, now at her office at Groote Schuur. I asked Tony to meet me there, as I drove in from Hermanus.

She saw me immediately and did a thorough examination. I saw a smile appear on her face "It's a spider bite". We had a good laugh. Never was I so pleased to have a spider bite.

Tony and I went off to celebrate over a cup of coffee.

# My Life, a Roller Coaster Ride

**Motor Shows.** At the end of 1990's and early 2000's my company had become involved in a rash of Motor Shows and events.

The Motor Show Organiser of the time was Roger Haugh. A handsome past master at putting on such Petro events.

The first was 'The Festival of Motoring' at the Killarney Race Circuit. A hands-on event for Cars and Motorcycles. Roger had sold 120 exhibition stands and set up a full programme of moving exhibitions, competitions and a GTI Jamboree.

**Boys and their Toys.** I had been brainwashed in my married life by a Rally driving husband and one son, Tony, both passionate and 'experts' on anything to do with motoring and events from Rallies to Formula 1. My other son, Peter preferred to invest in vintage cars, a Merc 280SL and an E-Type Jaguar, amongst others.

Husband, Peter Carr's cars always had a dashboard full of instruments and gadgets. Altimeters, Incline meters, rally odometers, various logbooks, clipboard and stopwatches. Any journey with him involved a flurry of referencing and recording. He knew the timing of every traffic light from home to office.

Like the Swiss trains, he would arrive at each robot exactly timed not to have to stop. On such journeys, traffic became a nuisance to his schedule as he had to speed up or slow down to be right every time.

**Peter and Trophy (centre)**
He represented Williams Hunt in the Mobilgas Economy Run in 1962 – and won.

# 5. The Move to Cape Town

He represented Williams Hunt in the Mobilgas Economy Run in 1962. He won. He got his picture below on a Hunts' Showroom poster holding the trophy next to his winning Chevrolet and showroom friends.

**Poster Boy.** When we moved house from Athol to Sandown, we found this poster on the wall above the bed of Regina, our housekeeper-nanny – much to his embarrassment - and pride. The whole family was very proud of him.

**The Cape Festival of Motoring** was held at the Cape Killarney Motor Racing Circuit. It was an easy one to promote. I signed up *The Weekend Argus* Motoring Pages as Media Sponsor. I booked a four-page tabloid loose insert and gave the Editor, Jonathon Hobday, the list of exhibitors for his sales staff to sell adverts to.

As usual, it worked this way, two thirds advertising and one third editorial – supplied by me. My editorial included the Programme of Events, motoring personalities and their participation, and unique points of interest. It was advertised as 'A Show for the whole Family'. So, we set up a supervised play area. Tony and Lee ran their usual Coffee Shop.

**Born to be wild.** I had my first thrilling Harley Davidson pillion ride twice round the circuit. Years before, I had hitched a motorcycle pillion ride from a stranger. After a long day exhibiting at the Rand Easter Show in Johannesburg (1970) I couldn't face the long walk up Yale Road to my parked car. So, I asked a mounted Traffic Cop at the gate, if he would give me a ride up the hill to my car. Gallantly he agreed to the amusement of his colleagues and others wishing it was them. As I was wearing my office 'uniform' of tight skirt and high heels, I had to sit side-saddle, and off we zoomed, with a happy wave of my spare hand and applause from the onlookers.

**Killarney drag racing.** Saturday afternoon was devoted to GTI Drag Racing. This was so popular, that we were engaged to organise and promote regular GTI Drag Races indefinitely. Having run the first one, I handed them over to Tony and Lee to continue, much to their delight.

Because of them, it became such a roaring success, that the Killarney Race Circuit terminated them, so to speak, and decided to run it themselves.

**Goodwood Motor Show.** The Killarney event led to another Motor Show at the Goodwood Showgrounds. Again, over a hundred show stands were sold and many events and competitions programmed. Several events in particular stand out in my memory.

## My Life, a Roller Coaster Ride

**Truck driving skills.** A competition for truck drivers in various categories of size and articulated trailers. We only staged the finals and were amazed seeing long trucks with longer trailers, reversing through challengingly narrow spaces.

There were Forklift skill demonstrations and races, A Motorcycle wheelie competition and motor sound systems.

**The motor sound competition.** Had to be held a fair distance from the main Expo stands, for obvious reasons. We are all familiar with noisy Boom-Boom sounds coming from passing cars. Not from the exhausts, but from very sophisticated sound systems.

Some could be described as 'The tail wagging the Dog'. More noise power than horsepower.

The competition rule states that the motor vehicle carrying the sound system had to be driven the last 100 metres to its allocated show spot. Some of the fanatical entrants had such massive sound equipment that the vehicle could barely move with the weight and arrived at the show on a flatbed trailer and driven the last measured metres to its spot for judging. They were allowed to set up and test their systems ahead of time. Imagine the noise. The organisers had thoughtfully allowed an earmuff supplier to set up shop and did good business on judging day.

With deafness assured in his future, the winner of the Sound competition boasted that his sound was equal to a Boeing taking off. What an ambition.

**Bug festival.** Now that I had taken on Motor Shows. I was approached by the Cape Town VW Beetle Club to promote the biennial Bug Fest being held in the park in Wynberg. What a delight this was.

Exhibits were open to any mini car. Mostly Beetles and Mini Minors but also a sprinkling of baby Renaults, baby Fiats and even a Fulda mobile bubble car.

Every car was a showpiece. A gem, polished to high gleam, inside and out and under bonnets and boots. Artistic hub caps, sun shields and paintwork in abundance. Fancy additions like turbo exhausts and doctored mufflers made each exhibit a novel show piece. In each case it appeared to be the demonstration of a love affair between owner and car. The owners almost all dressed themselves in colours and bling to match their little pets. Like at a dog show.

# 5. The Move to Cape Town

**Porcupine Beetle.** One interesting competition was how many people could fit into and over a Beetle, ending up looking like human porcupines. All participants had to be at least 1.5 metres tall and over eighteen years old. With seats removed and props inside to support the roof they fitted seven slim students lying flat inside and 50 slim men of varying heights on and over the Beetle, starting with a long rope linking two rows of the stronger men, standing upright and leaning, forming the spine front to back bumpers.

The next rows linked elbows and stood at ever-leaning angles around the sides of the car. They had practiced, so it only took seven muscle straining minutes for the outer formation of 43 to be completed with huffs and puffs and shouts of encouragement.

The judges double counted and set them free. The noisy and frantic nine minutes must have seemed like hours to the participants. The winner had 57 people counted.

**Bug jams.** Jamming competitions also took place. The winner had 12 slim students inside the gutted Beetle in under two minutes.

To advertise the Bug Festival, apart from press and radio, we had dressed up open mini cars with pretty girls holding banners, driving around the streets of Cape Town. The public rolled up Saturday and Sunday in their masses. Everyone walked around the show with big smiles on their faces.

**Upon reflection.** There comes a time in one's life to take stock. To recognise the need for clearing the mind. To change when the time comes, and to act upon it. Most of us get trapped in material things. A safe existence seems the sensible thing to do at our age. We hoard, collect, relax in set routines and are slaves to our diaries. Some have a fear of change and have lost their youthful sense of adventure. Retirement should not be an end but the beginning of a new kind of adventure.

**Decisive moment. I was about to turn 73.** It was early 2005. Like St Paul heading for Damascus, I had an epiphany. Out of the blue one day, with no pre warning to myself. I picked up the phone and resigned from everything with immediate effect.

I thought: 'I have nothing to lose and who knows what will follow?'

Having smoothed over many ruffled feathers, and some feeling of personal guilt, I knew I had done exactly the right thing. I knew something good would turn up.

\* \* \*

# Part 6
## Retirement Years and Writing

PROFILE

# Female dynamo winds down in Hermanus

**Avis MacIntyre**

One of the extraordinary entrepreneurial women this country produces from time to time has come to settle in Hermanus to manage one of the upper-end guesthouses in Voëlklip for a friend.

Nominated as one of 100 top women in the 1980s by the magazine *Fair Lady's Who's Who* of South Africa, Megan Carr has had an enchanted business career and in the course of it rubbed shoulders with the rich and famous, including Elizabeth Taylor, Richard Burton and ex-Beatle Ringo Starr.

She discovered her flair for organisation when she was a young mother of four children as a member of the exclusive Monday Club in Johannesburg in the 50s. Here 30 young socialites supported the Woodside Sanctuary and raised funds by bringing in unusual and adventurous activities - their goal being absolute excellence. One of the shows was a circus premier, Stars and Sawdust, which she and her closest friend, Adele Lucas spearheaded.

In the 60s she started working at the Chamber of Mines. This included taking visitors underground into the mines and among the dignitaries she accompanied were Britain's Harold McMillan and the UN's first secretary general, Vittorio Carpio from the Philipines.

Her knowledge of the hospitality industry grew in leaps and bounds as she organised top-drawer banquets and sporting events and was hurled head first into the delicate intrigues of protocol and fragile egos. From the formality of the mining industry she learned the fine art of writing excellent press releases from her perfectionist boss, and learning about public relations was very much a hands-on affair.

Her interest in what she was doing prompted her to do a marketing diploma and it was about this time that she moved on and joined forces with Adele Lucas in a promotions company. They came into the orbit of the soon to be famous hotel magnate, Sol Kerzner, who was a meticulous organiser and stickler for detail. As their expertise grew so did the promotions they were given and in the 1972 she decided to start her own business: Megan Carr Promotions.

"There was so much scope in those days because so few people were doing promotions seriously," she said modestly during a recent interview with the Hermanus Times. It was she who launched Oil of Olay with such success that it is still the top selling moisturiser in South Africa. Her radically different approach with a bevy of bandbox-beautiful, but at the same time, product-wise girls handing out orchids while they explained the product was a hit and the promotion was taken to five other countries.

Following the success of Oil of Olay came many other promotion jobs and Megan travelled all over the world promoting South African business.

She became involved in a charity promotion for Celebrity Tennis and was delighted that film stars Liz Taylor and Richard Burton, along with Ringo, were keen to attend.

She became the promotions consultant for Raymond Ackerman's Pick 'n Pay in 1978. "He was a meticulous, wonderful man to work for," she said of him, while he regarded Megan as an extension of himself - teaching general managers to be promotion conscious.

"Being a bit of a gambler has given me a wonderful life," she grins, eyes sparkling.

Throughout these high-flying fun times, although she divorced in 1975, she managed to keep her feet firmly on the ground, "To me family is supreme, the most important thing in life." She has two daughters and two sons and now boasts seven grandchildren.

After her years with Pick 'n Pay she decided to take a year's sabbatical and in the early 80s raised funds for the Wildlife Society.

At this time she was also a counsellor for Childline in Johannesburg which she did once a week for two years.

In 1992 she decided to move to Cape Town to "take it easy" but of course that wasn't to be. It wasn't long before she was deeply involved in media marketing and exhibitions. She created the Marketer of the Year Award in 1995 and the first one was presented to the Olympic bid committee headed by Raymond Ackerman and the next year it went to Maureen Thompson for the V&A Waterfront development.

The following year she became involved in the Alpha Mind Power seminars where she was put through memory tests on stage - and passed with flying colours every time.

Using mind over matter she has literally walked over burning coals without so much as a blister. Thousands of people attended the lectures she organised for the Australian mind power whizzman, Peter Heibloem who is a friend of hers to this day.

Newspaper cuttings fill dozens of scrap books that attest to a vibrant working life - "It's been so much fun, but it's time to slow down a bit now. Perhaps I'll have time to write my memoirs," she says before jumping up to say a cheery farewell to two happy departing guests.

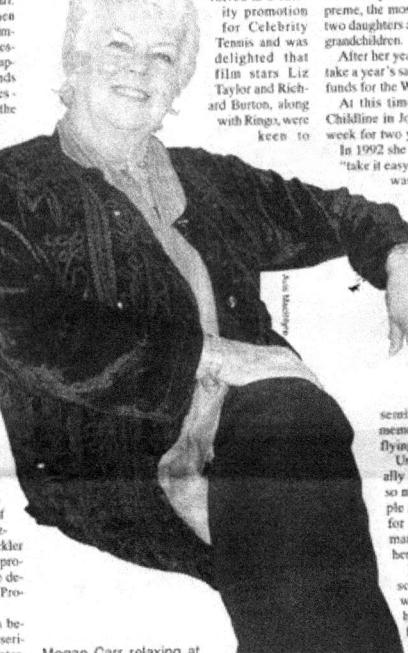

Megan Carr relaxing at the guest house which she manages in Voëlklip.

# My Life, a Roller Coaster Ride

## 6. Retirement Years and Writing

**2005 March.** The very next day, the Ides of March (mine, not Caesar's), my friend, Neil Malan phoned from Hermanus. He said, "Megs, drop everything I need you to come to Hermanus to help Barbara and me launch and market our new guest house".

Then he remembered to ask. "How free are you?" I said "You have no idea how perfect your timing is. When can I start?" He was surprised," How about tomorrow?", he joked; "Give it a try for three months until it gets going".

I locked up my Bonny Brook flat and started the following week. Three months turned into almost two wonderful years at 111 on 11th, till November 2006 when Neil leased the house out to the neighbouring Birkenhead Hotel.

### '111 on 11th' Guest House

Running the guest house, with staff of six kept me busy, but my bigger job was attracting house bookings. I had to bring this new accommodation into local awareness as well as further abroad.

The Rolls Royce Rally in the Park was next to 111 on 11th. The Rolls owners were our guests for a Coffee Break along their rally route which attracted a news article and public viewing in the park.

We occasionally hosted the Hermanus Supper Club, catered by me, and set up special promotional events for the Sanbona Nature Reserve to attract local buyers for the housing units. These events drew attention to our Guest House.

**Homeless.** Settled in Hermanus, one thing led to another. I again made a pivotal decision by selling my two Bonny Brook apartments in Muizenberg.

Tony was back to his property selling and got me excellent prices. So now I didn't have a back-up home in Cape Town, like burning one's bridges. It also gave me a fair retirement savings account to fall back on.

**Richard (Dick) Westcott.** A year earlier, 2004. Visiting the Malan's in Hermanus, I was introduced to the attractive and urbane Richard Westcott.

## My Life, a Roller Coaster Ride

The well-known Opening Bat cricketer of his time. Now, well into retirement, he had the time and inclination to court me with old world charm. He phoned several times a day. He'd journey all the way to Cape Town to take me to lunch at Kelvin Grove. almost weekly.

After my arrival in Hermanus in 2005, he delivered, or sent me a single rose, every week. Always with very dear notes and messages always addressed 'To a very special lady'. He introduced me to Hermanus life and the community.

My romantic life had been absent for many years, especially after my Mastectomy in 2002. By mutual consent, Richard's gentle courting was not going any further. I felt flattered and honoured by his attention. It also suited him that I was not seeking marriage.

We sometimes talked books. If I mentioned an out-of-print book I was looking for, he would scout local and Cape Town charity book shops till he found them. I was particularly excited when he found me Paul Gallico's *Love, let not Hunger*. A circus story. I love Circus. He also found a long out of print Lloyd C. Douglas's *Magnificent Obsession*, one of the books I live by about anonymous philanthropy. Often shared by me, so I never seem to have it on the shelf for reference. How lucky was I to have found such a book friend.

How did it end? He was older than me. Very sadly his health started deteriorating and he became shaky and had loss of balance. He had to stop driving. He had a Carer nurse move in. He sent me a note asking me not to call on him. He said he found his condition embarrassing and wanted me to remember him as he had been and not a wobbly, sick old man.

I understood and respected this until Ellen, his carer phoned me to say she thought he only had a few days to go. So, I visited him and indeed he was confined to bed and almost incoherent, but happy to see me. I just sat with him holding hands for an hour or so till he fell asleep. He died two days later.

Thanks to Barbara, Neil, Richard, and the *Hermanus Times* article, my new life in Hermanus felt good and took off well. As did the 111 on 11th Guest House.

**Publicity.** In promoting the guest house locally, I invited the *Hermanus Times* to do a story about this new elegant Hermanus accommodation. I would support it with an advert.

They agreed. I got the staff gathered in freshly pressed uniforms and flowers in the vases. But the reporter had other ideas. She was no less a

## 6. Retirement Years and Writing

person than the deputy editor of the *Hermanus Times*, Avis McIntyre, I gave her a tour of the house and introduced the staff, and we sat down for coffee, at which point she announced that she would do a story about the house, but her main interview would be about me.

After a two-hour interview over coffee, a half page story was published.

It was a thumbnail sketch of my life to date. I was seventy-three. After that, everyone in Hermanus knew me.

**Everest hero.** Avis was married to a man who was a born adventurer, Richmond McIntyre, a Hermanus businessman. After he successfully climbed Mount Everest on his own with only one Sherpa, I threw him a Press party at 111 on 11th.

Proud of him, Hermanus Street banners read 'Welcome home Everest hero. I have a memory of this irrepressible man, with his naughty smile, spread out on a couch, proudly displaying his bandaged feet hiding frostbitten toes.

**Awareness promotions** were organised, including a two-page supplement in The *Weekend Argus*, my old media friends.

We set up some interesting local functions, one of which would have a far-reaching effect in my life. The October 2006 Vintage Bentley Rally Organised by my friend John White, always accompanied by his artist wife Frederike` Stockhuizen, whose landscape paintings Gerry Leumann later bought for the walls of his house.

## My Life, a Roller Coaster Ride

**Vintage Cars in the Park.** It was at the 2006 Bentley Rally (previous page) that I met Gerry Leumann. First Bentley through the gates with his son, Adrian. I catered and, with Neil and Barbara, hosted the party of sixty-five international Bentley rallyists on a sunny day with the whales wagging their tails.

My position at 111 ended when Neil rented out the guest house to the neighbouring Birkenhead Hotel as an overflow annexe. Now I didn't have a home of my own to go to. What next?

Megan with Neil Malan, owner of 111 on 11th posing in front of a 1907 Rolls Royce Hearse, one of 23 Vintage Rolls Royces we hosted in the adjoining park for public viewing and coffee on their morning stop in Hermanus.

The tall Rolls in the middle is a 1907 Hearse. We also hosted Vintage Bentley Rallies.

# 6. Retirement Years and Writing

**7 Cliff Road,** Westcliff, Hermanus. I prefer to be busy. Right on time, a family friend in UK asked me to move into her holiday house in Westcliff, Hermanus, to project manage the renovations, getting it ready for sale. It was a seamless transition.

This house is a stunning, double storey, East facing residence, on the seafront. It was in very run-down condition.

Tony moved in with me to help. Within eight months it was perfectly renovated. I gave it a name 'Seventh Heaven' to help the sale along. We also did a holiday rental. The owner phoned to say that Lord Lytton and his family would be arriving from the UK, with friends, for ten days over Christmas and New Year. They would need all five bedrooms. I stocked up with his requested Colombard wine from Bouchard Findlayson Winery. Tony and I lived in the cottage in the garden.

**The mouse in the house.** An English Lord visiting? Probably some old hot potato, I wondered. To be sure that everything was perfect and no gaffes occurring, when he phoned from Somerset West to say they would arrive in an hour, I asked,"Lord Lytton, how we should address you?" He sounded young, thank heavens. He laughed and replied, "Call me Mickey, as in Mouse".

Suddenly we knew it would be a relaxed and happy Christmas and New Year visit. It seemed appropriate that our gardener was an elegant Malawian named 'Hopkins'.

After the lordly guests had left and the renovations on Cliff Road completed, the house was now ready for sale.

## 30. Pivotal Person Gerry Leumann:

**January 2007,** I was approached by Swiss, Gerold Leumann, participant in the October 2006 Vintage Bentley Rally, asking me to find him and Helen a house in Hermanus. They would visit in February to look around.

**Serendipity.** Whilst running 111 on 11th I had become friends with a bright young, whizz kid, Andrew Catlow. I had even organised his wedding to Ane` at 111 on 11th and was honoured to be seated at the bridal table.

He had become a regular visitor from the UK. One day he insisted I go with him to see a new spec house he'd seen being built high up in Voelklip, next to the Nature Reserve. It was nearing completion. Bauhaus style. Clean cut and with a stunning panoramic coastal view.

Andrew was considering making an offer on the house. The builders were putting in the finishing touches and the doors were open. We wandered in to have a look.

I, too, fell in love with it and thought 'That's a house I would love to live in'.

Gerry and Helen Leumann and granddaughter, Aline.

## 6. Retirement Years and Writing

When Gerry and Helen arrived in February 2007, Tony and I had set up seven sea-front properties, as specified, for them to view. It took the whole morning to process them. I then said I had one more house, away from the sea, for them to look at. I just happened to have ready, the keys of the newly completed house. The FOR SALE board was outside. They liked the look of it from the road. We walked up the stairs to the first floor, then out on to the terrace and the view. They held hands and said in one voice "This is it. We will take it".

Next day Gerry, having signed the documentation, then invited me to lunch at Harbour Rock as a 'thank you' for finding the perfect house.

Over lunch, he surprised me, asking, "When transfer comes through, will you move in and manage the property for us?" It was the perfect retirement job. Pure providence and perfect timing as I could move out of Cliff Road at exactly the time of transfer. Obviously, I accepted the offer and moved in during June 2007. The story continues.

**Selection of beds,** to me, is the most important aspect of a comfortable home. I bounced on every one of the six luxury beds and have lived with compliments on their comfort ever after.

I had to make only one change a year later when Gerry alerted me to the fact that Bruno, a special guest arriving soon, was two metres (6'6") tall and the regular King size bed in room two would be too short for him. So, I traded in the king size for a King X size I also had to get new linen to fit.

Big Bruno was also big in business.

He owned the Microsoft franchise for Europe.

I went shopping for all the house linen and napery, bathroom towels and toiletries, kitchen cutlery, crockery and glassware, for which didn't need the Leumann's approval.

Gerry and I had set up a household Bank account, with dual signatories on

Mini Meg and Big Bruno.

the cheques (remember cheques?). He co-signed the entire cheque book in advance, which simplified my shopping. I picked out every furnishing item for their approval. One stop shopping for the main furnishing items, to help Gerry and Helen in making their decisions. We did it in a morning.

**Parties.** Gerry, in typical Swiss fashion, was a creature of habit. In the first few years, he and Helen would arrive on a Tuesday. My son, Tony, would pick them up at the airport and bring them through mid-afternoon. The first night, we would all go out to dinner. The first Sunday in Hermanus, I would invite what became the same regular people to lunch. At first about twenty new friends. The number increased and varied over the next twelve years and increased to forty regulars and always a couple of new ones. The parties would then be divided into two parties. Luncheon first Sunday, Sundowners the following Friday.

The friends would include his Vintage car friends from Cape Town, Johannesburg and Elgin. He also, over time, gathered Swiss friends who were Hermanus swallows.

I catered breakfast for a house full of resident Swiss guests, and for all the parties and occasional lunches and dinners. Gerry was the perfect host, always circulating and making everyone feel welcome.

These three Bentleys belong to John White, Robert Middelmann and Stuart Maxwell. Gerry's 1930 Bentley was tucked away in the garage.

The first three years, Gerry kept his 1926 Bentley, from Switzerland,

Leumann House. My studio apartment was on the ground floor to the left of the front door. This house was my home from June 2007 - December 2018.

# 6. Retirement Years and Writing

here in the Hermanus house garage with the Land Rover.

The third year, he shipped all four tons of the Bentley, over to the UK for a full service. In 2010, we sent this 1926 Bentley back to Switzerland and he replaced it with a 1930 Bentley which stayed permanently in Hermanus.

He then acquired a red Austin Healey, which fitted him like glove.

He then replaced it with a handsome, sporty vintage Railton.(see below). Then came a bright red Ferrari – which he had 'wrapped' to black, which soon unwrapped itself back to reddish. So, he sold it and bought a black Ferrari. What else can a man do if the colour is wrong?

As he collected old and new cars, he regularly brought out, from Switzerland, Simon, a talented vintage car specialist mechanic to nurse the collection.

Bill Cunningham was Chairman of the Cape 'Crankhandle Club' and ran the Hermanus Car Club, so inevitably a friendship with Gerry developed.

**How did Bill meet Gerry?** When Gerry arrived in November 2010 for his regular summer visit, he timed the arrival of the 1930 Bentley for the following day. He was waiting impatiently on the terrace and supervised its offloading from the transport trailer, reversing backwards so it parked outside the garage, facing the road. He called Helen and me to come for a ride.

He turned the key, and it started perfectly. We turned right onto the road and started left and suddenly, it stopped. He jumped out and fiddled with everything and gave it a few more key turns but nothing. Being a fit and healthy seventy-eight-year-old, I ran up the hill to the house, gathered a ski rope, hopped into my Audi and offered to tow the four-ton Bentley.

Looking at the thin ski rope and then to the big Bentley, we had to laugh. There was no chance. I then I remembered Bill and his 'Crankhandle Club', living two kms away.

Leaving Gerry and Helen, I headed for Bill's house. Luckily, he was home. He had a stronger professional towing tape and even stronger towing car. I guided him to the two castaways and introduced them. Bill lifted the back and gazed in, fiddled with the on-off petrol switch, and 'voila' it started immediately. Gerry had got it wrong. Upon leaving the house, he had switched the petrol off instead of on. Bill and Gerry became friends for life.

## Farewell Adele

It was on a morning in June 2010 that Peter phoned to tell me that Adele had died of a heart attack while having a standard Stent procedure in hospital. An awful shock, hard to believe. I knew that she had cancelled a few days of office appointments to go for this procedure.

I remember feeling anxious about her, usually robust, health for the year running up to her death, but no warning that this could happen so suddenly. She was seventy-eight.

I wondered how I could come to terms with such a gap in my life. She was one of those people who seemed invulnerable.

Adele's memorial in their garden, was an emotional time with tears in our eyes as we spied her many hats waving in the trees and a single Piper playing. Des and Dawn Lindberg sang a specially composed song about

# 6. Retirement Years and Writing

her. I was one of the family and friends asked to tell a brief story about Adele, preferably 'typical and amusing'. I told this true story.

Adele, in the sixties, drove a clapped-out Morris Minor. Noisy and with very little power. Driving through Braamfontein one day, she jammed on the brakes at a red traffic light. Out of the left window she saw a red-faced traffic cop, leaning on the window, shaking his fist at her and obviously shouting. She pretended not to notice and looked away. When the light turned green, she hot footed the accelerator and spun off.

Further down the road she was waved to the side by the same traffic cop. She switched to her blonde-mode and said. "Oh Officer, I know I wasn't speeding". The furious officer agreed "No, you were certainly not speeding" he said, "You stopped on my foot".

No ticket was issued. What could he say?

She was incorrigible which is why we all loved her.

Bob, Adele's husband died 2012, two years after Adele.

**Below:** Richard Cuttler painted this portrait which hung at Reception at the Adele Lucas Promotions Reception at 75 Oxford Road, Rosebank.

# My Life, a Roller Coaster Ride

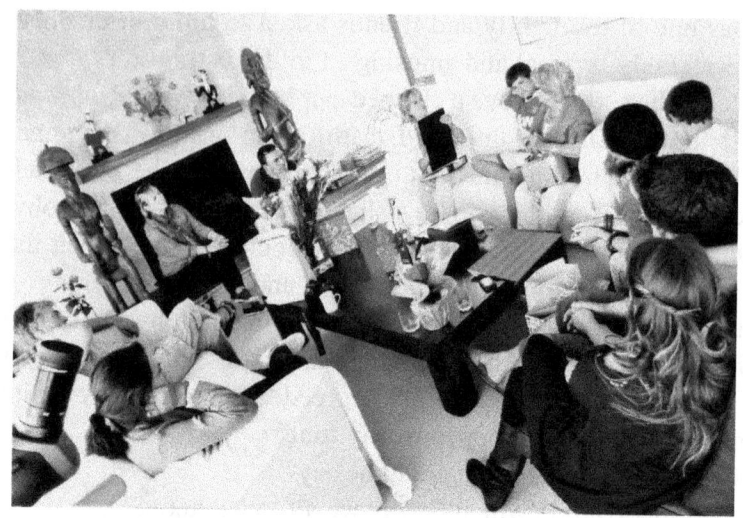

Top: Pressie time
Middle: Alex and Camilla
Bottom: Sebastian, Megan, Nicholas

## 6. Retirement Years and Writing

### 2012. My 80th Birthday

My 80th birthday was in two parts. The actual day I spent with Peter, Leanne, Seb and Nic at their house on the Vaal River. I asked Peter to take me for a ski. He did not look keen. I reminded him that it was my birthday wish. He reluctantly agreed. With the support of Seb and Nic, off we went out to the boat. All life-jacketed up.

Suffice it to say, my hands gave up with the strain of dragging me out of the water. I only made a few metres. I absolutely knew that once up, I would have had a good ski. The two teenagers patted me on the shoulders and said, "Well done for trying, Meg". ( See bottom left)

I'd had trouble crossing the line to eighty, so I called it '69 Again'.

My failed ski attempt was revealed when the photo of me ready to ski was flashed around at my Hermanus party the following week.

My two grandsons, Seb and Nic gave the age game away. They handed me huge A3 sized handmade cards, with best wishes at turning 80. I was 'outed'.

**Middle left, Alex and Camilla.** Making up A1 sized montages of photos, personalised for each family. I presented these as my gift to each of the four families. Plus, one for me, which hangs on the passage wall at the guest loo in my Fernkloof house. Guests going to the loo always take a little longer looking at the photos.

### 2013. Tony

Aah, sweet mystery of life – It took just seven weeks from …"Hi Mom, I'm coming to stay for a few days. I can take Gerry's cars for a run and charge them up whilst I'm there." To the dreaded words… ."he's gone." Those seven short weeks to his early death, had a profound effect on the lives of many people.

Tony had an engaging nature, and always willing, even if not always able, to help when needed. I think he needed to be needed to validate himself - to himself and to others.

**About Tony's last seven fateful weeks.** It was May 2nd 2013. I had just returned from visiting the family in Sandton for my 81st birthday. Tony had already arrived in Hermanus to sign a property deal. I immediately noticed that he was dragging one foot and his speech was slurred.

He said he had tripped and fallen. I had the irrational thought that he might have had a few beers. But when he took me to coffee in town next day, his driving was all over the place and he seemed spaced out. I asked him if he had taken some drugs. He was shocked at the question and said he was worried because he couldn't concentrate too well.

Monday 6th May, I took him to our regular doctor who diagnosed him as having had a mild stroke.

How is a mild stroke diagnosed? It is similar to a roadside drunk driving test, touching nose and walking a straight line, etc. The first question was "are you a smoker?" The answer was "yes" the doctor said, "you have had your last cigarette". He was right. Tony never ever again asked for a cigarette, having been a smoker for the past forty years.

The doctor said that because he hadn't had immediate stroke treatment, there was nothing to be done except keep him home and he would probably be fine after a few months or a year. This was shocking and hard to take, considering his youngish age of fifty-six.

I took him home. He seemed rather bewildered at the sudden turn of events in his life and the new limitations to his body and his lifestyle. The doctor made optimistic noises and had not given any instructions or warnings about his daily care – so we were just very careful and attentive. We were not warned that he might have loss of balance and fall.

When I phoned to tell Sean he immediately organised a second opinion and, two days later, Wednesday 8 May, he arrived to take Tony to a second examination. Tony was still able to walk but somewhat unsteadily. The examination and diagnosis were exactly the same as the other doctor. Also, with no recommendations for care or follow-up.

Two days later, I wasn't sleeping well, and I heard a thump in the night. Tony had fallen out of bed trying to go to the bathroom, he had bumped his head and couldn't get up off the floor. He just lay there shivering, cold and lonely in the night. I had to call in Michael, the neighbour, for help. We pulled the mattress on to the floor. He was such an inert weight that two of us battled to get him onto the mattress.

On Friday 10th, he had a minor seizure. I phoned for the ambulance and had him moved to the Provincial hospital for observation and care. He, and we, were all now in a panic. His good pal, Geoff rushed in from Cape Town and met us at the hospital and stayed over a few days to be with him. Carole and I visited several times a day.

# 6. Retirement Years and Writing

At midnight on Sunday, I was awoken with a call from the hospital. They asked the dreaded question "are you the next of kin of Anthony Carr?" 'Oh God, something's happened'. I thought, 'and he was all by himself'. But it was simply the duty doctor who informed me that they were transferring Tony to Tygerberg Hospital immediately that night for a brain and body scan.

Early next morning, Monday 14th, I packed a bag and drove to Cape Town to be near him.

Tuesday morning. I was just leaving Loader Street when I experienced a dizzy spell and racing irregular pulse. 'Oh no, not now'. Family friend, Carolyn (Lucas) Buckley insisted on driving me to the hospital to visit my boy. Geoff said he would do the afternoon visit and Peter was flying in from Johannesburg, and we would go together in the evening.

At this stage we knew that Tony was a really sick man. He now had to be helped to sit, eat, drink. He was connected to a 'bag' to relieve himself.

There was a Muslim man in the next bed whose whole family arrived for full visiting hours twice a day. Eight to ten of them standing round their relative's bed and talking quietly to the patient and each other. The patient's son, Muhamed, fussed around Tony if I wasn't there. He called the nurse when Tony was uncomfortable or needed the bedpan. He propped up his pillows and brought bottled water for him.

He told me they all prayed for him. I, the non-religious one, thanked him sincerely and said that I, too, would pray for his father. He laughed and said. "We pray five times a day". What could I say to that?

Next morning, Peter collected me from Loader Street, and we went to face the doctors on their morning rounds. They had done the scan in the night. They called us away from Tony's bedside into the passage which had a big TV screen on the wall.

Out of the ward's sight and earshot, the chief of hospital introduced himself and said he and the ward doctor would explain the results of the scan. The diagnosis was no need for technical.

**Prognosis.** Peter and I were in shock. He held my hand tightly. I asked what the treatment would be. The doctor didn't mince his words and said that there was no possible treatment. Only palliative treatment to keep him comfortable and out of pain. Our next obvious question was. "What is his prognosis?" The doctor answered, "He has about two to three weeks". Tony's forty years of smoking was the culprit.

# My Life, a Roller Coaster Ride

**Family conference.** We had a family conference and made our plans to bring him home. Carole, in Hermanus, under the guidance of Hermanus Hospice, would prepare the TV room in the house as a hospital room with a rail sided, levered bed. Hospice put her in touch with a nursing service for night nursing. Peter found a private ambulance service and arranged for them to pick up Tony on Friday morning, by which time the hospital room and nurse would be ready for him.

The minute we told Tony he was going home, he cheered up immediately, started eating and drinking and even joking through slurred words. It was a heart-rending moment. Carole, Pete, Andy and I knew we had made exactly the right decision.

**Camilla and Tony.** When Tony arrived home from Tygerberg, Camilla and Lee would visit to give him a hair trim, shampoo and manicure to make him feel good. With many laughs, they took him for rides down the road, sitting on the typist chair. We all resolved that we would make him comfortable, happy and very loved.

We notified all his friends, and the phone calls started pouring in from all over the country and other parts of the world.

When his friends asked him how he was, he would say "I'm feeling great. "I'm so happy to be home".

The house was filled with his beloved music, friends and neighbours visiting with plates of food and goodies. John O'Meara flew in from the river with a huge bunch of lilies.

In a nutshell, it can be truly said that the air of optimism and joy in our

I was holding Tony's hand when he died. Carole was with us.

# 6. Retirement Years and Writing

house kept Tony's spirits on a high and our hopes and energy charged up. Without doubt it gave him a few extra weeks of life at its best under the circumstances. He must have known because he started saying to me "Mom, please don't leave my side".

I phoned everyone I needed to. And the family decided to have a memorial wake, at home without delay, on the Saturday. It was almost a happy occasion with everyone talking about their memories of this lovely man.

My friend, Rex Gibson, said that he wanted to have a memorial just like that when his time came. And he did, nine years later.

We had found his favourite song and played it a lot before he died. And again at his wake 'I believe I can Fly – I believe I can reach the Sky'.

**Tony and the Dragon Boat Race.** Tony's Cape Town office colleagues often phoned and chatted to him during his illness. A few months after he died I received a phone call from his Infoprop Agency colleague and friend Pia Cornelius. She invited us to a Dragon Boat Race at Sandvlei in Lakeside, which is run annually for CANSA. Tony's Estate Agency had sponsored one of the boats in the name of Tony Carr (see below).

Gone Fishing. Sean, Carole, Nicola and Matthew casting Tony's ashes. Nicole, Beatrix and I watched from the Old Harbour wall above.

## My Life, a Roller Coaster Ride

The crew was a lively bunch of business professionals. Pia had decorated their Agency Pavilion with Tony's Real Estate bunting and board signs -

We all mused that when that number was called the message they would hear was "Hi, this is Tony. I am not available right now. Please leave your number and I will call you back.". The Tony Carr Team won the Dragon Boat Race challenge. Champagne was popped. Camilla said, "My dad helped them to win, didn't he?" I absolutely assured her that he did.

**How can you mend a broken heart?**
During Tony's short illness, I ignored my heart palpitations and dizziness and put them on the back burner. Ten days after Tony died, I awoke after midnight with what I thought was a heart attack. All the signs were there. I quickly swallowed some aspirin, unlocked the house doors, hung the panic button around my neck and got Carole's number ready on the cell phone, just in case. The attack passed.

Next morning, I decided to go to the Hermanus Medi Clinic outpatients for a check-up. I no longer trusted our doctor who had misdiagnosed Tony. I was on my way when I thought I would just let Carole know where I would be. She made me turn back to her house, bundled me into her car and insisted on driving me there. Always my rock.

Fortunately for me, the Cardiac Specialist just happened to dash into her office at the Clinic at that very time, on a Saturday, to pick up some papers. They persuaded her to have a look at me. She immediately planned for me to be admitted, next day. to the Vergelegen Cardio Unit, Somerset West, for an angiogram. I had to stay overnight to prepare for Monday morning tests.

The Angiogram tests showed my arteries to be healthy. So, they sent me for an ultrasound, which revealed what is called Cardiomyopathy. Or the Japanese word 'Taco Tsubo' which is the word for 'Octopus Trap' and which has come to describe a condition of heart muscle contraction which can be fatal or heal completely.

It is otherwise known as 'The broken Heart Syndrome'. Even now called by that name by such institutions as The Mayo Clinic and Johns Hopkins Hospital as a known phenomenon in cases of severe emotional shock and trauma. That one, I survived.

**'The Garage'.** In 2018, in my last year as Gerry's Property Manager, Bill Cunningham found an empty warehouse in the central industrial area in which to park some of the old cars which Gerry had bought. It could accommodate the five cars with ease.

# 6. Retirement Years and Writing

Bill and I decided to clean it up and make it comfortable. In the corner was a dusty old bar counter with six bar stools, which scrubbed and polished up nicely. The warehouse was a dismal place, so I decided to give it a facelift. I called in our Peter the Painter to paint white the dark grey walls. Bill organised professional cleaners to scrub the whole garage clean and get rid of the spiders. They even hosed down the wooden rafters.

The loo and shower were disinfected and scrubbed up. I put in fresh towels and hand washing liquid and lotion.

In the bar corner, I installed a small bar fridge, a coffee machine and fitted the kitchen out with crockery, cutlery, plates for take-aways. In the kitchen corner, washing up and cleaning materials and a bin were stowed under the sink. Under the bar counter, in closed containers, a supply of nuts and biscuits and a fully stocked wine rack.

Along the far wall was a workbench and toolbox. On the walls, I hung Bentley Tour posters and montages of photos of friends from the Vintage Rallies and Tours and Leumann family photos. Bill ordered a carpenter to install a ceiling over the bar and kitchen corner to make it cosy.

**Surprise!** We hadn't told Gerry what we were up to, readying the garage in time for his arrival. When he came in from the airport, he stopped by the garage to have his first look at his two new acquisitions, vintage cars fresh from the Labia family.

Expecting to see a grimy old warehouse, the shock and happy surprise on his face still lives with me. A love affair started as the garage took on a life of its own.

**'The Garage' turned into a club house.** Where friends and car fanciers could visit for a cup of coffee and biscuits, or wine and snacks at sundowner time, to talk about carburettor's, fuel injection and suspensions. It was always referred to as 'The Garage'.

**New Oldies**. Parked there were the two latest additions to Gerry's fleet. See next page a magnificent, 1907 De Dietrich. An open car with wide red studded leather seats a crank handle starter and dangling brass paraffin lamps. It had a totally removable canvas roof.

The other car in the garage, was a 1929 Fiat which had an interesting provenance. Both these cars had been owned by the Cape Town Labia family. This 1929 Fiat was one of only three of its kind in the world. It had been commissioned and given by the Italian Government to Count Natale Labia who was Italian Ambassador Plenipotentiary to South Africa from 1923.

# My Life, a Roller Coaster Ride

The other two original 1929 Fiats (DC1 and DC3) had been ceremoniously donated by Fiat. One to the Prime Minister of Italy, Benito Mussolini on his 1929 inauguration.

The other handed to Pope Pius X1 on his 1929 inauguration as first sovereign of Vatican City which was declared an independent state in Italy

All three, truly noble maroon and black extra-long beasts with a front driver's cab. Gerry's Fiat had a front, glassed-off compartment for the chauffeur and household valet. In the back, seating for five with an intercom button on the door for voice communication with the driver.

It seems that Italian chauffeurs are small and slim, because the tall and solidly built Gerry, couldn't fit behind the wheel to drive it. Swiss mechanic, Simon, had to do some fancy mechanics to move things around to make the extra space for Gerry.

Before leaving to return to Switzerland, in 2019, Gerry asked Carole to make up a flight of her suspended swallows to fly through the beams to decorate the ceiling. She had these installed before he returned a few months later, early 2020, strung up carefully not to place any above the precious cars in case one should come down in a Cape gale blowing through the double roller door.

When Gerry returned to Switzerland, we stored the old 1930 Bentley, his new 2017 Bentley sport and his new Ferrari in the garage, together with the two new oldies.

1929 Fiat.

Numberplate DC2

1907 De Dietrich

## 6. Retirement Years and Writing

### Final Retirement January 2019

**December 2018.** On my retirement, after twelve beautiful years as Property and Holiday Manager at Leumann House, the kind and thoughtful Gerry wrote me the most heartwarming letter of thanks for the many years of our association.

So detailed was it in its description of how I had made the lives of he and his late wife, Helen, their family and many guests pleasurable and trouble-free that I, in turn, realised that to have known such a fine man was a gift.

He called his life in Hermanus 'Paradise. He described how I introduced them into the Hermanus community and catered for their many parties and helped with bookings for anything from Game Reserves to Hair salons. Good times for all of us.

My departure was seamless. Carole and I simply exchanged places to live where we were both familiar with our new living space.

I immediately started to write the first of three books. The true South African true crime story *Shopping for a Killer*, *The 14 Marlbank Story* and finally, my autobiography *My Life, a Roller Coaster Ride*.

The first book's working title was 'Comedy of Errors', because of all the silly, careless mistakes which the millionairess murderer made and which got her, and her collaborators arrested within five days of the murder of her poor unsuspecting husband.

When retired editor, and friend, Rex Gibson offered to pre proof it for me, he recommended I change the title to *Shopping for a Killer*. "Much more dramatic", he said as he gave the story his stamp of approval.

Without any PR support from me, the PR professional, it didn't make me my million, but royalties did cover the costs.

I had engaged the services of professionals, Reach Publishers, who designed, proofed and prepared it for printing. Their editor thought my writing style was quirky, somewhat satirical and amusing.

**The 14 Marlbank Story.** I also wrote a family book about our happy 28 years at the Vaal River.

The book was A4 and 100 pages with lots of photos. It was a fun gift for all appearing in the inner pages and for other friends. I was now twice an author!

**Co-producers.** I was helped with the wrapping of the photos with the text in this book by Gerry's friend, and our house guest, Fritz Reust. Gerry

## My Life, a Roller Coaster Ride

Leumann was intrigued by it and insisted that Fritz order the printing of fifty copies as a gift to me.

My sincere thanks to Fritz and Gerry.

**2021. Gerry's illness.** Gerry had suffered lung tumours over his last five years. Carole and I suffered with him as he battled with breathing, even with the help of oxygen concentrator machines, over his last year in Hermanus.

It was 8th August 2021, when his older son, Stefan Leumann, phoned Carole to tell her that Gerry had died, surround by his family.

It hit us hard as we adored this man. Carole organised a Memorial to celebrate Gerry's life in Hermanus with the many friends he made here, in what he always called *'Paradise'*.

Carole setting up Zoom to share his memorial with his family in Switzerland, and friends. As we were in the middle of the Covid pandemic, our invitation was limited to fifteen friends and neighbours.

It was a very uplifting occasion as our eyes lingered on a huge picture of Gerry and his Bentley on the wall, and listened as people recalled many moving moments with this fine man.

After a year living at North Cottage, with its beautiful garden and stream running through it, I offered to move to the adjoining smaller two-bedroom South Cottage. This move suited the owners Dr. Andre` Hugo and his wife Lynn, as they needed it for family visits and also an Air B&B.

**Carole Carr and her grape mobile at the Steenberg Wine Bar outside the 1682 Restaurant.**

At about this time, Carole was commissioned by Graham Beck's architect

Carole Carr surveying her Steenberg Wine Bar Grape Installation.
The art sculpture was commissioned by the Graham Beck architecy, Richard Perfect.

# 6. Retirement Years and Writing

to produce a giant mobile of grapes to hang above his Wine Bar in Cape Town. This took four months to sculpt, drill, string and instal. Carole sold the Diwali lighting business and in 2013, she took on the Annie Sloan chalk paint franchise. She found a small shop in Dirkie Uys Street, Hermanus to set up her paint shop.

She had found an old plough in the Charity shop which gave her the idea to name the paint boutique 'The Plough Shed'.

This little gem became a hive of activity and almost a meeting place for a chat. Regular clients became pals.

She ran painting workshops and took on assignments, painting up old furniture to give it a fresh look. She found interesting pieces to chalk-paint and sell. I was fortunate enough to take turns minding the shop when Carole was out. She ran it profitably for two years till the Annie Sloan agent, contrary to the agreement, allowed a franchise to open in nearby Gansbaai. She realised that the area would not sustain two such businesses. Carole sold it and walked away. But it was a fun couple of years doing something different.

**2024. My home today.** Perfect for one with its two bedrooms en suite and spacious lounge looking onto a small courtyard, which I transformed into an enchanted garden. Hanging plant in the corner which became the nesting place for a family of Wagtails.

# My Life, a Roller Coaster Ride

**Uninvited Visitor.** In January 2022, the unthinkable happened right there in my living room. A Boomslang which attacked and gobbled up a tiny Wagtail chick, which had fallen out of the nest in my little garden.

I wrote a story about it and sent it to the local Village Newspaper. They published the story in its entirety on page 5, A full page with an extra picture they requested of me pointing to the hanging basket which housed the fated nest.I sent my newspaper story on to Gerry. He always loved getting my local news. ( See Appendix)

**My family has heart history.** My younger brother, Milton, having suffered Rheumatic Fever at sixteen, died of a heart attack at forty-seven. Father of four, he was a smoker and enjoyed the good life. He ran a highly successful printing and packaging business.

Younger brother, John, had a double bypass. That was in 1982. Since that time, he suffered several cardiac arrests, a further bypass and died of other problems after a bad fall in 2022 at the age of eighty-three. He was a father of two, a smoker all his life and a successful businessman.

My father, Alf Steer, at seventy, was on a world cruise with Mattie in 1970, when he suffered a massive heart attack as they disembarked the SS *Canberra* in Lisbon. He was taken to the British Hospital where he had the good fortune to be under the care of a superb Cardiologist. It was touch and go for him. Since then, he suffered a few heart scares.

He played a lot of golf and won the annual Seniors championship at the age of eighty-three. Executive Chairman of Haddon's, a JSE quoted company. He died at eighty-six of a heart attack.

**I was eighty-one when it happened to me.** A long story leading up to my first heart episode in 2013. After Tony's death, I suffered Taco Tsubo, Broken Heart syndrome. I was discharged from hospital, having been told that it was temporary and would heal itself in time. It did.

Five years later, the chest pains started. The Cardiologist diagnosed cardiomyopathy and referred me to a heart surgeon in Somerset West.

I did not go.

Four years after that, when the chest pains became frequent and unbearable, Dr. Barnard, and several Hermanus friends, referred me to Cardiologist Dr.Tjaart Venter at Vergelegen Cardiac Unit. By this time. I had turned ninety years old, enjoyed a huge birthday party, feeling lucky even to be alive, and worried about the misbehaving heart. I also felt silly to have delayed treatment for four years.

## 6. Retirement Years and Writing

**Dr. Tjaart Venter, Cardio Specialist** is in great demand, for very good reason. Appointments are like gold. When it comes to one's own health, waiting is hard.

A random thought. It struck me why, universally, doctors' Receptions are called 'Waiting Rooms' and we are 'Patients'. Patience?

I then had to play a different, supply and demand, waiting game. Firstly, in May, for an interview and evaluation, then in June, for pre TAVI tests and then weeks later, in July, for the ultimate procedure. I was feeling my mortality for the first time. While waiting at home, I packed a suitcase and had the Panic Button at the ready. I checked my Will and Living Will.

**Don't let me die before October.** The night before surgery, just as I was wondering about my chances of surviving the anaesthetic and surgery, Dr Venter visited me in the ward. I was not reassured as he asked about my next of kin, my Living Will and permission to cut me to insert the valve if the catheter didn't work. I signed a waiver for anything that could go wrong.

That's when I asked him to keep me alive till my book was done. He asked me about it, and I promised him that I would put him on page 401, which is where I would probably be by the time it was finished. He asked about my writing. I told him about my first book and he politely said he would like to read the true crime story.

**Are you St Peter?** The start of a busy 'day at the office' for the professionals. Anaesthetist, Dr. Andre Phillips' friendly Theatre Sister introduced herself and said she would be looking after me for the rest of the day. It felt good. In with a needle and I was out.

What seemed minutes later, I opened my eyes and there was the face of Dr. Phillips right in front of me. With a croaky voice I asked "Are you Saint Peter?" It made his day as they all laughed, and I knew I was OK.

Next day I was told that I had had a brief cardiac arrest during the procedure but they were happy to get me back with 'only one Zap' or words to that effect.

Dr Venter's assistant. Suné, phoned immediately I was out of Surgery, Carole to tell her it was completely successful. Carole phoned all the family and they all 'breathed a sigh of relief', I was told.

Apart from a temporary Pacemaker and one or two small issues, my recovery has been complete for over two years.

In my opinion this was a small miracle by a group of dedicated and talented people who worked their magic with a smile and infinite kindness.

## My Life, a Roller Coaster Ride

A class act. When I thanked them and remarked on the aura of peace and happiness around the Vergelegen Cardio Unit, Dr. Phillips remarked "When we arrive at work, we leave our egos outside the door. Everyone is important. We love what we do".

**Benita Januarie.** I had one little bonus gift which happened the last two days at the Clinic.

The 05.00 wake-up nurse arrived each day to do the usual Blood Pressure and Temperature. I noticed a sweet whistling sound coming from somewhere behind us.

I asked if she, too, could hear a whistling sound? She answered "It's me. I whistle". I asked her to whistle more. I was the only patient in the ward, so she closed the door and gave me a command performance. Firstly, a Frank Sinatra 'My Way' followed by Louis Armstrong's 'What a wonderful world'. I gave her a sitting ovation and said she had made my day. I asked her name, "I am Benita Januarie", she said, and wrote it on a paper napkin for me, together with her website! The whistling sound was mystical, musical and sweet like nothing I had ever heard. She told me that she whistles at concerts, had whistled on Radio Helderberg, and also in Church. She also does opera arias. I was enchanted with this tiny talented bird of a woman.

When she arrived next morning, my last morning at the clinic, she volunteered one more performance. All the many verses of Gounod's Ave` Maria, pitch perfect and simply beautiful. (It reminded me of my very first opera experience as a nineteen-year-old. It was Gounod's 'Faust' at the San Carlo Opera House in Naples, Italy, where I first heard the Ave` Maria). What a farewell gift to go with my new heart valve.

**After the Event** I left the clinic after a final check-up from Dr. Barry Barnard with an after-care prescription and no instructions about my health. That's how confident these guys are. But, as the new recipient of a foreign object in my little heart, I then wondered if I could continue my exercises on the vibrating Power Plate exercise machine. Should I go for walks? I didn't until these questions were answered at the six week thorough check-up with Dr. Venter. when he pronounced my new life sentence. "Your heart now working normally. You should be OK." Music to the ears. That day was Monday 15 August 2022, a very special day for me.

*Thank you, Dr. Venter. All credit to you and your amazing team.*

# 6. Retirement Years and Writing

## April 2022. My Ninetieth Birthday
### The family decided to celebrate it with a party

Thirty-eight guests arrived for a Birthday Lunch with all the bells and whistles arranged with a blue and white theme, by Carole. She has a natural eye for detail and included many surprises. Blue and white bunting, A huge silver blow up 90th balloon. Blue and white table setting. Blue and white balloons at the gate and up the stairs. And then guests arrived wearing a touch of blue.

Twenty-four of the guests were from the Carr, Steer, Lawley and Lucas families and their significant others. My niece, Leanne from U.S.A. and friend Robin Courage from UK, Di Valentine from Plett.

Many friends from Cape Town, Elgin and, of course, my friends from Hermanus. Carole and Peter made the main speeches. Sebastian and Alex made theirs, representing the seven grandchildren. Alex added her sweet poem. Andy had visited earlier from Johannesburg and stayed over for a few days. I had written a lengthy speech – but, fortunately for all, only remembered half of it. Patrick Chapment read out his birthday poem.

The Family. Back: Peter Carr, Christopher and Bridget Steer, Daniel Lawley, Megan, Sally Manson, John Steer, Leanne Scott Williams, Leanne Carr.
Middle: Matthew Harris. Front: Alex Carr, Sebastian Carr, Nicholas Carr, Carole Carr.

# My Life, a Roller Coaster Ride

Peter and Megan'.

Carole making her touching speech.

Bridget Steer brought a beautiful birthday cake.

Sebastian and Alex Carr.

# 6. Retirement Years and Writing

What I didn't forget was the births, in the sixties, of Bridget Steer and Diana and Garth Lucas who attended my birthday party. Diana with her husband Toby Chance and Garth with his daughter, Savannah.

Carolyn Lucas was one year old when I met her in 1961. She attended my 90th with her husband Michael Buckley, and their daughter, Ella, and her husband Peter.

John sadly died later that year. Carole's Matthew, a second-year student chef, was there, and helped with the food presentation. Sadly, Nicola didn't join us. Peter, Leanne, Sebastian and Nicholas were joined by Lee's sister Shelly. They travelled in from Plett and Cape Town

**Prezzie Time.** This was an entertainment in itself with everyone chipping in with remarks and jokes. Note the '90' balloon at the back. Diana (Lucas) Chance, in the white hat, was there with her husband, Toby (see below left)

Tony's family was not represented as Sean, Nicole and Beatrix had emigrated to Canada, and Camilla was unable to attend (later to emigrate to Australia). Danny and Crystal Lawley had flown in from Johannesburg. Danny had been my 'stepson' for forty-three years.

One of the best things about my party was that so many of the group had known each other for around fifty years but drifted apart in the natural course of life. Like all good friendships, catching up made the intervening years disappear.

I wish to thank all those who have touched my life. I am the richer for it.

My thanks to you, the reader. I hope you enjoyed the story as much as I did writing it.

**Love,
Megan**

# My Life, a Roller Coaster Ride

## Postscript

I have come to the conclusion that I have lived a charmed life. Whatever happened, I always seem to have landed on my feet. Just as my father prophesied. I am now 92 but don't feel 'old'.

I had a hard act to follow. My father was invalided out of the army with Blackwater Fever in 1918 at the age of 18. He therefore took health mattersv very seriously with a regime of diet and exercise. He won the Seniors Golf Tournament at 83. He died at 86. I followed his example, exercising and swimming from the age of four and later with friend Adele for over 30 years. I am now 92, and still going strong both physically and mentally agile.

A new study on ageing, as reported on CNN by Dr. Sanjay Gupta, also asserts that if you are a happy person, you will live longer, which is probably why I am still here.

My father started out as a journalist. As a potential father, he got a 'real job' in business and, at the age of sixty-eight, ended up Executive Chairman of the largest Printing Supply House in the Southern Hemisphere and quoted on the JSE.

Both my parents came from good stock. Obituaries in family archives mention success in business and prominent in community service. Even courage. We have a long distant relative, on my father's mother's Price family side. Thomas Price, a midshipman serving on board Admiral Horatio Nelson's flagship 'Victory' at the Battle of Trafalgar, 1805, received a cannon shot wound to his leg. A newspaper cutting tells of how the seventeen-year old whipped out his knife and cut off the damaged leg 'at the calf' 'with great composure', quoting "I will doctor myself". When the surgeon finally attended him, the leg was amputated at the knee 'without a groan' from Price. He was awarded a medal.

My mother Mattie's family, the Armours, have interesting history. Grandma Martha's brothers emigrated from Scotland to America. They both becames prominent millionaires in Armour Steel and Armour Canned Foods. Another Armour relative, Jeannie Armour, married the poet Robbie Burns who wrote about her 'My love is like a red, red rose...'.

In my lifetime, the most important change of all, is the equality of women in business and in the law. Leila Reitz and others, fought for the liberation of women in South Africa. In my twenties, women were expected to keep their place which, once married, was in the home and

## Postscript

not in business. School leavers were mostly directed to such careers as Secretarial services, Domestic Science or into the Nursing profession. It therefore took people like Adele and me to push the envelope and, through proving that women 'could do it', gradually the situation changed. But even now in 2025, there is still a way to go with the ongoing salary gap. Women are still being beaten up and killed by their partners. Of course, there has also been an increase in the abuse of drugs and alcohol hich has contributed to the problem and even used as an excuse. However I believe in the saying *In Vino Veritas*. What they do in their cups is actually who they really are.

One of my heroes is Helen Susman, the only, lonely, Progressive Member of Parliament, leading the movement against Apartheid.

A Post Script is a good place to complete this life story by telling, briefly, which episodes of my life, have been removed from the story.

When recommended to keep the book under 400 pages, I surgically removed 200 pages, before first handing the manuscript to Footprint Press. I removed certain personal stories relating to members of my family, which they did not want circulated outside the family. Then, after Footprint took over, many stories were shortened or removed altogether.

One story I cut out, told of two of two inventions which I designed and produced, and for which I registered patents, whilst enjoying one of my Vaal River sabbaticals. This is how it happened. To keep myself amused. I decided to make a two-metre long refectory table from some yellowwood planks which I had purchased and roof-racked to the river.

I purchased a circular saw, an electric drill, an orbital sander and overhead drill press. Already in the farm workshop was a workbench with a sturdy vice. I always kept a regular toolbox at the ready. And 'voila', a very nice table emerged, which Andy still has in her home.

Then, because I now had all the tools, I designed and produced a prototype of modular multi-part screening. It was inter-changeable and matching lattice screens. I then handed the very large set of prototypes to my industrial designer nephew to reproduce in fibreglass injection moulding. He didn't get around to it and I got too busy to follow up, but not before registering 'Lattice Design' with Spoor & Fisher, which paten registration lapsed after a year as not taken further.

Also, on a winter sabbatical at The Vaal, when my hands got chapped from the cold, I made a prototype of a hand softener. Menthol-cream-soaked gloves, which I Scotchgarded, to wear in bed and prevent the cream-soaked inners from marking the bed linen. I registered this invention under the name 'Softies'. (It was fairly soon after I had introduced Scotchgard into the South African market.) Again, I got too busy to follow it up. and the registration expired. Twenty years later one of the cosmetic companies marketed a similar product.

On yet another of my Vaal sabbaticals, because I love tomatoes, I made a half-acre tomato patch with a full ground irrigation system of punctured hose piping and water from the borehole. I planted rows of tomato seedlings under shadecloth. Beautiful tomatoes arrived. The universal principle clicked in. One third for the birds, one third for those who help themselves and one third for us and for sale. I had a regular customer, the roadside Fruit and Veg stall on the main road. I then planted seeds in rotation for a continuous supply. That one also bit the dust, so to speak, as the Joburg business was so demanding.

After the 1975 Vaal floods, the river emptied for a few days, so I took the opportunity, with my trusty staff and a handyman, to build up the river's edge with a wall and topped with a concrete footpath. But not before we fielded several bottles of beautifully mellowed wine, sunglasses and items which had fallen out of boats and which had become exposed on the dry riverbed. I also hung tyres against the new wall so boats could tie up without scratching.

Other stories I removed from the book, were my trips to Egypt, Italy and Switzerland with Carole, Ballooning at Chobe with John Roberts, and other adventures.

I cut out Peter's seasons of boat racing for under sixteens in a special class of boat for that age called Hotdog Racing. He almost always won his races.

And then there were some interesting men in my life, like John Laubscher who won the Mazda car agency for Anglo American. Surgeon, Ian Pepper. A long story. Mountaineer John Lange, who wrote the most wonderful love letters from wherever he was. In Matric, Pat Crozier, who had a passion for music and brought his wind-up record-player onto the school train, whose marvellous letter written in song titles became a victim of this self-editor's scalpel. And Rory Martin, who wrote me a letter a day at Matric time. I still have Pat's and Rory's letters in my journal.

I have written many poems and nonsense rhyme. I burst into verse at the drop of a hat. Now fancy that. I versify when I have something to say. A good way to vent, as in Donald Trump, or eulogise, talk nature or joke

# Postscript

about something. I wrote my version of Desiderata for my grandchildren and almost always say 'Happy Birthday' or send greetings in verse. I even thanked my TAVI heart surgeon in a poem. I handed over my puppy dog 'Rosebud', to Peter with full history and instructions for her care, in verse form. But all came a 'cropper' on this editor's cutting table. So I have enough stories for my next book.

**Where are they now?**
Tony – 'Gone Fishing' in 2013. Lee died rwo years after Tony. Sean, Nicole and Beatrix Kate have emigrated to Canada. Camilla and her partner, Lee, emigrated to Australia.

Carole lives in Hermanus, managing the Hermanus holiday life and property of a Swiss Swallow. She is also a qualified international Psych K online counseller. Matthew is a qualified Chef. Nicola is an artist. Carole and I enjoy each other's company daily.

Peter and Leanne live in Plettenberg Bay from where Peter runs his film company. Their two boys, Sebastian and Nicholas, now in business, live in Cape Town.

Andy lives in Johannesburg. She resigned from formal business to become a qualified Life Counsellor and continues with her ceramics and Raku. Alexandra lives with her fiancé Olli in Cape Town. They are both in the film business.

Daniel. Has a house in Johannesburg, but travels extensively with his wife, Crystal. He mentors young boxers.

Melanie lives in Scotland and plays a lot of golf.

Adele died in 2010 and Bob in 2012. Carolyn, Garth and Diana and their families, all live in S.A.

Megan. I live alone in Hermanus, with Carole living nearby. I enjoy writing, reading, music and gardening. My family and I remain close. Writing is my life and joy. I am toying with writing my next book, including many out-takes from this one (pity to waste them), and a collection of interesting theories (not conspiracy), anecdotes and answers to questions I have asked myself, and researched for answers. I have decided to call it 'Bedtime Stories for People Who Aren't very Tired'.

One of them is about 'Yawning'. So, before you do….thank you for joining me on this Roller Coaster Ride.

Megan

# My Life, a Roller Coaster Ride

My Father, Alf Steer. Still putting his 28th successive tournament.

# Appendix 1

## 83 and still putting on

Any gentleman who has reached the age of 83, would be excused if he sits back and enjoys life. But you will not find Mr. Alf Steer of Johannesburg, sitting, smoking his pipe, in his rocking chair. At 83, Mr. Steer is the oldest competitor in the 44th annual tournament of the Senior Golfers Union in Port Elizabeth..

Mr. Steer, who never received a golfing lesson in his life, is the holder of the Admiral Benson Putter for the oldest competitor to compete the tournament, and has set his sights on retaining it in the two day tournament tomorrow and Friday.

Mr. Steer has rubbed shoulders on the greens with many of South Africa's golfing greats including the legendary Bobby Locke and Gary Player. He adds, 'Gary was charming to play with and he gave me many useful tips on improving my game'.

I've always lived a healthy life and I suppose that has helped me still being able to play today.

When asked how long he plans to continue driving and putting, Mr. Steer said 'I know of many guys who wouldn't mind being accused by a jealous husband at a 100. So, here's hoping I'll be able to tee off on my 100th birthday'.

About his courtshp of Mattie: He always joked 'I chased her till she caught me".

\* \* \*

**Alf, Milton, John and Chris all enjoyed their golf.** When at the Vaal they would often spend a Saturday morning playing at the Emfuleni Golf Club, come home and spend the rest of the day analysing their shots over another couple of beers.

After leaving the Vaal property, aged 80, Alfie continued with his golf and, in fact, won the national Seniors' Championship in 1982 and again in 1983 when he defended his title. (See Left) a newspaper photo of him kneeling with his putter at the 18th hole in Port Elizabeth. When asked why he took up that pose he answered 'That is what Dennis Thatcher (husband of Margaret Thatcher) did when he won Seniors in England'.

# Appendix 2

**CITY OF CAPE TOWN**
OFFICE OF HIS WORSHIP THE MAYOR

14 October 1975

Mrs Megan Carr
P O Box 78630
SANDTON
2146

Dear Mrs Carr

Firstly may I congratulate you on your enterprise in arranging for the stars to visit South Africa. My wife and I were very pleased to have the opportunity of meeting Miss Taylor and Mr Burton. As agreed I would have great pleasure if you will kindly keep me posted about the possibility of them (or any other stars) visiting Cape Town in the future. Please be good enough to let me know what the conditions would be and what our commitments would be. I look forward to liaising with you in regard to any promotion you may have in mind.

Kind regards,

Sincerely

John Tyers
MAYOR

# Appendicies

# Appendix 3

STORES LTD/BPK
CLAREMONT MEDICAL CENTRE, MAIN ROAD, CLAREMONT, CAPE 7700

Tel. Add.: "Golvest" Cape Town  Telex 57-0013 Cape Town  P.O. Box 87 Claremont 7735  Phone 61-3030

4 October 1978

Dear Meg,

I have heard from Rex what a wonderful and successful trip you had, and I hope a lot will flow from it.

I was very impressed to hear about the Boys on the Border baking contest held at Norwood yesterday and the TV coverage we got. They are sending me down all details but I would like you to communicate the whole promotion to all the hypers, and let them know about it, because this is a very warm, sensitive area which we could work on, as you were working on the idea of messages to the boys on the border - is there any news on that? Please let me know.

Kindest regards.

Yours sincerely -

RAYMOND ACKERMAN

*Replied: 15.10.78*

MANAGING DIRECTOR R.D. ACKERMAN B.COM  DIRECTORS A. FINE  A.J. ROSIN B.COM. LL.B.  K.M. BLUMGART
D.C. COBB  R.P. DE WET B.COM. B.A. (HONS) C.A. (S.A.)  C.D.G. HURST F.C.A. (BRITISH)
H.S. HERMAN B.A. LL.B.

## Appendix 4

# Appendicies

# Appendix 5

**Pick 'n Pay Stores Limited**

Pick 'n Pay Centre, Corner of Main and Campground Roads, Claremont 7700
P.O. Box 57, Claremont 7735
Telephone: '65-5010 Telex: 57-20013

26 May 1983

Megan Carr
Chroma Video (Pty) Ltd.
Box 643
BERGVLEI
Tvl. 2012

Dear Megan,

I would just like to thank you for your excellent idea of putting the Open Letter on Video, and for the way it was executed.

It really has been extremely well received and I'm sure a lot of benefit will derive from this.

Thanks once again.

Kindest regards,

RAYMOND ACKERMAN

c.c. Allen Appel

# Appendix 6

**An experience for life to RE-CHARGE AND RE-ENERGISE**

**ALPHA MIND POWER**

**MAIN SEMINAR**
6 - 9 April Belmont Square Conf.Centre
Rondebosch
(Ample secure parking in the complex)
(NON RELIGIOUS. NON PHILOSOPHICAL)

**FREE LECTURE**

By Australian author & lecturer
**PETER HEIBLOEM**
As interviewed on M-Net's "Front Row",
Woman Today SAfm, Cape Talk & Punt Radio
And listen to Peter on Cape Talk after 1pm
Kieno's show on Tuesday 13 March.

Self Mastery.
- Dissipating stress and tension
- Going deeper into Alpha

**SATURDAY**
(8.30am to 9.30pm)

*Session 3 - Rapid Learning, Pain Relief*
- How to concentrate, improve understanding and memory while studying, reading or listening to a lecture, in Alpha.
- How to switch into Alpha quickly to be at your best.
- How to relieve headaches, migraines, aches and pains (eg backache, toothache).
- How to energise yourself to stay awake and alert for longer periods of time.

*Session 4 - Superior Goal Achievement*
- Applying mental rehearsal and the 3 Laws of the Mind in Alpha, for superior goal achievement.
- How to create your own life plan for successful living.
- Achieving excellence at sport, at work, at home.
- How to develop the two mental qualities exhibited by a genius.

to, and admire.

*Session 6 - Habit Mastery*
- How to lose or gain weight using your mind in Alpha.
- How to forego cigarettes, alcohol or drugs almost without effort.
- How to be decisive and fast acting and overcome your procrastination.
- How to eliminate fears and bad habits they create - (eg laziness, shyness, untidiness, fear of failure, fear of success, fear of rejection)

*Session 7 - Creativity & Intuition*
- Developing your own intuition and creativity, using precise Alpha techniques.
- How to communicate with others in Alpha.
- How to be inventive and have ideas that work.
- How to go into an imaginative and inspired inner dimension.

**SUNDAY**
(8.30am to 9.30pm)

*Session 8 - Beyond Your 5 Senses*
- How thoughts produce life - the metaphysics of the mind.
- How to develop your inner senses

others.
- How to accelerate your body's natural healing processes using your mind.

*Session 11 - Advanced Communication*
- How to counsel and help others using your creative mind.
- How to communicate your love to others using your thought.
- How to develop empathy, compassion and further expand your intuition.

*Session 12 - Advanced Intuition*
- Service - using your powers to help others - an extraordinary session.

**MONDAY EVENING**
(6.30pm to 11.00pm)

*Session 13 - Sleep & Creativity*
- How to solve problems and trigger creativity while you sleep.
- How to remember and understand dreams.
- How to awaken in the morning feeling refreshed and energised at the precise time you want.
- How to overcome sleeplessness, insomnia and disturbed sleep.

*Session 14 - A Journey in mind*
- Realising your great life goals. A vision for the future.
- Expanding your awareness as never before - a great climax to the Seminar.

To register for the next Seminar in your area contact:

**ALPHA MIND POWER**
P.O. BOX 30171
TOKAI 7966
TEL/FAX: 788-3564

**HEAD OFFICE**
1800 072 999

Appendicies

# Appendix 7

# Appendix 8

ST. JAMES'S PALACE
LONDON SW1A 1BS

From: The Assistant Private Secretary to HRH The Prince of Wales

16th July 1997

Dear Miss Carr,

Thank you for your letter of 30 June to The Prince of Wales, inviting him to visit the St Francis Adult Education Centre.

His Royal Highness was interested to read about your Centre. Sadly, however, the programme for The Prince of Wales's visit to South Africa does not allow the time for him to see the Centre for himself.

His Royal Highness has asked me to send you his warmest best wishes.

Yours sincerely,

Nicholas Archer

Miss Megan Carr

---

The British High Commissioner, Miss Maeve Fort
requests the pleasure of the company of

...... Ms. Megan Carr ......

at a buffet reception
in the presence of
His Royal Highness The Prince of Wales
on Wednesday 5 November 1997
at the South African Museum
from 11.45 am to 1.45 pm

Dress: Lounge Suit

R.S.V.P.
Tel: (021) 461-7220 ext 204
Fax: (021) 461-0017

S.A. Museum
25 Queen Victoria Street
Cape Town

Please bring this card with you

Appendicies

# Appendix 9

On my retirement 2018, Gerry's letter to me tells it all.

**Gerry Leumann**                                      **December 12, 2018**

Dear Megan

Our working relationship will end by December 31, 2018, after close to 12 years. In January 2007 I was able to acquire the house at 318 2nd Street, Hermanus. This was the beginning of our fruitful cooperation, when you decided to move in with us as our property manager.

You not only helped us to find a suitable home in this peaceful area, but also advised us on the outfitting of the house and interior decoration, located the shops to buy the right things and supervised delivery and installation of everything.

As we were swallows spending 4-5 months per year in Hermanus, you were looking after the house also in our absence, organized the right kind of craftsmen for renovation work and trained the maids in charge of cleaning, washing an0d all sorts of other household duties.

You organized the bookings for our frequent overseas guests, advised on sight seeings and excursions and created most delightful events for us and invited guests, up to 30 or 40 at some of the parties, so that we had nothing to do with the organisation and just could enjoy.

Your vast network in Hermanus and the whole country helped us a lot to feel welcome, and many of your friends became also ours.

You have been of invaluable service to us over these 12 years, and your loyalty and dedication is overwhelming.

I wish to thank you, also in the name of my late wife Helen, for everything you did for us. You enriched our lives and turned us into devoted lovers of South Africa and Hermanus. Thank you so much!

As a sign of our gratitude, I will pay for your Medical Aid during your retirement.

Kind personal regards,

*Gerry Leumann*

# Appendix 10

**In January 2021,** I had an uninvited visitor in my living room. A brown (female) Boomslang (Tree snake) which attacked and gobbled up a tiny Wagtail chick, which had fallen out of the nest in my little garden. The chick ran into my house when I opened the sliding door.

Always with a camera at the ready, I took a couple of photos of this scary scene just a metre away from my bare feet. I got the broom from the kitchen and swatted the snake. The slinky predator got the message and reversed out of the house, bird in mouth, and continued its breakfast outside. It then occurred to me to close the sliding door.

I then watched in anger as it proceeded to the hanging basket nest with the other chicks, which served the snake as breakfast 'seconds'

'.I wrote up a story about it and sent it to the local Village Newspaper. They published the story in its entirety, A full page with an extra picture they requested of me pointing to the hanging basket which housed the nest.

In January 2022, I sent my newspaper story on to Gerry

Hi Gerry,

Earlier I wrote you about my enchanted little 6 x 4 metre courtyard garden, filled with small trees and flowers.

I mentioned the tiny little Wagtail birds who checked the garden for safety and proceeded to build their nest in the hanging basket in the corner.

## Appendicies

For many weeks Carole and I followed the excitement and industry of the happy Wagtail couple as they went about building their home.

Last Wednesday Carole, Nixi and I sat sipping our sundowners and watched the Wagtail couple as they flew into the garden and hopped chair to chair and into the nest, feeding the open chick beaks small morsels of food. Each taking turns with visits about every ten minutes for hours. Magic moments.

Thursday morning, I heard loud bird screaming and tweeting – I knew something was wrong. The agitation was electrifying. I went to the lounge to see what was up. I opened the sliding door and saw the parent birds running round trying to protect their baby chick which was battling to walk on the lawn

It was almost as if they trusted me to help.. I assumed the tiny chick had fallen from the nest and couldn't yet fly. So small it could sit in my cupped hand.

The little chick ran into the house and hid under the couch. I gently scooped it up and put it down on the lawn next to its anxious parents. Just as I put it down, out of the garden corner shot a long snake snapping at the chick, which escaped and ran back inside again. Once again, the snake whiplashed after it and got it in its jaws, just a metre from where I stood. It started eating its prey immediately. In the picture, it looks like a bird with a very long tail.

I felt helpless, and in a rage, as I heard the little bones crunching. What to do? Automatic reaction. My camera? In the middle of all this drama, I picked up my cell phone, set 'Camera' and started snapping. In the picture, note more snake tail outside the door. At least 2 metres of her. (The Boomslang is highly venomou).

Sanity returning, I closed the door and debated what to do next.

As I watched, after a few moments, the snake returned to slide past the door and disappear behind the pot plants.

Next thing I saw it climbing the Hibiscus shrub next to the hanging basket and the nest. Of course, the Boomslang would be good at climbing trees. She wrapped self round the basket and her head went into the nest.

I ran out with the broom and hooked him off the nest and he plopped to the ground behind the flowerpots.

She then approached from the ground on the other side of the flowerpots, and simply stretched herself up to the nest – tail still on the ground, and got the other chicks. As she was doing this, I again hooked her off – but

# My Life, a Roller Coaster Ride

too late. She'd got them all. As the parents watched from the top of the chairs. At all times I knew where she was because the agitated parents showed me.

Finally, I went inside, closed the door and phoned Carole to call the snake man. He told Carole to tell me not to go near it as it sounded dangerous. Again, too late, but I was safe.

Carole arrived and gave me seven kinds of hell for going near the snake. Although at no time did I feel scared – only angry. She was absolutely right as this snake was really a bad one. Earlier in the week Carole had found a Cape Cobra in her back yard. She and the staff shooed it away. Snakes also get scared.

When snake man, Jonathon, arrived with his big bucket and a long pole with a hook at the end – it was only a couple of minutes before the villain was hooked and into his bucket. It seemed so easy. He estimated the Boomslang at about 2 metres long, and happily told me how a woman in Somerset West had died last week from a Boomslang bite. He also gave me hell for hitting it with the broom. He was not impressed that I had used the brush end to shoo it off.

When asked, Jonathan said he would release the snake up the mountain. Like the other Terminator - would it be back?

Sadly, our garden bird magic stopped Like Donald Trump – no more tweets.

That night when Carole, Nixi and I checked the nest – we found the most perfect little chick nest. Empty.

## Consolation.

Saturday, when I was feeling sad, I went into the garden and there, right next to the hanging nest, was the most perfect huge yellow Hibiscus bloom.

Was it Nature's message about the good things around us, and about life simply going on.

Kind regards,
Megan

# Appendicies

**Gerry's instant reply follows.**

Dear Megan,
What an exciting story! And Carole is right, of course, you should never have gone near the snake, but call the snake man instead immediately! But there is the bravery of the moment, the affect action, which takes over in such stressful situations. No time to think. You were lucky to get out of this incident without a scratch, which might have gone bad!

Some people have their own little angel watching over their shoulder and holding their magic hand over

*Se non è vero è en trovato*, as they say in Italy! Fun story, isn't it!

Thanks for sharing yours with me and kind regards,

Gerry.

He always loves my local news. Immediately and in character, Gerry came up with a snake story of his own.
]Reminds me of another snake incident.
A friend said that he broke his arm.
What happened, I asked, and he told me that he was in the shower when he heard his wife shrieking like crazy. So, he ran out of the shower and found her on the Patio. She said that she was moving the pot with the plants inside for protection from the cold, when a snake appeared out of the pot and fled into the living room and under the sofa. So, the man kneeled down to take a look

*Habe um halb Sechs Besuch, Reinhagens kommen auf einen Apero.*

Naked as he was, coming out of the shower. When he was well down on the floor peeking under the sofa, the dog came in and smelled on his naked being which stuck out like a fleshy bump.

The poor man, expecting the snake and with his nerves tense as violin strings, was so shocked when the cold dog nose touched his skin that he fainted.

The lady of the house, with her fainted husband on the floor and the snake somewhere in the room, immediately called 911. The ambulance arrived without delay and loaded the man on the stretcher.

They lifted him up, and just at that moment the snake appeared from under the couch. The paramedics were paralysed, they` let the stretcher go, the patient fell on the floor – and broke his arm.

## My Life, a Roller Coaster Ride

# **Desiderata**
(Ancient and wise script)
Megan's version for you my grandchildren.

Go calmly amid the noise and haste of life and discover
what peace and value there is in silence.
It is a wise Life Resolution
to be on good terms with everyone
whilst preserving your own fair judgment.

Speak the truth clearly, without fear or fuss.
Be a good listener – a good way to learn.
Even the dull and seemingly ignorant have their story to tell.

Avoid loud and aggressive people.
The empty barrel makes the most noise.
Their company diminishes the soul.

Comparisons are odious.
If you compare yourself to others, you may become vain or even disappointed,
for there will always be those who are less or greater than yourself.

Value your achievements.
You worked hard for them. Build on them.
They belong to you alone and are assets for life.

Write down all your innermost goals and desires.
Keep a Journal for reference.
Do it today

Write in your journal whenever planning and updating your career and life plans.
They do not necessarily have to be grand
But real and important to you.
As long as they are pursued with passion
from the heart and soul as well as the head,
The Universe will find a way to grant you these.
It works. Believe me.

Exercise caution in your business and social dealings
for the world is full of trickery and devious people.
More importantly,
let this not blind you to what virtue and generosity is also
everywhere to be found.

Always strive for high ideals.
Sadly, some people only manage empty self congratulation.
You should just be yourself, as best you can be.
Sincerity shines through.

Especially, do not fake affection. Nor be cynical about love
for when the going is tough and times are hard
real love endures above it all.

# **Appendicies**

Now that you are an adult
and taken on the full responsibilities of your life,
of course you can, and will, do it gracefully.

Nurture your strength of mind, spirit and resolve.
It comes in handy when the going gets tough and
you have hidden inner resources to draw upon.
Teach life values to your children when the time comes..

Don't distress yourself with unnecessary fears - or dark imaginings.
Many fears are born of fatigue or loneliness.
At times like this, search out the cause.
Think it through without self indulgence or self pity.
Work on a solution.

Fear has a job to do, to create sensible caution
but it should never rule your life.
Be gentle with yourself and work through it.

You are a precious child of the universe,
no less than the stars, moon, oceans and trees. You are part of it.
Whether it is clear to you or not, right now,
the universe is unfolding just as it should.
So just accept it, and be at peace.
Try and turn problems into advantages. Lessons.

Whatever your work, hopes and dreams are,
midst the noisy confusion of life,
Keep a level head and peace in your soul.
Keep your eye on the ball.

Never allow yourself to become disillusioned
or vengeful, it is a waste of time and energy.
It is not always people who let you down
maybe you misjudged and have let yourself down by
expecting too much of them.

The world, seemingly with all the sham, dishonesty,
confusion, hard work and broken dreams,
is still a beautiful and exciting world
full of adventures, surprises, challenges
and people who love you.
Be cheerful. Laughing takes less energy than anger.
Go on … just do it.


With my love and respect,
Megan - Morns.

My Life, a Roller Coaster Ride

## About the Author

**Megan Carr**, a woman of remarkable resilience, fearlessly entered the male dominated business and advertising world in late 1960s, at a time when societal norms dictated that a married women should not be allowed to have a career, but should focus on the home and children. In 1972, Megan divorced her husband (taboo at the time) with sole custody of their four children. Her purpose and determination in the face of the challenges ahead, is truly inspiring.

1972, Megan, newly divorced after eighteen years of marriage, embarked on her new path by establishing her company, Megan Carr Promotions (Pty) Ltd. She rented out her house and moved the family to a new apartment, a block away from the newly opened Sandton City where, eighteen months later, she leased half a floor to set up her offices. But before that, her first client was Oil of Olay. Its national launch, with real orchids, was an outstanding success, which rocketed the company into instant prominence. The business rolled in. She was on her way, in fact, she paved the way in this new field of live promotions. Despite a few hiccups along the road, MCP remained active for an impressive thirty-five years, a testimony to Megan's entrepreneurial skills and business acumen.

Megan met Adele Lucas when they were nineteen. It remained a close friendship through 58 years. The two women, in their separate fields of promotion, became regarded as pioneers in 'Below-the-Line' advertising, organising live events to support the print and radio media of the time, six years before the advent of TV. Their timing was perfect. With no precedents to follow, their unauthodox, and sometimes wild ideas worked.

They boldly 'did it their way'. And got it right

.Mentors and role models such as Leila Reitz "you don't have to be like a man to succeed in a man's world", Angus Collie, PR for the Chamber of Mines, who coached her in the art of PR and skills of Event Management and Sol Kerzner who, personally, coached Megan and Adele how to organise 'the perfect seminar. They never looked back and were soon accepted as equals in that hallowed man's world of business.

MCP clients included Southern Sun, Pick 'n Pay, Anglo American Properties – Cabana Beach, 320 West Street, Fiat, Leyland, Oil of Olay, JCI Platinum, Sterns, Ponte Towers, Wildlife Society, Penguin Books, Dewars and 100 Pipers Scotch Whisky, S.A. Breweries, KWV, SFW, Coca Cola,

# About the Author

Defy, Cerebos, Mercury Marine Outboards, and many more. Characters: The Wombles, Paddington Bear, Muppets and the Chitty Chitty Bang Bang machines.

Seminars: Alpha Mind Power, Brain Gym, Firewalking, Time Management, Quality Management, Mind Mapping. and Business events.

2005, semi retired, she moved to Hermanus and launched a Guesthouse for friends and Managed the property and holiday lives of a Swiss family. 2019 at the age of 87, she retired fully and wrote three books. A story about the family Vaal River days, a true S.A crime story 'Shopping for a Killer' (Amazon), and this Memoir.

The 14 Marlbank Story.

Shopping for a Killer.

My Enchanted Garden in Hermanus.

Patrick Chapman

Carolyn (Lucas) Buckley.

Alan Busuttil and Andy Carr.
Alan bought Megan's West cottage.

Savanna and Garth Lucas
Adele's son and granddaughter.

Peter Carr and Jacques Malan demolished the old middle house on the Vaal and built this in its place. Designed by Peter Carr.

www.ingramcontent.com/pod-product-compliance
Lightning Source LLC
Chambersburg PA
CBHW070835160426
43192CB00012B/2194